Lectio
(Pronounced: Leck – te[

MW01615245

Lectio Divina (from the Latin meaning "divine reading") is a contemplative way of reading the Bible. The practice dates back to the early centuries of the Christian Church and was established as a monastic practice by Benedict in the 6th century. It draws on the ways the Jews read the ancient Haggadah, a text during the Passover that retells the Exodus story. It is a telling and retelling of the story; thus, there is a lot of repetition involved.

If 2021 was about *quantity* (reading the entire Bible - Genesis to Revelation), then 2022 is about *quality*. Lectio Divina is a way of praying the Scriptures that leads us deeper into God's Word. We slow down. We read a shorter passage more than once. We chew it over slowly and carefully. We savor it. We open ourselves so that Scripture speaks to us in a new way with personal connection. We invite Jesus Christ, the Living Word, to touch our souls deeply.

So, Lectio Divina is not Bible study or even an alternative to Bible study but something altogether different. The practice understands Scripture as a meeting place for a personal encounter with the Living God. It operates very much on the emotional rather than the purely cerebral level. It is perhaps hearty rather than heady. Through it we allow ourselves to be formed in the likeness of Christ.

Lectio Divina is about communing with God, much like when we receive the Sacrament of Holy Communion. It's meant to be an intensely personal experience. Thus, we don't simply read the text; we think about it, we pray about it, we reflect on it, and we are silent with it, inviting the Holy Spirit to transform our hearts and minds in a whole new way.

We will be practicing Lectio Divina as a congregation as we read through the Gospel of John over the course of 44 weeks. In other words, as you are experiencing God's Word in a new way, you will have opportunity to share your thoughts, insights, and transformation with others at Faith Lutheran.

If this all sounds too mystical, rest assured that each day, as you are reading a Bible passage, you will also be invited to read some reflections from Chuck Swindoll, a winsome Bible teacher and story-teller of nearly 60 years. You are also encouraged to participate in a Life Group conversation, utilizing the reflections of Anglican Pastor NT Wright. Of course, each Sunday morning, you will also be encouraged and challenged from a Lutheran perspective.

 FAITH LUTHERAN CHURCH OF MCLEAN COUNTY 2022

CHARLES R. SWINDOLL

SWINDOLL'S
LIVING
INSIGHTS

NEW TESTAMENT COMMENTARY

JOHN

Tyndale House Publishers, Inc.
Carol Stream, Illinois

Swindoll's Living Insights New Testament Commentary, Volume 4

Visit Tyndale online at www.tyndale.com.

Insights on John copyright © 2014 by Charles R. Swindoll, Inc.

Designed by Nicole Grimes

Published in association with Yates & Yates, LLP (www.yates2.com).

Library of Congress Cataloging-in-Publication Data
Swindoll, Charles R.
 [Insights on John]
 John / Charles R. Swindoll.
     pages cm. — (Swindoll's living insights New Testament commentary ; Volume 4)
 Rev. and expanded ed. of: Insights on John. 2010.
 Includes bibliographical references.
 ISBN 978-1-4143-9379-7 (hc)
1. Bible. John—Commentaries. I. Title.
 BS2615.53.S95 2014
 226.5′077—dc23   2014020735

Previously published by Zondervan under ISBN 978-0-310-28435-2

Printed in China
25   24   23   22   21
 9   8   7   6   5

CONTENTS

AUTHOR'S PREFACE

For more than sixty years I have loved the Bible. It was that love for the Scriptures, mixed with a clear call into the gospel ministry during my tour of duty in the Marine Corps, that resulted in my going to Dallas Theological Seminary to prepare for a lifetime of ministry. During those four great years I had the privilege of studying under outstanding men of God, who also loved God's Word. They not only held the inerrant Word of God in high esteem, they taught it carefully, preached it passionately, and modeled it consistently. A week never passes without my giving thanks to God for the grand heritage that has been mine to claim! I am forever indebted to those fine theologians and mentors, who cultivated in me a strong commitment to the understanding, exposition, and application of God's truth.

For more than fifty years I have been engaged in doing just that—*and how I love it!* I confess without hesitation that I am addicted to the examination and the proclamation of the Scriptures. Because of this, books have played a major role in my life for as long as I have been in ministry—especially those volumes that explain the truths and enhance my understanding of what God has written. Through these many years I have collected a large personal library, which has proven invaluable as I have sought to remain a faithful student of the Bible. To the end of my days, my major goal in life is to communicate the Word with accuracy, insight, clarity, and practicality. Without informative and reliable books to turn to, I would have "run dry" decades ago.

Among my favorite and most well-worn volumes are those that have enabled me to get a better grasp of the biblical text. Like most expositors, I am forever searching for literary tools that I can use to hone my gifts and sharpen my skills. For me, that means finding resources that make the complicated simple and easy to understand, that offer insightful comments and word pictures that enable me to see the relevance of sacred truth in light of my twenty-first-century world, and that drive those truths home to my heart in ways I do not easily forget. When I come across such books, they wind up in my hands as I devour them and then place them in my library for further reference . . . and, believe me, I often return to them. What a relief it is to have these resources to turn to when I lack fresh insight, or when I need just the right story or illustration, or when I get stuck in the tangled text and cannot find my way out. For the serious expositor, a library is essential. As a mentor of mine once said, "Where else can you have ten thousand professors at your fingertips?"

In recent years I have discovered there are not nearly enough resources like those I just described. It was such a discovery that prompted me to consider becoming a part of the answer instead of lamenting the problem. But the solution would result in a huge undertaking. A writing project that covers all of the books and letters of the New Testament seemed overwhelming and intimidating. A rush of relief came when I realized that during the past fifty-plus years I've taught and preached through most of the New Testament. In my files were folders filled with notes from those messages that were just lying there, waiting to be brought out of hiding, given a fresh and relevant touch in light of today's needs, and applied to fit into the lives of men and women who long for a fresh word from the Lord. *That did it!* I began to work on plans to turn all of those notes into this commentary on the New Testament.

I must express my gratitude to both Mark Gaither and Mike Svigel for their tireless and devoted efforts, serving as my hands-on, day-to-day editors. They have done superb work as we have walked our way through the verses and chapters of all twenty-seven New Testament books. It has been a pleasure to see how they have taken my original material and helped me shape it into a style that remains true to the text of the Scriptures, at the same time interestingly and creatively developed, and all the while allowing my voice to come through in a natural and easy-to-read manner.

I need to add sincere words of appreciation to the congregations I have served in various parts of these United States for more than five decades. It has been my good fortune to be the recipient of their love, support, encouragement, patience, and frequent words of affirmation as I have fulfilled my calling to stand and deliver God's message year after year. The sheep from all those flocks have endeared themselves to this shepherd in more ways than I can put into words . . . and none more than those I currently serve with delight at Stonebriar Community Church in Frisco, Texas.

Finally, I must thank my wife, Cynthia, for her understanding of my addiction to studying, to preaching, and to writing. Never has she discouraged me from staying at it. Never has she failed to urge me in the pursuit of doing my very best. On the contrary, her affectionate support personally, and her own commitment to excellence in leading Insight for Living for more than three and a half decades, have combined to keep me faithful to my calling "in season and out of season." Without her devotion to me and apart from our mutual partnership throughout our lifetime of ministry together, Swindoll's Living Insights would never have been undertaken.

I am grateful that it has now found its way into your hands and, ultimately, onto the shelves of your library. My continued hope and prayer is that you will find these volumes helpful in your own study and personal application of the Bible. May they help you come to realize, as I have over these many years, that God's Word is as timeless as it is true.

The grass withers, the flower fades,
But the word of our God stands forever. (Isa. 40:8)

Chuck Swindoll
Frisco, Texas

THE STRONG'S NUMBERING SYSTEM

Swindoll's Living Insights New Testament Commentary uses the Strong's word-study numbering system to give both newer and more advanced Bible students alike quicker, more convenient access to helpful original-language tools (e.g., concordances, lexicons, and theological dictionaries). The Strong's numbering system, made popular by the *Strong's Exhaustive Concordance of the Bible*, is used with the majority of biblical Greek and Hebrew reference works. Those who are unfamiliar with the ancient Hebrew, Aramaic, and Greek alphabets can quickly find information on a given word by looking up the appropriate index number. Advanced students will find the system helpful because it allows them to quickly find the lexical form of obscure conjugations and inflections.

When a Greek word is mentioned in the text, the Strong's number is included in square brackets after the Greek word. So in the example of the Greek word *agapē* [26], "love," the number is used with Greek tools keyed to the Strong's system.

On occasion, a Hebrew word is mentioned in the text. The Strong's Hebrew numbers are completely separate from the Greek numbers, so Hebrew numbers are prefixed with a letter "H." So, for example, the Hebrew word *kapporet* [H3727], "mercy seat," comes from *kopher* [H3722], "to ransom," "to secure favor through a gift."

INSIGHTS ON JOHN

The Creator voluntarily became one of us in the person of Jesus Christ—who suffered as we suffer, who was tempted as we are tempted, and who endured injustice like we will never know, yet without sin. I am comforted to know that God understands and empathizes. Through His incarnation, we can appreciate His compassion more fully. Because He lived and died as a man, we can more easily accept that, in His resurrection, the Son is for us even while we feel abandoned, mistreated, or punished by God.

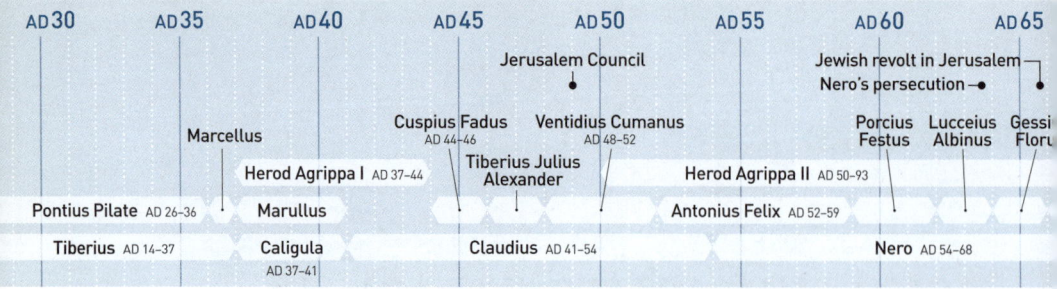

AD 30	AD 35	AD 40	AD 45	AD 50	AD 55	AD 60	AD 65

Jerusalem Council

Jewish revolt in Jerusalem
Nero's persecution →

Marcellus

Cuspius Fadus AD 44–46

Ventidius Cumanus AD 48–52

Porcius Festus

Lucceius Albinus

Gessi Floru

Herod Agrippa I AD 37–44

Tiberius Julius Alexander

Herod Agrippa II AD 50–93

Pontius Pilate AD 26–36

Marullus

Antonius Felix AD 52–59

Tiberius AD 14–37

Caligula AD 37–41

Claudius AD 41–54

Nero AD 54–68

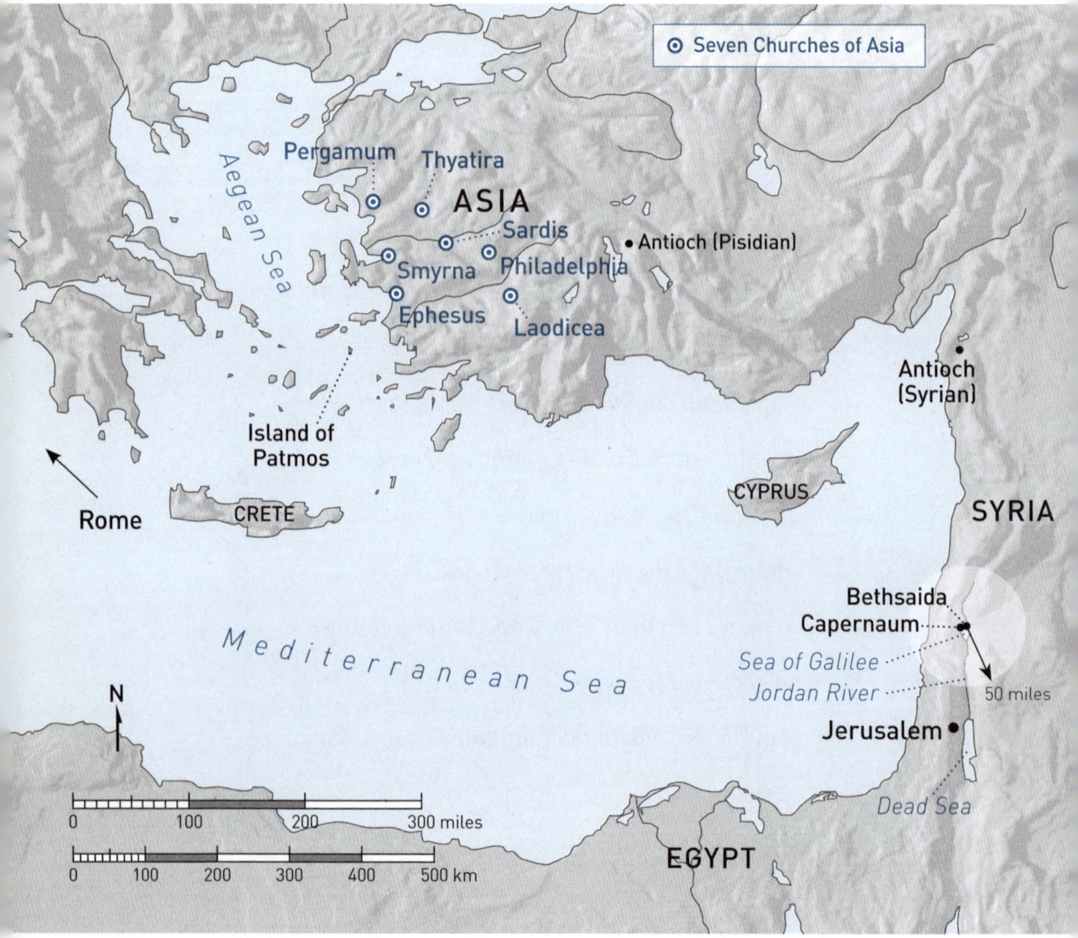

⊙ Seven Churches of Asia

Aegean Sea

Pergamum

Thyatira

ASIA

Sardis

• Antioch (Pisidian)

Smyrna

Philadelphia

Ephesus

Laodicea

Island of Patmos

Rome

CRETE

CYPRUS

Antioch (Syrian)

SYRIA

Bethsaida
Capernaum

Sea of Galilee

Jordan River

50 miles

N

Mediterranean Sea

Jerusalem •

Dead Sea

0	100	200	300 miles

0	100	200	300	400	500 km

EGYPT

John's World. Before he met Jesus, John probably thought he would spend his life tending the family fishing business in Bethsaida and travel no farther than 50 miles (80 km) from home. But the destruction of Jerusalem in AD 70 probably forced him to relocate to Syrian Antioch, where a large Gentile church continued to thrive. Then late in the apostle's life, Domitian exiled him to Patmos, where he penned Revelation. Tradition strongly suggests he spent the remainder of his life near Ephesus, ministering to the churches in Asia.

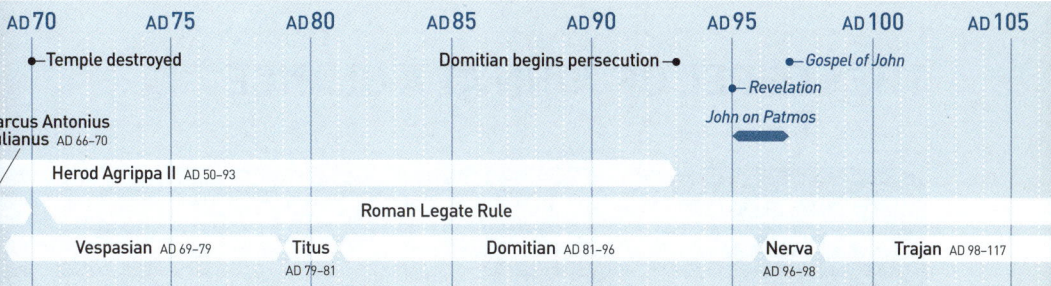

AD 70   AD 75   AD 80   AD 85   AD 90   AD 95   AD 100   AD 105

●—Temple destroyed   Domitian begins persecution —●   ●—Gospel of John

●—Revelation

John on Patmos

arcus Antonius
Julianus AD 66–70

Herod Agrippa II AD 50–93

Roman Legate Rule

Vespasian AD 69–79   Titus   Domitian AD 81–96   Nerva   Trajan AD 98–117
AD 79–81   AD 96–98

JOHN

INTRODUCTION

John had lived long enough to see it all, from the beginning all the way through to the end. As a brash, blustering young man, the idea of tramping around the wilderness of Judea after John the Baptizer appealed to him a great deal—so much so that the young fisherman left a thriving fishing enterprise in the hands of his brother, James, and abandoned his privileged status for the Baptizer's diet of locusts and wild honey . . . and for the chance to help prepare Israel for the coming of the Messiah. He helped the forerunner of the Messiah baptize thousands of repentant Jews, and supported the strange, Elijah-like figure as he called down judgment upon the corrupt leaders of the Jewish people.

Then, finally, the day came when John saw the long-awaited Anointed One. He looked nothing like what John had imagined, but the declaration of his wilderness mentor, John the Baptizer, was unequivocal: This was the One. He and another of the Baptizer's disciples decided to get a closer look, to follow Him home, to hear what He had to say about Himself and Israel. Before the dawn of the next day, he knew: They had found the Messiah.

The few years John spent with Jesus flew by in the beat of a lash, yet remained vividly clear in his mind for more than seventy years. During that short time with Jesus, he saw the man he thought would be a conquering super-David, the Savior of Israel, stripped, beaten mercilessly, and hung on a cross like a petty thug. He saw the sky darken as the Light of the world faded into death. Then he saw his hope resurrected to assume a more glorious form than he ever could have imagined, and he stood in awe as the presence of God filled the squabbling, self-promoting disciples and transformed them into the body of Christ—the bones and muscle, hands and feet of Christ.

THE GOSPEL OF JOHN AT A GLANCE

SECTION	PROLOGUE	PRESENTATION OF THE WORD	AUTHENTICATIO OF THE WORD
PASSAGE	1:1-18	1:19–4:54	5:1–12:50
THEMES	God in human flesh ——————— The evil-dominated world	Encounters with the Son of God	"His own" ——————— "The world"
KEY TERMS	Grace Receive The "Word" Flesh Life	Truth Baptize Testimony Believe Sign	Truly Glory Work(s) Judge
EMPHASIS	**PUBLIC SIGNS** • Water to wine (ch. 2) • Heals royal official's son (ch. 4)	• Heals invalid (ch. 5) • Feeds multitude (ch. 6) • Walks on water (ch. 6)	• Heals blind man (ch. 9) • Raises dead (ch. 11)
AUDIENCE	"THE WORLD"		
TIME	Prologue	Approximately 3 years	

CONFIRMATION OF THE WORD	VINDICATION OF THE WORD	
13:1–17:26	18:1–20:31	21:1-25
Love among believers Obedience Understanding Holy Spirit ―――――――― Persecution of the world Hatred Darkness Tribulation	The Son glorified Triumph over evil The ascension of Christ The commissioning of the disciples	
Glorify Comprehend Abide Hate Advocate	Follow Completed Manifest	

PRIVATE TALKS

- Heaven (ch. 14)
- Fruit (ch. 15)
- Promises (ch. 16)
- Prayer (ch. 17)
- Appearances (ch. 20)
- Commissioning (ch. 21)

BELIEVERS

Approximately 3 weeks	Epilogue

Then, as the blood of his martyred brothers and sisters yielded new believers, John nurtured them. As Paul, Barnabas, Silas, Apollos, Luke, Timothy, Titus, and a host of other missionaries zealously expanded the church westward, John anchored its foundation. As critics bashed, John defended. As imposters subverted, John exposed them. As false prophets misled, John refuted their heretical message. He condensed his teaching into three letters (1–3 John), which originally circulated within the churches of Asia Minor around AD 65.

Having outlived all his martyred peers, John was exiled by Emperor Domitian to the nearly barren isle of Patmos. There he saw the future of the world all the way to its destruction and re-creation, and then preserved everything he heard and witnessed in "The Revelation," which he sent as a letter to the churches of Asia Minor that were under his care. After Domitian's death in AD 96, John rested in the care of the church in Ephesus, which in turn enjoyed his gentle, grandfather-like shepherding.

The Synoptic Gospels, written as early as the AD 50s by Matthew, Mark, and Luke, had been staples of church teaching for decades. They told the story of Jesus from different perspectives, yet they chose to include many of the same events, largely taken from Jesus' ministry in Galilee. Decades later, when the elder John was in Ephesus, the church was no longer a budding movement, but an established community and system of thought. The challenges were different than when Christianity was in its infancy. The danger came less in the form of physical attacks or religious opposition, and more through philosophical corruption and theological compromise. Furthermore, the biography of Jesus lacked a much-needed cosmic dimension.

So, in the final years of John's life, after he had witnessed the most significant period of history the world has ever known and with the nearness of death giving memories an urgency to be shared, John wrote of his Master.

"THAT YOU MAY BELIEVE"

The Gospel of John is a masterpiece of storytelling. It is at once charming in its simplicity and challenging in its depth, a rare work of literature that fun-loving children and deep-thinking philosophers can share equally. John's God-breathed account of Christ's earthly ministry uses such elementary Greek, it reads like a child's primer and is often one of the first books novice learners of Koiné learn to translate. Yet philosophers and theologians spend lifetimes trying to fully comprehend the profound truths John presents.

John's Gospel presents God as Father more tenderly than any other book in the Bible. It boldly and unambiguously establishes the dual nature of Jesus Christ—fully God and fully human, perfectly united in one person. And it reveals the mystery of the Holy Spirit unlike any other Gospel. Moreover, John's narrative provides a broad range of practical lessons to guide the believer through life. Several passages come to our rescue when leading someone to faith in Jesus Christ, while others bring comfort and consolation when we are burying a cherished loved one. From the Gospel of John, we learn about our increasing estrangement from the world and our deepening intimacy with the Almighty, and we begin to appreciate the priority the Lord places on unity in the family of God.

Despite its intricacy and complexity, the Fourth Gospel is usually the first book of the Bible to be read by students and new believers. Martin Luther marveled over the dual nature of John's writing, admitting, "Never in my life have I read a book written in simpler words than this, and yet the words are inexpressible!"[1]

John's approach is deliberate. Under the inspiration of the Holy Spirit, he carefully crafted each sentence to unveil the fascinating mysteries of heaven in simple language, and he painstakingly chose which facts to relate and which to leave out. In his own words, "There are also many other things which Jesus did, which if they were written in detail, I suppose that even the world itself would not contain the books that would be written" (John 21:25). Rather than pen a document that quadrupled the size of the Old Testament, he chose the "less is more" approach. Instead of overwhelming us with volumes of information, he strategically chose which stories to relate in order to accomplish his primary purpose: "So that you may believe that Jesus is the Christ, the Son of God; and that believing you may have life in His name" (20:31).

WHY FOUR GOSPELS?

Why do we have four biographies of Jesus when one could have done the job just as well? Why not fourteen? In reality, we do not have four Gospels; we have one Gospel from four different vantage points. We have one biography from four writers, each providing his own unique perspective.

If we were to document the life of Jesus using only pictures, we could choose one of several possible methods. For example, we could use a motion picture camera to record every movement in detail, and—if the reel is long enough—replay His life from birth to death to resurrection and beyond. The running time of the film would exceed thirty-three years of non-stop viewing! Another method would be to capture key moments in still photographs—perhaps from several angles at once— and tell the story of His life in a photo essay. The benefits would be obvious. The story could be told briefly, yet adequately, allowing time to reflect on the details of the most important moments. In the case of the Gospels, we have four albums of Christ's life, put together by individuals who highlighted different, yet crucial, themes. Before John penned his account, these three were in circulation:

Matthew was a Jewish disciple of Jesus Christ who once earned his living as a tax collector, an official of the Roman government. Moved by the Spirit of God, he wrote a biography of Jesus from a Hebrew point of view, emphasizing the regal rights of Jesus as Messiah and legitimate King of Israel. Matthew traces Christ's genealogy from Abraham, through King David. It's a Jewish book written by a Jew to his fellow children of the covenant. Matthew's primary theme: *The Messiah has come.*

Mark was not one of the Twelve, but the son of a follower named Mary (Acts 12:12) and a close associate of Barnabas, Paul, and Peter. He presents Christ's ministry from a practical, action-oriented point of view in a narrative frequently punctuated by the phrase, "and immediately . . ." This style would have appealed to the can-do Romans of the first century, who respected deep thinkers but looked to men of action for leadership. Mark's Gospel shows Jesus to be the no-nonsense God-man who came from heaven to complete a task. "[He] did not come to be served, but to serve, and to give His life a ransom for many" (Mark 10:45). Mark's primary theme: *The Son of God came to seek, serve, and save.*

Luke was a physician, probably born and reared in Macedonia. He was a Gentile, not a Jew. He wrote to neither the spiritually privileged Jew nor the politically privileged Roman, but to common Greeks, most of whom had no power, no wealth, and no hope. Luke's Gospel highlights the humanity of Jesus, favoring the title "Son of Man" and providing details about His humble birth, His ordinary boyhood, His compassion for the poor and sick, and the global scope of His ministry. Luke's genealogy traces Jesus' lineage all the way back to Adam, the father of all humanity. Luke's primary theme: *The Son of Man came to redeem all of humanity.*

John certainly knew of the other Gospels and probably taught from them for many years before deciding under the guidance of the Holy Spirit that the biography of Jesus was still incomplete. The Christian world knew Jesus as the King of the Jews, Jesus as the servant, and Jesus as the Son of Man, but there remained a need to proclaim Jesus as the Son of God. John wrote his Gospel so that we would know that the Son of Man is God in human flesh—completely human, yet no less God than when, "in the beginning," He spoke the universe into existence.

The Gospel of John provides no genealogy, illustrating the fact that Deity has no beginning. The Gospel of John offers no childhood details and retells no parables,[2] perhaps to emphasize Jesus' transcendent nature as God. The Gospel of John bypasses Jesus' temptation in the wilderness, His transfiguration on the mountain, His commissioning the disciples after His resurrection, and His ascension from earth.

Instead, John writes from a philosophical and theological perspective, placing great emphasis on the miracles of Jesus, which he calls "signs." For John, the miracles were indicators of a supernatural happening, proof that what many considered to be theoretical truths were in fact tangibly real. The Word had become flesh to give all of humanity every reason to believe and to leave us with no excuse for doubt. John's primary theme: *The man we know as Jesus is none other than God on earth.*

- Matthew says, "This is the Messiah, the King; worship Him."
- Mark says, "This is the Servant who served humanity; follow Him."
- Luke says, "This is the only Man among men without sin; emulate Him."
- John says, "This is God in human flesh; believe in Him."

THE CRISIS OF FAITH

John declares, in effect, "I'm not writing merely to inform. I'm not writing merely to entertain. I'm writing to stir the heart of the reader to *believe*." The Greek word *pisteuō* [4100], translated "believe," appears 98 times in the Gospel of John—multiple times per chapter. But what does it mean to believe? Does it mean to believe in the historical personage of Christ, to accept the fact that a man named Jesus lived at some point in time? Does it mean to admire Him, or to emulate Him, or to take up His revolutionary cause? Does it mean to entertain warm feelings, or to venerate Him as more than human, or to devote time and energy in order to please Him?

THE GOSPEL OF JOHN

No. Those kinds of belief are good—some are even necessary. But the kind of belief John calls all his readers to embrace encompasses much more. First, the term *pisteuō* means "to acknowledge the truth as truth." When I say that I believe the book of John, I mean to say that I accept its content as truth. To believe in Christ is, first, to accept what He says as truth. Second, and more important, *pisteuō* means "to trust, to rely upon, to derive confidence in" something or someone. When I say *I believe in Jesus Christ,* I declare that I trust Him, I rely upon Him, I have placed my complete confidence in Him; everything I know about this life and whatever occurs after death is dependent upon His claims about Himself and how I respond to His offer of grace.

Here is how I respond: I believe in Jesus Christ.

Recently, churches all across the United States have experienced remarkable growth and the "megachurch" phenomenon has encircled the globe. It's exciting to see. However, the burgeoning numbers packing these sanctuaries include multitudes caught up in a movement, who listen week to week but have never given themselves over to the message of Jesus Christ and placed their absolute trust in Him. Many listen and learn and nod in agreement, but they do not *believe.* They have not submitted their hearts and wills to the truth of Jesus Christ— His identity as God and His offer of eternal life through faith alone.

Another important aspect of John's call to belief is that we are invited to believe in Jesus Christ, the person. Not merely His message, not merely His teaching, not merely His example, not merely His challenge to live a certain way. We are called first and foremost to believe in *Him.* This was the intellectual and moral crisis presented to people of all kinds in John's narrative, many of whom responded with *pistis* [4102]—belief, complete trust. Here are just six examples of people who responded positively to Jesus' message:

John the Baptizer
"I did not recognize Him, but He who sent me to baptize in water said to me, 'He upon whom you see the Spirit descending and remaining upon Him, this is the One who baptizes in the Holy Spirit.' I myself have seen, and have testified that this is the Son of God." (John 1:33-34)

Nathanael
Nathanael said to [Philip], "Can any good thing come out of Nazareth?" Philip said to him, "Come and see." Jesus saw Nathanael coming to Him, and said of him, "Behold, an Israelite indeed, in

whom there is no deceit!" Nathanael said to Him, "How do You know me?" Jesus answered and said to him, "Before Philip called you, when you were under the fig tree, I saw you." Nathanael answered Him, "Rabbi, You are the Son of God; You are the King of Israel." (John 1:46-49)

Peter

As a result of this [difficult teaching] many of His disciples withdrew and were not walking with Him anymore. So Jesus said to the twelve, "You do not want to go away also, do you?" Simon Peter answered Him, "Lord, to whom shall we go? You have words of eternal life. We have believed and have come to know that You are the Holy One of God." (John 6:66-69)

Martha

Martha said to [Jesus], "I know that he will rise again in the resurrection on the last day." Jesus said to her, "I am the resurrection and the life; he who believes in Me will live even if he dies, and everyone who lives and believes in Me will never die. Do you believe this?" She said to Him, "Yes, Lord; I have believed that You are the Christ, the Son of God, *even* He who comes into the world." (John 11:24-27)

Thomas

Then [Jesus] said to Thomas, "Reach here with your finger, and see My hands; and reach here your hand and put it into My side; and do not be unbelieving, but believing." Thomas answered and said to Him, "My Lord and my God!" Jesus said to him, "Because you have seen Me, have you believed? Blessed *are* they who did not see, and *yet* believed." (John 20:27-29)

John (the author of this Gospel)

Many other signs Jesus also performed in the presence of the disciples, which are not written in this book; but these have been written so that you may believe that Jesus is the Christ, the Son of God; and that believing you may have life in His name. (John 20:30-31)

SIGNS AND DISCOURSES

John's narrative is remarkable in several respects, not the least of which is its structure. The first verse of chapter 13 marks a dramatic shift in the story of Christ's earthly ministry so that the final eight chapters read very differently from the first twelve. Chapters 1 through 12 describe an extensive, very public ministry and message, whereas chapters 13 through 21 bring us behind closed doors to witness the private ministry of Jesus. Chapters 1 through 12 carry us through a period of more than three years, whereas chapters 13 through 20 span four days (followed by the epilogue, chapter 21, which took place within forty days of Christ's resurrection.) The first section highlights the miracles of Jesus, while the second section records His discourses with the Twelve.

JOHN 1–12	JOHN 13–21
3+ Years	3+ Days
Public Proclamation	Private Instruction
Spectacular Miracles	Intimate Discourses

Chapter 1 opens with the forerunner proclaiming the arrival of the Messiah and the baptism of Jesus, which is accompanied by the booming voice of the Father. In chapter 2, Jesus turns water into wine. In chapter 4, He heals an official's son. In chapter 5, He heals a paralyzed man. In chapter 6, He feeds more than 5,000 men and their families and walks across the surface of the Sea of Galilee. In chapter 9, He gives sight to a man who has suffered blindness from birth. His miracles reach a crescendo in chapter 11 with His raising a man from the dead. John calls these "signs" because they prove that Jesus, while completely human, is also more than human. He is the Son of Man who is also the Son of God.

Chapter 13 begins a relatively quiet period in the narrative, a calm before the great storm. Just before Jesus' arrest, trials, crucifixion, burial, and resurrection, He pulled His men aside for a final time of preparation. This was a review of His most important lessons before the great test, after which they would be sent out to minister without their Master's physical presence.

Chapter 13 describes servant-hearted love. Chapter 14 explains the promise of heaven, the unity of the Trinity, and the promise of the Spirit. Chapter 15 encourages the believer in a hostile world and emphasizes the need to abide in Christ. Chapter 16 warns of the certainty of challenges and persecution, and assures of the care of the Holy Spirit, the power of prayer, and the promise of victory. Chapter 17 relates Jesus' prayer for Himself, His disciples, and all future believers—a prayer that casts His vision for the church. Chapters 18 and 19 describe His Passion, then chapter 20 takes us behind closed doors for several private resurrection appearances to His closest followers. Chapter 21 allows us to witness the Lord's quiet fellowship with His disciples and His gentle restoration of Peter after his failure.

John did not structure his Gospel account haphazardly. The narrative unfolds much like the Christian life itself. Our initial, intriguing introduction to the Savior leads quickly to a call to believe and to follow. Understanding will come in time. This is not an intellectual decision but a moral one. Then, as we witness His power, hear His teaching, and experience life in His presence, our understanding deepens and our confidence grows. Gradually we become mature disciples, though never beyond the need for grace after failure.

In other words, John's account of Jesus' life and ministry on earth is no mere biography. The Gospel of John is an invitation to believe in the Son of God, to become His disciples, to deepen our understanding of His identity and mission, to grow in maturity, and to join Him in tending His sheep.

Now . . . let us behold "the Lamb of God, who takes away the sin of the world" (1:29)!

KEY TERMS IN JOHN 1:1-18

charis (χάρις) [5485] "grace," "joy," "divine kindness," "unmerited blessing"
The secular Greek definition is simply "rejoicing," and is associated with the feeling of joy. In the Old Testament, this feeling is most frequently associated with God's work of salvation, delight in His law, or His abundant provision at harvest. John draws heavily upon the joy of harvest time and wedding celebrations, both of which picture great blessing received as a gift. *See John 1:14, 16, 17.*

lambanō (λαμβάνω) [2983] "to receive," "to accept," "to hold to oneself"
In the literal sense, the term means to accept what has been offered. When used of a person, "to receive" is to welcome personal connection, as when a man or woman receives a partner for marriage, or when a host receives a houseguest. *See John 1:12, 16; 5:43; 13:20.*

logos (λόγος) [3056] "word," "message," "issue," "reasoning"
The most basic meaning of the term is "word," which can be a single term or an entire message, such as, "We received *word* of the army's victory." Greek philosophers adopted the term to describe the apparent logic that causes the universe to obey natural laws, such as gravity, mathematics, and morality. To them, the universe would fall into utter chaos were it not for this impersonal divine mind, which they named "the Word." John's Gospel claims that the divine mind is, indeed, personal and that He became flesh in the person of Jesus. *See John 1:1, 14; 12:48; 17:17.*

sarx (σάρξ) [4561] "flesh," "substance of the body," "earthly, tangible matter"
This word has three spheres of use: literal, technical, and philosophical. In the literal sense, "flesh" is merely muscle and sinew, as distinct from bone, blood, etc. It also acquired a technical nuance, closely related to the literal, to denote the material aspect of humanity. Greek philosophy and religion—especially the Gnosticism of John's day—eventually came to see everything tangible, including "flesh," as inherently evil.[1] John uses "flesh" to speak of humanity in the tangible realm for the express purpose of undermining the influence of Greek religion on Christian doctrine. *See John 1:13, 14; 3:6; 17:2.*

zoē (ζωή) [2222] "life"
At its most basic, the term refers to the physical vitality of a living being.[2] For Greek-speaking Jews, *zoē* is closely related to *hayim* [H2416], the Hebrew term for life, which they regarded as the supreme good of creation and a divine gift to be cherished, albeit shortened and corrupted by sin.[3] The Jewish notion of *zoē* carried with it the opportunity to enjoy *shalom* [H7965], "peace." *See John 1:4; 3:16; 11:25; 14:6.*

PROLOGUE (JOHN 1:1-18)

In 1964, Thayer S. Warshaw, an English teacher at Newton High School near Boston, worried that when public schools banned the Bible, students would be deprived of an important part of their culture. To make his point, he devised a quiz on common allusions to Scripture as they appear in secular literature and language. Despite their obvious intelligence and first-rate education, the majority of these college-bound students couldn't complete the following common expressions:

> "They shall beat their swords into plowshares." (63%)
> "Many are called, but few are chosen." (79%)
> "The truth shall make you free." (84%)
> "Pride goeth before a fall." (88%)
> "The love of money is the root of all evil." (93%)

Furthermore, several students at this nationally acclaimed school thought that Sodom and Gomorrah were lovers (rather than cities). Many named the four Gospels as "Matthew, Mark, Luther (rather than Luke), and John." According to these top-ranked students, Eve was created from an apple (rather than eating an "apple"), Moses baptized Jesus, Jezebel was Ahab's donkey (rather than his wife), and Jesus spoke in "parodies" (rather than parables).[4]

Around this same time, during the late 1950s and early 1960s, I had a close relationship with Campus Crusade for Christ. Some close friends of mine and I would talk to students on the campuses of the University of Oklahoma, Oklahoma State, and the University of Texas at Austin and in Arlington. As a conversation starter, we used a simple questionnaire, which included the question, "Who, in your opinion, was Jesus of Nazareth?" The most common response was, "The Son of God." That may surprise you, as it did me. I expected "a great teacher," or "the founder of Christianity," or "a martyr who died for his beliefs." However, when I asked the follow-up question—"How did you come to that conclusion?"—the most common response was, "I don't know." I find the same to be true among many Christians today. They know the right answer, but they don't know *why* the answer is true.

The apostle John wrote his account of Jesus' life to reveal the identity of Jesus so that we might respond in belief. He opens his Gospel with a prologue (1:1-18), which declares unambiguously that Jesus is God in human flesh. John then weaves this primary thesis through the rest of the narrative. Jesus claimed deity, His miracles supported His claim, His activities presupposed this truth, and His resurrection finally vindicated everything He said and did.

God in Human Flesh
JOHN 1:1-18

NASB

¹In the beginning was the Word, and the Word was with God, and the Word was God. ²ᵃHe was in the beginning with God. ³All things came into being through Him, and apart from Him nothing came into being that has come into being. ⁴In Him was life, and the life was the Light of men. ⁵The Light shines in the darkness, and the darkness did not ᵃcomprehend it.

⁶There ᵃcame a man sent from God, whose name was John. ⁷ᵃHe came ᵇas a witness, to testify about the Light, so that all might believe through him. ⁸ᵃHe was not the Light, but *he came* to testify about the Light.

⁹There was the true Light ᵃwhich, coming into the world, enlightens every man. ¹⁰He was in the world, and the world was made through Him, and the world did not know Him. ¹¹He came to His ᵃown, and those who were His own did not receive Him. ¹²But as many as received Him, to them He gave the right to become children of God, *even* to those who believe in His name, ¹³who were

NLT

¹ In the beginning the Word
    already existed.
The Word was with God,
    and the Word was God.
² He existed in the beginning with
    God.
³ God created everything through
    him,
    and nothing was created
        except through him.
⁴ The Word gave life to everything
    that was created,*
    and his life brought light to
        everyone.
⁵ The light shines in the darkness,
    and the darkness can never
        extinguish it.*

⁶God sent a man, John the Baptist,* ⁷to tell about the light so that everyone might believe because of his testimony. ⁸John himself was not the light; he was simply a witness to tell about the light. ⁹The one who is the true light, who gives light to everyone, was coming into the world.

¹⁰He came into the very world he created, but the world didn't recognize him. ¹¹He came to his own people, and even they rejected him. ¹²But to all who believed him and accepted him, he gave the right to become children of God. ¹³They are reborn—not with a physical birth

ᵃborn, not of ᵇblood nor of the will of the flesh nor of the will of man, but of God.

¹⁴And the Word became flesh, and ᵃdwelt among us, and we saw His glory, glory as of ᵇthe only begotten from the Father, full of grace and truth. ¹⁵John testified about Him and cried out, saying, "This was He of whom I said, 'He who comes after me ᵃhas a higher rank than I, for He existed before me.'" ¹⁶For of His fullness ᵃwe have all received, and ᵇgrace upon grace. ¹⁷For the Law was given through Moses; grace and truth ᵃwere realized through Jesus Christ. ¹⁸No one has seen God at any time; the only begotten God who is in the bosom of the Father, He has explained *Him.*

1:2 ᵃLit *This one* 1:5 ᵃOr *overpower* 1:6 ᵃOr *came into being* 1:7 ᵃLit *This one* ᵇLit *for testimony* 1:8 ᵃLit *That one* 1:9 ᵃOr *which enlightens every person coming into the world* 1:11 ᵃOr *own things, possessions, domain* 1:13 ᵃOr *begotten* ᵇLit *bloods* 1:14 ᵃOr *tabernacled;* i.e. lived temporarily ᵇOr *unique, only one of His kind* 1:15 ᵃLit *has become before me* 1:16 ᵃLit *we all received* ᵇLit *grace for grace* 1:17 ᵃLit *came to be*

resulting from human passion or plan, but a birth that comes from God.

¹⁴So the Word became human* and made his home among us. He was full of unfailing love and faithfulness.* And we have seen his glory, the glory of the Father's one and only Son.

¹⁵John testified about him when he shouted to the crowds, "This is the one I was talking about when I said, 'Someone is coming after me who is far greater than I am, for he existed long before me.'"

¹⁶From his abundance we have all received one gracious blessing after another.* ¹⁷For the law was given through Moses, but God's unfailing love and faithfulness came through Jesus Christ. ¹⁸No one has ever seen God. But the unique One, who is himself God,* is near to the Father's heart. He has revealed God to us.

1:3-4 Or *and nothing that was created was created except through him. The Word gave life to everything.* 1:5 Or *and the darkness has not understood it.* 1:6 Greek *a man named John.* 1:14a Greek *became flesh.* 1:14b Or *grace and truth;* also in 1:17. 1:16 Or *received the grace of Christ rather than the grace of the law;* Greek reads *received grace upon grace.* 1:18 Some manuscripts read *But the one and only Son.*

John's prologue offers four reasons to believe that Jesus Christ, the Word, is God:

- The Word is eternal; He had no beginning and He will have no end (1:1-2).
- The Word is the Creator; all things were made through Him (1:3).
- The Word is the Source of life; nothing remains alive apart from Him (1:4-13).
- The Word, though completely human, fully reveals the Father (1:14-18).

Before we examine each of these reasons in detail, read 1:1-18, and take note of John's deliberate progression from infinity and eternity down to the single individual, Christ, in whom resides all that is infinite and eternal.

EPHESUS: THE BIRTHPLACE OF "THE WORD"

JOHN 1:1

Around 500 BC, a Greek nobleman of Ephesus named Heraclitus taught that the universe operates according to a rational structure, a unified ordering principle, which we can discern if we carefully observe its patterns and solve its many riddles. According to this theory, all the laws of physics, mathematics, reason, and even morality can be traced back to this one ordering principle, which he called *logos*, "the Word."

Other philosophers, such as the Stoics, adopted this seminal idea and added their own doctrines, even going so far as to describe "the Word" as a divine animating (life-giving, life-moving) principle permeating the universe. Philo (20 BC—AD 50), a Jewish philosopher heavily influenced by Plato, taught that the *logos* was God's creative principle in the realm of pure thought, which cannot have any direct association with anything in the tangible realm of matter.

Ephesus was not only the birthplace of the *logos* idea; it had also become a celebrated repository of texts on Greek philosophy. By the time John lived and taught in Ephesus in the final decades of the first century, clashes with the priests of Artemis were a distant memory. In John's time, the philosophers of Greece, both ancient and modern, threatened to corrupt Christian doctrine. Some have suggested that John was overly influenced by the Greek *logos* idea, and have accused him of leaning toward Gnosticism. However, Greek philosophers would have strongly objected to the *logos* becoming flesh. John merely affirmed the parts of Greek philosophy that were valid in order to preach the truth of Christ on common ground.

— 1:1-2 —

The Word is eternal; He had no beginning and He will have no end.
In eternity past, before the beginning of anything—space, time, matter—in the indefinite expanse of timeless existence, in a beginning that had no beginning, "the Word" was existing in an eternal, infinite "present." The verb translated "was" is the imperfect past tense of the Greek verb *eimi* [1510], "to be." A literal rendering of John's first sentence is, "In the beginning, the Word was existing."

Why is this so important? Because John carefully crafted these initial sentences to establish an essential truth. He chose his words carefully and arranged them precisely to leave no room for misunderstanding. Before any conceivable point in the eternal past, the Word was already existing.[5] The Word, therefore, has no beginning. The Word has always existed.

Later in the prologue (1:14), we learn that the Word is Jesus Christ. The Greek term "Word" is *logos* [3056], which had been a profoundly significant concept among philosophers for at least three centuries before Christ. It referred to an uncreated divine mind that gives meaning and order to the universe. John essentially co-opted the concept, saying in effect, "The concept pagan philosophers have theorized about actually exists; He is God, and Jesus Christ is He."

Mark W. Gaither

The Library of Celsus. For centuries, various schools of Greek philosophy operated in Ephesus, attracting learners from around the Roman Empire. Then, in AD 110, the son of Roman consul Celsus Polemeanus began constructing this library in his father's honor. When completed in AD 135, it housed approximately 12,000 scrolls, which undoubtedly cemented the reputation of Ephesus as a major center of learning.

John continues to describe "the Word" by saying He was *with* God. The Greek preposition *pros* [4314], when used in this particular manner, represents familiarity. "The Word" and God the Father were existing closely together, sharing place, intimacy, and purpose. In fact, the intimacy and familiarity were such that "the Word was God." The Word and God share the same essence; therefore, all that is true of God is true of the Word.

Psalm 90 came from the pen of Moses and it celebrates the eternal existence of God, who has no beginning—unlike His creation.

> LORD, You have been our dwelling place in all generations.
> Before the mountains were born

> Or You gave birth to the earth and the world,
> Even from everlasting to everlasting, You are God.
> (Ps. 90:1-2)

The Hebrew word for "everlasting" is *olam* [H5769], which is probably derived from a similar word meaning "to hide." If an object is moved farther and farther away from an observer, it eventually vanishes from sight. It is beyond the vanishing point. A good paraphrase would render the idea this way: "From the vanishing point in the past to the vanishing point in the future, You have existed, Lord." A. W. Tozer captures the thought well in his book *The Knowledge of the Holy*:

> The mind looks backward in time until the dim past vanishes, then turns and looks into the future till thought and imagination collapse from exhaustion; and God is at both points, unaffected by either.
>
> Time marks the beginning of created existence, and because God never began to exist it can have no application to Him. "Began" is a time word, and can have no personal meaning for the high and lofty One that inhabiteth eternity.[6]

This is what John expresses about the Word. Then, to underscore and summarize his point, John adds, "He was in the beginning with God." In that eternal existence before time, the Word and God were together and they were the same being.

— 1:3 —

The Word is the Creator; all things were made through Him.
In 1:1-2, John states that the Word is Deity and then makes his case from the standpoint of time: Only God is eternal; and because the Word is eternal, He is God. In 1:3, the apostle establishes the deity of Christ from another perspective: creation. In the ancient mind—Hebrew and Gentile—everything that exists can be placed into one of two distinct categories:

"CREATED"	"NOT CREATED"
Things (or beings) that exist because they were created	Things (or beings) that were *not* created because they have always existed

Anything "not created"—that is, anything that was not brought into being—is deity. For the Hebrew in particular, only God was "not created." Therefore, anything said to be "not created" is, by definition, God.

JOHN'S PROLOGUE, AN ANCIENT RUBIK'S CUBE

JOHN 1:3

Why is John's prologue so important? Because false teachers—starting in John's day and persisting even now—claim that Jesus Christ is not God, coeternal and coexistent with the Father in eternity past. Many claim that He was the first created being—that the Father brought the Son into existence, and the Son then brought everything else into being. Arius, a third-century false teacher, was fond of saying, "There was a time when He was not."

This teaching continues today as official doctrine for the Church of Jesus Christ of Latter-day Saints (the Mormons) and the Jehovah's Witnesses, and both organizations have translated John's prologue to suit their theologies. However, John's prologue is not unlike a Rubik's Cube, the puzzle-toy popular in the early 1980s: You can't change one sentence of the prologue without causing logical problems with the others.

For example, Joseph Smith altered John's prologue in his *Inspired Version* of the Scriptures to support the notion that Christ is not God, but an exalted figure created by God before anything else:

> In the beginning was the gospel preached through the Son. And the gospel was the word, and the word was with the Son, and the Son was with God, and the Son was of God. The same was in the beginning with God. All things were made by him; and without him was not anything made which was made. (John 1:1-3, *Inspired Version*)

However, Smith failed to account for 1:3. According to his version, the Word created "all things." Furthermore, anything that "came into being"—that is, anything (or anyone) that had a beginning—was created by the Word. But if "there was a time when Christ was not," if He came into being at some point in time, this would mean that Jesus had to have created Himself before He existed.

If you think that sounds like nonsense, you're right. It *is* nonsense! Therefore, on this point we can agree: "Without him was not anything made which was made." The Son of God could not have made Himself, therefore He is God, and He created all things.

With this ancient worldview in mind, reread 1:3 carefully:

> All things came into being through Him, and apart from Him nothing came into being that has come into being.

John emphasizes the phrase "come into being," which he uses three times. Anything that "came into being" had a beginning. At one point it did not exist, and then it began to exist. John takes us back to eternity past, far beyond Genesis 1:1, to say that the Son of God was already existing. As "very God" (as the Nicene Creed puts it) who existed alone as "not created," He brought everything else that exists into being.

Why is this point so important? Because false teachers—starting in John's day and persisting even now—claim that Jesus Christ is not God, not coequal, coeternal, or coexistent with the Father in eternity past. Many claim that Christ was the first created being—that the Father brought the Son into existence, and the Son then created everything else. Arius, a third-century false teacher, was fond of saying, "There was a time when He was not." However, John points to the moment of creation to say that before anything existed, Christ, who is the Creator, called "all things" into being.

— 1:4-8 —

The Word is the Source of life; nothing remains alive apart from Him.

In 1:4, John's Gospel does something not done by the Synoptic Gospels (Matthew, Mark, and Luke). Matthew traces Christ's genealogy back to Abraham. Luke traces His roots to the first human, Adam. But John reaches beyond them to the creation of the universe. John states that in Jesus Christ was life and light, two images Moses used in reference to God in Genesis 1. The Creator spoke the universe into existence and then filled it with the light of His truth (Gen. 1:3). The Creator then began filling the earth with life: vegetation, sea creatures, birds, land animals, and His crowning achievement, humanity. He breathed His own life into the man and woman, who together bore His image.

John says, in effect, "In the beginning, God the Son created humanity and filled them with life. He then came to earth as a human to bring life again to humanity, which is spiritually dead because of sin." While it is true that John did not specifically mention the fall of humanity (see Gen. 3), it is safe to assume that by the end of the first century, the doctrine of human depravity was well understood by most. Nevertheless, John did highlight our desperate need for salvation by describing the world's reaction to the appearance of Life and Light.

John declares that the darkness of the world did not "comprehend" the Light. The underlying Greek word, *katalambanō* [2638], has a range of meaning depending upon the context and therefore has no direct English equivalent. The primary meaning is "to seize," "to attack," "to overpower," or "to hold without losing grip." However, as often happens in language, the literal definition eventually led to its metaphorical use, "to comprehend or understand." Which did John mean?

"The darkness did not overpower the Light," or "The darkness did not comprehend the Light"?

John could have intended a double meaning. In the end, darkness was not able to *suppress* the Light even by placing the Light in a tomb. However, the verses that follow appear to stress the mental deficiency of the darkness: its unwillingness to believe and therefore its *inability to comprehend*. Then, as the story of Jesus unfolds, John will show that truth is nonsense to a mind darkened by sin (8:44-45, 47; 14:17; 18:38).

John the Baptizer, the man Jesus called the greatest of all the prophets (Matt. 11:9-13), was no match for the darkness. Like Moses, Samuel, Elijah, Isaiah, Jeremiah, Ezekiel, Daniel, and all the luminaries of the Word throughout the centuries before him, John failed to enlighten humanity. After all, they were only human. The only hope for humankind was the Source of light, who can illumine every mind because He is more than human.

ILLUMINATING "LIGHT" IN BIBLICAL LITERATURE

JOHN 1:9

Some symbols are so universal, so common to human experience, they have the power to cross cultural and even linguistic barriers. Students of art and literature know these symbols as *archetypes*. Green, for example, symbolizes growth or new life. Winter alludes to death or hardship. In the Bible and other ancient literature, truth is often pictured as light. When someone gains wisdom, we say he or she has been "enlightened."

When Moses told the story of creation, he drew upon the literary symbol of light to communicate an important truth. Immediately after the formation of space and matter, the Lord filled the void and formless earth with light—literal light, yes, but not merely illumination. Before He fashioned physical sources of light on the fourth day—the sun, moon, and stars—He filled the universe with the light of His presence, with truth, the foundation upon which everything else would be built. Before giving the world order (dividing day from night, sky from earth, dry land from ocean), the Lord suffused every atom with His truth so that everything would reflect His character.

One day, perhaps sooner than we think, a new heaven and a new earth "will not have need of the light of a lamp nor the light of the sun, because the Lord God will illumine them" (Rev. 22:5). Evil will be gone and all of creation will again reflect the One in whom "there is no darkness at all" (1 Jn. 1:5). This is our hope because "these words are faithful and true!" (Rev. 22:6).

— 1:9-13 —

Verse 9 can be troublesome at first glance. It would seem to contradict what John had just declared in 1:5: "The Light shines in the darkness, and the darkness did not comprehend it." Read on and John's point becomes clearer. Now that the Source of light has come to earth and has illumined the minds of humanity, no one can legitimately claim ignorance. All who do not believe are without excuse. That is why, before His arrest, Jesus told His disciples,

> "If I had not come and spoken to them, they would not have sin, but now they have no excuse for their sin. He who hates Me hates My Father also. If I had not done among them the works which no one else did, they would not have sin; but now they have both seen and hated Me and My Father as well. But they have done this to fulfill the word that is written in their Law, 'THEY HATED ME WITHOUT A CAUSE.'" (John 15:22-25)

Let me illustrate John's point another way. Every modern house is connected to an electric grid, which provides all the energy necessary to illumine every dark corner. However, the people living in these homes can choose to live in the dark. The light is available but it isn't compulsory. The Source of light has come to the world and has illumined all minds; however, many choose to draw the shades and shun the light. Now that Christ has come, belief or unbelief is no longer a crisis of the intellect (if it ever was); it is a crisis of the will. When a darkened mind chooses to remain in darkness, no one is to blame but the individual making that choice.

Many have rejected the light; but many have chosen to receive it through faith—the choice to believe in Jesus Christ. John foreshadows the teaching of Christ in 3:1-21 by declaring that those who have chosen to believe are "children of God" as the result of supernatural birth from above. A natural birth is the result of two humans choosing to procreate. By contrast, spiritual birth is the result of God's sovereign choice.

— 1:14-18 —

The Word, though completely human, fully reveals the Father.
In our day, the influence of naturalism has so permeated culture that we have trouble accepting the deity of Christ. In John's day, most people had no problem accepting Christ's deity. They were more troubled by His humanity. The influence of Plato permeated every aspect of religion and philosophy so that anything tangible came to be seen as inherently

God with us

JOHN 1:14

The truth of Christ's dual nature, His unblemished deity and His complete humanity, is vitally important theologically, but it's crucial in a practical sense as well. When I am tempted to shake a fist at the heavens or wonder if God is being cruelly indifferent while I suffer down here on earth, John's Gospel reminds me of an important truth. When Adam brought sin into the world, and death with sin (Rom. 5:12), the Lord could have incinerated the world as just punishment and He would have been no less holy or righteous. But He didn't. Furthermore, when we sin—as individuals and collectively as humans—God has every right to turn His back and say, "Fine. Run the world your way. The mess you make of it is yours to bear." But He doesn't.

On the contrary, the Creator voluntarily became one of us in the person of Jesus Christ, who suffered as we suffer, who was tempted as we are tempted, and who endured injustice like we will never know—yet without sin. I am comforted to know that God understands and empathizes. Through His incarnation, we can appreciate His compassion more fully. Because He lived and died as a man, we can more easily understand and accept that, in His resurrection, the Son is for us even while we feel abandoned, mistreated, or punished by God.

evil. The great hope of Greek philosophers was to escape the foul, obnoxious material realm in order to commune with the divine mind, which existed only in the realm of pure ideas. In life, they tried to deny the body as a means of connecting with what they conceived of as god. They saw death as the liberation of the soul (the good aspect of man) from the prison of the body (the evil aspect of man). So, naturally, they recoiled from the notion that God would become anything genuinely physical.

To preserve the sinlessness of God, philosophers invented all kinds of myths to explain how Christ could appear human without actually having earthly material be a part of His nature. The most common, *Docetism*, suggested that He only *seemed* to be tangible, but was in fact a heavenly apparition. The so-called "Gnostic Gospels" tell stories of how Jesus created the illusion of eating food while never actually digesting it or needing to relieve Himself.

John's terminology was boldly offensive to these false teachers. He says, in effect, "The Word became meat." He lived among us in the material world. We literally saw Him, and heard Him, and touched Him. In 1 John 1:1, the apostle puts it in unmistakable terms: "What was from the beginning, what we have *heard*, what we have *seen* with our eyes, what we have *looked at* and *touched* with our hands . . ." (emphasis mine).

God didn't remain abstract. Having revealed Himself in dreams and visions, as supernatural fire in the midst of a bush, as an otherworldly glow above the ark of the covenant, and not content to send angels in His place, God became a man. A flesh, blood, and bone human being, who could be seen, heard, touched, and even smelled. The Son of God became a tangible representation of the Father in all His glory. If we have trouble understanding God the Father, we need only look to God the Son for all we need to know. Or, to summarize John: We saw His glory (1:14) and we received His fullness (1:16), because Christ has "explained" the Father (1:18). The Greek term translated "explained" describes what I am doing right now: expositing. The Son has exposited the Father far better than all the best commentators can explain Scripture.

• • •

People have always wondered, *What's God like?* Throughout Jesus' thirty-plus years on earth, you could have observed His visible presence. As Jesus conducted ministry among the inhabitants of Galilee,

Samaria, and Judea, the disciples could have said, "Come and see for yourself. He is the rabbi of this band of disciples; God is declared and displayed through Him." To this day, people struggle to know who God is and what He's like. We can point to Jesus Christ and say, "Get to know Him, and you will know God."

APPLICATION: JOHN 1:1-18

Five Qualities of Authentic Faith

What does it mean to be a genuine believer whose life is characterized by authentic faith? I find in John's Gospel five practical qualities that flow out of a life of trust in Christ.

First, *a genuine believer is not too independent to admit his or her own needs.* Throughout John's narrative, those who needed healing, or forgiveness, or enlightenment understood their own helplessness and came to Christ for help. While pride kept many trapped in their sin, others' vulnerability gave Jesus the opportunity to perform miracles in their lives.

Trust in the Lord should translate into vulnerability with others. Children long to hear their parents apologize after making a rash decision, or reacting harshly, or behaving hypocritically. Wives long for the Lord to break the wills of their husbands so they might finally hear the words, "Honey, I've reached the end of my rope. I need your help." Husbands long to have their wives give themselves without reservation, rather than remain locked away in towers of distance and distrust. Only when we trust the Lord enough to admit our weaknesses and our inadequacies will we enjoy intimacy with the people He has given to us as a blessing.

Second, *a genuine believer is not too busy to know the people around him or her.* People, not tasks, are the priority of believers living out their faith in truth. All too frequently, men and women *say* the people they love are more important than anything else, but then fail to express it or even feel appreciation until a loved one lies cold in a casket at the front of a church. Authentic trust in Christ recognizes the value of others, despite their failures or their shortcomings, and devotes adequate time to knowing them well.

Third, *a genuine believer isn't too proud to rely upon God's Word.*

Most churchgoers do their best to live in obedience to the Scriptures they know. Genuine faith, however, hungers to know as much about God's Word as possible because it doesn't trust in self. Genuine trust in Christ remains humbly devoted to knowing what *He* thinks about life and how *He* would have us live.

Fourth, *a genuine believer doesn't rely solely upon his or her own perspective.* Genuine believers have no trouble admitting the continuing impact of their sinful natures, and they do whatever is necessary to nullify its influence when making decisions. They seek truth in God's Word, they pray for the Holy Spirit's leading, they submit to the wisdom of mature counselors, and they remain sensitive to the constructive criticism of others—even their enemies.

Fifth, *a genuine believer doesn't take self or life too seriously.* That's not to suggest that life isn't serious or even dismal at times. Life in a fallen world can be hard! Nevertheless, genuine believers maintain a loose grip on the people they love and an even looser one on their possessions. They accept injustices and abuses and setbacks as confirmation they are on the right road to glory. They maintain a composed perspective, they refuse to allow bitterness to spoil their outlook, they choose joy, and they never pass up an opportunity to laugh. Believers can do this when they genuinely trust God as unfailingly good and utterly sovereign.

Of course, authentic belief in Jesus Christ has eternal implications. He came to seek and save the lost, to receive them to Himself, and to enjoy their worship forever. But genuine faith has profound implications for life here on earth. Our abundant life begins now.

PRESENTATION OF THE WORD (JOHN 1:19–4:54)

The world has never been kind to truth, or to the people who tell it. That's because shortly after the Word spoke the universe into existence and then filled it with light, sin plunged all of creation into darkness (Gen. 3). While darkness is indeed the absence of truth, make no mistake: The cause of this darkness is not ignorance; therefore, it cannot be overcome by education. People don't do bad things merely because they don't know any better. Evil is a deliberate choice. The darkness enveloping the world is the result of rebellion against its Creator. People resist the truth because they want only what they want, and they will tolerate no one—not even God—taking it away from them. Blinded by their own darkness, they truly believe they can defeat the Almighty and then shape their world according to their own desires.

It is true that the world needs to be enlightened, but darkened minds cannot and will not accept truth, even when it comes from God's lips to their ears, even when the signs of His presence among them are unmistakable. Darkened minds don't need more information. Only *re*-creation will solve the problem of evil—light from within, life from above.

John's Gospel opens with the dawn of re-creation. How will the world respond?

KEY TERMS IN JOHN 1:19–4:54

alētheia (ἀλήθεια) [225] "truth," "reality," "faithfulness"
The term is based on the ancient Greek concept of "nonconcealment" in the sense of transparency: things as they really are, not hidden or falsified.[1] Greek philosophers used the word to denote the true nature of something as opposed to its appearance. In this philosophical sense, "what truly is can then be equated with what is divine or eternal, in which one must share to be saved."[2] John draws upon these concepts and redefines the term to represent God's original created order, the universe as He originally conceived it before the Fall. See *John 1:17; 3:21; 4:23; 14:6.*

baptizō (βαπτίζω) [907] "to baptize," "to dip," "to immerse," "to wash"

The nonreligious use of this term describes the process of immersing something in water in order to remove impurities, thus it has washing or rinsing in mind. The word also describes "dipping" something in a solution for the purpose of dyeing. Old Testament worship used ceremonial rinsing as a means of gaining ritual purity, and eventually used whole-body washing as a rite of initiation for Gentiles (after circumcision for males) who wanted to be included in Abraham's Covenant. Thus, baptism became closely associated with repentance. *See John 1:26, 31, 33.*

marturia (μαρτυρία) [3141] "witness," "testimony," "report"

In the secular sphere, this term is a "declaration or confirmation of facts or events,"[3] commonly used in connection with legal proceedings. In ancient courts, the corroborating *testimony* of independent witnesses was considered virtually irrefutable. For John, the verb "to witness" and the noun "testimony" build upon the legal meaning to offer proof of what lies beyond the material realm, which can only be seen by the dead, who cannot return, and supernatural beings (the Lord and His angels). *See John 1:19; 3:33; 5:36; 21:24.*

pisteuō (πιστεύω) [4100] "to believe," "to accept as truth," "to commit one's trust"

In classical Greek usage, the term builds upon knowledge, adding to it obedience. One may receive knowledge of a certain truth and may even offer verbal agreement. But "trust" or "confidence" is not said to be present until one's behavior reflects that truth. For example, someone may verbally agree that air travel is safe; however, "trust" (as this Greek term defines it) occurs only when that person actually boards an aircraft. *See John 1:12; 3:16; 4:53; 20:31.*

sēmeion (σημεῖον) [4592] "sign," "authenticating mark," "token," "miracle"

The most basic meaning is "something that gives a true indication of something else." A road sign accurately indicates what lies ahead for the traveler. However, the Greeks gave the term special attention as a physical indication of divine will or supernatural omens. For example, lightning indicated the will of Zeus and thunder was a foreboding indication that he was about to speak through a "sign."[4] For the Jews, a "sign" was a physical manifestation of God's glory or a visual confirmation that a prophet was authentically from God. *See John 2:11, 23; 4:54; 12:37.*

A Man Sent from God
JOHN 1:19-34

NASB

¹⁹This is the testimony of John, when the Jews sent to him priests and Levites from Jerusalem to ask him, "Who are you?" ²⁰And he confessed and did not deny, but confessed, "I am not ᵃthe Christ." ²¹They asked him, "What then? Are you Elijah?" And he said, "I am not." "Are you the Prophet?" And he answered, "No." ²²Then they said to him, "Who are you, so that we may give an answer to those who sent us? What do you say about yourself?" ²³He said, "I am A VOICE OF ONE CRYING IN THE WILDERNESS, 'MAKE STRAIGHT THE WAY OF THE LORD,' as Isaiah the prophet said."

²⁴Now they had been sent from the Pharisees. ²⁵They asked him, and said to him, "Why then are you baptizing, if you are not the ᵃChrist, nor Elijah, nor the Prophet?" ²⁶John answered them saying, "I baptize ᵃin water, *but* among you stands One whom you do not know. ²⁷*It is* He who comes after me, the thong of whose sandal I am not worthy to untie." ²⁸These things took place in Bethany beyond the Jordan, where John was baptizing.

²⁹The next day he saw Jesus coming to him and said, "Behold, the Lamb of God who takes away the sin of the world! ³⁰This is He on behalf of whom I said, 'After me comes a Man who ᵃhas a higher rank than I, for He existed before me.' ³¹I did not recognize ᵃHim, but so that He might be manifested to Israel, I came baptizing

NLT

¹⁹This was John's testimony when the Jewish leaders sent priests and Temple assistants⋆ from Jerusalem to ask John, "Who are you?" ²⁰He came right out and said, "I am not the Messiah."

²¹"Well then, who are you?" they asked. "Are you Elijah?"

"No," he replied.

"Are you the Prophet we are expecting?"⋆

"No."

²²"Then who are you? We need an answer for those who sent us. What do you have to say about yourself?"

²³John replied in the words of the prophet Isaiah:

"I am a voice shouting in the wilderness,
  'Clear the way for the LORD's coming!'"⋆

²⁴Then the Pharisees who had been sent ²⁵asked him, "If you aren't the Messiah or Elijah or the Prophet, what right do you have to baptize?"

²⁶John told them, "I baptize with⋆ water, but right here in the crowd is someone you do not recognize. ²⁷Though his ministry follows mine, I'm not even worthy to be his slave and untie the straps of his sandal."

²⁸This encounter took place in Bethany, an area east of the Jordan River, where John was baptizing.

²⁹The next day John saw Jesus coming toward him and said, "Look! The Lamb of God who takes away the sin of the world! ³⁰He is the one I was talking about when I said, 'A man is coming after me who is far greater than I am, for he existed long before me.' ³¹I did not recognize him as the Messiah, but I have been baptizing with water so that he might be revealed to Israel."

NASB

bin water." [32]John testified saying, "I have seen the Spirit descending as a dove out of heaven, and He remained upon Him. [33]I did not recognize aHim, but He who sent me to baptize bin water said to me, 'He upon whom you see the Spirit descending and remaining upon Him, this is the One who baptizes bin the Holy Spirit.' [34]I myself have seen, and have testified that this is the Son of God."

1:20 aI.e. the Messiah   1:25 aI.e. Messiah
1:26 aThe Gr here can be translated *in, with* or *by*
1:30 aLit *has become before me*   1:31 aI.e. as the
Messiah   bThe Gr here can be translated *in, with* or
by   1:33 aI.e. as the Messiah   bThe Gr here can be
translated *in, with* or *by*

NLT

[32]Then John testified, "I saw the Holy Spirit descending like a dove from heaven and resting upon him. [33]I didn't know he was the one, but when God sent me to baptize with water, he told me, 'The one on whom you see the Spirit descend and rest is the one who will baptize with the Holy Spirit.' [34]I saw this happen to Jesus, so I testify that he is the Chosen One of God.*"

1:19 Greek *and Levites.*   1:21 Greek *Are you
the Prophet?* See Deut 18:15, 18; Mal 4:5-6.
1:23 Isa 40:3.   1:26 Or *in;* also in 1:31, 33.
1:34 Some manuscripts read *the Son of God.*

John the Baptizer is a shadowy figure in the minds of many Christians. Most could fit all they know about him on one side of a 3 x 5 card with plenty of room to spare. Clearly, he baptized people. Some know he lived in the desert and subsisted on a diet of locusts and honey. Those interested in theology know he was the forerunner of the Messiah. And . . . that is about all most people know. Yet Jesus said of him, "Among those born of women there has not arisen anyone greater than John the Baptist!" (Matt. 11:11).

The Gospel of John gives us very little information about the man, where he came from, and what he was like as a person. This is, of course, intentional. The lack of information serves an important purpose for John, which we will soon discover. We must look to the Gospels of Matthew, Mark, and Luke for details.

Dr. Luke, a physician by training, was interested in the humanity of the men and women surrounding Jesus. From him we learn that John was born the only child to an aging priest, Zacharias, and his post-menopausal wife, Elizabeth. His birth attracted the attention of everyone in the Judean hill country, not only because it was miraculous, but also because John was set aside from day one to be a Nazirite. He was not to cut his hair, or touch anything dead, or partake of anything from the grapevine—no wine, no grapes, no raisins (see Num. 6:2-6). He had been chosen by God, even before his conception, to be the prophesied forerunner of the Messiah (see Isa. 40:3-5; Luke 1:14-17).

John the Baptizer didn't grow to manhood in the court of a palace.

Luke says, "The child continued to grow and to become strong in spirit, and he lived in the deserts until the day of his public appearance to Israel" (Luke 1:80). Don't misunderstand—this was not a desert like Palm Springs. John grew up among dust and rock and scrub bushes and heat and the scarcity of everything, including food and water. However, in the silence and solitude, and in the simplicity of those difficult days, John communed with the Author of truth. He was filled with the Holy Spirit from his earliest years (Luke 1:15), and he lived by the foundational principle of God's kingdom—a standard Israel failed to heed centuries before: "Man does not live by bread alone, but man lives by everything that proceeds out of the mouth of the LORD" (Deut. 8:3).

When John came out of the wilderness to confront and convict the nation of Israel, how different he was from the religious leaders people were used to hearing! He "was clothed with camel's hair and wore a leather belt around his waist, and his diet was locusts and wild honey" (Mark 1:6). While the Sadducees, Pharisees, chief priests, scribes, and

Todd Bolen/BiblePlaces.com

The Judean Wilderness. While most rabbis enjoyed the creature comforts of resplendent robes, rich food, secure dwellings, and political protection, John chose the austere life of the wilderness south of Jerusalem. Though not completely barren, the land did not yield sustenance easily. Living in the wilderness not only protected John from his political and religious enemies; it taught him complete dependence upon God for every physical need.

Herodians[5] were robed in finery and nourished with meat and wine, John stood gaunt from ascetic living and leathery from the sun. And his message was just as unadorned and unyielding as his appearance. When Sadducees and Pharisees, practitioners of hypocritical religion, came to him for a showy baptism of counterfeit repentance, he would have none of it . . . and he told them so! "You brood of vipers, who warned you to flee from the wrath to come? Therefore bear fruit in keeping with repentance; and do not suppose that you can say to yourselves, 'We have Abraham for our father'; for I say to you that from these stones God is able to raise up children to Abraham" (Matt. 3:7-9).

How the religious elite hated him! And they would have killed him were he not protected by the wilderness and surrounded by growing multitudes of people who were genuinely repentant of their sin.

While John the Baptizer was as extraordinary as any mere human could be, he was nonetheless just a man. Therefore, John introduces him as simply "a man sent from God, whose name was John" (1:6). John 1:19-34 will show us what made this mere man so special.

— 1:19 —

The issue of truth was important to the apostle John—it appears repeatedly in his account of Jesus' ministry on earth. In this first episode, John the Baptizer is challenged by "the Jews," the religious leaders who ruled Israel through the temple in Jerusalem. Their principle concern was that of authority: Who has the right to proclaim truth? Take note of their questions:

"Who are you?" (1:19)

"What then? Are you Elijah?" (1:21)

"Are you the Prophet?" (1:21)

"Who are you, so that we may give an answer to those who sent us? What do you say about yourself?" (1:22)

"Why then are you baptizing, if you are not the Christ, nor Elijah, nor the Prophet?" (1:25)

The real question they were asking was, "Who do you think you are?" According to the world's standard, whoever wields the greatest power has the right to determine what truth is and who gets to proclaim it. But according to the standard of religion, only those who are worthy can be a source of truth, and we should only listen to those who pass religious muster.

Religion

JOHN 1:19

If I could eradicate religion from churches, I would do it. That sounds odd, doesn't it? If you were to ask the average person, "Is a Christian religious?" the answer would likely be, "Sure!" And they would be correct according to Webster's definition: "relating to or manifesting faithful devotion to an acknowledged ultimate reality or deity; devoted to religious beliefs or observances."[6] In theory, Christianity is religious devotion to Jesus Christ. In practice, religion takes on a life of its own, such that we become devoted to "beliefs and observances" instead of to the person, Jesus.

Years ago, someone coined an aphorism to address the issue: "Christianity is not a religion; it's a relationship." The Lord invites us into a personal relationship with Himself, not onto the treadmill of religious activity. God offers to transform us into the likeness of Christ, yet many Christians attempt to reform themselves through religious devotion.

"Religion" demands that we strive and labor, hoping to find God and gain His affection or approval. Religion suggests we can earn what God desires to give us and keeps us too busy to enjoy a personal relationship with the Almighty. Religion encourages comparisons, fuels pride, and turns unified communities into complex caste systems. Religion brings out the worst in people rather than their best.

Because "devotion to religious beliefs or observances" invariably distracts us from devotion to Jesus Christ, I hope to convince all believers to reject religion. In the absence of religion, we're forced to accept our helplessness and to receive God's favor as a gift. Without the self-aggrandizing treadmill of religion, we must humble ourselves and call upon the Spirit of God to make us good. Without religion, we have no hope but to respond to God's offer to become our friend, our advocate, our Savior, our Lord.

This strange-looking, ultra-dogmatic wilderness preacher was an enigma to the religious elite. This man who preached in the rugged regions of Judea claimed neither power nor worthiness. The thought of celebrity turned him off. In fact, he took great care to strip himself of all credentials:

> "Who are you?" "I am not the Christ." (1:19-20)
> "Are you Elijah?" "I am not." (1:21)
> "Are you the Prophet?" "No." (1:21)
> "What do you say about yourself?" "I am a voice . . ." (1:22-23)

He refused to make himself of any account, choosing instead to clarify his role. He said, in effect, "I am not the source of truth; I simply bear witness to the One who is the Truth."

— 1:20 —

When pressing John for his credentials, the emissaries of the temple ran down a religious checklist: Christ? Elijah? The Prophet? Some other authority?

John answered their first question before they had a chance to ask, "Are you the Christ?"

"Christ" is the Greek translation of the Hebrew term *mashiach* [H4899], "Messiah," which means "anointed one." In the Old Testament, the king of Israel was chosen by God. Then, in a public ceremony, a priest anointed the chosen one's head with olive oil, thus making him the "anointed one." However, no king ever lived up to his calling—not even King David, with his terrible downfall (2 Sam. 11:1–12:15). For centuries, prophets proclaimed the eventual rise of a larger-than-life figure known as "the Anointed One," a king who would please God perfectly, lead the nation to claim all of the covenant promises, and even rule over the whole world (Ps. 2). By the first century, the Jews expected him to be an impressive political powerhouse and military genius who would rid them of Roman rule and then usher them into an unprecedented time of prosperity.

John fiercely denied being the Messiah.

— 1:21 —

By asking if he were Elijah, the religious leaders wanted to know if John the Baptizer was the same Old Testament prophet who, instead of dying, was carried off to heaven in a fiery chariot (2 Kgs. 2:11-12). The prophet Malachi later predicted that an Elijah-like figure would announce the imminent arrival of the Messiah (Mal. 3:1; 4:5-6). Many took the prophet's words literally and expected the return of the actual man.

Although John the Baptizer was indeed the fulfillment of Malachi's prophecy (see Matt. 11:14), he was not the revered seer of old himself.

When the religious leaders asked the Baptizer if he were "the Prophet," they had the prophecy of Moses in mind (Deut. 18:15-19). Moses was referring to the Messiah, but most Jews in the first century accepted the notion that the Prophet and the Messiah were two different men. It's still a common misunderstanding among Jews today.

The wilderness preacher was indeed a genuine prophet; however, he was not *the* Prophet.

— 1:22-23 —

Having run down the list of known possibilities, the religious leaders continued to press the issue by asking if John were some other kind of authority, perhaps someone they failed to anticipate.

Again John denied any kind of personal credentials. The bizarre-looking man was clear about his role, and the Gospel of John faithfully reflects his message.

> He came as a witness, to testify about the Light, so that all might believe through him. He was not the Light, but *he came* to testify about the Light. (John 1:7-8)

> John testified about Him and cried out, saying, "This was He of whom I said, 'He who comes after me has a higher rank than I, for He existed before me.'" (John 1:15)

To avoid any mistaken notion that he was of any importance whatsoever, John described himself as merely "a voice." Not as a prophet, though he was one. Not as a remarkably worthy man of God, though he was. Not even as a man to be noticed, though he was certainly that! Simply "a voice."

John the Baptizer's self-description was drawn from a well-known prophecy (Isa. 40:3), which in turn drew upon a familiar image. When a monarch traveled to a particular region, it was rarely unplanned. A forerunner would first go and announce the imminent arrival of the king. The city would then be prepared and the route cleared of anything that would slow the king's chariot or make the journey unpleasant. The forerunner was simply a voice, having no authority of his own. If people chose to heed his message, it would be because they revered the coming king.

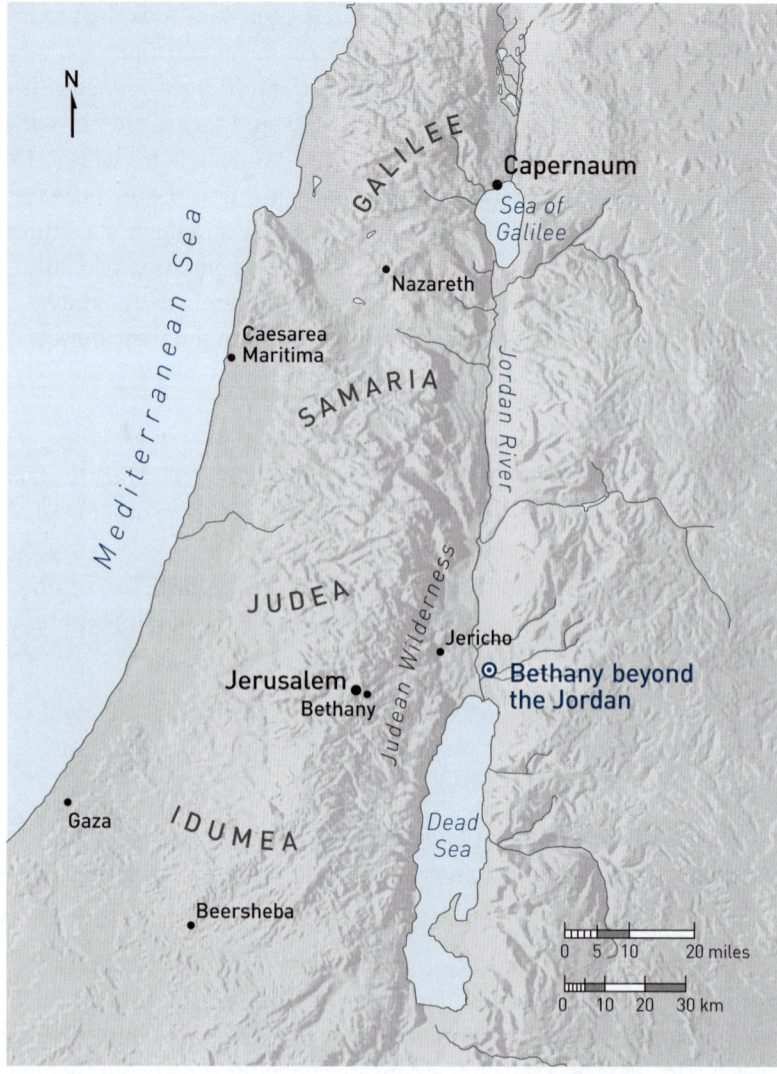

Bethany beyond the Jordan. Residents of Jerusalem knew Bethany as the town less than two miles east of the city wall. Bethany beyond the Jordan, on the other hand, lay 23 miles away on the eastern side of the Jordan Valley. This is where John the Baptizer called Jews to repent of their sins and submit to the rite of baptism.

— 1:24-28 —

The Pharisees cared most about rules, regulations, rituals, and rights. They established themselves as religious authorities and jealously guarded their power. They were disturbed by John's hubris in baptizing people without the proper credentials, without regard for the proper use of the rite, and without following their established procedures.

Jewish baptism was a rite in which a new Gentile convert to Judaism was ceremonially immersed in pure water as a symbolic, once-for-all cleansing from sin before entering the Hebrew covenant community. It was supposed to be administered by priests, not by a wild-eyed, locust-eating firebrand from the wilderness. It was intended for Gentile proselytes, not Jews already born into Abraham's covenant with God. It was to be done in pure water in the temple or synagogue, not in the muddy Jordan River. But these were all man-made rules.

John gave the rite of baptism a new application. He called Jews to a baptism of repentance, saying, in effect, "Because of your sin, you are outside of Abraham's covenant with God. You must repent like a Gentile and come to God as if for the first time." As a result, they came in droves! Nevertheless, John admitted that his baptism was merely symbolic and quickly turned the discussion away from water baptism itself—which pointed to the Messiah—toward the One he had come to announce. After all, he was merely a witness to the truth, not the source of truth. He was only the lampstand, not the light.

— 1:29 —

The day following John's selfless denial of any credentials and his relentless deflection of glory away from himself, the moment for which he

We cannot know the precise location of John's ministry along the Jordan River; we know only that he baptized near the town of Bethany (beyond the Jordan). Because the Jewish ritual of baptism at Gentile conversion involved complete immersion, John likely chose a slow portion of the river where the waters ran at least waist deep.

had been born suddenly arrived. He saw Jesus and identified Him, not as the King of Israel, the Prophet, or even the Messiah, but first as "the Lamb of God," a clear reference to the Passover lamb (Exod. 12:1-13) and Isaiah's messianic imagery (Isa. 53:7).

— 1:30-31 —

John's honesty is startling. On the one hand, he freely talks of his receiving revelation directly from God—a privilege reserved for prophets—and on the other, he admits that he did not recognize his relative as the Messiah. According to Luke 1:36, their mothers were related, so their families must have mingled before. Undoubtedly, Elizabeth told her son the story of Mary's visit many times throughout the years (cf. Luke 1:39-56). Yet, he did not "recognize" (the same Greek word as "know" in 1:26) His true identity.

Rather than try to explain how or why John the Baptizer did not recognize the Messiah before, and instead of searching for clever interpretations, let's focus on John's primary point: Jesus Christ, though equal with God in every respect, did not appear on the surface to be an extraordinary man. He was a man among men, a Jewish son of a Jewish mother, reared in an obscure town far from the center of religious activity. He was remarkable in that He had never sinned and He was extraordinary in His understanding of Scripture and spiritual matters, but He possessed none of the traits we expect from leaders: no movie-star good looks, no halo, no spotless robe trimmed in gold . . . He didn't even have an agent or a publicist!

But make no mistake; He is the Word, the Author of truth in a human body. However, as He stood among His fellow humans, no one recognized Him. No one connected the dots. And let's be honest: Truth often stares us in the face and we fail to acknowledge Him.

— 1:32-34 —

We know from the other Gospels that John baptized Jesus, but the apostle John leaves it out of this account. The incident was undoubtedly well known to him and his audience, and omitting it serves his purpose better. In describing this scene, he has taken great care to stress the superiority of Jesus Christ and to emphasize the Baptizer's role as a witness. Perhaps this is why we see the phrase "baptize in water" three times in connection with the Greek word *oida* [1492], "to know, to recognize."

> "I baptize in water, but among you stands One whom you do not know." (John 1:26)

"I did not recognize Him, but so that He might be manifested to Israel, I came baptizing in water." (John 1:31)

"I did not recognize Him, but He who sent me to baptize in water said to me, 'He upon whom you see the Spirit descending and remaining upon Him, this is the One who baptizes in the Holy Spirit.'" (John 1:33)

Just as light was a classic image for truth, water had long been a symbol of life. John's baptism in water was merely symbolic of what was to come, and it took place in the context of spiritual blindness. Then Jesus, the Word, stepped onto the scene baptizing in the Holy Spirit—authentic, abundant *life*—thus proving His identity as the Messiah (Isa. 11:1-10; 42:1; Ezek. 36:27; 39:29; Joel 2:28). The genuine source of truth has arrived and He baptizes in eternal life. There can be no more convincing proof of His true identity than this.

The Gospel writer closes the episode as he opened it: "This is the testimony of John . . . 'I myself have seen, and have testified that this is the Son of God'" (1:19, 34).[7]

• • •

John the Baptizer said, in effect, "Christ is the light; I am merely the lampstand." The purpose of a lampstand is to hold up the light so that everything is illuminated. No matter how expensive or how beautiful a lampstand may be, it's useless without a light. This is a crucial distinction when serving God in ministry, one the religious authorities in Jerusalem didn't understand. John, however, never forgot his role and his purpose. He refused to allow anyone to overlook the message by focusing on the messenger. And that is what made him an exceptionally extraordinary man among men.

APPLICATION: JOHN 1:19-34
Common People, Uncommon Message

As I reflect on the witness of John the Baptizer, this strange Elijah-like figure calling to Israel from the wilderness, I observe four truths that are helpful for us today, especially those engaged in ministry.

First, *John was extraordinary, but he was only human.* The unusual wilderness preacher was an extraordinary man in most respects. He renounced most of what his contemporaries would have considered reasonable comforts. He chose a diet of locusts and wild honey, and wore camel's hair and leather instead of linen and wool. He called Jews to approach their God as though they were Gentile converts, and he called the religious establishment to account for their hypocrisy and crimes. John was not a man like others in his day. He was altogether unique. Most would even say he was weird. Nevertheless, he—like his spiritual predecessor Elijah—was "a man with a nature like ours" (Jas. 5:17), who needed a Savior. John, like all of humanity, faced judgment at the end of his days on earth. In this respect, he was only human . . . just an ordinary man.

This gives us hope. John had the Holy Spirit dwelling within him; those of us who are in Christ have the Holy Spirit dwelling within us. John was given an extraordinary, countercultural message from God; the gospel is an extraordinary, countercultural message from God. John stood apart from his world in order to reach it more effectively; we have been called to do the same (John 17:15-18). John spoke the truth boldly despite the risk of suffering persecution from the enemies of truth; we have the same opportunity virtually everywhere we turn.

In a very real sense, we all have the opportunity to be uncommon men and women because the Lord has given us every advantage John enjoyed.

Second, *John was a lamp, but he was not the light; he was a voice, but he was not the Word.* While John amassed a large, loyal following, he never allowed his admirers to mistake the messenger for the message. Oswald Sanders writes, "That man is most successful who attaches the affection of his followers more to Christ than to himself."[8] This means if you lead a discipleship group, it's not to revolve around you; the members must never doubt it points to our Savior. If you have a pulpit, the pulpit doesn't revolve around you; it's a lamp from which the Word shines. And the congregation is not comprised of "your people"; they are the flock of God. Sanders continues, "He can rightly draw encouragement from the fact that his service has been fruitful and appreciated, but he must sedulously refuse to be idolized!"[9]

Third, *John was useful, but he was not indispensable.* Those who become "successful" in ministry, specifically those who attract a great following, face a particular danger. If they are not careful, they begin to believe their own press; that is, they allow the well-intentioned encouragement of others to become the basis of their own perspective. And it isn't long before they believe they are indispensable to the Lord's work.

What about you? Are you serving on a committee and feel that it cannot function without you? Are you leading others and feel that the goals will not be met without your direct involvement? Must you have a hand in everything that occurs around you for fear that nothing will be done "right" otherwise? Are you that controlling? How comfortable are you allowing subordinates to have a vision for your organization that is greater than your own? Are you one of those who justifies a non-stop schedule with the old excuse, "I'd rather burn out than rust out"?

Let's face it; cemeteries are full of people who thought they were indispensable.

Fourth, *John was effective, but he remained humble.* John effectively fulfilled the role for which he was called by God and he knew he was successful in completing the task given to him, yet he remained humble.

Humility does not lead us to feel inferior or to doubt our own worth. Self-loathing is not the path to humility. Thinking too little of ourselves is actually a form of pride. On the contrary, humility is seeing ourselves as God sees us. Humility is understanding our place in the Lord's plan while giving preference to the welfare of others over self. Mostly, humility is recognizing the Lord as the one and only worthy object of worship.

John put it succinctly when he said, "He must increase, but I must decrease" (John 3:30). Let his attitude become our testimony. Those truly sent from God exalt the One who sent them, and they diminish the one who is sent.

Five Who Followed in Faith
JOHN 1:35-51

NASB

35 Again the next day John was standing ᵃwith two of his disciples, 36 and he looked at Jesus as He walked, and said, "Behold, the Lamb of God!" 37 The two disciples heard him speak, and they followed Jesus. 38 And Jesus turned and saw them following, and said to them, "What do you seek?"

NLT

35 The following day John was again standing with two of his disciples. 36 As Jesus walked by, John looked at him and declared, "Look! There is the Lamb of God!" 37 When John's two disciples heard this, they followed Jesus.

38 Jesus looked around and saw them following. "What do you want?" he asked them.

NASB

They said to Him, "Rabbi (which translated means Teacher), where are You staying?" [39] He said to them, "Come, and you will see." So they came and saw where He was staying; and they stayed with Him that day, for it was about the [a]tenth hour. [40] One of the two who heard John *speak* and followed Him, was Andrew, Simon Peter's brother. [41] He found first his own brother Simon and said to him, "We have found the Messiah" (which translated means [a]Christ). [42] He brought him to Jesus. Jesus looked at him and said, "You are Simon the son of [a]John; you shall be called Cephas" (which is translated [b]Peter).

[43] The next day He purposed to go into Galilee, and He found Philip. And Jesus said to him, "Follow Me." [44] Now Philip was from Bethsaida, of the city of Andrew and Peter. [45] Philip found Nathanael and said to him, "We have found Him of whom Moses in the Law and *also* the Prophets wrote—Jesus of Nazareth, the son of Joseph." [46] Nathanael said to him, "Can any good thing come out of Nazareth?" Philip said to him, "Come and see." [47] Jesus saw Nathanael coming to Him, and said of him, "Behold, an Israelite indeed, in whom there is no deceit!" [48] Nathanael said to Him, "How do You know me?" Jesus answered and said to him, "Before Philip called you, when you were under the fig tree, I saw you." [49] Nathanael answered Him, "Rabbi, You are the Son of God; You are the King of Israel." [50] Jesus answered and said to him, "Because I said to you that I saw you under the fig tree, do you believe? You will see

NLT

They replied, "Rabbi" (which means "Teacher"), "where are you staying?"

[39] "Come and see," he said. It was about four o'clock in the afternoon when they went with him to the place where he was staying, and they remained with him the rest of the day.

[40] Andrew, Simon Peter's brother, was one of these men who heard what John said and then followed Jesus. [41] Andrew went to find his brother, Simon, and told him, "We have found the Messiah" (which means "Christ"*).

[42] Then Andrew brought Simon to meet Jesus. Looking intently at Simon, Jesus said, "Your name is Simon, son of John—but you will be called Cephas" (which means "Peter"*).

[43] The next day Jesus decided to go to Galilee. He found Philip and said to him, "Come, follow me." [44] Philip was from Bethsaida, Andrew and Peter's hometown.

[45] Philip went to look for Nathanael and told him, "We have found the very person Moses* and the prophets wrote about! His name is Jesus, the son of Joseph from Nazareth."

[46] "Nazareth!" exclaimed Nathanael. "Can anything good come from Nazareth?"

"Come and see for yourself," Philip replied.

[47] As they approached, Jesus said, "Now here is a genuine son of Israel—a man of complete integrity."

[48] "How do you know about me?" Nathanael asked.

Jesus replied, "I could see you under the fig tree before Philip found you."

[49] Then Nathanael exclaimed, "Rabbi, you are the Son of God—the King of Israel!"

[50] Jesus asked him, "Do you believe this just because I told you I had seen you under the fig tree? You will see

greater things than these." ⁵¹ And He said to him, "Truly, truly, I say to you, you will see the heavens opened and the angels of God ascending and descending on the Son of Man."

1:35 ªLit *and*   1:39 ªPerhaps 10 a.m. (Roman time)   1:41 ªGr *Anointed One*   1:42 ªGr *Joannes* ᵇI.e. Rock or Stone

greater things than this." ⁵¹ Then he said, "I tell you the truth, you will all see heaven open and the angels of God going up and down on the Son of Man, the one who is the stairway between heaven and earth.*"

1:41 *Messiah* (a Hebrew term) and *Christ* (a Greek term) both mean "anointed one."   1:42 The names *Cephas* (from Aramaic) and *Peter* (from Greek) both mean "rock."   1:45 Greek *Moses in the law.*   1:51 Greek *going up and down on the Son of Man;* see Gen 28:10-17. "Son of Man" is a title Jesus used for himself.

The Cold War was never more frigid than during the 1970s. It seemed that nothing would stop the creeping spread of communism. One by one, capitalist nations in Europe, Asia, and Africa either crumbled before the Soviet military or fell under the spell of socialism. Few in the United States feared a military assault from the East. The true threat of communism would come from within.

That's when I happened to read a series of lectures by Douglas Hyde, a lifelong communist who had renounced his party affiliation and spent the remaining years of his life exposing communist techniques for recruiting members and building them into leaders. As I read *Dedication and Leadership Techniques*, I discovered that no new recruit was treated as insignificant. Quite the opposite. The party demanded total commitment and expected great things from each member. And the scope of their ambition was nothing less than to change the world. Karl Marx wrote, "Philosophers have only *interpreted* the world, in various ways; the point, however, is to *change* it."[10] He closed his manifesto with the passionate call to action, "[Working class people] have nothing to lose but their chains. They have a world to win."[11]

To our shame as Christians, communists did a better job selling their failed world system than we have done in proclaiming the good news. They were bold, where we have remained timid. If I learned nothing else from Hyde's book, I learned this: Small expectations arouse a weak response; great expectations inspire heroic action.

Jesus set out to change the world, beginning with a handful of unremarkable men. And from the beginning, He had great expectations.

— 1:35-39 —

Reading John 1:19-51, one might think the apostle John had torn four pages out of his personal diary:

1:19—"This is the testimony of John . . ."
1:29—"The next day . . ."
1:35—"Again the next day . . ."
1:43—"The next day . . ."

He presents four consecutive days in simple, chronological order based on his personal observation of the events. On the first day, John the Baptizer announced the imminent revelation of the Messiah. On the second day, the Baptizer identified Jesus as the Messiah. On the third and fourth days, Jesus called His first five disciples, which the Gospel writer describes in quick, rapid-fire succession.

With each encounter, there is the presentation of truth, an initial response from the hearer, and then a decision to believe and follow. The pattern is set; however, within this pattern, each response to the truth is as individual as the man, and the Lord engages each man individually.

In this first encounter, Andrew and another disciple (whom I believe to be John) had been following the wilderness preacher when they saw their mentor point to Jesus and then declare Him to be the long-anticipated Hebrew Messiah, the man who would save the world from sin. Immediately, they moved toward Jesus to learn more.

The phrase "they followed Jesus" is both literal and figurative. Jesus was walking somewhere and the two men trailed after Him. In the ancient world, disciples literally "walked after" a teacher to observe His life as well as listen to His teaching. When Jesus noticed the two men, He asked, "What do you seek?" which was to ask, "What are your intentions?" In other words, "Are you here to ask a question, or are you indicating a desire to become my disciples?" When they asked Him where He lived, they confirmed their intention to begin following Him from then on.

I love His response: "Come, and you will see." Such simple words would have lifelong meaning.

In 1:38-39, John uses one of his favorite terms three times. The Greek word *menō* [3306] means "to stay, to live, to remain still, to endure." Later, Jesus commanded His disciples (probably in Aramaic) to "abide in Me," which John renders in Greek using *menō*.

John recalls that the two men remained with Jesus the rest of the day because it was the "tenth hour." According to the Roman timekeeping system, which marks the beginning of the new day at midnight, they would have arrived at His home at 10 a.m. By Jewish reckoning, however, a new day starts at 6 a.m., which would have them arriving at 4 p.m. John clearly used the Jewish system when recounting the events of Jesus' arrest and trials, so the same is probably true here. Furthermore, the Roman system was only used for official government business; Roman sundials, for example, marked noon with the number VI, not XII.[12]

Because the hour was late, they very likely reclined at Jesus' table, talked into the night, and lodged with Him until the next morning. It must have been magnificent for them to spend those hours alone with the God-man Himself!

— 1:40-42 —

After leaving the home of Jesus, Andrew's first act was to find his brother, Simon. Although Simon was a principle owner of a fishing enterprise in Galilee, more than 70 miles north of Jerusalem, he was undoubtedly nearby, perhaps visiting the temple. Andrew announced that he had found the Messiah and brought his brother to see Jesus. (Andrew apparently had a habit of introducing others to Jesus; see 6:8-9 and 12:20-22.).

When Jesus looked at Simon, He immediately looked deep within him. We can only guess what He saw or why He said what He did. Jesus changed the man's name from Simon, which is derived from the Hebrew word *shama*, "to hear." His name would be changed to *Kepha*, the Aramaic word for "stone." (John transliterated the name as "Cephas" for Greek readers). However, Greeks would know him by their word for "stone," *Petros*, or Peter.

John's narrative never fully explains the significance of this encounter or the reason for the changed name. This, however, is certain: Jesus saw people not as who they were, but as who they would ultimately become. And the same is true today . . . for you and for me.

— 1:43-44 —

After meeting Peter, Jesus "purposed to go into Galilee," which was a journey of about three days. John, Andrew, and Simon were all residents of the same fishing village in Galilee. This was also the home of Philip, who was probably in Jerusalem for the same reason as Peter. John doesn't tell us how Jesus knew Philip. All we know is that Jesus looked for him with the express purpose of calling him to be a disciple. He apparently followed without hesitation or reservation.

— 1:45-50 —

Philip's first act as a disciple was to find his friend Nathanael. Philip identified Jesus in three ways:

- "Him of whom Moses in the Law and also the Prophets wrote"
- "Jesus of Nazareth"
- "The son of Joseph"

Of course, Jesus was not the physical son of Joseph, and the Gospel writer knew this. Philip either spoke in ignorance at the time or he meant "a member of the Joseph household." Surnames were not common in the ancient world. People were most commonly identified by their family association (even slaves) and their place of origin. Jesus was from Nazareth and was reared in the household of Joseph.

Earlier that day, Nathanael had sought solitude in the shade of a fig tree. The Talmud (the collected writings of Jewish scholars on practical living) encouraged men to meditate under a large tree, reading and reflecting on the Scriptures, at least once each day. It's likely that Nathanael was doing just that. Philip's description of Jesus would only influence a man who had studied "the Law and the Prophets" and was looking for the Messiah.

Nathanael's response was incredulous: "Can any good thing come out of Nazareth?" Nazareth was considered a no-account town, not far from Bethsaida. Recent archaeological discoveries suggest the town housed a garrison of Roman soldiers, and where you find a town full of bored soldiers, you find a nesting ground for vice and immorality. In addition, many Jews believed that contact with Gentiles rendered them ritually unclean.

Jesus didn't rebuke Nathanael. Instead, He peered into the man's soul and called Nathanael an honest, forthright Israelite. Then, to

Saints Like Me

JOHN 1:45-50

The disciples have been presented to us throughout history as saints, which creates a certain holier-than-us image that can leave us feeling inferior. How can we ever measure up to that?

When I was a child, our family attended a church named for St. Andrew, and it featured a statue that represented exactly what you would think of as a saint. The man wore sandals and long, flowing robes. His hands were folded and he bore the face of a determined yet gentle leader. I couldn't resist touching the statue and, in my little mind, thinking Wow! Saint Andrew! He seemed larger than life.

As I matured, I learned that the biblical account of Andrew does not portray anyone particularly remarkable. In fact, if you were hiring someone to lead your company, you probably would not hire Andrew. He was timid. Unimpressive. A follower. A man standing in the shadow of his more charismatic brother, Simon. Andrew, like all of the disciples, was anything but heroic, and certainly not saintly. They were far from the flawless specimens of perfection we tend to imagine. Instead, they were like us. Confused, called to fulfill roles far beyond their abilities, weighed down by all sorts of flaws, and hindered by individual quirks. To put it candidly, they were saints just like you and me!

In time, the disciples became great men of God. The Lord chose them, transformed them, equipped them, trained them, and then empowered them to make disciples of all nations. All they did was believe and follow. Even I can do that!

Todd Bolen/BiblePlaces.com

Hebrew culture celebrated the fig tree as a symbol of protection or covering (1 Kgs. 4:25; Mic. 4:4; Zech. 3:10). Indeed, the thick foliage of a mature tree offered a cool retreat for quiet reflection on Scripture, or perhaps an afternoon nap.

help Nathanael overcome his sincere skepticism, Jesus offered a small measure of supernatural evidence. The response was both immediate and enthusiastic. Nathanael's confession reveals a remarkable depth of understanding and an impressive breadth of scope. He understood both the theological and practical implications of Jesus' identity. He is both the Son of God and the King of Israel.

Nathanael's heart was thoroughly prepared to receive the truth because he had been earnestly studying the Scriptures and searching for the Messiah. So, once Jesus removed a legitimate obstacle to belief, Nathanael believed at once. Others will prove to be quite the opposite; the most astounding displays of supernatural power will not move them to believe because they stubbornly choose to reject the truth standing before them.

— 1:51 —

Jesus' final words in this episode reveal His ultimate purpose for coming into the world. It was to bridge the great schism that sin created between heaven and earth. This is a reference to Genesis 28:12, in which Jacob dreamt of a ladder stretching from earth to heaven and angels using it to move between the separated realms. Jesus announced that He is that ladder. What had been a dream is now a reality. Undoubtedly, this held special significance for Nathanael, as a son of Jacob, as a sinful man, and as an earnest student of "the Law and the Prophets."

• • •

Throughout this segment of John's narrative (1:35-51), the Greek word *heuriskō* [2147], "to locate by searching," appears five times:

- Andrew **found** Simon, claiming to have **found** the Messiah (1:41).
- Jesus **found** Philip (1:43).
- Philip **found** Nathanael, claiming to have **found** the Messiah (1:45).

Ironically, it's unclear who found whom. From a human perspective, the men found one another. However, the heart of each man had been providentially prepared for the moment that Jesus met him.

APPLICATION: JOHN 1:35-51
Evangelism Illustrated

Clearly, the Gospel writer's primary purpose was not to outline different models of evangelism; however, it is worth noting the different means by which the first five disciples were found and brought to faith in Christ. Their stories highlight an important truth: no one method of evangelism will be effective for all, because each of us is different. This passage illustrates four popular means of calling individuals to follow Jesus Christ.

1. Mass Evangelism (1:35-39)
"Mass evangelism" refers to one gifted person proclaiming the good news to audiences who have not yet received the gift of eternal life. John the Baptizer was the evangelist of the first century. And he pointed to Jesus Christ and proclaimed, "There is the Messiah, God's Lamb! Follow Him." More recent examples would be John Knox, John Wesley, George Whitefield, Dwight L. Moody, Billy Sunday, and Billy Graham. They preached to large gatherings of nonbelievers and multitudes were converted and became disciples of Jesus Christ.

2. Personal Evangelism (1:40-42)
Personal evangelism takes place when a person shares the good news of Jesus Christ with a friend or loved one. It is perhaps the most common

and effective means by which people come to know the Lord, because they hear the gospel from someone they already know and trust and respect. Unfortunately, personal evangelism is dreadfully underutilized. Many believers fear the dreaded question, "How can I be saved?" They would rather invite others to church, or better, hire someone else to do evangelism.

Fortunately, personal evangelism training programs are inexpensive and readily available, and students emerge feeling confident and eager.

3. Contact Evangelism (1:43-44)

Contact evangelism, like personal evangelism, takes place when one individual shares the gospel with another, only in this case, the two may not have established a rapport. We have no record of contact between the two men before Jesus "found" Philip. It is quite possible the Lord had been talking to Philip for several days or weeks and then called him to become a formal disciple. However, it is equally likely that "found" is John's shorthand for a first-time conversation that resulted in Philip's immediate decision to believe (not unlike 4:7-45). Upon his believing, Jesus called him to follow as a disciple.

I wholeheartedly believe in "divine appointments" in which a person's heart is prepared and the Lord places a willing messenger in his or her path. Contact evangelism doesn't seek to convince another to believe; contact evangelism merely assists a willing heart to receive the gift of eternal life. However, belief may not occur right away. Many people who became Christians later in life admit to hearing the gospel five or six times (sometimes *more*) before believing.

4. Word Evangelism (1:45-51)

The power of God's Word dare not be underestimated. Many people have come to know the Lord merely from reading Scripture, recognizing their need, and then kneeling in prayer all alone, even before setting foot in a church. In 1898, two traveling businessmen recognized the power of the Bible to penetrate the hearts of nonbelievers and then founded an organization that is best known for its effective use of Word evangelism. We know them as The Gideons International. Their program of placing Bibles in hotels, hospitals, and schools has been the means of many people trusting Jesus Christ and becoming His disciples.

When sharing a meal with fellow believers for the first time, I love to ask the question, "How did you come to know Jesus Christ?" Their stories never fail to fascinate. I am constantly amazed by the variety of means used by the Lord to bring His own to faith.

How did *you* come to trust in the Savior? How has it influenced *your* preferred method of evangelism?

Wine . . . Coins . . . and Signs
JOHN 2:1-25

NASB

¹On the third day there was a wedding in Cana of Galilee, and the mother of Jesus was there; ²and both Jesus and His disciples were invited to the wedding. ³When the wine ran out, the mother of Jesus said to Him, "They have no wine." ⁴And Jesus said to her, "Woman, ᵃwhat does that have to do with us? My hour has not yet come." ⁵His mother said to the servants, "Whatever He says to you, do it." ⁶Now there were six stone waterpots set there for the Jewish custom of purification, containing ᵃtwenty or thirty gallons each. ⁷Jesus said to them, "Fill the waterpots with water." So they filled them up to the brim. ⁸And He said to them, "Draw *some* out now and take it to the ᵃheadwaiter." So they took it *to him.* ⁹When the headwaiter tasted the water which had become wine, and did not know where it came from (but the servants who had drawn the water knew), the headwaiter called the bridegroom, ¹⁰and said to him, "Every man serves the good wine first, and when *the people* have ᵃdrunk freely, *then he serves* the poorer *wine; but* you have kept the good wine until now." ¹¹This beginning of *His* ᵃsigns Jesus did in Cana of Galilee, and manifested His glory, and His disciples believed in Him.

¹²After this He went down to

NLT

¹The next day* there was a wedding celebration in the village of Cana in Galilee. Jesus' mother was there, ²and Jesus and his disciples were also invited to the celebration. ³The wine supply ran out during the festivities, so Jesus' mother told him, "They have no more wine."

⁴"Dear woman, that's not our problem," Jesus replied. "My time has not yet come."

⁵But his mother told the servants, "Do whatever he tells you."

⁶Standing nearby were six stone water jars, used for Jewish ceremonial washing. Each could hold twenty to thirty gallons.* ⁷Jesus told the servants, "Fill the jars with water." When the jars had been filled, ⁸he said, "Now dip some out, and take it to the master of ceremonies." So the servants followed his instructions.

⁹When the master of ceremonies tasted the water that was now wine, not knowing where it had come from (though, of course, the servants knew), he called the bridegroom over. ¹⁰"A host always serves the best wine first," he said. "Then, when everyone has had a lot to drink, he brings out the less expensive wine. But you have kept the best until now!"

¹¹This miraculous sign at Cana in Galilee was the first time Jesus revealed his glory. And his disciples believed in him.

¹²After the wedding he went to

Capernaum, He and His mother and *His* brothers and His disciples; and they stayed there a few days.

¹³ The Passover of the Jews was near, and Jesus went up to Jerusalem. ¹⁴ And He found in the temple those who were selling oxen and sheep and doves, and the money changers seated *at their tables.* ¹⁵ And He made a scourge of cords, and drove *them* all out of the temple, with the sheep and the oxen; and He poured out the coins of the money changers and overturned their tables; ¹⁶ and to those who were selling the doves He said, "Take these things away; stop making My Father's house a ᵃplace of business." ¹⁷ His disciples remembered that it was written, "ZEAL FOR YOUR HOUSE WILL CONSUME ME." ¹⁸ The Jews then said to Him, "What sign do You show us ᵃas your authority for doing these things?" ¹⁹ Jesus answered them, "Destroy this ᵃtemple, and in three days I will raise it up." ²⁰ The Jews then said, "It took forty-six years to build this ᵃtemple, and will You raise it up in three days?" ²¹ But He was speaking of the ᵃtemple of His body. ²² So when He was raised from the dead, His disciples remembered that He said this; and they believed the Scripture and the word which Jesus had spoken.

²³ Now when He was in Jerusalem at the Passover, during the feast, many believed in His name, observing His signs which He was doing. ²⁴ But Jesus, on His part, was not entrusting Himself to them, for He knew all men, ²⁵ and because He did not need anyone to testify concerning man, for He Himself knew what was in man.

2:4 ᵃLit *what to Me and to you* (a Hebrew idiom) 2:6 ᵃLit *two or three measures* 2:8 ᵃOr *steward* 2:10 ᵃOr *have become drunk* 2:11 ᵃOr *attesting miracles;* i.e. one which points to the supernatural power of God in redeeming grace 2:16 ᵃLit *house* 2:18 ᵃLit *that You do these* 2:19 ᵃOr *sanctuary* 2:20 ᵃOr *sanctuary* 2:21 ᵃOr *sanctuary*

Capernaum for a few days with his mother, his brothers, and his disciples.

¹³ It was nearly time for the Jewish Passover celebration, so Jesus went to Jerusalem. ¹⁴ In the Temple area he saw merchants selling cattle, sheep, and doves for sacrifices; he also saw dealers at tables exchanging foreign money. ¹⁵ Jesus made a whip from some ropes and chased them all out of the Temple. He drove out the sheep and cattle, scattered the money changers' coins over the floor, and turned over their tables. ¹⁶ Then, going over to the people who sold doves, he told them, "Get these things out of here. Stop turning my Father's house into a marketplace!"

¹⁷ Then his disciples remembered this prophecy from the Scriptures: "Passion for God's house will consume me."*

¹⁸ But the Jewish leaders demanded, "What are you doing? If God gave you authority to do this, show us a miraculous sign to prove it."

¹⁹ "All right," Jesus replied. "Destroy this temple, and in three days I will raise it up."

²⁰ "What!" they exclaimed. "It has taken forty-six years to build this Temple, and you can rebuild it in three days?" ²¹ But when Jesus said "this temple," he meant his own body. ²² After he was raised from the dead, his disciples remembered he had said this, and they believed both the Scriptures and what Jesus had said.

²³ Because of the miraculous signs Jesus did in Jerusalem at the Passover celebration, many began to trust in him. ²⁴ But Jesus didn't trust them, because he knew all about people. ²⁵ No one needed to tell him about human nature, for he knew what was in each person's heart.

2:1 Greek *On the third day;* see 1:35, 43. 2:6 Greek *2 or 3 measures* [75 to 113 liters]. 2:17 Or *"Concern for God's house will be my undoing."* Ps 69:9.

Jesus attended a wedding in Cana and helped the family of the groom avoid the embarrassment of a social faux pas. But Jesus' simple act of kindness was much more—it was a sign. Soon after this, Jesus railed against corruption in the temple. But it was no mere protest against obvious injustice; one prophecy was fulfilled and another announced.

— 2:1-2 —

Scholars have scratched their heads for years over the opening words of this episode in Jesus' ministry: "On the third day . . ." The third day in connection with what? It can't be the third chronological day in John's narrative. Four days have already elapsed:

- Day 1 – The religious leaders confront John the Baptizer (1:19-28).
- Day 2 – John the Baptizer identifies Jesus as the Messiah (1:29-34).
- Day 3 – Andrew and John (the apostle) begin following Jesus (1:35-42).
- Day 4 – Peter, Philip, and Nathanael are found (1:43-51).

"On the third day" most likely means on the third day after the events of 1:45-51, after He had "purposed to go to Galilee." Or perhaps this was the third day after His arrival in Galilee. Regardless, Jesus was again in the region of His upbringing. Cana was about four miles from Nazareth, and this was quite likely the wedding of a close family member. This would explain His mother's proactive role at the feast.

Weddings in those days were different than they are today in the West. Marriages in the ancient Near East were arranged by the parents, a contract was prepared, vows were spoken in the synagogue, tokens were exchanged, and then the man and woman returned to their respective homes. Although legally considered married, they lived apart during a betrothal period, which lasted no less than two months and could be as long as a year.

At the end of the waiting period, the groom would take to the streets with his friends, usually at night, in a torch-lit procession from his home to the bride's in a grand parade accompanied by pomp and color and singing. After speeches of goodwill and blessings pronounced over the couple, the groom took his bride home, where family and friends feasted for as long as a week. The groom's family was expected to provide enough food and drink for everyone.

— 2:3-4 —

At this particular wedding feast, the family hadn't planned very well. They didn't have enough wine to serve their guests the entire time, which was a major breach of etiquette. To this day in the East, hospitality is considered a sacred duty and, in some cases, a cause for legal action if withheld! Something needed to be done, so Mary turned to her son for help.

Three words or phrases need explanation, mostly because the language and culture is foreign and could lead to misinterpretation.

"Woman . . ." To all husbands and sons: I encourage you to avoid this term of address. It doesn't go over well in English. In the culture of first-century Galilee, however, it was very polite, much like addressing a woman as "Ma'am."

"What does that have to do with us?" The Greek behind this phrase is based on a Semitic expression, literally, "What to me and to you?" It can be a sharp rebuke (Judg. 11:12; 2 Sam. 16:10; 1 Kgs. 17:18; 2 Chr. 35:21) or a gentle request to be left out of a matter (2 Kgs. 3:13; Hos. 14:8).

"My hour has not yet come." Jesus made several references to His "hour" or His "time." Five times He says the time has not yet come (2:4; 7:6, 8, 30; 8:20); three times He declares that the time has come (12:23; 13:1; 17:1). These expressions are always references to the time of His glorification.

Those who accepted Jesus as the Christ were correct to anticipate that the promised King would receive God's glory and then bring glory to the nation (e.g., Isa. 60). Just *how* that was to happen was poorly understood by everyone but Jesus. This conflicting expectation appears frequently throughout John's narrative, beginning with this incident just days after John the Baptizer officially announced the identity of the Christ.

Mary knew before anyone else that her son was the Messiah. For years, she and Joseph endured scorn and ridicule and misunderstanding for apparently conceiving Jesus during their betrothal. For decades, she waited patiently to share her wonderful secret with the world. It's likely she saw the present crisis as a perfect opportunity for Jesus to burst onto the political scene, stir the people to action, and begin His campaign to claim the throne of David.

Jesus' response clarified three misconceptions. First, the Messiah's glory would come at the expense of His death, not as the result of a dazzling show of power. Second, the Messiah's glory would come from

God, not from people. And third, the Messiah's glory would take place on the Father's timetable, not anyone else's.

Mary may not have understood the full significance of her son's correction, but she got the message: He knows His destiny, and He's in charge.

— 2:6-10 —

The fact that Jesus did act and that it was by supernatural means tells us that He didn't object to His mother's request. Having addressed her misguided motivation, He delighted to help the host family. He instructed the servants to fill six stone water jars, each of which held 18–27 gallons (80–120 liters). This would provide more than 150 gallons (580 liters) of wine. That's enough for 2400 one-cup servings.

Turning water into wine was, by this time in history, a clichéd, sleight-of-hand parlor trick. Today, it would be like pulling a rabbit out of a top hat. Conjurers in pagan temples used special pitchers with hidden chambers to create the illusion of pouring either water or wine at will. I see Jesus revealing His sense of humor in choosing to solve the family's problem by actually doing what others could merely simulate.

SEVEN "SIGNS" OF THE SON OF GOD				
Sign	Reference	Description	Sign	Significance
1	2:1-11	Turned water into wine	Power over shame	Jesus is the source of life.
2	4:46-54	Healed royal official's son	Power over distance	Jesus is the giver of grace.
3	5:1-17	Healed infirm man by the Pool of Bethesda	Power over disease	Jesus is the giver of grace.
4	6:1-14	Fed a hungry multitude	Power over insufficiency	Jesus is the Word of God.
5	6:15-21	Walked on the Sea of Galilee and calmed a storm	Power over nature	Jesus is the Creator.
6	9:1-41	Gave sight to a man born blind	Power over sin	Jesus is the Truth.
7	11:17-45	Raised Lazarus from the dead	Power over death	Jesus is the hope of resurrection.

He left no room for trickery. While he stood back—perhaps even while reclining at table in the other room—the servants handled the jars, fetched the water, and drew the sample. Then, somewhere between the jars and the wedding coordinator, the miraculous transformation took place.

Note that the provision of wine was abundant and the quality of the wine was excellent. Take note of the Lord's motivation as well: This was a simple act of kindness done for the sake of love for His friends. He didn't make this a sideshow spectacle. In fact, it appears the only people who knew about it were those who had already believed in Him as the Christ. The "headwaiter" didn't even know what had happened.

— 2:11-12 —

John concludes the vignette with a comment and a transition to the next scene. He calls this miracle of Jesus the first of many "signs." The supernatural display of power attested to His identity as God. Moreover, it was symbolic of what He had come to do: to transform all who believe in Him. While the time for Jesus' "glory" had not come, His disciples witnessed it nonetheless. And their faith was strengthened as a result.

Afterward, Jesus and His disciples—five of them at this point— enjoyed a time of family reunion in Capernaum, roughly 18 miles northeast of Cana. Because Joseph is not mentioned by any Gospel after Jesus' twelfth year (Luke 2:41-52), most interpreters conclude that he had died. Mary probably lived with one of Jesus' half-brothers.

— 2:13-14 —

An unknown period of time had gone by; we have no way of knowing how long. Unlike Luke, whose chronicle reads more like a traditional history—chronological and event-driven—John's narrative is more philosophical and driven by a central theological purpose: to prove that Jesus is the Son of God. Therefore, some episodes appear out of chronological order, organized by topic rather than by time or place.

In John's Gospel, the Feast of Passover is a signpost along the journey through Jesus' life, and it plays a crucial role in the narrative. Earlier, John the Baptizer called Jesus "the Lamb of God" (1:29, 36). John does not use the term again, but he does use symbolism to identify Jesus as the true sacrificial lamb and the ultimate fulfillment of the Passover festival.

Passover goes back to the time in Egypt when Moses was given instructions to prepare a lamb a certain way and to honor the Lord's presence by spreading its blood on the lintel and doorposts of every Israelite's house. When the death angel moved through Egypt to take the life of the firstborn male in each household, he passed over every home bearing the blood of a sacrificial lamb.

By the first century, the festival was very different. It hardly resembled the solemn event of Israel's exodus from bondage in Egypt. The priesthood was completely corrupt and the temple had been polluted by the priests' greed. The courts of the complex had become a mixture of flea market and stock market. This so-called "Annas Bazaar" was named for Annas, a godfather-like figure who once held the office of high priest but had been deposed by the Roman government more than fifteen years earlier. Since that time, he ruled through a successive series of puppet priests, most of them his sons, and continued to run a well-established con game on a grand scale. Put bluntly, he was corrupt to the core.

Throughout the year, but especially at Passover, all Jewish males were expected to visit the temple, to pay the tax required by the Law of Moses, and to sacrifice an animal. On Passover, the sacrifice was to be a lamb, and as always, it had to be without blemish or defect. Moreover, the tax had to be paid in shekels, not in foreign currency, which bore images forbidden by the Law.

Annas and his cronies set up stations in the temple courts for the purpose of exchanging foreign currency for shekels—for an exorbitant fee, of course. Then, he supplied sacrificial animals, for which he charged top price. If someone brought his own animal, an inspector would judge it unfit and offer another in trade . . . for additional cash. Undoubtedly, the inferior animal would become some other man's "superior" sacrifice later on. What a racket!

During the Passover festival, the population of Jerusalem would swell to more than 250,000 males. Josephus put the total number of people (males and their families) close to three million![13] Obviously, the money-making potential of the temple was staggering.

This is what Jesus had seen each year as He and His family visited the temple to celebrate festivals, observe sacrifices, and glorify God. This year, like all the others, He found not a place of worship, but a shameless sham—a shrine to greed and a sanctuary for thieves. Only this year, something was different.

— 2:15-17 —

Before the official beginning of His ministry, Jesus visited the temple as a worshiper in His Father's house. But the time had come for Him to enter as the Messiah, the owner and ruler of the place. In fulfillment of prophecy (Mal. 3:1-4), His first official act was to purge His temple of a stubborn infestation.

Jesus' disciples stood back—probably in stunned silence. With mouths wide open, they stared astonished as Jesus tossed furniture like toothpicks and slung coins like seeds. The lash of His whip sent livestock scurrying behind their unclean owners as the temple Owner's voice echoed through the courts, "Take these things away!" And the disciples remembered Psalm 69:9, "Zeal for Your house has consumed me."

— 2:18-19 —

Once the commotion died down, the inevitable confrontation came. Jesus was not surprised. He knew it would happen . . . and where it would lead Him.

The religious leaders knew the Scriptures too. Concerned with the issue of authority—just as they were with the Baptizer in the Judean wilderness—they said, in effect, "If you're declaring Yourself to be the Messiah by this act, authenticate Yourself with a series of miracles." John uses the term "sign" here, just as he did in 2:11, because Jesus was not opposed to offering a miracle as a seal of authenticity under the right circumstances (2:23). In this case, however, the burden of proof was not His to bear. *He* was not in violation of the Law. *His* actions were not blatantly immoral. The rightness of His actions was authority enough. So instead, Jesus gave them a veiled response. Only a perceptive hearer would comprehend it, and none of them qualified. In fact, His own disciples didn't understand His true meaning until after His resurrection.

John highlights this tendency of Jesus more than the other Gospel writers. Jesus didn't waste His words on people who didn't want to hear. In fact, He didn't speak in order to convince the skeptic or sway the dissenter. His words were intended to divide His audience into two groups: receptive hearts and hard hearts. He understood that hearing Him is not an intellectual process, but a crisis of the will. Several times throughout the story when Jesus says something cryptic, some people *think* they understand Him and turn away, while others admit their confusion and draw nearer.

— 2:20-22 —

Just as Jesus expected, the religious authorities took His challenge literally. They completely missed His point.

The temple was constructed to be the dwelling place of God—not that He needs a structure! God is omnipresent—present everywhere simultaneously. He ordered the temple constructed to house the special manifestation of His presence, a supernatural light called the *shekinah,* "glory." In the Old Testament, this light appeared in a bush to Moses (Exod. 3:1-3), it led the Israelites through the wilderness in a pillar (Exod. 13:21-22), and it settled on Mount Sinai before the Israelites (Exod. 19:18; 24:17). When the tabernacle was constructed—and later the temple—the *shekinah* hovered over the ark of the covenant behind a thick veil in the most holy place (Exod. 25:22; Lev. 16:2). The Lord did this for the benefit of His people, to affirm His presence among them as their one and only God.

Unfortunately, because of the people of Israel's repeated and persistent failure to worship Him exclusively and because of their immorality and rebellion, the *shekinah* had long ago departed (Ezek. 10:18). While God's love for Israel never faded, and He continued to guide the nation after its return from exile, the temple had not been the dwelling place of God for centuries. When Jesus issued His challenge to the religious leaders, it's as though He were pointing to His own chest to say, *"This is the authentic dwelling place of God."*

— 2:23-25 —

John concludes this part of the story on a positive note. While the religious leaders had remained defiant and rejected their High Priest, many others believed. John adds that those who believed did so by "observing" Jesus' signs. The Greek word translated "observing" is *theōreō* [2334], from which we derive our word "theory." The term means "to come to understand as the result of perception."[14]

• • •

Throughout this section (1:19–4:54) and the next (5:1–12:50), John is careful to show that Jesus is unlike any religious or political leader the world has ever known. His power and authority come from a different realm, one that stands in stark contrast to the system of this world that is corrupt with sin. People of the world seek charismatic leaders who will lead them where they already want to go. Consequently, worldly leaders usually derive their power and influence from popular support. But not this Man; not this King.

Jesus simply presented Himself in truth; some will believe in Him and some will not. He performed miraculous signs, not to convince skeptics or sway dissenters, but to signal His own arrival as Messiah. He offered "signs" to prompt willing, prepared hearts to respond. Furthermore, He wasn't depending upon a favorable response from anyone—the religious leaders or the masses—to complete His mission. He wasn't running for election; He didn't need popular support to claim the throne; He had no plans to train an army. He didn't entrust Himself, His mission, or His future to humanity; He trusted His Father, and then He invited humanity to trust Him.

There have been courageous men and women who have led in this way; long before Jesus arrived, they spoke the truth and led those whose hearts resonated with that truth. Some amassed great hoards of followers. Most were ignored or martyred. All of them died. But Jesus is different, and His kingdom is different.

APPLICATION: JOHN 2:1-25

Keeping Your Temple Clean

John tells the story of Jesus cleansing the temple in Jerusalem to establish three primary truths:

1. *God owns His temple, not priests.* He called priests to steward the temple and to help people approach Him as He has commanded.
2. *God's Word is the only authority recognized in the temple, not the high priest or any other designated position.* Anyone acting contrary to His Word has no authority.
3. *God's Son came to claim ownership of the temple, and the religious "authorities" rejected Him.* This point is repeated often in John's narrative and ultimately leads to the final rejection of Jesus as the Messiah.

This incident also illustrates a practical truth for believers: *God's temple is sacred ground, a dedicated place of meeting between the Lord and His people.* In the Old Testament, the Lord used a physical structure for that purpose; first a tabernacle, which the Hebrews called the "tent of meeting," and then a permanent building in Jerusalem. The Lord was very specific about reserving everything in the temple for the purpose of worship. Once Jesus completed His work of atonement for the sins of the world, the place of meeting changed, but the standards remain the same. Believers are now His temples (1 Cor. 6:19-20), and we are to remain no less sanctified.

What do you think the Lord wants to drive out of your temple?

While the Lord wants the temple of your body to be clean, the task is not yours to complete. Note that the corruption in the temple was not removed by any mere mortal; God in human flesh confronted and removed the impurity—as only He can. Our role is to submit to His cleansing process; first by refusing to tolerate the presence of corruption, then by asking Him to remove it.

Here is a simple prayer to help you get started:

Lord, I recognize You as the Owner of my temple. I willingly submit to the authority of Your Word. I confess that I have allowed the corruption of _____ to take up space that is reserved for worshiping You. I freely admit that I do not have the power to remove it on my own. Please cleanse me, even if I must endure hardship or suffer affliction in the process. Grant me the courage to remain steadfast as You work. Grant me patience to endure the process and provide extra encouragement when my patience wears thin. Then let me rejoice when Your temple is again pure. I make the same request as David did so many years ago: Create in me a clean heart, O God (Ps. 51:10).

I ask this in the matchless name of Jesus, Amen.

Brainstorming the New Birth
JOHN 3:1-21

NASB

[1] Now there was a man of the Pharisees, named Nicodemus, a ruler of the Jews; [2] this man came to Jesus by night and said to Him, "Rabbi, we know that You have come from God *as* a teacher; for no one can do these [a]signs that You do unless God is with him." [3] Jesus answered and said to him, "Truly, truly, I say to you, unless one is born [a]again he cannot see the kingdom of God."

[4] Nicodemus said to Him, "How can a man be born when he is old?

NLT

[1] There was a man named Nicodemus, a Jewish religious leader who was a Pharisee. [2] After dark one evening, he came to speak with Jesus. "Rabbi," he said, "we all know that God has sent you to teach us. Your miraculous signs are evidence that God is with you."

[3] Jesus replied, "I tell you the truth, unless you are born again,* you cannot see the Kingdom of God."

[4] "What do you mean?" exclaimed Nicodemus. "How can an old man go

NASB

He cannot enter a second time into his mother's womb and be born, can he?" 5 Jesus answered, "Truly, truly, I say to you, unless one is born of water and the Spirit he cannot enter into the kingdom of God. 6 That which is born of the flesh is flesh, and that which is born of the Spirit is spirit. 7 Do not be amazed that I said to you, 'You must be born ªagain.' 8 The wind blows where it wishes and you hear the sound of it, but do not know where it comes from and where it is going; so is everyone who is born of the Spirit."

9 Nicodemus said to Him, "How can these things be?" 10 Jesus answered and said to him, "Are you the teacher of Israel and do not understand these things? 11 Truly, truly, I say to you, we speak of what we know and testify of what we have seen, and you do not accept our testimony. 12 If I told you earthly things and you do not believe, how will you believe if I tell you heavenly things? 13 No one has ascended into heaven, but He who descended from heaven: the Son of Man. 14 As Moses lifted up the serpent in the wilderness, even so must the Son of Man be lifted up; 15 so that whoever ªbelieves will in Him have eternal life.

16 "For God so loved the world, that He gave His ªonly begotten Son, that whoever believes in Him shall not perish, but have eternal life. 17 For God did not send the Son into the world to judge the world, but that the world might be saved through Him. 18 He who believes in Him is not judged; he who does not believe has been judged already, because he has not believed in the name of the ªonly begotten Son of God. 19 This is the judgment, that the Light has come into the world, and men loved the darkness rather than the Light, for their deeds were evil. 20 For everyone who does evil hates the Light, and

NLT

back into his mother's womb and be born again?"

5 Jesus replied, "I assure you, no one can enter the Kingdom of God without being born of water and the Spirit.* 6 Humans can reproduce only human life, but the Holy Spirit gives birth to spiritual life.* 7 So don't be surprised when I say, 'You* must be born again.' 8 The wind blows wherever it wants. Just as you can hear the wind but can't tell where it comes from or where it is going, so you can't explain how people are born of the Spirit."

9 "How are these things possible?" Nicodemus asked.

10 Jesus replied, "You are a respected Jewish teacher, and yet you don't understand these things? 11 I assure you, we tell you what we know and have seen, and yet you won't believe our testimony. 12 But if you don't believe me when I tell you about earthly things, how can you possibly believe if I tell you about heavenly things? 13 No one has ever gone to heaven and returned. But the Son of Man* has come down from heaven. 14 And as Moses lifted up the bronze snake on a pole in the wilderness, so the Son of Man must be lifted up, 15 so that everyone who believes in him will have eternal life.*

16 "For this is how God loved the world: He gave* his one and only Son, so that everyone who believes in him will not perish but have eternal life. 17 God sent his Son into the world not to judge the world, but to save the world through him.

18 "There is no judgment against anyone who believes in him. But anyone who does not believe in him has already been judged for not believing in God's one and only Son. 19 And the judgment is based on this fact: God's light came into the world, but people loved the darkness more than the light, for their actions were evil. 20 All who do evil hate the light

does not come to the Light for fear that his deeds will be exposed. ²¹But he who practices the truth comes to the Light, so that his deeds may be manifested as having been wrought in God."

3:2 ᵃOr *attesting miracles*   **3:3** ᵃOr *from above*   **3:7** ᵃOr *from above*   **3:15** ᵃOr *believes in Him will have eternal life*   **3:16** ᵃOr *unique*, only one of His kind   **3:18** ᵃOr *unique*, only one of His kind

and refuse to go near it for fear their sins will be exposed. ²¹But those who do what is right come to the light so others can see that they are doing what God wants.*"

3:3 Or *born from above;* also in 3:7.   **3:5** Or *and spirit*. The Greek word for *Spirit* can also be translated *wind;* see 3:8.   **3:6** Greek *what is born of the Spirit is spirit*.   **3:7** The Greek word for *you* is plural; also in 3:12.   **3:13** Some manuscripts add *who lives in heaven.* "Son of Man" is a title Jesus used for himself.   **3:15** Or *everyone who believes will have eternal life in him*.   **3:16** Or *For God loved the world so much that he gave*.   **3:21** Or *can see God at work in what he is doing*.

I have a close personal friend who was born when he was twenty-seven years old. It all started when he was an earnest ten-year-old who wanted to know God. Two years later, he found out that the way to know God was to join a church (or so he thought). And that's what he did. He joined a church and was baptized . . . but nothing changed. Three years later he began to develop as a young man. He had drives and pressures and interests that were—to put it delicately—not godly. So he tried another approach. Really, it was the same approach, just through another church. He walked down an aisle, joined the church, and was baptized a second time.

This particular church taught that the only effective way to know God is reform yourself, mostly by giving up things you desire. So he did. He gave up alcohol, which had become a regular part of his life. He gave up smoking. He gave up playing cards. He gave up dancing. He even stopped dating, which was no small sacrifice for a 15-year-old boy. But he thought, *To know God, it's worth it.*

After all that, he still didn't know God, so he began to wonder, *Is God really knowable?*

After two years of faithful giving up and dogged obedience to rule and regiment, he tried another approach. Well, actually, it was the same approach with yet another church. He walked down front, joined the church, and was that very night baptized a third time. A few months passed and, much sooner than before, he realized that his condition was just as hopeless as it had always been. No change. So, in his own words, he "kissed it all off and ran wild."

He attended a university and quickly partied himself out of the school. He joined the military and served his country faithfully between drunken benders. After his discharge, he met a nice woman and married her, but soon their marriage was coming unraveled. He landed a good job and tried his best to live well, but eventually decided the effort was a total waste. Finally, he adopted a familiar motto and gave himself to fulfilling it: "Live fast, play hard, die young, and leave a good-looking corpse!"

People don't actually live by that philosophy for very long; either because they don't live very long or because they discover what a precious gift this life really is. A brush with death sent my friend digging through his old sea bag for a little New Testament given to him by the Gideons when he was issued his uniform years before. He pulled it out and started reading right away, from the beginning: Matt. 1.

By the time he reached chapters 5, 6, and 7, he fell into a deep despair. He knew he couldn't keep the standard Jesus set while preaching His "Sermon on the Mount." So he skipped to Mark only to find more commandments. That only intensified his guilt. He then turned to Luke. More commandments he knew he couldn't keep.

Confused, frustrated, and miserable, he turned to John. And in the third chapter, he was hooked. He stumbled upon an intriguing conversation between Jesus and a deeply religious man, who seemed to share his struggle. It wasn't until that moment that my friend recognized his problem. He had been born wrong the first time. What he needed was a whole new start. A different start. A birth of another kind. So, like a child, he got on his knees and prayed, "Lord, if You accept me like I am, I'll accept You like You are. And I'll expect from You a new birth." That changed everything!

My friend was born again . . . born from above. At the age of 27, he discovered the difference between religion and regeneration.

— 3:1-2 —

Here we meet another man confused in his religion. If Judaism had an office like that of pope, Nicodemus (Greek for "conqueror of the people") would have been the ideal candidate. As we observe his encounter with Jesus, we discover that he possessed three outstanding qualifications that made him one of the most impressively religious men alive.

"A man of the Pharisees" (3:1). The most likely meaning of the term "Pharisee" is "separated one." Many trace their roots to Daniel and his three friends, who refused to partake of their captors' food (Dan. 1:8-19) or worship the king as a god (Dan. 3:1-30) while in exile in Babylon. Having been taken from the Promised Land and cut off from their temple, they clung to the Law as a means of preserving their identity as distant sons of Abraham.

But after more than six-hundred years, this admirable loyalty to nationalism and devotion to the Law had taken on a life of its own. Pharisees had become a tight-knit brotherhood, a political and religious party that had earned the respect of their fellow Jews. They were meticulous expositors of Scripture and worked tirelessly to apply the general principles of the Law to everyday life. For example, the Law stated that every Israelite was to set aside the seventh day of the week for resting the body and refreshing the soul (Exod. 20:10-11). So that everyone would know how to apply the Law in their culture and to "rest" as they should, the Pharisaic rabbis added a long list of specific prohibitions. Later, this oral tradition of the Pharisees would be preserved in a document called the Mishnah, which contains twenty-four chapters just on how to keep the Sabbath.

No one rivaled the Pharisees in being religious. No one could!

"A ruler of the Jews" (3:1). Before the Jews were exiled to Babylon, a king ruled the nation of Israel. After their return to the Promised Land, they were subject to foreign governors and looked to the high priest for leadership. By the first century, when Rome dominated Israel, the high priest shared power with a council of seventy men who were experienced statesmen and notable religious figures. This ruling council of "elders," called the Sanhedrin, served as Israel's Parliament/Congress and Supreme Court.

Not only was Nicodemus a devoutly religious man; he was a leader of religious men.

"The teacher of Israel" (3:10). John uses the definite article, indicating that Nicodemus was more than merely one teacher among many in Israel. There was no rabbinical position or political office called "the teacher of Israel," so this was either Jesus' personal opinion or, more likely, the general opinion of his peers. Jesus found irony in the man's reputation, suggesting Nicodemus was regarded by most to be the preeminent voice of religious teaching in Israel.

The fact that Nicodemus came to see Jesus under cover of darkness suggests he was concerned about being seen with Him. The images of night and darkness are menacing in John's Gospel (9:4; 11:10; 13:30; 19:39). Open confrontation in the temple proved to be embarrassing for the religious leaders, so Nicodemus may have been sent by his peers to negotiate privately. His opening lines show all the grace and dignity of a man on a diplomatic mission. It's also possible he came in all sincerity to investigate the popular and controversial rabbi from Galilee, perhaps in the spirit of professional courtesy if not personal curiosity.

— 3:3 —

John may have summarized this conversation for the sake of brevity while keeping the general flavor of the encounter. The Lord quickly bypassed the flattering approach and cut straight to the heart of the matter. This was no common Jew sitting in front of Him; this was a remarkably astute theological mind. And Jesus saw through him with supernatural, spiritual X-ray vision.

Jesus put before the teacher a theological proposition, using fresh terminology. This is the first instance of the phrase, "born again." This was not a concept familiar to scholars of the Hebrew Scriptures. In the Greek language in which John wrote this story, the words are charged with multiple layers of meaning, all of which reveal a simple yet profound truth that invites closer investigation. John foreshadowed this concept in his prologue:

> But as many as received Him, to them He gave the right to become *children of God*, even to those who believe in His name, who were *born, not of blood nor of the will of the flesh nor of the will of man, but of God.* (1:12-13, emphasis mine)

The Greek word *anōthen* [509], translated "again," can have several meanings, but the most common rendering is "from above." Similarly, we might say someone "received help from above," meaning that God helped him or her. However, here it very likely has an intended double meaning, bringing both "from above" and "again" together to illustrate a profound truth.

In the words of Merrill Tenney, "Birth is our mode of entrance into the world and brings with it the potential equipment for adjustment to the world."[15] It is passing from one kind of life and from one environment to another. "To be born again, or 'born from above,' means a transformation of a person so that he is able to enter another world and adapt to its conditions. . . . To belong to the heavenly kingdom, one must be born into it."[16] Moreover, our own birth is not something we can accomplish ourselves. We cannot conceive ourselves and we cannot become ready for birth on our own. Physical birth is the result of two people deciding to procreate and then joining their bodies as God designed. Spiritual birth is similar in that the newborn is not able to bring about his or her own birth; it must be done on his or her behalf. But, unlike physical birth, spiritual birth is strictly the work of God (1:12-13).

Jesus made this different kind of birth a requirement for citizenship in the "kingdom of God," a phrase rarely used in John's Gospel. As a politician, Nicodemus cared about the crisis in Israel; God's kingdom had been reduced to a province of Rome. Furthermore, he expected the Messiah to be a military commander and political ruler, who would transform Israel into a dominant world power and economic power-house. This new requirement grabbed his attention and his demeanor shifted dramatically. He dropped his flattering facade and engaged Jesus in thoughtful debate.

— 3:4-5 —

When Nicodemus heard the new requirement, "must be born *anōthen*," he deliberately focused on the "again" nuance of the phrase. Perhaps with tongue in cheek, he stretched the image out of shape. Don't forget; this is no imbecile sitting across from Jesus. This is a brilliant theo-logian, skilled in the art of debate, addressing what he undoubtedly saw as a young upstart. His question said, in effect, "What a ludicrous proposition!"

Jews in his day called Gentile converts to Judaism "newborn chil-dren," a charming expression for those who had just begun their new life as "sons of the covenant" and heirs to the blessings of Abraham's offspring. Men were circumcised and all converts were baptized in water. Nicodemus didn't misunderstand Jesus' imagery; he objected to the notion that only Gentile converts can take part in the coming earthly kingdom under the Messiah. This would leave Jews—the very people God had preserved for Himself through the centuries (Pss. 106:5; 135:4)—out of the promises made to Abraham (Gen. 12:1-3; 15:18-21).

Of course, this was not Jesus' point at all. Nicodemus' perspective was limited to the earthly plane, the physical dimension. To help the old theologian see, Jesus offered two illustrations (3:6-8 and 3:14-15). To twenty-first century Westerners, both appear more cryptic than to those living in the first. The concepts would have been very familiar to Nicodemus.

Before we examine these two illustrations, note the parallelism be-tween 3:3 and 3:5. This common literary device of Hebrew poets is a helpful means of interpretation for us today.

"Truly, truly, I say to you, unless one is *born again* he cannot see the kingdom of God." (John 3:3, emphasis mine)

"Truly, truly, I say to you, unless one is *born of water and the Spirit* he cannot enter into the kingdom of God." (John 3:5, em-phasis mine)

The ministry of John the Baptizer was well-known to everyone in Jerusalem, including this rabbi. John called Jews to a "baptism of repentance" in which Jews were to come to God as if for the first time, like Gentile converts. But remember—John's baptism was only a *symbol* of new life (1:31-33); the baptism of Jesus is a baptism of actual life . . . abundant life, spiritual life, life made possible only through the Holy Spirit. Furthermore, connecting the concepts "born *anōthen*" and "born of water and the Spirit" should have sparked the rabbi's memory of a familiar Old Testament promise:

> "I will take you from the nations and gather you from all the countries; then I will bring you to your land. I will sprinkle you with pure water and you will be clean from all your impurities. I will purify you from all your idols. I will give you a new heart, and I will put a new spirit within you. I will remove the heart of stone from your body and give you a heart of flesh. I will put my Spirit within you; I will take the initiative and you will obey my statutes and carefully observe my regulations. Then you will live in the land I gave to your fathers; you will be my people, and I will be your God." (Ezek. 36:24-28 NET)

Unless one is born "from above" through the cleansing work of the Spirit of God within, he or she cannot enter God's kingdom.

— 3:6-8 —

Jesus' first illustration reveals a radical difference between religion and regeneration. His second illustration (3:14-15) explains how regeneration works.

Flesh produces flesh. Spirit produces spirit. Spiritual life is a mystery to the physical realm. It cannot be obtained through physical means. The Spirit of God, the Source of all spiritual life, cannot be impressed to give life as a reward; He cannot be bribed, or flattered, or tricked into giving life in exchange for sacrifice; and He will not sell eternal life, which is priceless, for anything temporal, which is ultimately worthless.

Religion is man-made. Religion is of the physical realm: impressive on earth, rubbish in heaven.

— 3:9-13 —

Let's give Nicodemus credit. While many rejected Jesus outright, Nicodemus tried to understand Jesus' message and wrestled with the issue of His identity. The smooth-talking statesman had become a stammering pupil. On the surface, his problem appeared to be lack of understanding, but Jesus dug deep to find the real source of his struggle. Note the progression:

"[You] . . . do not *understand* . . ." (3:10),

"you do not *accept* . . ." (3:11),

"how will you *believe* . . . ?" (3:12).

First, Jesus was incredulous that spiritual matters would be so foreign to the mind of Israel's leading spiritual teacher. If the shepherd is blind, the flock is doomed!

Second, the real struggle for Nicodemus and the people he represented was their refusal to affirm the truth of eyewitness testimony. In the ancient world, there was no stronger evidence than the corroborating testimony of multiple witnesses.

Third, Jesus acknowledged that spiritual realities are more difficult to believe than truths that can be perceived with the senses;

"SON OF MAN"

JOHN 3:13-14

Jesus frequently referred to Himself as "Son of Man," which was a particularly meaningful title with roots deep in the soil of Israel's Scriptures. First, Jesus used it to call attention to His own humanity, which is feeble and fragile (Job 25:6; Pss. 8:4; 144:3; 146:3; Isa. 51:12; cf. Matt. 26:41; Mark 14:38). Ezekiel used the title ninety times, usually in reference to his own human weakness (e.g., Ezek. 2:1). Jesus is human, and He suffered the pains of humanity, most especially in the ordeal of the cross.

More significantly, "Son of Man" is the title given by Daniel to the messianic figure in his vision. He was "One like a Son of Man," who received from the "Ancient of Days" everlasting dominion over all the earth, to rule as its king (Dan. 7:13).

Jews of Jesus' time struggled to understand the dual image of the Messiah presented in prophecy. Many theologians then, as now, suggested that perhaps the Messiah is really two individuals, one who dies as the "suffering servant" and another who resurrects the first and then reigns as supreme king. By no coincidence then, the title "Son of Man" appears thirteen times in John's Gospel (John 1:51; 3:13-14; 5:27; 6:27, 53, 62; 8:28; 9:35; 12:23, 34; 13:31) and always in conjunction with Jesus' claim to deity. It was Jesus' way of identifying Himself as the sole Messiah.

nevertheless, the heart of the matter is credibility. Who are you going to trust?

Finally, Jesus claimed to be an eyewitness to heavenly truths, having seen what physical eyes cannot see. A mere human cannot physically ascend to heaven to witness spiritual realities, but God *can* descend physically to testify to humanity. Not only *can* God come to earth as a man, He *did* come to earth as a man. That is why Jesus used the familiar Old Testament idiom "Son of Man" to refer to Himself.

— 3:14-15 —

Jesus drew upon a familiar episode in Israel's history (recorded in Num. 21:4-9) to illustrate how regeneration takes place. When this episode occurred, the Israelites had experienced God's miraculous deliverance from slavery in Egypt: ten plagues, the parting of the Red Sea, a pillar of cloud and pillar of fire to lead them. Yet they began to grumble and complain. Eventually, God decided to discipline His disbelieving, disobedient people with an affliction of venomous snakes. As people began to die, Moses interceded. In response, the Lord instructed him to fashion a bronze snake and set it on a pole so that those who were bitten could look up at it. He then promised that when a person looked upon the bronze representation of his or her affliction, the venom would lose its effectiveness (Num. 21:8-9). Just as God had promised, the plan worked. Not only did the people survive the affliction; they also gained a powerful object lesson in repentance.

The Israelites' experience in the desert was a foreshadowing of what Jesus did for all people when He was "lifted up" on a cross (see also 2 Cor. 5:21). When we acknowledge our sin, take complete responsibility for our guilt, and come to the Lord for healing, the poison of evil loses its power to kill.

— 3:16-17 —

Because Nicodemus was thoroughly familiar with Old Testament Scripture and he knew well Israel's history of disbelief, this brief allusion prepared him to see the spiritual truth he had been missing all his life. It was not a new truth; it had been plainly visible for any who desired to see:

Regeneration occurs through belief.

John 3:16 is perhaps the most well-known verse in all of Scripture, and for good reason. The truths contained in this summary statement are life altering, even for those who are earnestly religious. Let me examine the verse phrase by phrase.

"For God so loved the world." Religion likes to pretend its God is good and loving, but in reality, all religious devotion is fueled by a secret dread that God is looking for an excuse to condemn those who do not please Him. While a holy God must punish sin in accordance with justice, He does not delight in destroying what He created and crafted with such care. God is the Author of life; sin is the cause of destruction.

"That He gave His only begotten Son." The Greek phrase translated "only begotten" is *monogenēs* [3439], which was an idiom based on an ancient custom called "primogeniture." Put simply, the eldest son in a family, the "firstborn," was entitled to receive the greatest share of the inheritance. If he was the only son, "the only-born" (*monogenēs*), he obviously received everything. As often happens in language, a familiar expression gradually loses its literal meaning as it becomes more common in legal or technical circles. For example, a "writ of habeas corpus" is a legal document that says the government must have evidence of a crime before arresting someone. *Habeas corpus* is Latin for "you have a body." While the expression originally applied to murder cases, it eventually became a general principle for any kind of alleged crime. In the same way, the term *monogenēs* lost its literal connotation in favor of the legal meaning: "sole heir." So, *monogenēs* is best translated "one and only."

"That whoever believes in Him." The Greek term is *pisteuō* [4100], "to believe as true, to trust, to place confidence in" (see Introduction, "The Crisis of Faith," p. 9). When one trusts in God's gift rather than his or her own merit, eternal life flows like water. What simplicity!

To Nicodemus, a man who spent most of his life honing his religious skills, meticulously fulfilling every perceived expectation of goodness and righteousness, this news could have come as either a wonderful relief or an exasperating disappointment. Pride is the determining factor.

"Shall not perish." "Perish" is translated from the passive form of the Greek word *apollumi* [622], meaning "to be destroyed, to be utterly lost." Trusting in the Son of God saves the believer from the penalty of sin. This is a promise. Good deeds cannot make the promise more secure, and moral failure cannot nullify it. We are saved by God's grace through faith alone (cf. Eph. 2:8-9). What security!

"But have eternal life." We are destined to die physically and we exist in a kind of living death in the meantime. While nothing will halt the process of decay, and nothing will prevent the end of physical life,

God's grace will not allow death to reign supreme. Evil will not have the final word. Life—eternal, incorruptible, abundant life—is offered to all who will receive it through faith. What grace!

Jesus reveals the true nature of God. He longs to see His creation saved from the just penalty of sin to thrive forever in His presence. Therefore, the Son of God came to earth to save all humanity from judgment. What hope!

— 3:18-21 —

As Jesus concluded His discourse, He helped Nicodemus see the connection between belief and salvation, and between unbelief and condemnation. Snake-bitten Israelites could escape death simply by trusting the word of God through Moses. Because the remedy was easily accessible and completely free, it cannot be said that anyone was condemned by God. If someone died, his or her death was the just penalty of sin. However, God did not condemn. The person condemned himself or herself by choosing not to believe God's Word or by refusing His grace.

Jesus then drew upon the image of light to illustrate the power of truth to prompt obedience. Those who genuinely believe the truth will obey it. Jesus didn't come to teach that obedience to the commandments of God is worthless or that evil deeds don't matter. On the contrary, obedience is crucial. If an Israelite genuinely believed the Word he or she heard through Moses, following instructions would naturally follow. Belief and obedience go together.

Nicodemus—the very personification of religion—had removed belief from the equation. But trying to achieve salvation through obedience is impossible, and it always leads to hypocrisy and despair. Religion is ultimately nothing more than faith in self, trusting one's own ability to be good enough to impress God. Sooner or later, the religionist's deeds will be exposed for what they are: the fruit of pride.

• • •

What could be less complicated than belief? What could be more effortless than faith? There's nothing to achieve, no quest to complete, no challenge to overcome, no method to master, no merit to earn. We have only to trust the One who made us, who loves us, and who satisfied all of God's expectations on behalf of all humanity.

Unfortunately, humanity is chronically religious. Most people will opt for religion over regeneration. Pride is not only powerful; it's blinding.

Second Kings 18 describes a time in Israel's history, several centuries after the death of Moses, long after the affliction of the snake had passed, when Hezekiah, a righteous king, led his people away from religion and toward genuine belief in God.

> [Hezekiah] removed the high places and broke down the *sacred* pillars and cut down the Asherah. He also broke in pieces the bronze serpent that Moses had made, for until those days the sons of Israel burned incense to it; and it was called Nehushtan ["a piece of bronze"]. He trusted in the LORD, the God of Israel. (2 Kgs. 18:4-5)

For seven hundred years, the Israelites had been dragging that hunk of bronze around the desert, though the Conquest, and into the Promised Land. They preserved it through invasion, famine, civil war, and the rise and fall of kings. The Israelites turned the bronze symbol of their ancestors' faithlessness into a superstitious good luck charm. They even "burned incense to it." As all people are prone to do, they set aside confident trust in their God for something tangible, something they thought they could manipulate or control.

The same lack of belief occurred in John's time, just as it did in ages past and still occurs today. Churches are filled with men and women who are clinging tightly to their precious trinkets or trusting in their own moral merits. Pride reigns supreme. According to Jesus, they have judged themselves and have therefore decided their own eternal destinies.

Do not say, "May God have mercy on their souls." He already has. The condemned have judged themselves.

APPLICATION: JOHN 3:1-21

You Must Be Born Again

When Israel's finest example of religious devotion visited Jesus, he was surprised to hear that his preeminent status and his impressive list of qualifications failed to earn him a place in God's kingdom. Jesus said, "You must be born *anōthen*" (3:7). This simple statement confronted a significant misconception held by Nicodemus and all religious people.

Salvation requires a second birth "from above," because we are powerless to save ourselves. Moral perfection is the standard and we have all fallen short (Rom. 3:23); therefore, we cannot become good enough to earn our place in heaven. Fortunately, the penalty for sin has been paid in full by Jesus Christ. Rather than try to overcome evil on our own, we must respond to His free gift of eternal life with complete trust that He alone will save us (Eph. 2:8-9).

Salvation cannot be earned; it can only be received as a free gift. We accept God's gift of salvation by faith alone in Christ alone for the forgiveness of our sins. If you would like to enter a relationship with your Creator by trusting in Christ as your Savior, here is a simple prayer you can use to express your faith:

Dear God,

I know that my sin has put a barrier between You and me. Thank You for sending Your Son, Jesus, to suffer the penalty of my sin by dying in my place so that barrier would be removed. I trust in Jesus alone for the forgiveness of my sins. In doing that, I also accept His free gift of eternal life, which is mine forevermore by Your grace.

Thank You.

In Jesus' name,
Amen.

The Preacher Who Lost His Congregation
JOHN 3:22-36

NASB

22 After these things Jesus and His disciples came into the land of Judea, and there He was spending time with them and baptizing. 23 John also was baptizing in Aenon near Salim, because there was much water there; and *people* were coming and were being baptized— 24 for John had not yet been thrown into prison.

25 Therefore there arose a discussion on the part of John's disciples with a Jew about purification. 26 And they came to John and said to him,

NLT

22 Then Jesus and his disciples left Jerusalem and went into the Judean countryside. Jesus spent some time with them there, baptizing people.

23 At this time John the Baptist was baptizing at Aenon, near Salim, because there was plenty of water there; and people kept coming to him for baptism. 24 (This was before John was thrown into prison.) 25 A debate broke out between John's disciples and a certain Jew* over ceremonial cleansing. 26 So John's disciples came to him and said, "Rabbi, the man you met on the other side of

"Rabbi, He who was with you beyond the Jordan, to whom you have testified, behold, He is baptizing and all are coming to Him." ²⁷John answered and said, "A man can receive nothing unless it has been given him from heaven. ²⁸You yourselves ᵃare my witnesses that I said, 'I am not the ᵇChrist,' but, 'I have been sent ahead of Him.' ²⁹He who has the bride is the bridegroom; but the friend of the bridegroom, who stands and hears him, rejoices greatly because of the bridegroom's voice. So this joy of mine has been made full. ³⁰He must increase, but I must decrease.

³¹"He who comes from above is above all, he who is of the earth is from the earth and speaks of the earth. He who comes from heaven is above all. ³²What He has seen and heard, of that He testifies; and no one receives His testimony. ³³He who has received His testimony has set his seal to *this*, that God is true. ³⁴For He whom God has sent speaks the words of God; ᵃfor He gives the Spirit without measure. ³⁵The Father loves the Son and has given all things into His hand. ³⁶He who believes in the Son has eternal life; but he who does not ᵃobey the Son will not see life, but the wrath of God abides on him."

3:28 ᵃLit *testify for me* ᵇI.e. Messiah 3:34 ᵃLit *because He does not give the Spirit by measure* 3:36 ᵃOr *believe*

the Jordan River, the one you identified as the Messiah, is also baptizing people. And everybody is going to him instead of coming to us."

²⁷John replied, "No one can receive anything unless God gives it from heaven. ²⁸You yourselves know how plainly I told you, 'I am not the Messiah. I am only here to prepare the way for him.' ²⁹It is the bridegroom who marries the bride, and the best man is simply glad to stand with him and hear his vows. Therefore, I am filled with joy at his success. ³⁰He must become greater and greater, and I must become less and less.

³¹"He has come from above and is greater than anyone else. We are of the earth, and we speak of earthly things, but he has come from heaven and is greater than anyone else.* ³²He testifies about what he has seen and heard, but how few believe what he tells them! ³³Anyone who accepts his testimony can affirm that God is true. ³⁴For he is sent by God. He speaks God's words, for God gives him the Spirit without limit. ³⁵The Father loves his Son and has put everything into his hands. ³⁶And anyone who believes in God's Son has eternal life. Anyone who doesn't obey the Son will never experience eternal life but remains under God's angry judgment."

3:25 Some manuscripts read *some Jews.*
3:31 Some manuscripts do not include *and is greater than anyone else.*

If you want a lively discussion at your next dinner gathering, ask the following questions: "Except for Jesus Christ, who is the greatest person who ever lived? What made him or her great?" I guarantee the second question will quickly dominate the conversation, because we all have our own way of measuring greatness, and we rarely agree with the standards of others.

Jesus answered that question. As He reviewed history from the dawn of time, He bypassed Abraham, the father of faith, and Moses, the instrument of God to deliver His covenant people out of bondage. He omitted David, the rugged and humble shepherd, the champion war-rior, the greatest of Israel's kings. He ignored Daniel, perhaps the most powerful and influential man in the world, a leading figure in two of the world's greatest empires, and a faithful prophet of God. He skipped over Noah, Samuel, Solomon, Isaiah, and every notable figure in secu-lar history. Instead, Jesus boldly named a contemporary: "Truly I say to you, among those born of women there has not arisen anyone greater than John the Baptist!" (Matt. 11:11).

John didn't have the qualities of greatness we prize most in the people we admire. He didn't move among the rich and famous, the proud and powerful; he chose the solitude of the desert. He didn't cultivate a suave image; he wore camel's hair and leather. He didn't rise through the ranks of politics and society to become a pied piper of men; he confronted and offended and spoke the truth without apol-ogy. Adjectives to describe John would be austere, ascetic, aggressive, animated . . . and *weird*. Regardless, Jesus, who measures greatness on a different scale, called John the greatest man who ever lived.

John was born to be the forerunner, and he fulfilled his role fault-lessly. The forerunner of the Christ had three primary responsibilities:

1. The forerunner was to *clear the way*. His job was to remove ob-stacles regarding the Messiah from people's minds. Jews had come to expect a powerful hero on a white horse, brandishing a sword, inspir-ing courage, and rousing national zeal. They looked for a Messiah to overthrow Rome, establish His kingdom, usher Israel into a new era of military and economic abundance, conquer the world, destroy evil, and then rule with perfect justice. Indeed, King Jesus will do just that . . . eventually. First, however, He must destroy evil in the hearts of His people, and He must establish His reign there before conquering a square inch of land.

2. The forerunner was to *prepare the way*. With false notions pushed to the side, John prepared hearts by calling them to repentance.

3. Then, the forerunner was to *get out of the way*. He had to decrease, so that Jesus could increase (John 3:30). That is what made him great.

— 3:22-24 —

"These things" refers to Jesus' cleansing of the temple (2:13-17), His confrontation with the religious leaders (2:18-22), His public ministry (2:23), and His dialogue with Nicodemus (3:1-21). In the flow of John's narrative, the Baptizer had his ministry in the wilderness of Judea (1:19-36) while the Messiah conducted His in Galilee and the temple

(1:37–3:21). John then builds a sense of drama in how he sets the time and place of the next incident.

Judea was clearly the Baptizer's territory. Jesus and His disciples came into Judea, where they not only lingered, they even baptized! Meanwhile, John and his disciples continued their ministry of baptism in Aenon (based on the Greek word for "fountain") near Salim (the Hebrew and Aramaic term meaning "peace"). Both places were undoubtedly familiar to first-century readers.

— 3:25-26 —

John's wilderness disciples had been engaged in the ministry of baptism, which drew inspiration from the Old Testament and the ceremonial washing of Gentile converts. Furthermore, Pharisees had raised ritual purification to high art, so naturally John's activity would spark a number of theological discussions. The specifics of this particular conversation are not important to the Gospel writer; the confrontation merely called attention to a problem, as the Baptizer's disciples saw it. The multitudes that once flocked to John were now going to Jesus.

John's response demonstrates why Jesus considered him the greatest man since Adam. Not only did John avoid following his ego into a trap, he corrected his disciples by clarifying four points:

1. All leaders serve at God's pleasure (3:27).
2. John's ministry had always been to introduce Jesus as the Christ (3:28-30).
3. Jesus Christ is the author of truth; opposing Him is to oppose reality (3:31-34).
4. The Son of God is the supreme ruler of all that exists; opposing Him is to choose His wrath (3:35-36).

— 3:27 —

All leaders serve at God's pleasure.
John is absolute in his statement. It's no mistake to take it literally or to apply it to anything imaginable. Authority, grace, income, possessions, even our next breath—all these things and hundreds more are gifts above and beyond anything we deserve. Everything belongs to the Lord and He has the sovereign right to give or take as He desires, including authority to lead. Because all authority derives from God's sovereign choosing, no leader can legitimately claim any entitlement to his or her position. Those who claim to exercise authority by "divine right" fail to acknowledge their duty to God and become guilty of pride.

— 3:28-30 —

John's ministry had always been to introduce Jesus as the Christ.
John must have been incredulous that his disciples failed to hear his primary message or understand his very purpose for being. He had clearly stated that he was not the Messiah, but the forerunner. He then drew upon a familiar first-century image to explain his own attitude, which should have been that of his disciples as well.

The "friend of the bridegroom" in ancient Near East culture held considerably more responsibility than the "best man" today. In addition to helping the bridegroom prepare his home for the eventual day when the bride would come to stay, he helped direct the wedding feast at the end of the betrothal period. His most significant duty was to guard the bridal chamber during the feast, especially after the bride had slipped into the room unnoticed by the guests. No one except for the groom was allowed to go near the bridal chamber. When the "friend of the groom" heard the groom's voice, he stood aside. His joy was complete when the groom arrived.

— 3:31-34 —

Jesus Christ is the author of truth; opposing Him is to oppose reality.
Jesus Christ, the Son of God, does not have His origin on earth. While He is completely human in every respect, He is not merely human. We came into being upon conception; He has no beginning because He is of heaven. Consequently, the truth He proclaims is firsthand knowledge, not something he received from some other source. The Baptizer reminded his disciples that their shared mission is to proclaim the truth of God. One cannot proclaim the truth and oppose the Word, who *is* God. Likewise, to believe Jesus is to affirm the truth of God.

— 3:35-36 —

The Son of God is the supreme ruler of all that exists; opposing Him is to choose His wrath.
John the Baptizer concluded his correction with a chilling warning. The Greek term translated "wrath" is *orgē* [3709].

A God of love must also have the capacity for anger. However, the wrath of God is not the kind of bellowing anger we have come to associate with abusive people. Paul described the Creator's response to sin using the Greek word *orgē*, which means "upsurging." When used to describe wrath, it is a passionate expression of outrage against wrongdoing. In this context, it pictures the passionate righteous anger of God cresting the walls of heaven and spilling over onto earth. And while it is indeed a passionate, upsurging response, it is completely consistent with God's character, which is also love. Without question, His wrath is fearsome, yet it is also controlled, deliberate, measured, and utterly just. His wrath is nothing less than a reasonable expression of His righteous character and His unfailing love when confronted with evil.

No Jew would admit to disbelieving God. However, because Jesus is the Word of God, failing to trust Him is the same as choosing to disbelieve God. And Hebrew history is replete with warnings and illustrations of people falling under the wrath of God for failure to believe. John said to his students, in effect, "Don't forget that this 'rival' you are prepared to oppose is none other than God in human flesh; to oppose Him is to rebel against the Almighty."

• • •

Charles Haddon Spurgeon was the greatest preacher of his day. At the age of twenty, without any formal theological training, he drew overflowing crowds at the historic New Park Street Chapel in London. Eventually, the five-thousand-seat Metropolitan Tabernacle was constructed to accommodate the multitudes who came to hear him. From the time Spurgeon was twenty-seven until the end of his life, every seat was filled and another thousand people stood virtually every Sunday.

Based on his study of Spurgeon's writings and career, Helmut Thielicke wisely wrote in his book *Encounter with Spurgeon,*

> Success exposes a man to the pressure of people and thus tempts
> him to hold on to his gains by means of "fleshly" methods and
> practices, and to let himself be ruled wholly by the dictatorial
> demands of incessant expansion. Success can go to my head,
> and will unless I remember that it is God who accomplished his
> work, that He can continue to do so without any help, and that
> He will be able to make out with other means whenever He "cuts
> me down to size."[17]

History has affirmed that Spurgeon was a fairly great man himself. However, it was his deference to Jesus Christ that made him so. Like John the Baptizer, he recognized his need to decrease so that the Son of God might increase.

APPLICATION: JOHN 3:22-36

How to Become Great

When I hear someone described as "great" at something, such as music, sports, writing, leadership, or some other endeavor I admire, that's my cue to watch and learn. I want to know what he or she does right. According to Jesus, John the Baptizer was a great man—greater than any other person in history. With an endorsement like that, I want to know what made him great!

This portion of the narrative describes John's reaction to a prickly situation in the life of a leader: the success of another leader. Because difficulties often reveal the character of a person, this incident provides an opportunity to observe John up close and then glean several principles that will help us imitate his kind of greatness.

First, *all leaders serve at God's pleasure (3:27)*. Everyone at one time or another has been overlooked, ignored, underappreciated, or unjustly passed over for a promotion or an honor. It's difficult to watch another succeed, especially when you are stuck in a cycle of setbacks. John wasn't threatened by the success of another. On the contrary, he rejoiced in it. In doing so, he echoed the psalmist, who wrote,

> For not from the east, nor from the west,
> Nor from the desert *comes* exaltation;
> But God is the Judge;
> He puts down one and exalts another.
> (Ps. 75:6-7)

That's an essential perspective to keep when you're struggling to succeed, and even more so when you're on top of the world. All who serve do so at God's pleasure.

Second, *joy comes from serving God, not from one's title or job description (3:28-29)*. Let's face it: Titles and job descriptions are worth a lot in our culture. Pride craves the approval of others, and people in powerful positions get plenty of applause and affirmation. John, however, refused to fall into that trap. He found his joy in serving His Lord, fulfilling a role that brought glory to God rather than himself. John's illustration describes the best friend of a groom delighted to have completed his task and then stepping aside for the groom.

Titles and honors come and go. Our relationship with the Lord will stand forever, bringing more joy than we can describe.

Third, *genuine humility calls attention to Christ, not to self (3:30-34).* There's a sad misconception among some Christians that genuine humility stems from feelings of worthlessness. They mistakenly think that "decreasing" self will "increase" Christ. Frankly, that sounds more like depression than joy. Truth be told, the focus of attention is still self.

John regarded the exaltation of Christ as the source of his joy. F. B. Meyer writes, "The only hope of a decreasing self is an increasing Christ."[18] Don't waste time trying to decrease yourself by looking super-humble. That's focusing on the wrong object. You'll dig yourself into a hole trying to act humble, appear humble, and sound humble. Before long, you'll be the proudest one in the church. Instead, stand aside. Forget yourself as you exalt Christ. Turn glory toward Him. And without your ever knowing it, humility will have emerged naturally.

As you seek to apply these three principles, beware of two common traps: envy and jealousy. People often confuse these two fears because both are fueled by the dread of not having.

Envy has empty hands and wants them full.
Jealousy has full hands and never wants them empty.

Envy languishes in self-pity because it doesn't have what others have.
Jealousy rants in paranoia because it fears losing what it feels unworthy to own.

John the Baptizer avoided both traps. He clutched nothing and released everything to the Lord: his following, his popularity, his will. He recognized that God owns it all and deserves all the glory. He knew that we find the greatest joy in fulfilling our purpose: "to glorify God, and to fully enjoy Him forever."[19] Is it any wonder Jesus considered him great?

Water for a Thirsty Woman
JOHN 4:1-42

NASB [1]Therefore when the Lord knew that the Pharisees had heard that Jesus was making and baptizing more disciples than John [2](although Jesus

NLT [1]Jesus* knew the Pharisees had heard that he was baptizing and making more disciples than John [2](though Jesus himself didn't baptize

NASB

Himself was not baptizing, but His disciples were), ³He left Judea and went away again into Galilee. ⁴And He had to pass through Samaria. ⁵So He came to a city of Samaria called Sychar, near the parcel of ground that Jacob gave to his son Joseph; ⁶and Jacob's well was there. So Jesus, being wearied from His journey, was sitting thus by the well. It was about ᵃthe sixth hour.

⁷There came a woman of Samaria to draw water. Jesus said to her, "Give Me a drink." ⁸For His disciples had gone away into the city to buy food. ⁹Therefore the Samaritan woman said to Him, "How is it that You, being a Jew, ask me for a drink since I am a Samaritan woman?" (For Jews have no dealings with Samaritans.) ¹⁰Jesus answered and said to her, "If you knew the gift of God, and who it is who says to you, 'Give Me a drink,' you would have asked Him, and He would have given you living water." ¹¹She said to Him, "ᵃSir, You have nothing to draw with and the well is deep; where then do You get that living water? ¹²You are not greater than our father Jacob, are You, who gave us the well, and drank of it himself and his sons and his cattle?" ¹³Jesus answered and said to her, "Everyone who drinks of this water will thirst again; ¹⁴but whoever drinks of the water that I will give him shall never thirst; but the water that I will give him will become in him a well of water springing up to eternal life."

¹⁵The woman said to Him, "ᵃSir, give me this water, so I will not be thirsty nor come all the way here to draw." ¹⁶He said to her, "Go, call your husband and come here." ¹⁷The woman answered and said, "I have no husband." Jesus said to her, "You have correctly said, 'I have no husband'; ¹⁸for you have had five

NLT

them—his disciples did). ³So he left Judea and returned to Galilee.

⁴He had to go through Samaria on the way. ⁵Eventually he came to the Samaritan village of Sychar, near the field that Jacob gave to his son Joseph. ⁶Jacob's well was there; and Jesus, tired from the long walk, sat wearily beside the well about noontime. ⁷Soon a Samaritan woman came to draw water, and Jesus said to her, "Please give me a drink." ⁸He was alone at the time because his disciples had gone into the village to buy some food.

⁹The woman was surprised, for Jews refuse to have anything to do with Samaritans.* She said to Jesus, "You are a Jew, and I am a Samaritan woman. Why are you asking me for a drink?"

¹⁰Jesus replied, "If you only knew the gift God has for you and who you are speaking to, you would ask me, and I would give you living water."

¹¹"But sir, you don't have a rope or a bucket," she said, "and this well is very deep. Where would you get this living water? ¹²And besides, do you think you're greater than our ancestor Jacob, who gave us this well? How can you offer better water than he and his sons and his animals enjoyed?"

¹³Jesus replied, "Anyone who drinks this water will soon become thirsty again. ¹⁴But those who drink the water I give will never be thirsty again. It becomes a fresh, bubbling spring within them, giving them eternal life."

¹⁵"Please, sir," the woman said, "give me this water! Then I'll never be thirsty again, and I won't have to come here to get water."

¹⁶"Go and get your husband," Jesus told her.

¹⁷"I don't have a husband," the woman replied.

Jesus said, "You're right! You don't have a husband—¹⁸for you have had husbands, and the one whom you now have is not your husband; this you have said truly." ¹⁹The woman said to Him, "ᵃSir, I perceive that You are a prophet. ²⁰Our fathers worshiped in this mountain, and you *people* say that in Jerusalem is the place where men ought to worship." ²¹Jesus said to her, "Woman, believe Me, an hour is coming when neither in this mountain nor in Jerusalem will you worship the Father. ²²You worship what you do not know; we worship what we know, for salvation is from the Jews. ²³But an hour is coming, and now is, when the true worshipers will worship the Father in spirit and truth; for such people the Father seeks to be His worshipers. ²⁴God is ᵃspirit, and those who worship Him must worship in spirit and truth." ²⁵The woman said to Him, "I know that Messiah is coming (He who is called Christ); when that One comes, He will declare all things to us." ²⁶Jesus said to her, "I who speak to you am *He*."

²⁷At this point His disciples came, and they were amazed that He had been speaking with a woman, yet no one said, "What do You seek?" or, "Why do You speak with her?" ²⁸So the woman left her waterpot, and went into the city and said to the men, ²⁹"Come, see a man who told me all the things that I *have* done; this is not ᵃthe Christ, is it?" ³⁰They went out of the city, and were coming to Him.

³¹Meanwhile the disciples were urging Him, saying, "Rabbi, eat." ³²But He said to them, "I have food to eat that you do not know about." ³³So the disciples were saying to one

five husbands, and you aren't even married to the man you're living with now. You certainly spoke the truth!"

¹⁹"Sir," the woman said, "you must be a prophet. ²⁰So tell me, why is it that you Jews insist that Jerusalem is the only place of worship, while we Samaritans claim it is here at Mount Gerizim,* where our ancestors worshiped?"

²¹Jesus replied, "Believe me, dear woman, the time is coming when it will no longer matter whether you worship the Father on this mountain or in Jerusalem. ²²You Samaritans know very little about the one you worship, while we Jews know all about him, for salvation comes through the Jews. ²³But the time is coming—indeed it's here now—when true worshipers will worship the Father in spirit and in truth. The Father is looking for those who will worship him that way. ²⁴For God is Spirit, so those who worship him must worship in spirit and in truth."

²⁵The woman said, "I know the Messiah is coming—the one who is called Christ. When he comes, he will explain everything to us."

²⁶Then Jesus told her, "I Am the Messiah!"*

²⁷Just then his disciples came back. They were shocked to find him talking to a woman, but none of them had the nerve to ask, "What do you want with her?" or "Why are you talking to her?" ²⁸The woman left her water jar beside the well and ran back to the village, telling everyone, ²⁹"Come and see a man who told me everything I ever did! Could he possibly be the Messiah?" ³⁰So the people came streaming from the village to see him.

³¹Meanwhile, the disciples were urging Jesus, "Rabbi, eat something." ³²But Jesus replied, "I have a kind of food you know nothing about."

³³"Did someone bring him food

another, "No one brought Him *anything* to eat, did he?" [34]Jesus said to them, "My food is to do the will of Him who sent Me and to accomplish His work. [35]Do you not say, 'There are yet four months, and *then* comes the harvest'? Behold, I say to you, lift up your eyes and look on the fields, that they are white for harvest. [36]Already he who reaps is receiving wages and is gathering fruit for life eternal; so that he who sows and he who reaps may rejoice together. [37]For in this *case* the saying is true, 'One sows and another reaps.' [38]I sent you to reap that for which you have not labored; others have labored and you have entered into their labor."

[39]From that city many of the Samaritans believed in Him because of the word of the woman who testified, "He told me all the things that I *have* done." [40]So when the Samaritans came to Jesus, they were asking Him to stay with them; and He stayed there two days. [41]Many more believed because of His word; [42]and they were saying to the woman, "It is no longer because of what you said that we believe, for we have heard for ourselves and know that this One is indeed the Savior of the world."

4:6 ªPerhaps 6 p.m. Roman time or noon Jewish time 4:11 ªOr *Lord* 4:15 ªOr *Lord* 4:19 ªOr *Lord* 4:24 ªOr *Spirit* 4:29 ªI.e. the Messiah

while we were gone?" the disciples asked each other.

[34]Then Jesus explained: "My nourishment comes from doing the will of God, who sent me, and from finishing his work. [35]You know the saying, 'Four months between planting and harvest.' But I say, wake up and look around. The fields are already ripe* for harvest. [36]The harvesters are paid good wages, and the fruit they harvest is people brought to eternal life. What joy awaits both the planter and the harvester alike! [37]You know the saying, 'One plants and another harvests.' And it's true. [38]I sent you to harvest where you didn't plant; others had already done the work, and now you will get to gather the harvest."

[39]Many Samaritans from the village believed in Jesus because the woman had said, "He told me everything I ever did!" [40]When they came out to see him, they begged him to stay in their village. So he stayed for two days, [41]long enough for many more to hear his message and believe. [42]Then they said to the woman, "Now we believe, not just because of what you told us, but because we have heard him ourselves. Now we know that he is indeed the Savior of the world."

4:1 Some manuscripts read *The Lord.* 4:9 Some manuscripts do not include this sentence. 4:20 Greek *on this mountain.* 4:26 Or "The *'I AM' is here*"; or "*I am the* LORD"; Greek reads "*I am, the one speaking to you.*" See Exod 3:14. 4:35 Greek *white.*

Expert instructors know that if a student is to master a new skill, his or her training must include balanced portions of three essential elements: theory, practice, and inspiration. These can come in any order and through a variety of means, but no training is complete without all three. Theory without practice is pointless. Practice without theory is frustrating. Theory and practice without inspiration is drudgery. Leave out any one element and students are almost certain to fail or quit.

Once John the Baptizer announced Jesus as the Messiah, the Lord wasted no time calling disciples. Within forty-eight hours, five hand-selected students had begun training for the transformation of the

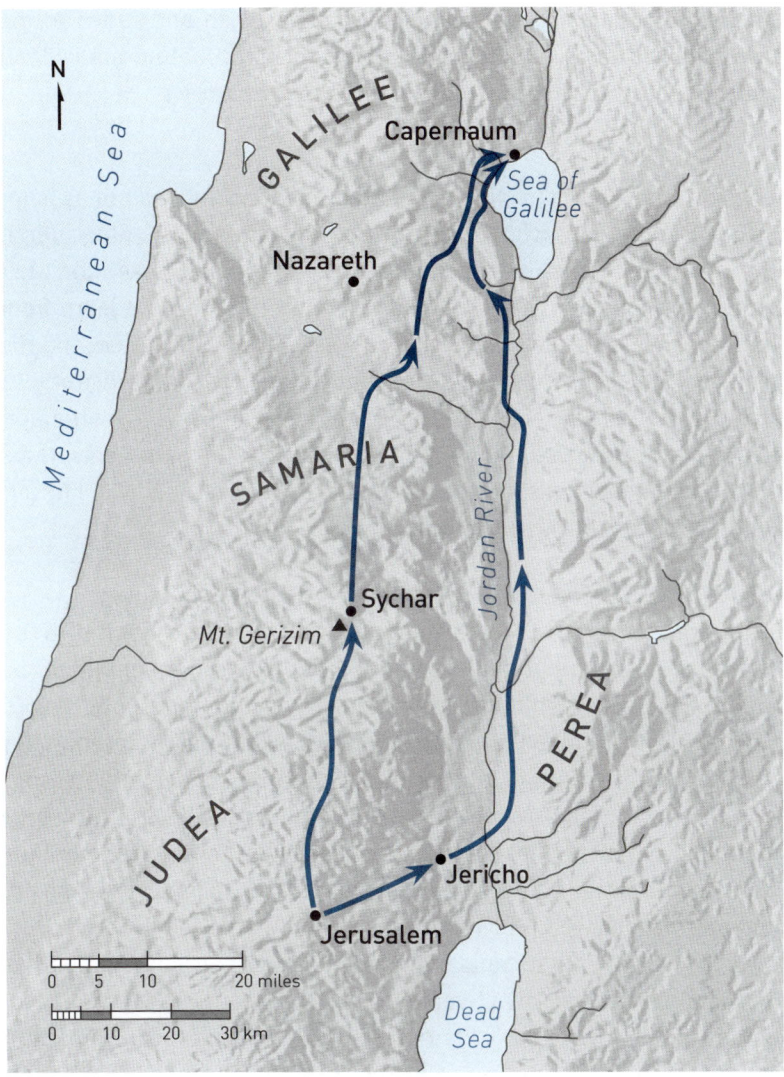

N

Jews traveling between Judea and Galilee usually avoided Samaria, a land they considered defiled by Gentile intermarriage and religious syncretism. Rather than walk on impure soil, they descended the mountains surrounding Jerusalem to the Jordan Plain, journeyed along the eastern shore of the Jordan River, and then turned west into Galilee. Jesus, however, chose a direct route from Jerusalem to Cana, which took Him through the Samaritan town of Sychar.

world. They had seen Jesus perform miracles (2:1-12), they had experienced His passionate desire for revival (2:13-25), and they had heard Him preach and teach (3:1-36). The time had come for them to glimpse their future as evangelists. Jesus the Jewish reformer would become Jesus the missionary and show His students how to reach the world outside of Judaism. Between Galilee to the north and Judea to the south, a lost and forsaken people lived in a spiritual no-man's-land called Samaria, and they needed to hear the good news.

— 4:1-3 —

Trying to trace Jesus' movements in the Gospel of John is not as help-ful as it is in Luke, which provides more geographical information. However, the Synoptic Gospels (Matthew, Mark, and Luke) don't tell us nearly as much about the Lord's ministry in Judea. We learn from John that Jesus traveled frequently between Galilee and Judea, and His reasons for moving from one region to the other varied significantly. In this case, He sensed that His ministry in Judea was attracting attention for the wrong reasons. While truth will always stir controversy, Jesus was not interested in squaring off with the Pharisees—at least not yet, not until it served His ultimate purpose (15:22-25).

— 4:4 —

The phrase "had to" is translated from a Greek verb meaning "to be necessary." Anyone unfamiliar with Samaria's history who might be looking at a map would not see anything peculiar about John's word choice. Draw a straight line from Jerusalem to Cana (4:46), account for the hilly terrain, and a stopover in Sychar appears perfectly reason-able. However, John's choice of words would have been provocative to any Jewish reader. Jews despised Samaritans. To them, Samaritans were idolatrous half-breeds—ethnically polluted, religiously confused, and morally debased. During a particularly dark period in Israel's his-tory, the Hebrew inhabitants of this region intermarried with Gentiles and established their own temple to rival the one in Jerusalem. Conse-quently, Jews—particularly Pharisees—would not set foot on Samaritan soil and, frankly, there was no love lost on the part of the Samaritan people either.

To avoid "contamination," most Jews traveling between Galilee and Judea chose to cross the Jordan River and go around Samaria to the east rather than journey straight through. So to say, "*It was necessary to pass through Samaria*," suggests that the need was not geographical.

— 4:5-6 —

John locates the Samaritan city of Sychar not in terms of its geographic location, but by its historic relevance. This parcel of land was signifi-cant in Israel's history as a place purchased by Jacob (who was later

A BRIEF HISTORY OF TEN "LOST" TRIBES

JOHN 4:4

Originally, the Hebrew nation settled the Promised Land and thrived for several centuries as twelve tribes united by worship in one tabernacle, which was located in Shiloh, about ten miles from Mount Gerizim. Eventually, Israel's third king, Solomon, constructed a permanent temple in Jerusalem.

Shortly after Solomon's death, the northern ten tribes rejected the legitimate successor to the throne, chose an idolatrous rebel general to lead them, formed a separate nation, and claimed the name "Israel" for themselves. The southern tribes of Benjamin and Judah remained loyal to Solomon's son and became known as "Judah." North and South fought intermittently for the next 200 years, until Israel was distracted by repeated assaults by the Assyrian king Pul (also known as Tiglath-pileser; see 2 Kgs. 15:19-20, 29; 1 Chr. 5:26; Isa. 9:1). Finally, Shalmaneser (2 Kgs. 17:3-6) and his successor, Sargon, finished off Israel by deporting the ten tribes and intermarrying them with other conquered nations, virtually breeding them out of existence. After 721 BC, only a small remnant of the ten tribes remained in the northern territory, and most of them began to intermarry with Gentiles.

After the people of Judah, who became known as "Jews," were exiled to Babylon (605–586 BC) and later returned under the leadership of Ezra and Nehemiah, they found the northern region inhabited by "Samaritans," who were of both Hebrew and Gentile heritage. Tensions mounted when the Samaritans opposed the rebuilding of Jerusalem and the temple, and the final breach occurred when the Samaritans built their own temple on Mount Gerizim, claiming that it was the authentic place of worship, rather than Jerusalem.

renamed "Israel") and given to his sons (Gen. 33:18-21). This was also the place where the bones of Joseph were laid to rest after Israel's exodus from Egypt (Josh. 24:32). John's mention of the well is no accident either. Samaria had no major rivers to supply water, only wadis (natural drainage channels), which brought seasonal rains and then dried up for months at a time. Jeremiah used the wadi as an image of deceit (Jer. 15:18). The historic location and the presence of Jacob's well gave Jesus (and therefore John) another perfect opportunity to draw upon the familiar symbol of life: water.

The sixth hour in Jewish reckoning was about noon. Early in May (during the barley harvest), the sun would have been high and the weather hot and dry. Jesus and the disciples had been traveling throughout the morning and needed food and water to continue their journey. While Jesus rested by the well, probably in the shade, His students went in search of food (4:8).

— 4:7-8 —

As John tells the story—this portion of which he had to have heard from Jesus—the appearance of the woman appears coincidental. Again, those familiar with the customs of the day would immediately notice two ominous details. First, she came alone. Women generally came to the well in groups, not only to share the labor of drawing water, but to socialize. Second, she came during the heat of the day. The best time to carry a one-bath jar holding 5 gallons (19 liters) of water, weighing approximately 40 pounds (18 kilograms), was early in the morning or just before sundown. The circumstances appear curious and add to the impression that the meeting was not accidental—the meaning of "had to" (4:4) becomes a little clearer now.

Jesus broke with the tradition of His day by speaking to the woman and politely asking her to draw Him some water from the well. While Jesus would never break a commandment or behave immorally, He routinely flouted (and sometimes appeared to take special delight in) the nonsensical customs of religion. He had come to redeem this woman and He knew how to reach her. She wore the emotional armor of a woman beaten down by the morality of the righteous. He honored her closely guarded vulnerability by appealing to her kindness.

As we read how Jesus engaged the woman in conversation, take note of a repeated cycle. Six times Jesus appealed to the woman, and six times she attempted to deflect the discussion:

- Jesus appealed to her kindness (4:7), and the woman responded defensively (4:9).
- Jesus appealed to her curiosity (4:10), and the woman responded sarcastically (4:11-12).
- Jesus appealed to her spiritual need (4:13-14), and the woman focused only on physical needs (4:15).
- Jesus appealed to her personal interest (4:16), and the woman responded with a half-truth (4:17).
- Jesus appealed to her conscience (4:17-18), and the woman raised a controversial issue (4:19-20).
- Jesus appealed to her will (4:21-24), and the woman tried to delay any decision (4:25).

— 4:9 —

The woman's response was defensive. The way John records her words reveals how shocked she was. She asked, literally, "How do You, being a Jew, ask for a drink from me, being a woman, a Samaritan?" The tone of her question asked, in effect, "What are you doing asking me for a drink?! You, a Jew, despise me as a non-Jew, as a woman, and as a Samaritan. You can't instantly overcome centuries of barriers like that."

John underscores the racial prejudice for anyone who might have missed the source of her tension.

— 4:10 —

Jesus didn't react to the woman's defensiveness. Instead, He said, in effect, "If you really knew who you were talking to, *you* would be asking *Me* for a drink, and I would give you *living* water." The structure of the sentence in Greek emphasizes the adjective "living."

"Gift of God"? "Know who He is"? "Living water"? What an enigmatic statement! Jesus deliberately laced His comment with enticing phrases and then delivered it with casual ease. This was no less outrageous than if I were to drop the following line into normal conversation: "Well, back on Mars, where I'm from, everyone has free cable TV." People would think I was joking.

He clearly intended to excite her curiosity.

— 4:11-12 —

She showed a quick wit by responding with sharp sarcasm. A modern version of her line might be, "Hey, man, the waters in this well run deep and clearly your bucket doesn't go all the way down! So where do you plan to get this water, the *living* kind?" She also reacted to Jesus' insinuation that He's someone special by drawing upon the history of the site.

This was a very intelligent woman with a delightful sense of humor; however, a rough life had ground her wit to a razor's edge. Undoubtedly, many men had charmed her and then left her broken. Now, any man who thinks he's God's gift should think again. Most men would have gotten the message and backed off. But Jesus didn't want to use her like other men used her.

— 4:13-14 —

Jesus bypassed her sarcastic assault and then appealed to her spiritual need. She needed new life. Sin had destroyed her old life, both in the theological sense and in the emotional. She had long since stopped living and was merely existing. Furthermore, her death-like life would soon end in eternal death.

Jesus played upon images of well water, which is stagnant, and running water, which is "living," to describe the kind of life available to those who believe in Him. Those who trust in Christ never need to look outside themselves for satisfaction because He dwells within them, supplying every emotional and spiritual need. They will never be without water again.

— 4:15 —

Either the woman was spiritually tone-deaf, or she was deliberately avoiding the real issue. Very often people avoid talking about spiritual matters because physical needs are easier to satisfy and frequently provide the illusion of deeper satisfaction. That's what drives all sorts of compulsions and addictions. People also avoid spiritual discussions because they are too painfully personal. They have learned to cope with their hopelessness; they don't want anyone upsetting the delicate balance they have worked so hard to achieve. So the woman took the conversation back into the shallows, where she was more comfortable.

— 4:16 —

Jesus put an end to her coy bantering with an innocent request. At the surface level, He appealed to her personal interest. In most any other conversation, no one could have taken offense. But Jesus knew the dilemma it posed for her. She undoubtedly felt stung and probably made the connection between "thirst" and her current living arrangements.

Of course Jesus knew her situation. He knew all about her promiscuous life. And He went directly for her need. He appealed to her deepest personal longing.

The woman responded evasively. She hoped to shift the topic of conversation to the acceptable side of her half-truth: "I don't have a husband (in the traditional sense of the word)."

— 4:17-18 —

Jesus used His supernatural knowledge to take the conversation below the surface. He set aside all fun and games in order to appeal to her conscience. It is noteworthy that He didn't condemn her or shame her or exploit her sinfulness. He merely stated the truth and let it stand on its own. The man she was living with was not her husband, but the sixth temporary man in a long line of temporary men. Despite that ugly reality, Jesus found a way to commend her for the truthful half of her half-truth.

The woman obviously didn't feel so threatened as to run away. Exposing the source of someone's shame too quickly leaves him or her feeling emotionally stripped naked, and the only natural response is to run for cover. But Jesus' timing was perfect. He had already established a rapport. He allowed the woman to see His genuine concern for her as a person, not an object. He treated her with uncommon dignity and spoke compassionately to her spiritual need. He didn't allow her to distract Him from the real issues involved, including her attempt to flatter Him and then engage in a pointless theological debate.

— 4:19-20 —

"Oh, you've been to seminary. You must be extremely smart. Let me ask you something I've always wondered about. How do you reconcile the great existential problem of God's sovereignty and the free will of man?" Only in her culture, the great debate revolved around the most appropriate place to worship an omnipresent God.

— 4:21-24 —

I wish I could think on my feet as quickly as Jesus. He neither indulged her ruse nor ignored her question. He used her distraction to get the conversation back to the real issue. Her problem—as with most people in John's account—was not intellectual, but volitional. Jesus responded by appealing to her will. He presented three issues to challenge her.

First, *the physical location of worship is of secondary concern to God.* A temple is given for the benefit of man, not God. A temple merely serves to focus our wandering attention. Many Jews faithfully worshiped God when moved thousands of miles from the Jerusalem temple, even as it lay in ruins.

Second, *the object of worship is primary in heaven—but it had become secondary in Samaria.* Make no mistake, the Samaritan temple was designed and built in direct opposition to the reconstruction efforts of Ezra and Nehemiah. And the men who built it did not know the one true God. Jesus didn't shy away from the uncomfortable truth: The Samaritans were indeed idolatrous.

Third, *the quality of worship is the true measure of devotion to God.* Even as Jesus spoke to the woman in Samaria, the Jewish religious leaders were polluting the temple with their money-changing schemes. Therefore, the temple in Jerusalem was no better or worse than the one on Mount Gerizim. The Lord wants genuine, Spirit-empowered worship.

— 4:25-26 —

The woman fell back to her last line of defense, one commonly used today: delay. She tried to backpedal out of the conversation, claiming that all matters of theology are moot until the Messiah comes to resolve them. The Samaritans expected a Messiah like Moses—more teacher and prophet, less ruler and priest (Deut. 18:15-18). According to this line of reasoning, "No one can really say what is truth and what isn't until this great Teacher comes to reveal all things."

This attempt to back out of the conversation played perfectly into Jesus' hands. John's description of the encounter builds toward a climax. The Lord successfully bypassed all of her defenses in order to lay the ultimate truth before her. He said, in effect, "Good! You don't have to wait any longer. I am the Messiah, and I am here just as promised."

In the Greek, the phrase "I am" is particularly emphatic: *egō eimi* [1473, 1510]. It harkens back to God's self-identification to Moses: "I AM WHO I AM" (Exod. 3:14). Both Jews and Samaritans understood Jesus' meaning. In fact, the religious leaders accused Jesus of blasphemy for claiming to be God because of His repeated use of the "I am" formula (6:48; 8:18, 24, 28, 58; 10:7, 11; 11:25; 13:19; 14:6; 15:1-3; 18:5-8).

— 4:27-30 —

The return of the disciples and their apparent shock over Jesus' obvious breach of Jewish etiquette could have been awkward, but John doesn't tell us. All we know is that the woman forgot all about her original task and ran back to the town to confer with her own religious authorities.

The construction of the Greek sentence anticipates a negative response: "He couldn't possibly be the Christ, could He?" But then she presented evidence to suggest that she, in fact, did believe Jesus to be the Messiah. Remarkably, the details she so painfully avoided discussing earlier had become a joyful confirmation of her spiritual hope.

Her testimony had a positive effect. The people of her town were compelled to meet the man who might possibly be their Savior.

— 4:31-34 —

The interlude between Jesus' discussion with the woman and His ministering to the rest of the town allows us to see why John included this particular incident in his Gospel. Jesus "had to pass through Samaria" (4:4) to redeem this particular woman, who brought her entire town to Christ with her testimony. And, just as importantly, He "had to pass through Samaria" in order to give His disciples crucial training in evangelism (4:34-38). Reaching the lost was Jesus' purpose for coming to earth and the destiny of His disciples. Moreover, this encounter provided a tangible lesson on the first rule of the new kingdom: *Obeying the Word of God is more important and more satisfying than fulfilling any mere physical need* (Deut. 8:3; Matt. 4:4; Luke 4:4).

— 4:35-38 —

Jesus then turned toward the fields of barley (the poor man's grain) and noted how their color had faded from green to light brown. "White for harvest" is an exaggeration, meaning "extremely ripe." If the grain isn't harvested in time, the seed pods fall off the stalks, which is a tragic and humiliating blunder by the farmer. Jesus thought of evangelism as harvesting what God had nurtured and ripened, and He called the disciples to harvest the men and women God had prepared.

— 4:39-42 —

John, a master storyteller, turns from Jesus' lecture back to the living illustration He had orchestrated. The entire town of Samaritans followed the woman's witness to discover the Savior for themselves. What an unusual "evangelist" the woman was! She had no wholesome roots. She had no seminary training. She knew little theology. She couldn't explain why Jesus must be the Messiah. She merely reported her personal encounter.

The response of the Samaritans stands in sharp contrast to that of the religious leaders in Jerusalem. Unlike the theologically trained Jews running the temple, the hated "half-breeds" welcomed Jesus and asked Him to teach. And, as a result of hearing Him, "many more believed."

John concludes the lesson on evangelism with a telling statement by the newly harvested Samaritans. While the woman's testimony brought them to hear Christ, it was their own encounter with the Word that caused them to trust Jesus as their Savior.

APPLICATION: JOHN 4:1-42

The Few, the Humble, the Reapers

As John told the story of Jesus and the Samaritan woman, he consciously emphasized the sharp distinction between the attitudes and actions of Jesus and those of His disciples. Their dissimilarity is especially clear in the interlude between His conversation with the woman and His greeting the townspeople. While the woman witnessed to the town leaders, the Lord impressed upon His disciples the urgent need for laborers to harvest souls ripened by the Holy Spirit. The disciples illustrate several attitudes that frequently keep us from entering the fields of harvest. Three come to mind.

First, *we are put off by prejudice or bigotry.* The disciples saw Jesus talking to a Samaritan woman—to them, she was as low on the social ladder as one can descend—and they simply could not believe it. Let's face it; we care about the salvation of some people more than others. Our Creator, however, doesn't rank people on a scale of worthiness. We are *all* unworthy of salvation, yet equally loved by Him.

Second, *we are consumed with the mundane details of life.* The disciples couldn't stop thinking about food long enough to notice their Master's excitement. They left Him weary, hungry, and thirsty from travel; they returned to find Him brimming with energy. Anyone the least bit perceptive should have set aside the food and asked the Lord what made Him so cheerful. But not those self-serving, shortsighted disciples.

We spend most of our day dealing with the so-called necessities of life: fixing meals, keeping schedules, making a living. When is the last time you set aside time and made specific plans to share the good news at work or with someone you've become friends with in your neighborhood or community?

Third, *we are lulled into inaction by the promise of tomorrow.* The disciples didn't appreciate the urgency of their call. Jesus used a popular catchphrase among farmers in His day, "Four months, and then comes the harvest," to rouse them into action. He said, in effect, "Not four months . . . NOW! The time is now!"

We procrastinate. We presume upon tomorrow. In the meantime, death continues to reap. Moreover, the time before the end of days grows shorter.

I notice that people actively engaged in evangelism lack many of the attitudes that destroy churches. The joy of their call keeps them from arguing over the worth of people. The priority of their call inspires them to handle the details of life quickly and move on to more pressing matters, such as the ingathering of souls. The urgency of their call prods them to overcome procrastination and to make the most of the present opportunities. These people have neither the time nor the energy to waste on anything but the call to reap the harvest. However, they didn't overcome negative attitudes and *then* heed the call.

If you will allow me to switch metaphors, people actively engaged in evangelism are like people on the front lines of battle. One of my Marine Corps friends, who had seen more than his share of combat, once remarked, "The men on the front lines never complained about the food; it was the guys farthest from the battle who grumbled the most when standing in the chow line!" Life-and-death struggle has a way of keeping things in perspective.

The principle remains the same for evangelism. If we wait until prejudice, pettiness, or procrastination are no longer issues, we will never enter the harvest. We are called to reap; therefore, we must obey. Once we have moved into the front lines, nagging hindrances quickly fade away.

Healing at a Distance
JOHN 4:43-54

NASB

43 After the two days He went forth from there into Galilee. 44 For Jesus Himself testified that a prophet has no honor in his own country. 45 So when He came to Galilee, the Galileans received Him, having seen all the things that He did in Jerusalem at the feast; for they themselves also went to the feast.

46 Therefore He came again to Cana of Galilee where He had made the water wine. And there was a royal official whose son was sick at Capernaum. 47 When he heard that Jesus had come out of Judea into Galilee, he went to Him and was imploring *Him* to come down and heal his son; for he was at the point of death. 48 So Jesus said to him, "Unless you *people* see ªsigns and wonders, you *simply* will not believe." 49 The royal official said to Him, "ªSir, come down before my child dies." 50 Jesus said to him, "Go; your son lives." The man believed the word that Jesus spoke to him and started off. 51 As he was now going

NLT

43 At the end of the two days, Jesus went on to Galilee. 44 He himself had said that a prophet is not honored in his own hometown. 45 Yet the Galileans welcomed him, for they had been in Jerusalem at the Passover celebration and had seen everything he did there.

46 As he traveled through Galilee, he came to Cana, where he had turned the water into wine. There was a government official in nearby Capernaum whose son was very sick. 47 When he heard that Jesus had come from Judea to Galilee, he went and begged Jesus to come to Capernaum to heal his son, who was about to die.

48 Jesus asked, "Will you never believe in me unless you see miraculous signs and wonders?"

49 The official pleaded, "Lord, please come now before my little boy dies."

50 Then Jesus told him, "Go back home. Your son will live!" And the man believed what Jesus said and started home.

51 While the man was on his way,

NASB

down, *his* slaves met him, saying that his [a]son was living. [52]So he inquired of them the hour when he began to get better. Then they said to him, "Yesterday at the [a]seventh hour the fever left him." [53]So the father knew that *it was* at that hour in which Jesus said to him, "Your son lives"; and he himself believed and his whole household. [54]This is again a second [a]sign that Jesus performed when He had come out of Judea into Galilee.

4:48 [a]Or *attesting miracles* **4:49** [a]Or *Lord* **4:51** [a]Or *boy* **4:52** [a]Perhaps 7 p.m. Roman time or 1 p.m. Jewish time **4:54** [a]Or *attesting miracle*

NLT

some of his servants met him with the news that his son was alive and well. [52]He asked them when the boy had begun to get better, and they replied, "Yesterday afternoon at one o'clock his fever suddenly disappeared!" [53]Then the father realized that that was the very time Jesus had told him, "Your son will live." And he and his entire household believed in Jesus. [54]This was the second miraculous sign Jesus did in Galilee after coming from Judea.

I am not a "faith healer." I don't hold services in which sick people stand in line, waiting for a touch on the forehead and a shout. I can't heal anyone, nor am I a "conduit" of God's healing power. Frankly, the supposed healings performed by certain notable figures bear little resemblance to the "signs" offered by Jesus and His apostles. However, this is not to say I don't believe in supernatural healing. I do. In fact, I can recall many examples in which the healing power of God left doctors speechless.

On one occasion, a close friend developed a malignancy on the side of his tongue. By the time it was diagnosed, it had spread to the lymph nodes and through a part of his upper torso. As a father of four with a full life and a promising career ahead, he found it necessary to prepare a will, get his house in order, and begin the process of turning his business over to associates.

Several of his friends, including me, were not able to go be with him right away, so we agreed to pray for him. Though we were all separated by many miles, we faithfully prayed and began asking God for a miracle, if that would be His will. We asked that the Lord be glorified in the healing and continued life of this friend. To be perfectly honest, none of us knew the Father's will for our friend—but we all agreed that our God was able. Furthermore, we loved the man, and we desperately wanted God to snatch him from the jaws of death.

A palpable sense of assurance enveloped us like a warm blanket. Though we hadn't even met to pray together, we were confident that God would intervene in some unusual way. And did He ever!

Within a matter of days, our friend stepped off a plane in Rochester,

Minnesota, for more scans, further examination, refined diagnoses, and if needed, a more aggressive treatment. If anyone could help him, it would be those experts at the Mayo Clinic. And to the stunned amazement of the four-physician team, as further X-rays and scans were taken, no trace of the disease could be found. The obvious explanation was that the original diagnosis was incorrect, but the records were double-checked and the same conclusion reached. His widespread malignancy was unmistakable . . . but all the tumors were now gone. Furthermore, annual re-checks confirmed that they were gone for good.

What happened? Clearly and miraculously, God healed the man.

I have other examples that are no less dramatic. Admittedly, I know of only a handful of cases in nearly fifty years of ministry. Far less than I would have hoped for . . . but, as a fellow minister friend of mine is fond of saying, "If they happened every day, we'd call 'em 'regulars,' not 'miracles.'" Make no mistake: God can and does heal today. And there is no need to find someone with a supposed "gift" to make it happen. He has given us unrestricted access to the throne room of heaven. We are invited to come directly to the Almighty with our most pressing problems and distressing afflictions, and He has promised to hear all of our concerns and to receive our requests with compassion. However, we must keep in mind that the Lord will do what *He* determines to be right, which may not be what we want or request. At that point, our trust in Him faces its greatest challenge.

— 4:44-46 —

After two days of ministry, Jesus continued on to Galilee, where He had spent His childhood.

Jesus had warned His disciples with the statement, "A prophet has no honor in his own country" (see Matt. 13:57; Mark 6:4; Luke 4:24), especially when ministering in the region near his boyhood home. In this case, John is reflecting on the success among the "foreign" Samaritans and granting us access to Jesus' inner life. While the present visit was a congenial time among the Galileans, who were perhaps proud of their hometown hero, the Lord kept their goodwill in perspective. When people get what they want, belief comes easily. How will they respond when confronted with the truth? When the true Messiah confronts the "messiah" of their expectations, which will they choose? The days ahead will become a clash of wills—human expectations versus God's sovereignty. Jesus' encounter with the royal official illustrates the faith response He desires.

— 4:46-47 —

John sets the location as Cana, the location of Jesus' first "sign." A royal official appears to have been conducting business in Cana when he heard that Jesus had returned from Judea. John tells us that the man's home was in Capernaum, an important town on the north shore of the Sea of Galilee, roughly eighteen miles away (about six hours on foot, two hours by chariot).

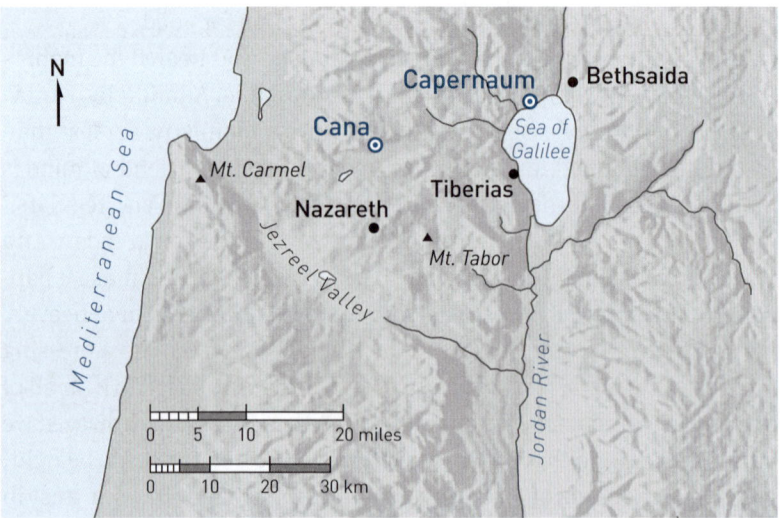

The royal official located Jesus in Cana, but his son lay dying in Capernaum, roughly eighteen miles away. Jesus healed the man's son with a mere word, proving that distance cannot diminish His power.

The term translated "royal official" is *basilikos* [937] in Greek, which generally refers to something or someone associated with royalty—royal clothing (Acts 12:21), royal territory (Acts 12:20), royal law (Jas. 2:8). The man may have been a member of Herod Antipas' extended family; however, it's more probable that he was serving as an official in the royal court. Regardless, he was a man of influence, wealth, and privilege, who wielded significant authority.

We can be certain that his coming to see Jesus did not go unnoticed. And his demeanor did not fit his station. His son lay dying in Capernaum and he "was imploring" Jesus to make the journey. This is a good rendering of the Greek imperfect verb tense, which describes action that is either ongoing or repetitive. In the urgency of his son's illness, the official cast off any dignity and "kept on begging" the Lord to come.

— 4:48 —

Jesus responded with a rebuke, which appears harsh. "You people" is just the plural "you" in the Greek, identifying the man with a group. Who, specifically, is unclear. Galileans in general? People associated with the royal family? Because the man was an aristocratic Jew, it's very likely he was one of the Sadducees, who didn't believe that God intervened in human affairs. They believed each person creates his own fate and therefore deserves whatever fate he receives, including illness, poverty, and death. To have a Sadducee begging Jesus for a miracle was a notable irony.

Because the man was a Galilean standing among Galileans, it's also likely that Jesus was noting a subtle pattern in their thinking that would become unmistakable later on (6:26-27). The man desperately wanted Jesus to "*come down* and heal his son" (emphasis mine). This suggests that he saw a limitation in Jesus' power, one that prevented His healing over a great distance. Furthermore, he presumed to tell Jesus *how* to conduct the healing rather than simply entrusting the care of his son to the Lord. And, most significantly, he sought Jesus as a means to get what he wanted, not as the Messiah who is worthy of worship.

— 4:49-50 —

The royal official would not relent. Facing this kind of desperate situation, he was not an aristocrat, or an official, or a Sadducee, or even a Galilean. He was first and foremost a father, sick with worry over his dying son. Jesus used the man's vulnerable state of mind to teach him genuine belief. He said, in effect, "Go about your business; your son is fine."

John says the man "believed the word that Jesus spoke." How significant! "Belief" is a key feature in John's narrative; however, "belief" is not necessarily trust in Jesus as Messiah and Savior. When John uses the verb "believe" without an object—as in, "Many people believed" (1:7, 50; 3:12, 15; 4:41)—he describes saving faith, trust in Jesus as Savior. The same is true of the phrase, "believe *in Him*" (3:16-17, emphasis mine). The man believed what Jesus said to be true, which is an important first step, but not the same belief that saved the Samaritans (4:41).

Clearly, the Lord's word was enough for this father. John says he "started off," or "carried on." It's the very same verb for "go" the Lord used earlier.

— 4:51-52 —

Someone reading this too quickly might think the phrase "started off" in 4:50 means the man started off for home. A natural response would be to rush home to verify that the boy was indeed better. But a close examination of the details tells a different story. The man didn't race off to Capernaum. He went about his business in Cana. How do we know? By putting several clues together.

As mentioned earlier, Capernaum was no more than six hours away on foot, two hours by chariot. (Rich people didn't walk when they had the means to ride!) As the man journeyed home, his servants met him with the news that his son had recovered. Note the time of the healing: the seventh hour (1 p.m.) . . . *yesterday*. The father didn't start out for home until *the day after* his encounter with Jesus.

Jesus said, "Go about your business," and the man did just that!

— 4:53-54 —

When the man realized that his son's fever broke at the very hour Jesus declared the boy healed, the man "believed." Note the absence of any direct object. Whereas before he "believed the word that Jesus spoke," now he simply "believed." This is the kind of faith that brings a person into a right relationship with God though His Son, Jesus. It moves beyond mere acceptance of His message to trust in Jesus Himself as Savior, Messiah, Son of God.

The man believed in the Savior, along with his whole household.

• • •

We know from the other Gospel accounts that Jesus performed many more signs in Galilee and Judea, and that His growing fame brought multitudes seeking physical and spiritual healing. Before long, a movement began to form as followers fell in behind the rabbi from Nazareth, who also happened to be a descendant of David. They believed His words, and they appeared to believe in Him. They were also looking for a king to lead them. But would they accept the kingdom He promised, or did they want a king of their own making?

As Jesus turned toward Jerusalem, His followers faced a difficult choice.

APPLICATION: JOHN 4:43-54

Easy Believing versus Saving Faith

When D. James Kennedy wrote the text for *Evangelism Explosion,* a wonderful evangelism training program, he was careful to clarify what we mean by the invitation, "Believe in Jesus." He first describes what saving faith is *not.*

> The first thing people mistake for saving faith is this: an intellectual assent to certain historical facts. Some people believe in Jesus Christ the same way they believe in Napoleon or George Washington. They believe He actually lived. He was a real person in history, but they are not trusting Him to do anything for them now.[20]

Kennedy calls this kind of belief "mere intellectual assent." He then describes another kind of belief that falls short of saving faith. "Temporal faith" is a step in the right direction, yet it still falls short.

> We might say that when you trusted in the Lord for your finances you had a financial-faith. You trusted in the Lord to take care of your family—you could call that family-faith. You trusted in the Lord to help you with your decisions—you might call that deciding-faith. On trips you had traveling-faith.
>
> There is one element all these things have in common. They are temporal. . . . But saving faith is trusting in Christ to save you—to save you eternally.[21]

John's story of a father desperate to see his deathly ill son restored to health illustrates the difference between authentic saving faith and other kinds of belief. When Jesus assured the man that his son would live, he "believed the word that Jesus spoke" (4:50). He believed that Jesus would grant his request. Temporal faith. Later, when he realized that his son's miraculous recovery coincided with Jesus' word, "he himself believed" (4:53). He then believed in Jesus as Messiah, accepting as true all the Lord's claims and trusting the Savior for salvation.

What is the nature of your belief? Do you call upon the Lord to save your finances, or restore the health of someone you love, or to keep your family from harm? If so, don't stop! He wants us to come to Him with all our sorrows and cares. The Lord desires to become an integral part of our everyday experiences. But don't stop there. Don't let the extent of your trust end with temporal matters.

Jesus told Nicodemus, "This is how God loved the world: He gave his one and only Son, so that everyone who believes in him will not perish but have eternal life" (John 3:16, NLT). Each one of us is sick with the terminal disease of sin. And justice demands punishment for sin, which is eternal separation from God. Because Jesus, the Savior, paid the penalty for our sin, we may have eternal life . . . by trusting in Jesus to save us.

That's the kind of belief Jesus calls us to exercise. That's *saving* faith.

AUTHENTICATION OF THE WORD (JOHN 5:1–12:50)

The Lord's ministry began well. A bold announcement by John the Baptizer immediately yielded five disciples with unreserved commitment to following the Son of God. His turning water into wine strengthened His disciples' faith. He taught Nicodemus, performed signs in Jerusalem, redeemed a Samaritan town, and healed the nobleman's son, all of which resulted in multitudes from every quarter of Israel trusting Jesus as Savior. While the Lord's ministry had not been without conflict, the general response to the Word had been belief. Then, like the first chill of winter on an autumn breeze, something began to change. Not everyone believed right away. A few began to oppose Him openly . . . followed by more. The Son of God came to the world to shine the light of truth, yet some minds remained darkened. Instead of uniting Israel, the Word began to create sharp divisions.

The human author of Hebrews called the Word of God a double-edged sword, a blade sharp enough to divide anything into its constituent parts (Heb. 4:12). Dividing is, after all, the purpose of a sword. Moreover, this sword—the Word—is "able to judge the thoughts and intentions of the heart." In other words, while truth enlightens willing hearts, it also proves some hearts to be willfully darkened. So it should be no surprise that when the Word became flesh, the world began to divide in response to Him.

In this section of John's narrative (John 5:1–12:50), Jesus will offer five more "signs" authenticating Himself as the promised Messiah, as well as God in human flesh. Each sign identifies the Son of God more clearly than the one before it until the truth is unmistakable . . . to willing hearts, hearts prepared to receive Him. The truth of Jesus Christ will also authenticate those who were given to Him (6:37, 39; 17:2, 6, 9, 24). The words and deeds of Jesus will separate believers from "the world," identifying them as His own—trusting souls He promised to preserve until the last day.

As believers are separated from their unbelieving peers, "the world" in John's narrative begins to take on a more menacing character. In the first section (1:19–4:54), "the world" refers to all of humanity, whom God loves and sent His Son to save (1:29; 3:16-19; 4:42). In the second section (5:1–12:50), the Lord continues to illumine "the world"; however, as John warned his readers earlier (1:10), "the world" begins to reject Jesus, while "His own" continue to believe, although with fragile faith and feeble understanding. After the second section, "the world" becomes the Lord's expression for all those who reject the Word (14:17, 27, 30-31; 15:18-19; 16:8, 20-21, 28, 33; 17:5-6, 9-11, 13-18, 21, 23-25), thus proving themselves to be overt enemies of God and His elect.

By the end of Jesus' public ministry, the line between believers and nonbelievers was unmistakable. Like a sword, the Word had divided Israel down the middle.

Modern culture judges the quality of leaders by their ability to unite people. However, if I've learned anything from my years in pastoral ministry, it's that truth does not unite people; it divides them. In fact, the easiest way to unite people is to hide the truth, to tell them what they want to hear. History has proven that the most effective way to build a large following is to sell an image. Create one symbol for people to rally around and another for them to hate. Make your symbols bold, make your message simple, tailor it to the deepest needs of people, convince them that following you will solve all their problems and—whatever you do—keep the real truth hidden. That will require absolute, totalitarian control. Furthermore, you'll have to make an example of truth-tellers, but your reward will be immense power in the form of a large following.

Truth, on the other hand, does not tend to attract large followings. On the contrary, truth draws enemies like a magnet in a box of nails. That's why godly leadership requires courage, tenacity, resiliency, and most of all, humility. A proclaimer of truth cannot worry about image or applause, polls or popularity; he or she must be content to present the truth, allow it to stand on its own—let it attract or repel whomever it will—and then accept personal rejection as the most probable outcome.

If this was the experience of the Word—divine Truth in human flesh—you can be certain it won't be any different for you.

amēn (ἀμήν) [281] "amen," "truly," "surely," "certainly"

Amēn is simply a transliteration of a Hebrew exclamation, which people uttered to affirm a pronouncement of God or to confirm the acceptance of a divine directive (Deut. 27:15; cf. 1 Kgs. 1:36; 1 Chr. 16:36; Neh. 5:13). Jesus used *amēn* to indicate that His next statement was new revelation from God, which also bore His own stamp of authority as the Son of God. *See John 5:19; 6:53; 8:51; 12:24.*

doxa (δόξα) [1391] "glory," "good reputation," "token," "miracle"

This noun derives from the verb *dokeō* [1380], "to believe, to think." Secular Greek literature uses the term to mean "opinion," which can be either positive or negative.[1] New Testament literature uses *doxa* exclusively in a positive sense. First-century Jews chose *doxa* to translate the Hebrew term *kabod* [H3519], the Old Testament term for the radiant splendor of God's character, which He often manifested as light (the *shekinah*). Therefore, the New Testament closely associates *doxa* with the visible expression of God's presence. *See John 1:14; 2:11; 11:40; 17:5.*

ergon (ἔργον) [2041] "work(s)," "deed(s)," "doing"

Fundamentally, this term can refer to effort, the result of one's effort, or both simultaneously. The "works" of God can be seen in the creation of the universe and His continued involvement with creation in the form of provision and protection. The "works" of humanity can be either tangible, such as art, construction, and farming, or intangible. Intangible "works" of people usually have a moral connotation and might just as well be translated "good deeds." These efforts contribute to the working of God in the universe and, as such, they please Him. *See John 5:36; 6:29; 9:3; 10:25.*

krinō (κρίνω) [2919] "to judge," "to separate and select," "to assess," "to decide"

The literal meaning is "to sift and separate in order to isolate the components of a mixture." The primary use is metaphorical in the sense of "sifting through the details to arrive at a conclusion." In terms of a person, the idea is to sift the details of his or her life in order to examine them and render a decision about his or her character. The nouns *krisis* and *krima* both derive from this verb, but have slightly different meanings. *Krisis* [2920] is the act of judging. *Krima* [2917] is the result of judgment, which might be either a verdict or a sentence. *See John 3:17; 5:30; 12:47; 16:11.*

An Exposé of Legalism
JOHN 5:1-18

NASB

¹After these things there was a feast of the Jews, and Jesus went up to Jerusalem.

²Now there is in Jerusalem by the sheep *gate* a pool, which is called in ᵃHebrew ᵇBethesda, having five porticoes. ³In these lay a multitude of those who were sick, blind, lame, and withered, [ᵃwaiting for the moving of the waters; ⁴for an angel of the Lord went down at certain seasons into the pool and stirred up the water; whoever then first, after the stirring up of the water, stepped in was made well from whatever disease with which he was afflicted.] ⁵A man was there who had been ᵃill for thirty-eight years. ⁶When Jesus saw him lying *there,* and knew that he had already been a long time *in that condition,* He said to him, "Do you wish to get well?" ⁷The sick man answered Him, "Sir, I have no man to put me into the pool when the water is stirred up, but while I am coming, another steps down before me." ⁸Jesus said to him, "Get up, pick up your pallet and walk." ⁹Immediately the man became well, and picked up his pallet and *began* to walk.

Now it was the Sabbath on that day. ¹⁰So the Jews were saying to the man who was cured, "It is the Sabbath, and it is not permissible for you to carry your pallet." ¹¹But he answered them, "He who made me well was the one who said to me, 'Pick up your pallet and walk.'" ¹²They asked him, "Who is the man who said to you, 'Pick up *your pallet* and walk'?" ¹³But the man who was healed did not know who it was, for Jesus had slipped away while there was a crowd in *that* place. ¹⁴Afterward Jesus found him in the temple and said to him, "Behold, you have

NLT

¹Afterward Jesus returned to Jerusalem for one of the Jewish holy days. ²Inside the city, near the Sheep Gate, was the pool of Bethesda,* with five covered porches. ³Crowds of sick people—blind, lame, or paralyzed— lay on the porches.* ⁵One of the men lying there had been sick for thirty-eight years. ⁶When Jesus saw him and knew he had been ill for a long time, he asked him, "Would you like to get well?"

⁷"I can't, sir," the sick man said, "for I have no one to put me into the pool when the water bubbles up. Someone else always gets there ahead of me."

⁸Jesus told him, "Stand up, pick up your mat, and walk!"

⁹Instantly, the man was healed! He rolled up his sleeping mat and began walking! But this miracle happened on the Sabbath, ¹⁰so the Jewish leaders objected. They said to the man who was cured, "You can't work on the Sabbath! The law doesn't allow you to carry that sleeping mat!"

¹¹But he replied, "The man who healed me told me, 'Pick up your mat and walk.'"

¹²"Who said such a thing as that?" they demanded.

¹³The man didn't know, for Jesus had disappeared into the crowd. ¹⁴But afterward Jesus found him in the Temple and told him, "Now you are well; so stop sinning, or some-

become well; do not sin anymore, so that nothing worse happens to you." ¹⁵The man went away, and told the Jews that it was Jesus who had made him well. ¹⁶For this reason the Jews were persecuting Jesus, because He was doing these things on the Sabbath. ¹⁷But He answered them, "My Father is working until now, and I Myself am working."

¹⁸For this reason therefore the Jews were seeking all the more to kill Him, because He not only was breaking the Sabbath, but also was calling God His own Father, making Himself equal with God.

5:2 ^aI.e. Jewish Aramaic ^bSome early mss read *Bethsaida* or *Bethzatha* 5:3 ^aEarly mss do not contain the remainder of v 3, nor v 4 5:5 ^aLit *in his sickness*

thing even worse may happen to you." ¹⁵Then the man went and told the Jewish leaders that it was Jesus who had healed him.

¹⁶So the Jewish leaders began harassing* Jesus for breaking the Sabbath rules. ¹⁷But Jesus replied, "My Father is always working, and so am I." ¹⁸So the Jewish leaders tried all the harder to find a way to kill him. For he not only broke the Sabbath, he called God his Father, thereby making himself equal with God.

5:2 Other manuscripts read *Beth-zatha;* still others read *Bethsaida.* 5:3 Some manuscripts add an expanded conclusion to verse 3 and all of verse 4: *waiting for a certain movement of the water,* ⁴*for an angel of the Lord came from time to time and stirred up the water. And the first person to step in after the water was stirred was healed of whatever disease he had.* 5:16 Or *persecuting.*

The quintessential legalists of Jesus' day were the Pharisees, a brotherhood of experts in religion.

Legalism is an enemy. I declare that not just on the basis of Scripture; I have discovered its spirit-smothering capacity through experience. As a young believer seeking companions to share my spiritual journey, I found myself surrounded by a group of legalists and, without realizing it, I began to embrace their views. I started gauging the quality of my spiritual life and the lives of others by a list of dos and don'ts, measuring everyone's worth in terms of performance and achievement. I wanted to pursue spiritual excellence, but I thought I could do it on my terms, as though righteousness depended completely upon my efforts. Instead of experiencing greater joy in my relationship with Christ, I became critical and judgmental. I gradually turned into a harsh, negative, rigid spirit. Freedom was gone. Worship was flat. Service was drudgery. I didn't realize it at the time, but that environment of legalism was smothering me.

Because legalism is a subtle, silent killer, we need to understand our enemy before we confront it. We need to know what it is, how it appears, and why it is wrong.

What is legalism?

Legalism is the establishment of standards carefully selected by people for the purpose of celebrating human achievement under the guise of pleasing God. Legalism is righteousness as defined by humans, who frequently cite God as the source of the standard. In reality, the standards come from culture, tradition, and most frequently the personal preferences of those who maintain positions of power or influence.

Legalism is based on lists (legalists love their lists!). If you do keep every item on the list of dos and don'ts, you're deemed spiritually acceptable. But if you don't follow the prescribed standard, you are judged unworthy of God's favor and others' approval. Naturally, legalists always think they know how God judges and they are more than willing to act on His behalf.

How does legalism appear?

Legalism almost always adorns itself in the regal robes of religious garb, and it brandishes the credentials of religious organizations. This is not to condemn Christian organizations or the clothes they wear— I am merely pointing out that legalists are drawn to them and have successfully infiltrated churches, missions, parachurch organizations, charities, and schools. When they do, they use religious trappings to convince others that their own agendas have God's approval. Eventually, followers begin to fear the disapproval of the leaders, who become more and more visible and controlling as the Lord fades into obscurity.

Why is legalism wrong?

Legalism denies God's grace and presumes to earn His favor through deeds. It is a man-made righteousness that exalts humanity rather than the Lord. Legalism produces either pride or depression in the people under its spell—pride for those who keep the list to their own satisfaction, depression for those who recognize their utter inability to keep the list perfectly. Criticism is the primary motivation. The goal of legalism is to *give* as much criticism as possible and to avoid *receiving* it at all costs.

Legalism is wrong because it produces in people what the Lord desires least: pride, self-loathing, hypocrisy, and self-righteousness.

— 5:1-2 —

After Jesus had ministered in Galilee for some time, which could have been several weeks or even months, He traveled to Jerusalem to observe "a feast of the Jews." John doesn't tell us which feast, probably because it doesn't contribute to his purpose, unlike the Passover (2:23; 6:4; 11:55), which is profoundly meaningful to his case. He merely tells us why Jesus came to Jerusalem. In the beginning of His ministry, He traveled to the capital city only for the purpose of worship in keeping with Jewish law. Eventually, He would enter the city to claim it as the King of Israel. But not yet.

When Jesus earlier cleansed the temple (2:13-22), He claimed ownership of Judaism's most visible symbol. His purpose was to restore worship. Here, on His next visit to Jerusalem, He claimed ownership of Judaism's most treasured institution: the Sabbath. His purpose on this occasion was to restore grace.

www.HolyLandPhotos.org

The pool described by John bears a striking resemblance to a complex of two pools surrounded by five colonnades to the north of Herod's temple, which is visible here at left. The complex appears to have been a sanitarium, known in the Greek world as an *asklēpieion*. The Greeks believed Asclepius, the god of medicine, to be a kind, gentle healer. The three towers in the center of the photo mark the northwest corner of the temple complex.

When Jesus arrived in Jerusalem, He apparently visited the sanitarium that lay in the shadow of the great temple built by Herod. The temple authorities, especially the Pharisees among them, would never have entered the place and probably rebuked any Jew who did.

— 5:3-4 —

A portion of 5:3-4 doesn't appear in the earliest Greek manuscripts. Most likely, an early scribe added the text as a clarification based on his knowledge of the tradition.

The name *Bethesda* is a kind of play on words, meaning "house of grace" or "house of outpouring [water]." A curious blend of Hebrew religion and Greek superstition held that an angel of God periodically stirred the waters and promised healing to the first invalid able to pull himself into the pool. (We now know that the pools were periodically fed by an underground spring that caused the surface to stir.) There could not have been a more fitting image of legalistic religion in all of Israel. Around the symbol of life lay desperately sick people, waiting for the chance to participate in a pathetic race of invalids to the water, in which healing went to the least needy person among them.

"House of grace"? Hardly!

— 5:5-6 —

As Jesus visited weary patients who were vainly trying to heal themselves, He found a man who had been sick for thirty-eight years, which was longer than the average life expectancy for a male in the first-century Roman Empire. He had been sick for literally a lifetime. So, Jesus' question sounds absurd: "Do you wish to get well?"

John states that Jesus "knew" the man's history of illness. Either someone had informed the Lord earlier, or He exercised supernatural awareness (1:47-48; 4:17); John does not say. The question was Jesus' first words to the man and was probably intended to get his attention before leading him (and us) toward an important truth.

— 5:7-8 —

The man's reply is telling. The Koiné Greek language often used word order for the sake of emphasis. In this case, the man stressed the word "man"—he did not have a man to help him. He clearly recognized his own helplessness; however, the object of his faith was confused. He hoped for a bit of superstition, perhaps because the temple of Herod had failed him. Generally accepted theology held that illness was the result of God's judgment for sin (9:2); he would not have found much sympathy in the temple.

Furthermore, he looked to humanity to help him win his absurd race for healing, obviously having lost hope of ever seeing God's grace. For him, as for many in our own day, "God helps those who help themselves."

— 5:8-9 —

Jesus didn't preach. He didn't correct the man's failing theology. He didn't lecture him on grace. People who lack hope don't need more knowledge; they need compassion. Jesus gave the man what he lacked and so desperately needed. He gave him grace in the form of a command: "Get up, pick up your pallet and walk."

Disease and Desperation

JOHN 5:7-8

The scene by the pool of Bethesda must have been a soul-rending experience for any visitor with the capacity for empathy.

When I served on the island of Okinawa, I was a member of the Third Division Marine Corp band. On one particular occasion, we were invited to a leprosarium on the north end of Okinawa to play a concert. The memory of those men and women will never leave me. Mangled bodies stumbled and pushed and pulled themselves along, each one bearing remnants of a human face. They sat in neat rows of chairs provided for them and they listened in rapt attention to our music. I could barely play my instrument through the sadness weighing upon my heart, seeing bodies horrifically distorted by Hansen's disease. I'll never forget the sound of their applause, which they offered by banging stumps of limbs together or tapping their crutches on the floor or against their chairs.

I would have given almost anything to have the power of healing that day. What a joy it must have been for Jesus to reach down into the sea of human depravity and snatch a soul from the clutches of disease. I sometimes wonder why He didn't clear the area around the pool of Bethesda instead of choosing just one man. Even so, He left the pristine realm of heaven to become one of us, to share our suffering, to experience death, and ultimately to end the tyranny of evil through His own sacrifice. And one day soon, Jesus will empty the hospitals, the leper colonies, and even the graveyards of the world. Then we will live in a world without darkness, sin, suffering, disease, and death. We have His promise on that. And I, for one, passionately anticipate that glorious day!

"Immediately" the man's body responded to the healing power of Jesus. The man responded to the words of his Lord. John's description of the scene is undoubtedly a deliberate understatement. I'm sure that after nearly four decades of atrophied limbs and withered hope, the man skipped, ran, leaped, and did cartwheels around that wretched pool. He must have been a sight!

Just as the reader might begin to celebrate the man's healing, John's aside drops like a wet blanket. He says, in effect, "Oh, by the way, *it was the Sabbath*." Anyone who knew anything about Pharisees understood the significance of that simple statement. His literary killjoy foreshadows a bizarre twist to the story.

— 5:10 —

While John doesn't interrupt the logical flow of the story, there is an apparent change of scene. The man was probably carrying his bedroll home, or perhaps to the temple, where he would partake of the feast for the first time in many years. He was scolded by "the Jews" (John's term for "religious authorities") for carrying something on the Sabbath, which was strictly forbidden by tradition but perfectly acceptable by the Law of Moses given the extraordinary circumstances.

This is a perfect example of the legalist's obsession with the letter of the law while ignoring the inspiration (or the "spirit") of the law. The Pharisees strictly applied the words of Jeremiah, "do not carry any load on the sabbath day" (Jer. 17:21), but failed to recognize the context. Jeremiah complained because the seventh day in Jerusalem was business as usual, like any other day. Later, Nehemiah would take the same stand by ordering the doors of Jerusalem to be closed on the last day of the week, "so that no load would enter on the sabbath day" (Neh. 13:19).

The Lord instituted the Sabbath as a gift. He ordered a day of rest to rejuvenate the bodies and minds of His people. More importantly, it was given in order to break the day-in, day-out cycle of routine so that people would not forget that *God* is the ultimate source of their sustenance; their labors are but a means of His provision. The Sabbath gave people permission to stop work so they would not neglect a vital need: worship. We are created for worship; therefore, worship is good for us. But the Pharisees turned this wonderful gift of God into a burden, an occasion for severe criticism, an excuse to exercise power, and yet another opportunity to remind themselves and everyone else of their superior moral worth.

THE HEBREW SABBATH

JOHN 5:10

According to Exodus 20:11, the Hebrew people were to stop all work on the Sabbath because the Creator "rested" after the sixth day of creation. Because He was tired? Of course not! Omnipotence never needs to rest. The Hebrew term translated "rest" is *shabat* [H7673], which means "to cease." The Lord ceased work because His creative work was complete, at which time He called His creation "good." By sundown on the sixth day, He had provided everything His creatures—including humans—would need to thrive and to fulfill their created purpose. He created humanity to worship and enjoy Him forever.

God set aside the seventh day—the Sabbath, the "ceasing-time" as it were—to be a perpetual gift that commemorates the Lord's creation of the world and celebrates His provision. He intended it to be a time of rest, feasting, enjoying family, and—more than anything—celebrating His provision and protection. However, by the time of Jesus, the Pharisees had turned this wonderful gift of grace into a toilsome, tedious burden.

To the simple command "rest," the Pharisees added a long list of specific prohibitions. And, just in case they overlooked something, they established thirty-nine categories of forbidden activities: carrying, burning, extinguishing, finishing, writing, erasing, cooking, washing, sewing, tearing, knotting, untying, shaping, plowing, planting, reaping, harvesting, threshing, winnowing, selecting, sifting, grinding, kneading, combing, spinning, dyeing, chain-stitching, warping, weaving, unraveling, building, demolishing, trapping, shearing, slaughtering, skinning, tanning, smoothing, and marking.

The long list of prohibited activities made life more difficult for people by forbidding even the simplest common-sense activities (see also Matt. 12:1-2, 10; Luke 13:14-17; John 9:14-16). By focusing on the letter of the Law, the Pharisees turned a day of rest into a tedious burden!

— 5:11-13 —

The healed man explained the extraordinary reason for his minor violation of the Pharisees' rules: "He who made me well was the one who said to me, 'Pick up your pallet and walk.'" But take note of the glass-half-empty perspective of the Pharisees, which would be comical if it weren't so appalling: "Who is the man who said to you, 'Pick up your pallet and walk'?"

I think any normal person would have been at least a little intrigued by the man's instant healing. But the Pharisees bypassed an opportunity to celebrate the grace of God in order to ferret out a potential threat to their authority.

Imagine you had a neighbor who had been paralyzed from the neck down by an accident more than thirty years ago. One Sunday morning, just after six o'clock, the sound of a lawnmower jolts you from a deep, satisfying sleep. Annoyed, you bolt to the front door to see who would be so insensitive as to rattle every window on the block with that infernal noise so early on a day of rest. Upon seeing your formerly paralyzed friend gleefully mowing his lawn in perfect health, what do you think you would say? If you're a normal person, you'd say, "Hank! What happened? How are you not paralyzed?!" But if you're a Pharisee, you'd scream, "Hank! It's Sunday morning! Turn that thing off!"

Instead of looking for a wonder-worker to praise, the Pharisees went in search of a troublemaker to censure.

— 5:14 —

John wrote that Jesus "found" the man in the temple, which strongly suggests He had been looking for him, not that He just happened to see him. According to Old Testament Law, a person healed of leprosy was to be examined by a priest and declared "clean" (Lev. 14:1-27; Matt. 8:4; Mark 1:44). It's possible the Pharisees added this requirement to other ailments. Or the man was simply grateful to worship alongside his Jewish brothers. Regardless, the man was in the right place and Jesus found him.

Some have taken Jesus' warning to mean that sin had caused the man's illness, but Jesus later denied a *moral* cause-effect relationship between sin and physical disabilities (John 9:3). A simpler explanation is that Jesus knew the man's heart. Having delivered the man from his physical affliction, Jesus sought to save the man from eternal spiritual suffering. The "worse" Jesus had in mind was hell. Jewish theology of the day correctly taught that sin deserves punishment; however, the rabbis incorrectly attributed physical illness to God's wrath. The true and ultimate punishment for sin is eternal torment after death.

— 5:15 —

The man's response to Jesus' incredibly generous gift of grace is perplexing. Rather than defend Jesus' deed, he appears to use it for political advantage. He says, in effect, "I didn't want to violate your rules—that man told me to do it. And who was I to question someone with the power to heal? Your argument is with him, not me!"

The Greek word rendered "went away" is better translated "went after" and usually indicates purpose. It's a common expression in the Synoptic Gospels for discipleship. One "goes after" a mentor in order to learn from him. The man turned away from following Jesus and affirmed his allegiance to the Jewish leaders. His response to Jesus proved quite different from that of another man healed by the Lord (9:13-34).

— 5:16 —

John closes the story with two comments that explain the source of a growing tension between Jesus and the religious authorities. Their dispute is no mere squabble among theologians. The issue at stake is authority. Jesus cleansed the temple with divine authority; as the Son of God, He owns the house of God (2:16). The religious authorities had usurped the Lord's ownership of His own house and tenaciously resisted His confrontation of their sin.

On this occasion, and others to follow, Jesus confronted the religious authorities on their perversion of God's Law. This particular healing begged the question, "Who owns the Sabbath?" The religious authorities claimed ownership of the Sabbath by objecting to Jesus "doing these things" (implying more acts of grace than this particular healing), activities the Pharisaic *tradition* forbids on the seventh day.

— 5:17-18 —

Jesus responded to the religious leaders' false claim in two ways: first by refuting their self-serving definition of "work," and then by claiming ownership of the Sabbath as God.

He began by pointing out that God had never stopped "working." This goes to the root of the religious leaders' theological presumption that "work" includes any kind of activity. They pointed to Exod. 20:9-11 as precedence, which in turn points to Gen. 2:3 (see the feature "The Hebrew Sabbath" on page 115).

Having refuted the faulty theology of the religious leaders, Jesus equated His act of grace with God's continuing "work." This was an outright claim to ownership of the Sabbath. Because the Law came from God, God cannot be condemned by the Law. The Son of God was merely continuing to do what He, as the Creator, had been doing since the seventh day of creation.

His point was not lost on the religious authorities. They resented His challenging their illegitimate authority and they rejected His claim of equality with God. This precipitated their plot to kill Him.

• • •

The Word didn't become flesh to establish a new religion. He became one of us to restore a broken relationship. He came to restore the true worship of God, which doesn't presume to earn His blessing through good deeds but rejoices in the unmerited favor He delights to give. Unfortunately, the roots of pride run deep into our flesh; therefore, the ability to accept grace does not come naturally, only supernaturally.

APPLICATION: JOHN 5:1-18

Waging War on Legalism

Legalism is a silent killer. Like carbon monoxide, it is odorless, colorless, tasteless, and has the power to lull the mind into a deep sleep from which it will never emerge. So, I never recommend a person remain in a place where the poison of legalism has displaced the fresh air of grace. One individual cannot rescue an organization that is permeated with legalism. He or she can only escape, leave the poison behind, and seek a place of grace. Then, as the dulling effects of legalistic religion wear off, he or she can call others to follow. But no one, not even the fully recovered, should ever reenter such a place.

However, we have a responsibility to respond to legalism when it seeks to invade places of grace. Pastors, teachers, and leaders must confront legalism aggressively by taking specific action. I find in John 5:1-18 three responses to legalism in the words and deeds of Christ.

First, we must *expose* legalism. The truth of the gospel—the good news of God's grace received through faith—must refute the claims of tradition, custom, or any other standard of righteousness not explicitly taught in Scripture. And where Scripture is clear, it must be applied to call people to celebrate the Spirit of God living within them through joyful obedience.

Second, we must *combat* legalism. Legalism is an enemy that cannot be met with violence; however, like in any war, we must fight with courage and conviction, recognizing that combat requires toughness. Without setting aside kindness, we must be willing to confront the legalist with his or her lies. In the words of Jess Moody, the author of *A Drink at Joel's Place,*

The only way to live with such a person as this is to be intolerant of his intolerance. . . . If you resist him in this fashion you can expect him to come at you like a bull elephant with a mad on.

He'll speak to you and of you like eight thunderstorms but you must keep up the pressure because it is the only way to break his precast psychic mind-set.

His rhino charge will come at you with bullying fascism. There is no fence limiting the lies he will tell to bring you down.

As Paul says, he will "spy out your liberty" and do everything in his power to enchain you and break your spirit. You simply must not let him overwhelm you. Every time he slaps you, hit him in return with a great big dose of love. If you keep it up he will either repent or crucify you.[2]

Third, we must *overcome* legalism. We do that by proclaiming grace louder, more often, in more places, and to more people than the false prophets of legalism. People only choose bondage when they fear that freedom is unreachable, impossible, unaffordable, or unreal. Once people experience grace and learn that it can be theirs, legalism doesn't stand a chance.

The Claims of the Christ
JOHN 5:19-30

NASB

[19]Therefore Jesus answered and was saying to them, "Truly, truly, I say to you, the Son can do nothing of Himself, unless *it is* something He sees the Father doing; for whatever ªthe Father does, these things the Son also does in like manner. [20]For the Father loves the Son, and shows Him all things that He Himself is doing; and *the Father* will show Him greater works than these, so that you will marvel. [21]For just as the Father raises the dead and gives them life, even so the Son also gives life to whom He wishes. [22]For not even the Father

NLT

[19]So Jesus explained, "I tell you the truth, the Son can do nothing by himself. He does only what he sees the Father doing. Whatever the Father does, the Son also does. [20]For the Father loves the Son and shows him everything he is doing. In fact, the Father will show him how to do even greater works than healing this man. Then you will truly be astonished. [21]For just as the Father gives life to those he raises from the dead, so the Son gives life to anyone he wants. [22]In addition, the Father judges no one. Instead, he has given the Son absolute authority

NASB

judges anyone, but He has given all judgment to the Son, ²³so that all will honor the Son even as they honor the Father. He who does not honor the Son does not honor the Father who sent Him.

²⁴"Truly, truly, I say to you, he who hears My word, and believes Him who sent Me, has eternal life, and does not come into judgment, but has passed out of death into life. ²⁵Truly, truly, I say to you, an hour is coming and now is, when the dead will hear the voice of the Son of God, and those who hear will live. ²⁶For just as the Father has life in Himself, even so He gave to the Son also to have life in Himself; ²⁷and He gave Him authority to execute judgment, because He is ᵃthe Son of Man. ²⁸Do not marvel at this; for an hour is coming, in which all who are in the tombs will hear His voice, ²⁹and will come forth; those who did the good deeds to a resurrection of life, those who committed the evil deeds to a resurrection of judgment.

³⁰"I can do nothing on My own initiative. As I hear, I judge; and My judgment is just, because I do not seek My own will, but the will of Him who sent Me.

5:19 ᵃLit that One   5:27 ᵃOr a son of man

NLT

to judge, ²³so that everyone will honor the Son, just as they honor the Father. Anyone who does not honor the Son is certainly not honoring the Father who sent him.

²⁴"I tell you the truth, those who listen to my message and believe in God who sent me have eternal life. They will never be condemned for their sins, but they have already passed from death into life.

²⁵"And I assure you that the time is coming, indeed it's here now, when the dead will hear my voice—the voice of the Son of God. And those who listen will live. ²⁶The Father has life in himself, and he has granted that same life-giving power to his Son. ²⁷And he has given him authority to judge everyone because he is the Son of Man.* ²⁸Don't be so surprised! Indeed, the time is coming when all the dead in their graves will hear the voice of God's Son, ²⁹and they will rise again. Those who have done good will rise to experience eternal life, and those who have continued in evil will rise to experience judgment. ³⁰I can do nothing on my own. I judge as God tells me. Therefore, my judgment is just, because I carry out the will of the one who sent me, not my own will.

5:27 "Son of Man" is a title Jesus used for himself.

As a distinguished-looking gentleman stood behind a microphone to rally his people in the name of Allah, he praised Jesus as a genuine prophet, a wise teacher, and a worthy example of human goodness. However, he then declared with remarkable confidence that this same Jesus never claimed to be anything more than a man—that He never claimed to be God. While it is true that no one ever recorded the exact phrase "I am God," Jesus boldly asserted His deity in such precise, unambiguous terms that His enemies were outraged, calling Him a blasphemer for "making Himself equal with God" (John 5:18). The magnitude of Jesus' many claims may have eluded this Muslim leader, but His enemies understood His meaning completely.

When Jesus went to the pool of Bethesda in Jerusalem and chose to heal a superstitious invalid, He knew it would attract the attention of the religious authorities. Sure enough, after scolding the man for carrying his pallet, they hunted Jesus down and denounced Him for violating their rules. Their real purpose was to eliminate a threat to their authority; however, they masked their true intent by pretending to uphold God's preeminence in the Sabbath. Jesus didn't avoid the surface issue. He first corrected their faulty theology, and then He addressed the real question at hand: *Who owns the Sabbath?* The Lord answered that question with six specific claims:

(1) He is equal with God (5:19-20),
(2) He is the giver of life (5:21, 26),
(3) He is the final judge (5:22-23),
(4) He will determine the eternal destiny of humanity (5:24),
(5) He will raise the dead (5:25-29), and
(6) He is always doing the will of God (5:30).

— 5:19-20 —

Jesus is equal with God.
When Jesus said, "My Father is working until now, and I Myself am working" (5:17), the religious leaders understood exactly what He meant. He was "calling God His own Father, making Himself equal with God" (5:18). The speech that follows presents the truth of His deity in terms no one in His day could mistake.

Jesus began with a double *amēn* [281], meaning "it is true, it is true." He then claimed equality with God, calling Himself the Son of God and referring to God as His Father. While Father and Son are distinct persons, Father and Son are equal and unified. As such, the Father and the Son cannot act in opposition to one another.

The Son is the perfect revelation of the Father here on earth in human form. Everything He does reflects the intentions and actions of the Father. Moreover, what the Father knows, the Son knows, because they are one being; therefore, they share the same mind.

— 5:21 —

Jesus is the giver of life.
In order to be able to give life, you must be the Source of life. This would be an outrageous claim for any mere human. Doctors can give medicine or administer treatment in order to delay death, but they cannot give life to a dead body. Prophets in the Old Testament had been the

human instruments of divine power in raising the dead, but none of them dared claim credit. Only God can create something from nothing and then fill it with life.

We are never more helpless than when a loved one dies. If our loved one is sick, we can bring medicine. If our loved one is weary, we can offer rest. If our loved one is discouraged, we can provide encouragement and consolation. If our loved one is destitute, we can provide financial support. But what happens if he or she dies? All we can do is mourn our loss. Only God has the power to restore life.

— 5:22-23 —

Jesus is the final judge.

Ask anyone, "Who is the final judge of man?" and seldom will the answer be anything but "God." Only God can discern the intentions of the heart, because He is omniscient. Only He can weigh the value of a person without being hypocritical, because He is perfectly righteous. Only He can decide the fate of humanity, because He made us and He is sovereign.

The Father has delegated all judgment to the Son, because the Son is equal with the Father. Consequently, Jesus claimed to deserve the same honor due the Father.

— 5:24 —

Jesus will determine the eternal destiny of humanity.

Jesus again punctuated a statement with a double *amēn*, "truly, truly." Usually, Jesus called for belief in Himself (3:16); in this case, He called for belief in the Father to reinforce the theme of complete unity of Father and Son. To believe in one is to believe in the other, because the two persons are one. Furthermore, this belief impacts one's eternal destiny (3:18).

— 5:25-29 —

Jesus will raise the dead.

Again, the double *amēn*, "truly, truly," places emphasis on the immediate statement in which Jesus claims to be the one who will summon the dead to final judgment.

His phrasing in 5:25 is interesting because the verb "to hear" takes a double meaning. "The dead [all of humanity that has died] will hear the voice of the Son of God . . ." but only "those who hear" will receive life. The first "hearing" is literal; that is, mere exposure to the sound of His voice. The second has to do with comprehending the message and believing it. The irony, of course, is that dead people cannot hear anything. His statement has both a present and a future aspect. He will summon the dead to judgment on the final day; however, the "dead"—those who have no spiritual life in Him—can receive life now.

Jesus validated His qualification to be the judge of all humanity because He is both the Son of God, who can give life, and the Son of Man, who experienced life as a human, yet without sin.

— 5:28-29 —

In describing the fate of humankind, Jesus explained the two possible destinies: "life," which is eternal life, or "judgment." Taken by itself, this statement would appear to declare that one's eternal destiny is determined by his or her deeds; that is to say, bad deeds lead to judgment while good deeds result in life.

It is true that the basis of judging will be one's behavior, whether good or evil. The Greek term for "judgment" in 5:24 and 29 is *krisis,* the noun form of the verb *krinō,* "to judge, to divide, to assess, to decide" (see Key Terms, p. 107).

Theoretically, a person can go to trial before the Judge and, if he or she is found to be morally perfect, gain eternal life. However, in a practical sense, no one is morally perfect. Therefore, to face judgment without grace is to face condemnation. Consequently, Jesus uses the two ideas interchangeably; judgment *is* condemnation. His point then is to avoid judgment altogether . . . by grace that is received through belief (5:24).

— 5:30 —

Jesus is always doing the will of God.
Jesus' final claim links His actions on earth to the will of the Father in heaven. Everything the Son does reflects the intentions of the Father, because they are one being.

Note the sudden shift in perspective. Throughout the speech, Jesus referred to Himself in the third person, using the titles "Son of God" and "Son of Man." As He transitioned from this portion of the speech (5:19-30) to the next (5:31-47), He restated His original claim, "the Son can do nothing of Himself, unless it is something He sees the Father doing" (5:19), only in the first person: "I." His point is clear. He was not referring to some other person; He made these claims about Himself.

• • •

Stop for a few moments and seriously consider these six claims. Think of the best person in all of history (other than Jesus Christ), living or dead. Imagine him or her standing before you to make a speech having these six points:

- I am equal with God the Father.
- I am the giver of life.
- I am the final judge over all of humanity.
- I hold the destinies of every human in my hand.
- I will raise the dead.
- Everything I do is the will of God.

How would you respond?

Of all the great philosophers, teachers, artists, and statesmen who ever lived, none would dare make such claims unless he or she were either completely insane or shamelessly evil. Not unless He was indeed God in human flesh.

APPLICATION: JOHN 5:19-30
Declarations That Demand Response

Jesus declared six truths about Himself in John 5:19-30, all of which point to a single overarching declaration that demands a response.[3] Jesus claimed equality with God, which left humanity no room for compromise, no middle ground to stand upon. We must choose to believe or reject His declaration.

If you choose to reject His claim to deity, then you must choose between two alternative explanations. Either Jesus knew His claims were false, or He did not. If He deliberately misrepresented Himself, then He was a liar of the worst kind, evil to the core for demanding the worship of His peers. If, on the other hand, a mere man genuinely believes he is God, then that man has completely lost his mind; he is utterly insane. Therefore, if Jesus was wrong about His identity, He was neither a good man nor a teacher worth hearing. None of His words would be trustworthy.

If you choose to believe His claim to deity, then you have to choose between another pair of alternative responses: rebellion or trust. Accepting the fact of Jesus' deity without trusting Him for salvation puts you in no better position than that of demons. They believe in the reality of God . . . and shudder with hatred and fear (Jas. 2:19). It is possible to believe in the existence of God and even accept the truth of His becoming a man in the person of Jesus Christ yet reject His offer of grace and suffer the just penalty of sin.

How is this possible? By trusting the false claims of religion instead of receiving God's gift of grace. Religion is nothing more than the attempt of humanity to gain entrance to heaven on one's own terms, primarily by achieving enough goodness through one's own efforts. Sadly, the road to hell is jammed with people who proudly trust in their own goodness rather than humbly admitting their moral poverty and receiving eternal life as a gift.

The response demanded by the Lord is to accept the claims of Jesus as true and to place complete trust in Him, receiving His gift of eternal life. Of all the alternatives, it's the only logical thing to do.

Witnesses for the Defense
JOHN 5:31-47

NASB

31 "If I *alone* testify about Myself, My testimony is not ªtrue. 32 There is another who testifies of Me, and I know that the testimony which He gives about Me is true.

33 You have sent to John, and he has testified to the truth. 34 But the testimony which I receive is not from man, but I say these things so that you may be saved. 35 He was the lamp that was burning and was shining and you were willing to rejoice for ªa while in his light.

36 But the testimony which I have is greater than *the testimony of* John; for the works which the Father has given Me to accomplish—the very works that I do—testify about Me, that the Father has sent Me.

37 And the Father who sent Me, He

NLT

31 "If I were to testify on my own behalf, my testimony would not be valid. 32 But someone else is also testifying about me, and I assure you that everything he says about me is true. 33 In fact, you sent investigators to listen to John the Baptist, and his testimony about me was true. 34 Of course, I have no need of human witnesses, but I say these things so you might be saved. 35 John was like a burning and shining lamp, and you were excited for a while about his message. 36 But I have a greater witness than John—my teachings and my miracles. The Father gave me these works to accomplish, and they prove that he sent me. 37 And the Father who sent me has testified about me himself. You have never heard

has testified of Me. You have neither heard His voice at any time nor seen His form. [38] You do not have His word abiding in you, for you do not believe Him whom He sent.

[39] [a] You search the Scriptures because you think that in them you have eternal life; it is these that testify about Me; [40] and you are unwilling to come to Me so that you may have life. [41] I do not receive glory from men; [42] but I know you, that you do not have the love of God in yourselves. [43] I have come in My Father's name, and you do not receive Me; if another comes in his own name, you will receive him. [44] How can you believe, when you receive [a] glory from one another and you do not seek the [a] glory that is from the *one and* only God? [45] Do not think that I will accuse you before the Father; the one who accuses you is Moses, in whom you have set your hope. [46] For if you believed Moses, you would believe Me, for he wrote about Me. [47] But if you do not believe his writings, how will you believe My words?"

5:31 [a] I.e. admissible as legal evidence   5:35 [a] Lit *an hour*   5:39 [a] Or (a command) *Search the Scriptures!*   5:44 [a] Or *honor* or *fame*

his voice or seen him face to face, [38] and you do not have his message in your hearts, because you do not believe me—the one he sent to you.

[39] "You search the Scriptures because you think they give you eternal life. But the Scriptures point to me! [40] Yet you refuse to come to me to receive this life.

[41] "Your approval means nothing to me, [42] because I know you don't have God's love within you. [43] For I have come to you in my Father's name, and you have rejected me. Yet if others come in their own name, you gladly welcome them. [44] No wonder you can't believe! For you gladly honor each other, but you don't care about the honor that comes from the one who alone is God.*

[45] "Yet it isn't I who will accuse you before the Father. Moses will accuse you! Yes, Moses, in whom you put your hopes. [46] If you really believed Moses, you would believe me, because he wrote about me. [47] But since you don't believe what he wrote, how will you believe what I say?"

5:44 Some manuscripts read *from the only One.*

Throughout human history, civilized cultures have maintained order by creating laws and then enforcing those laws through a court system. While these systems of justice have varied widely, and some have undoubtedly been more effective than others, their purpose has basically been the same: to discover the truth in any given matter. At least, that is their stated purpose. As we have all seen at one time or another, the truth is quite irrelevant to a judge or jury who refuses to accept facts.

While Jesus had not yet been hauled into court, He was nonetheless on trial. The temple officials had found a man breaking their tradition, who in turn pointed an accusing finger at Jesus (John 5:11). Then, an initial confrontation only added to their list of alleged crimes; Jesus immediately accepted responsibility for breaking with tradition and then, in addition to that, claimed to be equal with God (5:17-18).

John presents the dialogue between Jesus and the officials in

Legalists . . . You Gotta Love 'Em

JOHN 5:31-47

The uncomfortable space "between a rock and a hard place" is such familiar ground for a pastor, I keep a pillow there. I'm never sure how long my next stay is going to be. The "hard place" is life in the real world; the "rock" is usually the naive expectations placed upon a pastor by well-meaning legalists.

Take, for instance, the issue created by an ashtray I used to keep in my study at the church. Long before "smoke-free" became fashionable, it was not uncommon for people to light up a cigarette when emotions ran high. This was especially true for non-Christians and new believers. As you can imagine, people frequently end up in my study when they've reached the end of their rope. And I decided long ago that when someone is wracked with pain over the loss of a child or devastated by an affair, it's the wrong time to focus on the health risks of tobacco and the need to steward God's gift of life.

One church member was deeply troubled by the idea of a pastor keeping an ashtray in his study, so she confronted me. "Why? Why would you have an ashtray where you prepare sermons and minister to God's people?" I wanted to tell her I didn't want God's people putting out their cigarettes on the carpet.

I learned many years ago that most legalists mean well. Most of them sincerely think the world should operate according to their standard of right and wrong in matters where the Bible is silent. I also learned that once you have explained your position, no amount of debate will satisfy. Legalism is not a difficulty that can be overcome with more information. Only grace can do that. Show legalists lots of love and lots of acceptance, despite their criticism. Jesus confronted the legalists of His day because He is God; their spiritual growth is His responsibility. Eventually, as the Holy Spirit brings maturity, legalism fades. Our job in the meantime is to present the truth in love and then shower them with grace.

summary form rather than chronologically. The Lord's interaction with the religious authorities occurred over several days or even weeks, which 5:18 summarizes. After the first confrontation, we see the passing of time and a steady escalation of resentment on the part of the temple officials. John describes this extended time with verbs in the "imperfect" tense, which the Greek language uses to describe ongoing, habitual, or iterative action. The officials were continually "*seeking* all the more to kill Him" because He was continually or repetitively "*breaking* the Sabbath," "*calling* God His own Father," and "*making* Himself equal with God." Eventually, this growing tension led to what may be called a "drumhead trial."[4] Rather than hauling Jesus into court, the temple officials brought the makeshift courtroom to Jesus. They assumed the role of judge and hoped the jury of public opinion would side with them.

Jesus met their challenge with a declaration of truth in the form of six bold claims to deity (5:19-30). His sudden shift in perspective from third person ("Son of God" and "Son of Man") to the first person ("I") in 5:30 marks a transition in His rebuttal.

Now, having established His premise, the Lord began to call witnesses to support His claims. Before closing His case in 5:47, Jesus will have called five witnesses to the stand:

Witness #1: God the Father (5:32, 37-38)
Witness #2: John the Forerunner (5:33-35)
Witness #3: Jesus' "signs" (5:36)
Witness #4: The Scriptures (5:39-44)
Witness #5: Moses (5:45-47)

— 5:31 —

Jesus opened His case by quoting a guiding principle of Jewish court procedure, which stems from the Law of Moses (Deut. 17:6; 19:15). The testimony of a defendant is not considered valid unless it is supported either by undisputed fact or reliable testimony. Moreover, testimony must come from more than one witness. Jewish courts accepted corroborating testimony from multiple witnesses as indisputable proof—truth that could not be denied.

— 5:32, 37-38 —

John, translating the Aramaic words of Jesus, could have chosen either of two Greek words for "another," *allos* [243] or *heteros* [2087]. The two words are basically synonymous with a slight nuance. Whereas *heteros* means "another of a different sort," *allos* means "another of the same sort." This "another" is, of course, God the Father (5:36-37). Without denying complete unity or oneness with the Father, Jesus treated the Father's testimony as independent. If His accusers objected, they would be admitting that He and the Father are indeed one being. By failing to object, His accusers had to receive the independent testimony of the Almighty into evidence.

Jesus was referring to more than nine centuries of prophecy, which He had fulfilled precisely. He even fulfilled details of prophecy over which He had no control (humanly speaking), such as the manner, time, and place of His birth (Isa. 7:14; Dan. 9:25; Mic. 5:2). His judges and jury included scribes, men who had dedicated their lives to preserving Scripture and had quite naturally become experts in its interpretation and application. The Pharisees devoted their lives to meticulous obedience to the Law, believing that the moral purification of Israel would hasten the coming of the Messiah. Unfortunately, like most religious people, these men preserved and transmitted truth on a daily basis yet failed to live it.

— 5:33-35 —

Earlier, the religious authorities sought out John the Baptizer because his widespread ministry caused Jews to begin looking for the Messiah. His impact was so profound that few doubted his status as a genuine prophet of God (Matt. 14:5; 21:26; Mark 11:32; Luke 20:6). However, the excitement he stirred was short-lived. He was the lamp, not the light. He was the forerunner, not the Christ. John completed His mission by introducing the Messiah and then stepped aside. But Jesus was not the Messiah Israel wanted. He came to establish a different kind of kingdom, not one that would raise an army, overthrow Rome, conquer the world, and usher Israel into a new golden age of power and prosperity. At least not yet. The true Messiah—as opposed to the messiah of selfish expectations—came to conquer hearts. He came to transform hearts of stone into hearts of flesh, which would then beat in perfect rhythm with the Law (Jer. 31:31-33; Ezek. 11:19-20; 36:26).

— 5:36 —

While John had been a powerful witness and an authentic voice for God, he never performed miracles (John 10:41). Jesus, however, performed many "signs" (2:23; 3:2), including the dramatic miracle that sparked His current trial. These miracles do not establish His deity by themselves; other mere mortals have been the means by which God accomplished supernatural "works." However, miracles had long been accepted as God's stamp of approval on the miracle-worker's message. Jesus' signs authenticated His message: *I am equal with the Father.* Furthermore, the miracles were consistent with the character and plans of God.

— 5:39-44 —

The verb "to search" can be translated either as a command or as a statement. The NASB elects to render the verb as a statement; however, I believe Jesus issued a challenge: "Go ahead, search the Scriptures!" His point was twofold. First, Jesus' challenge anticipated the conclusion they would reach if they dared take the message of Scripture at face value. If they remained intellectually honest, the Old Testament would lead them to the conclusion that He is undoubtedly the Son of God. Second, these practitioners of religion searched the Word of God for criteria by which they could merit their own salvation and failed to encounter the Word Himself, who promised to give them righteousness by grace, through belief. He challenged the religious experts to continue their vain quest while alluding to the grave consequences of their stubbornness. Rather than read Scripture as a means of knowing God, they made the Law their god.

Jesus supported His accusation first by contrasting His motivation with theirs: Whereas He doesn't seek the approval of men (implying that He seeks only the approval of God), the religious authorities daily sacrifice their love of God for the admiration of people. Jesus then pointed to the absurdity of their accepting teachers who made a name for themselves while rejecting the One who glorifies the Father.

— 5:45-47 —

Jesus' fifth and final witness is none other than Moses, the man revered by every Jew as a founding father of their faith and the greatest of all the prophets. Only the coming "greater prophet," the Messiah (see Deut. 18:15-19), would surpass the great Moses. Moreover, it was the writings of Moses the temple officials had twisted into a religion of works and had perverted to become their means of rejecting the Christ. You will recall that it was Jesus' supposed violation of Moses' Law that drew them in the first place.

Moses never intended the Law to become an end unto itself. The Law cannot become the means of a self-made righteousness, because no one can keep it perfectly. Therefore, the Law can only indict, never justify. On the contrary, Moses predicted the failure of the Israelite people and promised a Savior to lead them . . . *if* they would heed His words.

• • •

Why didn't the religious leaders believe these witnesses to the truth of Jesus Christ? Jesus named two interrelated reasons:

1. *They were unwilling* (5:40-43). Accepting Jesus as the Son of God is not an intellectual problem; it's a crisis of the will. Like many court cases in history, the judge and jury received only those facts that supported their foregone conclusion and cast the others aside.
2. *They were proud* (5:43-44). Pride is the secret virtue of all religion, and glory is its reward. Those who achieve man-made righteousness would rather reject the truth of God's grace than give up their glory.

The religious leaders rejected Jesus not because they were unable to believe but because they were unwilling. Inability to believe is the result of a dull mind, which the disciples struggled to overcome for much of Jesus' ministry on earth. The Lord is remarkably patient with our weaknesses, as John illustrates in the next segment of his narrative. Unwillingness to believe, on the other hand, is the result of pride; and pride invariably leads to destruction.

APPLICATION: JOHN 5:31-47

Five Reasons, Two Obstacles, and One Way

Jesus gave the Pharisees five reasons to believe He is the Son of God, five appeals to authorities they claimed to respect. Despite this and other irrefutable evidence proving Jesus' deity, the Pharisees remained intractable.

Be on the lookout for such people as you move through life. Some are genuinely curious about Jesus Christ and their questions can become an opportunity to lead them to faith in Him (1 Pet. 3:15). But don't be fooled. Not every debate about spiritual matters is prompted by curiosity; more often than not, religious debate is merely the ruse of the rebellious. People will engage you in debate for no other purpose than to challenge the truth, not to understand and believe. It's part of a clever game they play with themselves. Their purpose for debating a believer is to pretend they have good reason to remain on their present course; if the Christian cannot refute their objections or offer a compelling reason to believe in Christ, they don't feel obligated to submit control of their lives to anyone else. In reality, they cannot tolerate the Christian's firm belief that God, not humanity, controls the destiny of the universe. By the end of the debate, the Christian is exhausted and the rebel feels vindicated . . . for a while. Soon, he or she compulsively engages another unwary believer, driven by the same need as a boy whistling past the graveyard.

Here are a few ways to know when a rebel wants to play "convert-me-if-you-can":

- The person challenges you with a negative opinion about God, or some other theological concern, and then expects you to talk him or her out of it. (For example, "God doesn't care about people or He would end all suffering.")
- The person presents a theological conundrum that has no definite answer. (For example, "What about those who never heard about Jesus?")
- The person presumes to judge the goodness of God by human standards, especially his or her own. (For example, "I can't believe in a God who would send someone to hell.")
- The person tries to convince you that your faith is irrational or that God does not exist.
- The person shifts the conversation to another issue whenever you begin making headway on the first.
- The person becomes angry and belligerent or resorts to name-calling.
- The person wants to compare qualifications or casts doubt upon yours.

If you suspect you're in a debate with a rebel, politely end the conversation. You might even offer your reason for cutting it short. The temptation to continue can be enticing, but never once have I seen someone argued into the kingdom. At best, you can only argue to a stalemate because with a rebel the challenge is not the intellect; it's the will. If you must leave him or her with something, let it be a testimony of your own experience. Few people can refute that.

On the other hand, genuinely curious people listen rather than argue. They question rather than challenge. They are receptive and humble, not argumentative and brash. They accept that some questions cannot be answered adequately and they respect the occasional "I don't know." They respond positively to empathy, whereas rebels are unaffected by compassion. And, best of all, with genuinely curious people, the conversation naturally flows into a presentation of the gospel. Not everyone acts upon the good news right away, but those who want to know the truth will at least hear it without a fight.

God's Specialty: Impossibilities
JOHN 6:1-21

NASB

¹After these things Jesus went away to the other side of the Sea of Galilee (or Tiberias). ²A large crowd followed Him, because they saw the ᵃsigns which He was performing on those who were sick. ³Then Jesus went up on the mountain, and there He sat down with His disciples. ⁴Now the Passover, the feast of the Jews, was near. ⁵Therefore Jesus, lifting up His eyes and seeing that a large crowd was coming to Him, said to Philip, "Where are we to buy bread, so that these may eat?" ⁶This He was saying to test him, for He Himself knew what He was intending to do. ⁷Philip answered Him, "Two hundred ᵃdenarii worth of bread is not sufficient for them, for everyone to receive a little." ⁸One of His disciples, Andrew, Simon Peter's brother, said to Him, ⁹"There is a lad here who has five barley loaves and two fish, but what are these for so many people?" ¹⁰Jesus said, "Have the people ᵃsit down." Now there was much grass in the place. So the men ᵃsat down, in number about five thousand. ¹¹Jesus then took the loaves, and having given thanks, He distributed to those who were

NLT

¹After this, Jesus crossed over to the far side of the Sea of Galilee, also known as the Sea of Tiberias. ²A huge crowd kept following him wherever he went, because they saw his miraculous signs as he healed the sick. ³Then Jesus climbed a hill and sat down with his disciples around him. ⁴(It was nearly time for the Jewish Passover celebration.) ⁵Jesus soon saw a huge crowd of people coming to look for him. Turning to Philip, he asked, "Where can we buy bread to feed all these people?" ⁶He was testing Philip, for he already knew what he was going to do.

⁷Philip replied, "Even if we worked for months, we wouldn't have enough money* to feed them!"

⁸Then Andrew, Simon Peter's brother, spoke up. ⁹"There's a young boy here with five barley loaves and two fish. But what good is that with this huge crowd?"

¹⁰"Tell everyone to sit down," Jesus said. So they all sat down on the grassy slopes. (The men alone numbered about 5,000.) ¹¹Then Jesus took the loaves, gave thanks to God, and distributed them to the people. Afterward he did the same with the

seated; likewise also of the fish as much as they wanted. [12] When they were filled, He said to His disciples, "Gather up the leftover fragments so that nothing will be lost." [13] So they gathered them up, and filled twelve baskets with fragments from the five barley loaves which were left over by those who had eaten. [14] Therefore when the people saw the [a]sign which He had performed, they said, "This is truly the Prophet who is to come into the world."

[15] So Jesus, perceiving that they were [a]intending to come and take Him by force to make Him king, withdrew again to the mountain by Himself alone.

[16] Now when evening came, His disciples went down to the sea, [17] and after getting into a boat, they *started to* cross the sea to Capernaum. It had already become dark, and Jesus had not yet come to them. [18] The sea *began* to be stirred up because a strong wind was blowing. [19] Then, when they had rowed about [a]three or four miles, they saw Jesus walking on the sea and drawing near to the boat; and they were frightened. [20] But He said to them, "It is I; [a]do not be afraid." [21] So they were willing to receive Him into the boat, and immediately the boat was at the land to which they were going.

6:2 [a]Or *attesting miracles* 6:7 [a]The denarius was equivalent to a day's wages 6:10 [a]Lit *recline(d)*
6:14 [a]Or *attesting miracle* 6:15 [a]Or *about*
6:19 [a]Lit *25 or 30 stadia* 6:20 [a]Or *stop being afraid*

fish. And they all ate as much as they wanted. [12] After everyone was full, Jesus told his disciples, "Now gather the leftovers, so that nothing is wasted." [13] So they picked up the pieces and filled twelve baskets with scraps left by the people who had eaten from the five barley loaves.

[14] When the people saw him* do this miraculous sign, they exclaimed, "Surely, he is the Prophet we have been expecting!"* [15] When Jesus saw that they were ready to force him to be their king, he slipped away into the hills by himself.

[16] That evening Jesus' disciples went down to the shore to wait for him. [17] But as darkness fell and Jesus still hadn't come back, they got into the boat and headed across the lake toward Capernaum. [18] Soon a gale swept down upon them, and the sea grew very rough. [19] They had rowed three or four miles* when suddenly they saw Jesus walking on the water toward the boat. They were terrified, [20] but he called out to them, "Don't be afraid. I am here!*" [21] Then they were eager to let him in the boat, and immediately they arrived at their destination!

6:7 Greek *Two hundred denarii would not be enough.* A denarius was equivalent to a laborer's full day's wage. 6:14a Some manuscripts read *Jesus.* 6:14b See Deut 18:15, 18; Mal 4:5-6.
6:19 Greek *25 or 30 stadia* [4.6 or 5.5 kilometers].
6:20 Or *The 'I AM' is here;* Greek reads *I am.* See Exod 3:14.

Sometime after His clash with the religious elite in Jerusalem, Jesus returned to Galilee, where events gave Him an opportunity to offer His disciples a divine perspective on earthly challenges. This was to be a crucial lesson for the men He would later commission with the words, "As the Father has sent Me, I also send you" (John 20:21).

Sometimes, life on planet Earth can be a demoralizing struggle. Some challenges loom larger than our meager resources, some demands far outweigh our ability to meet them, some answers float high above our intellectual reach, and some problems are too complex to solve. Let's face it; the world is big and we are small. And to make matters worse, we are naturally predisposed to think only on the horizontal plane. Nothing is impossible for God, yet we habitually think in terms of what *we* have to offer and what can be accomplished through *natural* means.

Some might call this a lack of faith or a failure to believe, but not John the apostle. He remembered a time when a small band of men had chosen to believe in the Son of God and had left everything behind to follow Him, yet frequently struggled to understand Jesus' words and repeatedly failed to comprehend what they saw Him do. Theirs was a completely different problem from the lack of belief Jesus encountered among the religious leaders in Jerusalem. The disciples failed to understand what they saw and heard, yet chose to believe in the Son of God; the temple officials understood better than anyone who Jesus claimed to be, yet chose to reject Him. Disbelief and ignorance are distinct problems, and Jesus handled them accordingly. He condemned disbelief, while He patiently transformed the minds of struggling believers.

THE JEWISH CALENDAR AND FESTIVAL CYCLE

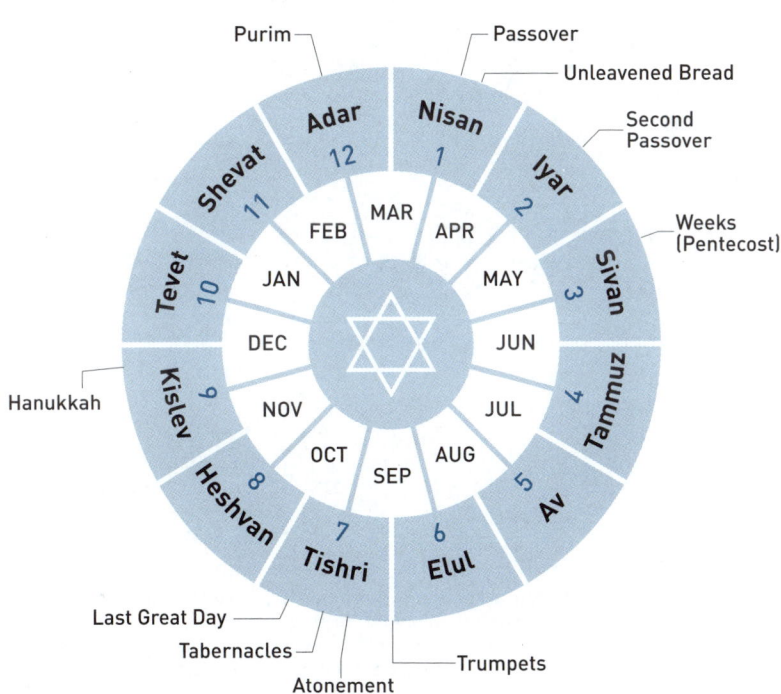

— 6:1-3 —

Several months passed after the events of 5:1-47. John tells us that Passover (March–April) was not far in the future (6:4), so if the "feast" mentioned in 5:1 was the Feast of Tabernacles (September–October), the time is not likely to have been less than six months. The Jews observed both Hanukkah (November–December) and Purim (February–March) in the interim, but neither celebration required people to travel to Jerusalem. During this time, the Lord continued to minister in Judea and Galilee.

As He healed the sick and proclaimed the good news, multitudes began to follow. In fact, they didn't merely follow; they relentlessly dogged His every movement. The other Gospels tell us that the disciples had just completed an extensive preaching tour of their own and were in need of rest and encouragement (Mark 6:30-31), so He took them to a "secluded place" somewhere in the wilderness east of Bethsaida (Luke 9:10). But they still couldn't escape the crowds. The Lord knew the vast majority of the people sought Him for selfish gain and nothing more; nevertheless, unlike His disciples, He felt compassion for them, even when they became a nuisance.

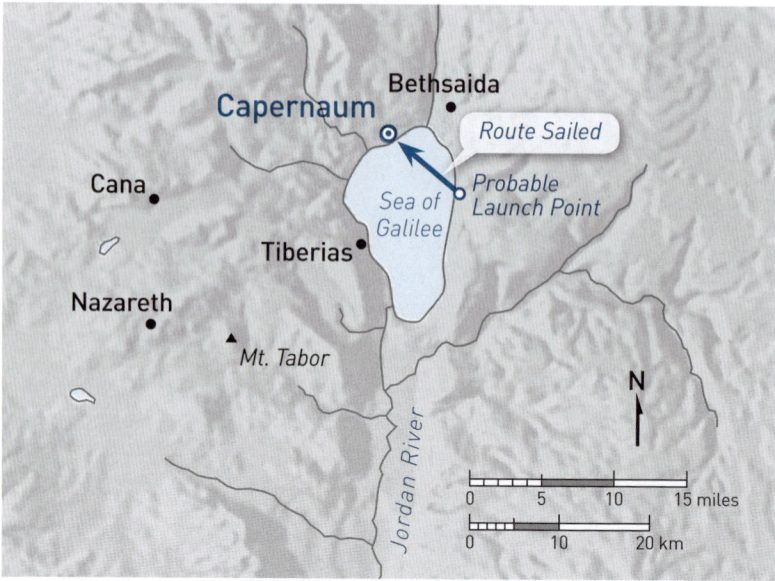

Jesus fed a multitude of followers somewhere in the hill country northeast of the Sea of Galilee. According to other Gospels, He then commanded His disciples to set sail for Capernaum. Unfortunately, a strong wind—most likely from the west (Matt. 14:24)—impeded their progress so that the men were "straining at the oars" (Mark 6:48).

— 6:4 —

John occasionally includes a time reference in his narrative. His reference to the coming Passover tells us something about the people's frame of mind, much like our beginning a story with the words, "Christmas was just around the corner and . . ." Passover was just around the corner and a large congregation of Hebrews had gathered in the wilderness. In such a setting, Moses, paschal lambs, unleavened bread, the wilderness wanderings, and manna would have mingled easily in the minds of everyone present. Jesus recognized an opportunity and decided to make the most of it. In a single miraculous "sign," He would teach His disciples a valuable lesson, clearly define His mission on earth, winnow the multitude for authentic believers, and set a course for Calvary.

— 6:5-6 —

Having retreated no less than four miles into the wilderness, Jesus "lift[ed] up His eyes" (cf. 4:35) to see the multitude approaching. According to Matthew, the crowd numbered five thousand men plus their wives and children (Matt. 14:21); perhaps there were as many as ten thousand people in all. Upon seeing the multitude, Jesus selected a specific disciple: Philip. His purpose was to "test" His students.

Peirazō [3985], the Greek word for "test," has a wide range of meaning that includes both positive and negative connotations. Jesus was *tempted* throughout His ministry (Heb. 2:18; 4:15), most directly by Satan, whom Matthew called *peirazōn*, "the tempter." But the term can also be positive. For James, faith reaches full maturity through *trials* (Jas. 1:2-3, 12), a disposition that agrees with Peter (1 Pet. 4:12-13). Therefore, the nature of a "test" depends upon the intent of the person conducting it. In this case, Jesus saw an opportunity to let His disciples fail so that He might strengthen them.

Jesus chose Philip for the test because he was the statistical pessimist of the group. It's a common problem. Every group has at least one, and most everyone has a fair amount of Philip in them. While Jesus' opening question was earnest, it was nonetheless intended to reveal a specific attitude. All the while, of course, Jesus knew what He was going to do, which is a crucial part of the lesson.

— 6:7 —

Philip didn't answer the question he was asked. Jesus asked about "where"; Philip answered with "how much." A *denarius* was a Roman silver coin, roughly equal to one day's wages for a common, semi-skilled laborer (Matt. 20:2-13). He quickly estimated the buying power of 200 days' wages, which was perhaps the amount they had in the treasury. Although this sum was considerable, it was paltry compared to the need.

Philip looked at the problem in terms of meeting the minimum requirement. If "a little" for each person was impossible, abundance was not even worth considering. Statistical pessimists think like that.

— 6:8-9 —

While Philip calculated, Andrew quietly moved through the crowd. While Philip didn't look beyond his own means, Andrew considered the possibility that the people might provide for themselves with a little leadership. But the people had little or nothing. He sheepishly mentioned one little boy's sack lunch, containing "five barley loaves and two fish."

Everything about Andrew's statement emphasizes inadequacy. The Greek term for "lad" is a double diminutive; he was "a little boy." In terms of provision, little children were of no use at all. His few "barley loaves" were common to the Mediterranean diet. They would have been leavened at least a little, formed into little disks about 4 or 5 inches (10 to 13 centimeters) in diameter, and then baked. And the Greek term for "fish" is the diminutive form of a word meaning "little fish." They were small, seasoned, sardine-like fish, included for the sake of flavor. This was, after all, a small boy's lunch, so there was not much to work with. While it harkened back to a similar experience with Elijah (2 Kgs. 4:42-44), the proportions in this case were extreme.

While Andrew faithfully reported what provision he had found, his final comment revealed his own limited perspective: "but what are these for so many people?"

— 6:10-11 —

I imagine the Lord flashing a reassuring grin as He instructed His disciples. In the vernacular of the day, He said, "Have the people recline." The posture for eating back then was leaning back on one elbow.

Imagine the scene. The disciples organized the people into groups of fifty (Mark 6:39; Luke 9:14) and instructed them to prepare for a meal. No one saw any food and the disciples had no idea how the people would be fed. Once the organization was complete, the Lord placed the little sack lunch in front of Him and gave thanks. I imagine the disciples

GOD'S SPECIALTY: IMPOSSIBILITIES | JOHN 6:1-21

sneaking glances at one another as Jesus was praying, "Thank You, Father, for the food this large gathering is about to enjoy . . ."

Jesus then multiplied the meager offering. Again, imagine the scene. He broke one lunch into two, then again, and again, and again. He divided the lunch many thousands of times over a period of hours, assuming He worked alone. And each person received more than "a little"; they all received "as much as they wanted." For most of them, this was their first complete meal in a long while. Leftovers were not a common sight in ancient times.

— 6:12-13 —

John never includes details without good reason. The offering had been meager, the miracle dramatic, and the provision abundant, but the lesson was not yet complete. The Lord instructed each of the twelve men to collect the leftovers. Each of the disciples took a wicker basket called a *kophinos*—typically used to carry one person's provisions for a journey of two or three days (Judg. 6:19; Ps. 81:6)—and collected enough uneaten scraps to provision each of the twelve.

At the end of the day, the disciples' lesson should have been clear. The size of a challenge should never be gauged in terms of our capability. What we have to offer will never be enough. God never calls us to provide; that's His responsibility. Instead, He calls us to commit whatever we have—even if it's no more than a sack lunch. His call comes with a promise: *You take care of the addition, I'll be in charge of the multiplication, and the mission I've invited you to join will be accomplished.*

— 6:14-15 —

John comments briefly on the response of the people, which is important to the story later on. The Lord performed this "sign" to instruct the people as well as His disciples. There in the wilderness, having consumed miracle bread to their stomachs' delight, they recognized Jesus as "the Prophet" (Deut. 18:15-18; John 1:21).

Jesus rejected the path to the throne taken by most earthly kings. He refused to ride the swell of popular support into Jerusalem. He knew His path to be the way of suffering, as it had been prophesied for centuries and planned from the beginning by the Father (John 18:36). Moreover, He knew the people had been prompted by their stomachs rather than their hearts. Jesus chose not to address the crowd immediately; instead, He retreated further into the wilderness hill country.

— 6:16-18 —

As evening fell, the crowd dispersed and the disciples boarded their fishing boat for Capernaum as they had been instructed by the Lord (Matt. 14:22-23; Mark 6:45-46). Jesus perceived them (supernaturally, no doubt—see Mark 6:48) struggling to stay afloat and on course in the wee hours of the morning (Matt. 14:25). A fierce squall had descended on the sea as often happens. The Sea of Galilee is situated 686 feet (209 meters) below sea level in a deep rift between the Arabian Desert and the Mediterranean Sea. Winds frequently whip down through the gorge and turn the Sea of Galilee very choppy, which would have been a nightmare for the crude sailing boats of the first century. As one commentator notes, "Even today the situation is similar. Power boats periodically are warned to remain docked as the winds whip the water into foamy white caps."[5]

— 6:19-21 —

The men put all their strength against the oars to make landfall at Capernaum, but the winds resisted them for hours. This is another vivid example of human inadequacy. By contrast, Jesus demonstrated mastery over the elements by walking across the water to rescue them.

When Jesus reached the boat, He calmed them by declaring, *Egō eimi*, "I AM." He followed this with a short command—literally, "Stop fearing." And when He stepped into the vessel, they were "immediately" at their destination. John offers this without explanation or comment, presumably because the point is clear. Jesus once again brought His abundant power to the rescue of human inadequacy, turning an impossible situation into an opportunity to strengthen the confidence of His believers.

• • •

The disciples should be commended for continuing to trust the Lord despite their still-dull minds. While they continued to trust Jesus, tragically they failed to gain any insight from the "sign" they had witnessed only hours before in the wilderness. According to Mark, "their heart was hardened" (Mark 6:52). This idiom didn't mean they were unkind or cruel (as it does in English). Rather, their reasoning and emotions were resistant to development. We would say they were "thickheaded." Nevertheless, Jesus remained patient with His disciples. If He rebuked them at all, He was gentle (Matt. 14:31).

The people who had been fed in the wilderness were thickheaded as well, but for completely different reasons. Upon landing in Capernaum, Jesus would confront their selfish motives head-on.

APPLICATION: JOHN 6:1-21

Miracle Math

Philip faced a math problem he couldn't solve one early spring day in Galilee. Jesus looked down the slope of a mountain to see a multitude of empty stomachs. Immediately, He challenged Philip with the task of feeding them. The poor disciple didn't need a calculator to figure out that no natural solution to the problem existed. In fact, a quick estimate gave proof enough that Jesus' challenge could not be met with the money they had on hand.

Sooner or later, every believer will face a test that mathematics has declared impossible. How should we respond? As I observe Philip, Andrew, the other disciples, the little boy, and Jesus, I find a model of faithful obedience worth emulating. Consider the following steps the next time a math problem challenges the work of God.

First, *acknowledge your own inadequacy and the Lord's omnipotence.* Perhaps Philip could have responded to Jesus' directive by saying, "Lord, we don't have the ability to accomplish what you have asked, but nothing is too difficult for You." This is not shrinking from a challenge or shirking responsibility. There's nothing ungodly about acknowledging the size of the challenge. We need only remember that the Lord's power is always greater, no matter what difficulty we face.

Second, *be certain the challenge before you glorifies the Lord, obeys one of His commands in Scripture, or helps to fulfill a Scriptural mandate (such as the Great Commission).* The Lord never challenged His disciples to demoralize them. The impossible task He gave to Philip did have a solution, albeit a supernatural one. And the same is true with us. Jesus issued a command just before ascending to take His place in glory: to "make disciples of all the nations" (Matt. 28:19-20). Humanly speaking, this is an impossible task. He might as well ask us to dip the Pacific Ocean dry with a teaspoon. It can't be done . . . naturally. Nevertheless, if He has commanded something, it can be done . . . supernaturally.

The difficulty we face today is that we generally do not receive personal commands from the Lord, such as "Build a multipurpose facility for neighborhood outreach." How much easier ministry would be if He would simply send instructions via FedEx. Instead, He communicates His vision and His values through the Bible. Therefore, we must work together and keep one another honest as we put our plans to the test.

Does the challenge glorify God? Does the challenge obey a command of Scripture? Does the challenge fulfill a Scriptural mandate?

Third, *give the challenge back to the Lord as an opportunity for Him to accomplish it on your behalf and to receive glory for the victory.* The Lord delights in accomplishing the impossible on our behalf and sharing the spoils of victory, especially when the triumph is the result of obedience. How much pleasure Jesus would have received if Philip had said, "Lord, this is far more than we can handle, but nothing is too difficult for You. How will You feed this multitude?"

Fourth, *do what you can, supply what you have, put forward your effort, then allow the Lord to multiply it (or not) at His discretion.* The Lord did not materialize food out of thin air—although He could have. Instead, He used the meager lunch of an unassuming, inconspicuous little boy . . . and He multiplied it. Jesus doesn't need help. He can do anything and everything Himself. Nevertheless, He calls us to do our part—not for His sake, but for ours. He invites us to become a part of His plan as a means of grace, so that when the victory is won we can say together, "*We* triumphed!"

By the end of day, as the disciples gathered the surplus of food, the solution to the mathematical problem was obvious. Jesus said, in effect, "You do the addition, I'll take care of the multiplication, and everything I have commanded you will be accomplished . . . with plenty left over."

Bread Delivered from Heaven
JOHN 6:22-71

NASB

22 The next day the crowd that stood on the other side of the sea saw that there was no other small boat there, except one, and that Jesus had not entered with His disciples into the boat, but *that* His disciples had gone away alone. 23 There came other small boats from Tiberias near to the place where they ate the bread after the Lord had given thanks. 24 So when the crowd saw that Jesus was not there, nor His disciples, they themselves got into the small boats, and came to Capernaum seeking Jesus. 25 When they found Him on the other side of

NLT

22 The next day the crowd that had stayed on the far shore saw that the disciples had taken the only boat, and they realized Jesus had not gone with them. 23 Several boats from Tiberias landed near the place where the Lord had blessed the bread and the people had eaten. 24 So when the crowd saw that neither Jesus nor his disciples were there, they got into the boats and went across to Capernaum to look for him. 25 They found him on the other side of the lake and asked, "Rabbi, when did you get here?"

the sea, they said to Him, "Rabbi, when did You get here?"

²⁶Jesus answered them and said, "Truly, truly, I say to you, you seek Me, not because you saw signs, but because you ate of the loaves and were filled. ²⁷Do not work for the food which perishes, but for the food which endures to eternal life, which the Son of Man will give to you, for on Him the Father, God, has set His seal." ²⁸Therefore they said to Him, "What shall we do, so that we may work the works of God?" ²⁹Jesus answered and said to them, "This is the work of God, that you believe in Him whom He has sent." ³⁰So they said to Him, "What then do You do for a sign, so that we may see, and believe You? What work do You perform? ³¹Our fathers ate the manna in the wilderness; as it is written, 'HE GAVE THEM BREAD OUT OF HEAVEN TO EAT.'" ³²Jesus then said to them, "Truly, truly, I say to you, it is not Moses who has given you the bread out of heaven, but it is My Father who gives you the true bread out of heaven. ³³For the bread of God is ᵃthat which comes down out of heaven, and gives life to the world." ³⁴Then they said to Him, "Lord, always give us this bread."

³⁵Jesus said to them, "I am the bread of life; he who comes to Me will not hunger, and he who believes in Me will never thirst. ³⁶But I said to you that you have seen Me, and yet do not believe. ³⁷All that the Father gives Me will come to Me, and the one who comes to Me I will certainly not cast out. ³⁸For I have come down from heaven, not to do My own will, but the will of Him who sent Me. ³⁹This is the will of Him who sent Me, that of all that He has given Me I lose nothing, but raise it up on the last day. ⁴⁰For this is the will of My Father, that everyone who beholds the Son and believes in Him will have eternal life, and I Myself will raise him up on the last day."

²⁶Jesus replied, "I tell you the truth, you want to be with me because I fed you, not because you understood the miraculous signs. ²⁷But don't be so concerned about perishable things like food. Spend your energy seeking the eternal life that the Son of Man* can give you. For God the Father has given me the seal of his approval."

²⁸They replied, "We want to perform God's works, too. What should we do?"

²⁹Jesus told them, "This is the only work God wants from you: Believe in the one he has sent."

³⁰They answered, "Show us a miraculous sign if you want us to believe in you. What can you do? ³¹After all, our ancestors ate manna while they journeyed through the wilderness! The Scriptures say, 'Moses gave them bread from heaven to eat.'*"

³²Jesus said, "I tell you the truth, Moses didn't give you bread from heaven. My Father did. And now he offers you the true bread from heaven. ³³The true bread of God is the one who comes down from heaven and gives life to the world."

³⁴"Sir," they said, "give us that bread every day."

³⁵Jesus replied, "I am the bread of life. Whoever comes to me will never be hungry again. Whoever believes in me will never be thirsty. ³⁶But you haven't believed in me even though you have seen me. ³⁷However, those the Father has given me will come to me, and I will never reject them. ³⁸For I have come down from heaven to do the will of God who sent me, not to do my own will. ³⁹And this is the will of God, that I should not lose even one of all those he has given me, but that I should raise them up at the last day. ⁴⁰For it is my Father's will that all who see his Son and believe in him should have eternal life. I will raise them up at the last day."

41 Therefore the Jews were grumbling about Him, because He said, "I am the bread that came down out of heaven." 42 They were saying, "Is not this Jesus, the son of Joseph, whose father and mother we know? How does He now say, 'I have come down out of heaven'?" 43 Jesus answered and said to them, "Do not grumble among yourselves. 44 No one can come to Me unless the Father who sent Me draws him; and I will raise him up on the last day. 45 It is written in the prophets, 'AND THEY SHALL ALL BE TAUGHT OF GOD.' Everyone who has heard and learned from the Father, comes to Me. 46 Not that anyone has seen the Father, except the One who is from God; He has seen the Father. 47 Truly, truly, I say to you, he who believes has eternal life. 48 I am the bread of life. 49 Your fathers ate the manna in the wilderness, and they died. 50 This is the bread which comes down out of heaven, so that one may eat of it and not die. 51 I am the living bread that came down out of heaven; if anyone eats of this bread, he will live forever; and the bread also which I will give for the life of the world is My flesh."

52 Then the Jews *began* to argue with one another, saying, "How can this man give us *His* flesh to eat?" 53 So Jesus said to them, "Truly, truly, I say to you, unless you eat the flesh of the Son of Man and drink His blood, you have no life in yourselves. 54 He who eats My flesh and drinks My blood has eternal life, and I will raise him up on the last day. 55 For My flesh is true food, and My blood is true drink. 56 He who eats My flesh and drinks My blood abides in Me, and I in him. 57 As the living Father sent Me, and I live because of the Father, so he who eats Me, he also will live because of Me. 58 This is the bread which came down out

41 Then the people* began to murmur in disagreement because he had said, "I am the bread that came down from heaven." 42 They said, "Isn't this Jesus, the son of Joseph? We know his father and mother. How can he say, 'I came down from heaven'?"

43 But Jesus replied, "Stop complaining about what I said. 44 For no one can come to me unless the Father who sent me draws them to me, and at the last day I will raise them up. 45 As it is written in the Scriptures,* 'They will all be taught by God.' Everyone who listens to the Father and learns from him comes to me. 46 (Not that anyone has ever seen the Father; only I, who was sent from God, have seen him.)

47 "I tell you the truth, anyone who believes has eternal life. 48 Yes, I am the bread of life! 49 Your ancestors ate manna in the wilderness, but they all died. 50 Anyone who eats the bread from heaven, however, will never die. 51 I am the living bread that came down from heaven. Anyone who eats this bread will live forever; and this bread, which I will offer so the world may live, is my flesh."

52 Then the people began arguing with each other about what he meant. "How can this man give us his flesh to eat?" they asked.

53 So Jesus said again, "I tell you the truth, unless you eat the flesh of the Son of Man and drink his blood, you cannot have eternal life within you. 54 But anyone who eats my flesh and drinks my blood has eternal life, and I will raise that person at the last day. 55 For my flesh is true food, and my blood is true drink. 56 Anyone who eats my flesh and drinks my blood remains in me, and I in him. 57 I live because of the living Father who sent me; in the same way, anyone who feeds on me will live because of me. 58 I am the true bread that came down from heaven. Anyone who eats

of heaven; not as the fathers ate and died; he who eats this bread will live forever."

⁵⁹These things He said in the synagogue as He taught in Capernaum.

⁶⁰Therefore many of His disciples, when they heard *this* said, "This is a difficult statement; who can listen to it?" ⁶¹But Jesus, conscious that His disciples grumbled at this, said to them, "Does this cause you to stumble? ⁶²*What* then if you see the Son of Man ascending to where He was before? ⁶³It is the Spirit who gives life; the flesh profits nothing; the words that I have spoken to you are spirit and are life. ⁶⁴But there are some of you who do not believe." For Jesus knew from the beginning who they were who did not believe, and who it was that would ªbetray Him. ⁶⁵And He was saying, "For this reason I have said to you, that no one can come to Me unless it has been granted him from the Father."

⁶⁶As a result of this many of His disciples withdrew and were not walking with Him anymore. ⁶⁷So Jesus said to the twelve, "You do not want to go away also, do you?" ⁶⁸Simon Peter answered Him, "Lord, to whom shall we go? You have words of eternal life. ⁶⁹We have believed and have come to know that You are the Holy One of God." ⁷⁰Jesus answered them, "Did I Myself not choose you, the twelve, and *yet* one of you is a devil?" ⁷¹Now He meant Judas *the son* of Simon Iscariot, for he, one of the twelve, ªwas going to betray Him.

6:33 ªOr *He who comes* 6:64 ªOr *hand Him over*
6:71 ªOr *was intending to*

this bread will not die as your ancestors did (even though they ate the manna) but will live forever."

⁵⁹He said these things while he was teaching in the synagogue in Capernaum.

⁶⁰Many of his disciples said, "This is very hard to understand. How can anyone accept it?"

⁶¹Jesus was aware that his disciples were complaining, so he said to them, "Does this offend you? ⁶²Then what will you think if you see the Son of Man ascend to heaven again? ⁶³The Spirit alone gives eternal life. Human effort accomplishes nothing. And the very words I have spoken to you are spirit and life. ⁶⁴But some of you do not believe me." (For Jesus knew from the beginning which ones didn't believe, and he knew who would betray him.) ⁶⁵Then he said, "That is why I said that people can't come to me unless the Father gives them to me."

⁶⁶At this point many of his disciples turned away and deserted him. ⁶⁷Then Jesus turned to the Twelve and asked, "Are you also going to leave?" ⁶⁸Simon Peter replied, "Lord, to whom would we go? You have the words that give eternal life. ⁶⁹We believe, and we know you are the Holy One of God.*"

⁷⁰Then Jesus said, "I chose the twelve of you, but one is a devil." ⁷¹He was speaking of Judas, son of Simon Iscariot, one of the Twelve, who would later betray him.

6:27 "Son of Man" is a title Jesus used for himself.
6:31 Exod 16:4; Ps 78:24. 6:41 Greek *Jewish people;* also in 6:52. 6:45 Greek *in the prophets.* Isa 54:13. 6:69 Other manuscripts read *you are the Christ, the Holy One of God;* still others read *you are the Christ, the Son of God;* and still others read *you are the Christ, the Son of the living God.*

Roughly twenty to twenty-five times each week, people are compelled to engage in a particular activity and they will sacrifice almost anything for the opportunity. For most, it is a top priority. Chances are, you have already done it once today and you will likely do it again before the end of another day. We do this activity alone, but prefer to share it with company. We include this activity in almost every festive occasion we plan and, sometimes, it *is* the festive occasion!

By now, you've probably guessed that I'm referring to *eating*. Not only do we depend on food for survival; we celebrate it as art, savor it as luxury, share it as communion, and even abuse it as therapy. I have never seen a travel brochure that didn't highlight the importance of what you would be eating and how often. Food is the primary subject of countless magazines, books, websites, and television shows. We even have entire channels—more than one!—dedicated to the preparation and consumption of nourishment, twenty-four hours each day, seven days each week, all year round.

Those of us who benefit from twenty-first century abundance cannot fully appreciate the perspective of people struggling to survive in first-century Galilee, Samaria, and Judea. Spending time in developing countries, where one's next meal is never guaranteed, would help us appreciate the significance of Jesus' miraculous provision of food in the wilderness. John emphasizes the fact that each person received as much as he or she desired, and that the provision of food exceeded their capacity to eat. Undoubtedly, for many of them this was the first time in a long time they had gone to bed on a full stomach. Finally, after so much suffering under the iron rule of Rome, after so much deprivation at the hands of unjust aristocrats, after so much corruption in the temple, God had sent a Savior. Jesus, the healer, the provider, the reformer, the King! Certainly, His arrival signaled the beginning of a revolution that would end poverty, restore justice, and usher the kingdom of God into another golden era. This was, after all, the promise of God (Deut. 30:9-10; Isa. 9:7; Jer. 29:14, 30:3, 18; 32:44; Ezek. 37:24-26). Finally, the Messiah had come and He brought with Him *abundance!* Perhaps as many as ten thousand men, women, and children wondered where the Christ would lead them next and how He would go about claiming His throne.

We cannot be too critical of that multitude in the wilderness. They woke up hungry the following morning, just like each of us will tomorrow. While most had returned to their homes, many searched the hill country on the northeastern shore of the Sea of Galilee for their new-found provider and leader. But they were disappointed to discover their meal ticket had departed.

— 6:22-25 —

Matthew and Mark tell us that the Lord sent the disciples ahead to Capernaum while He dispersed the crowd. The great majority of them left, perhaps for their homes, but a contingent remained behind seeking Jesus. They had seen the Twelve put out to sea without the Lord and no other boat remained, so they assumed He was still enjoying solitude in the surrounding hill country. Eventually, they realized He had left, so they boarded small boats that were moored nearby.

The boats had come from Tiberias, a city on the western shore of the Sea of Galilee, founded by Herod Antipas and named for Emperor Tiberius, the heir of Caesar Augustus' titles and power. Because it had been built on the site of Jewish burial grounds, religious Jews refused to live there, which left it open to Hellenized Jews and Herod's political allies.

The people either heard the Lord's instructions to the disciples or presumed He would go to Capernaum next. The synagogue there was a center of Jewish teaching for the region. The people were surprised to find Jesus so far from where He was last seen in so short a time, but their question suggests more than a desire to know when He had arrived or how. Based on Jesus' response, they wanted to know why He was there (and not, perhaps, where they thought He should be) and why He had deliberately eluded them.

Barry Beitzel

The Jewish synagogue fulfilled many of the same functions in the local community as the modern-day Christian church: worship, instruction, and fellowship. Jesus, as an exceptionally popular rabbi, taught at the synagogue in Capernaum. Today, this white limestone synagogue from the fourth century rests on the foundation of the black basalt synagogue Jesus knew in His day.

— 6:26-27 —

Jesus responded to the spokesmen of the multitude with an indict-ment, one resonating with the words of Moses (Deut. 8:2-3). God's cov-enant people wandered the desert because they failed to trust Him. They shrank back from the Promised Land because the physical chal-lenges loomed like giants before them. During their forty years in the wilderness, the Lord sustained them with manna, "bread from heaven" (Exod. 16:4; Ps. 105:40), while teaching them that true sustenance is the Word of God. Where the Israelites failed, Jesus triumphed (Matt. 4:4), and He deeply desired them to learn from His victory.

Jesus contrasted physical food, which is the result of work and per-ishes quickly, with spiritual food, which comes by grace and lasts for-ever. Both are necessary, for they fulfill two legitimate human needs; life cannot continue without either. However, our fallen, fleshly nature craves one to the exclusion of the other. The distinction between "food which perishes" and "food which endures to eternal life" is, of course, symbolic. Physical food represents any and all things that satisfy le-gitimate bodily desires: nourishment, clothing, shelter, medicine, sex, exercise, rest. Spiritual food, on the other hand, represents the need of the human soul to be sustained by its Maker.

Jesus challenged the crowd to stop working for food that perishes and to devote equal passion to fulfilling the hunger of their souls. He said, in effect, "Just as God physically sustained the Hebrews in the wilderness and called them to be filled with His Word, so I met your physical need yesterday and now call you to receive spiritual nourish-ment." Note the irony of the Lord's invitation: "*Work* . . . for food which endures to eternal life, which the Son of Man will *give* to you." This paradox echoes the invitation of God in Isa. 55:1: "Come, buy wine and milk without money and without cost."

— 6:28-29 —

These people's first response to Jesus' offer of grace is especially amus-ing in Greek. My translation and emphasis mimics the structure of the Greek sentence: "What shall we *do* to *work* the *works* of God?" They completely missed His point. They ignored "give" and pounced on "work."

They were so consumed by physical concerns they couldn't compre-hend Jesus' figurative language. John uses this breakdown in communi-cation to illustrate the nature of spiritual blindness, which is caused by one's stubborn fixation on physical, earthly matters. When the world

Signs of Our Times

JOHN 6:28-29

When I lived in California, a friend of mine illustrated the absurdity of human nature by taking me on a hair-raising ride.

I lived in a city that was then encircled and crisscrossed by freeways still under construction. Sometimes, while riding bumper-to-bumper along a narrow asphalt road, I was tempted to slip onto one of those unfinished superhighways, but I restrained myself. One day, I sat in the passenger seat while a friend of mine drove. He turned to me and said, "Chuck, I want to show you something you're not going to believe." Then he turned off the road, down a little ditch, and onto this pristine yet-to-be-opened highway.

Despite my protests, he mashed the accelerator and off we went at seventy miles an hour down this new freeway. Soon a big sign came into view: "Construction Traffic Only." I grew tense, but he kept going. Then another sign: "Danger." My heart started pumping faster. Then another: "Bridge Under Construction," highlighted with giant flashing arrows. By now, I barely noticed my white-knuckle grip on the door handle; meanwhile, my friend never slowed down.

Finally, he screeched to a halt. As we got out of the car, I silently gave thanks and followed him past a set of wooden barricades. We stood at the end of a half-completed overpass, a precipice that would have launched us into a chasm of debris a hundred feet below.

My friend pointed in one direction and said, "You see that litter over there?" I nodded. "That's where a car landed night before last. Two people were killed right there." He pointed to another spot. "You see that right there? Two more people on a motorcycle. Both killed."

In the passing of a few days, two people drove down that highway, ignored all the signs, disregarded the barricade, and plunged to their deaths, taking two others with them. It's unlikely both committed suicide. They did with their vehicles what many do in life: They failed to heed obvious warnings and then paid an awful price.

The Old Testament sage is correct: "There is a way which seems right to a man, but its end is the way of death" (Prov. 14:12).

fell into darkness, it ceased to comprehend the light (John 1:5). Those who choose to serve the fallen world system become increasingly self-absorbed, proud, shortsighted, and unable to look up long enough to comprehend such things as spiritual hunger and God's grace. As the conversation continues, the tension between Jesus' figurative language and the spokesmen's literal interpretation strains to the point of breaking. They are proven to be absurdly obtuse.

Jesus extended His earlier paradox. The only "work" required is belief in the Son, which involves no work at all.

— 6:30-33 —

On the surface, this demand for a "sign" is a bizarre shift in attitude from the day before when these same people had exclaimed, "This is truly the Prophet who is to come into the world" (6:14). But it's really an extension of their earlier perspective. Note their emphasis on "do" and "work." Note also their requirement for belief: "so that we may see, and believe." Their "belief" in the wilderness was no less temporal and earthbound than their hunger. No sooner had the image of Jesus' "sign" faded from their corneas than the need to see again returned. Ironically, they cited the provision of manna through Moses as precedent for their request!

Jesus responded with a double *amēn* [281] to place emphasis on the statement to follow. He then corrected their faulty memory of Hebrew history. Moses did not provide anything; God provided the manna. The plural pronoun "you (all)" links the identity of his listeners with that of their "fathers," the ancient Hebrews who received the manna and still failed to trust their God. Jesus again associated the provision of manna with God's grace, the greater portion of which was the provision of His Word (Deut. 8:2-3). This is also an allusion to the Father's provision of His Word in human flesh, the Son of God Himself.

— 6:34-35 —

The people's request is similar to that of the Samaritan woman by the well. When offered living water that permanently quenches thirst, she replied, "Give me this water, so I will not be thirsty nor come all the way here to draw" (John 4:15). While her response was coy, she nonetheless comprehended Jesus' spiritual language. By contrast, the inclusion of "always" in the response here suggests that these people did not. Therefore, Jesus made Himself unmistakably clear. In a single sentence, He linked the concepts of belief, bread, eternal life, and Himself.

— 6:36-40 —

The people said earlier that, for them, seeing is believing (6:30). After they had been given a sign, they asked for a sign. Having seen Jesus, they refused to believe. Jesus rebuked them for their unbelief and then presented a different perspective on the relationship between "signs" and belief.

These people claimed that a miraculous sign would give them the ability to believe. According to Jesus, faith responds to God when He reveals Himself. The presence of God, then, becomes a sort of litmus test. Those who are His respond in belief and are attracted to Him, while those who are not respond in disbelief and reject Him. Jesus, who is God in human flesh, came to earth to gather His own, who can be identified by their belief in Him.

— 6:41-42 —

The "grumbling" of the disbelieving Jews resembled the grumbling of their ancestors in the wilderness. They complained about having no food, so the Lord provided bread from heaven. Then they complained about having only manna, so the Lord provided quail (Exod. 16). The manna was both His provision of grace and a test (Exod. 16:4; Deut. 8:16). How they received the manna and whether they followed the Lord's instructions revealed the genuineness of their faith.

While Jesus was speaking of His miraculous conception and natural birth—the means by which God became flesh—these people did not accept the truth of His coming from heaven. Jesus' family had probably visited Capernaum often. What is more, His brothers apparently made the city their home (John 2:12). These people had seen Jesus during His boyhood and thought they knew all about His roots. To them the phrase "came down out of heaven" suggested that something suddenly and mysteriously materialized out of thin air, which clearly hadn't happened.

— 6:43-51 —

"Eating" is the image He used to illustrate a spiritual truth: people must appropriate His sacrifice through belief. As "the Lamb of God who takes away the sin of the world" (1:29), He would become the sacrifice of atonement, which would pay the penalty of sin on behalf of the whole world. However, only those who believe in Him, receive this gift, and then apply it to their sins will benefit.

This truth was illustrated in the first Passover. The Israelites had been instructed to sacrifice a lamb on behalf of the whole household, apply its blood to the doorposts and lintel of the house, prepare the meat for consumption, and remain inside as the death angel descended upon Egypt. Those who did not apply the blood mourned the death of their firstborn sons. Those who appropriated this symbol of atonement to their homes were spared. As they ate the flesh of the paschal lamb, the death angel passed over their homes (Exod. 12:3-49).

At some point in His ministry, Jesus began teaching through parables—symbolic stories using familiar images to teach spiritual truths. He explained to His disciples the reason for this change: "I speak to them in parables; because while seeing they do not see, and while hearing they do not hear, nor do they understand" (Matt. 13:13). Parables allowed the observer to see what his or her heart chose to see, which was guided by his or her belief in Jesus.

Sometimes preachers are guilty of overextending their illustrations. If a speaker is not careful, he or she can allow a metaphor to take over the lesson and unintentionally teach error. This is not the case with Jesus, however. He intentionally pressed his metaphor to extremes to achieve two objectives. First, He left any reasonable person without excuse for adopting a physical interpretation of His teaching. How absurd to think He had cannibalism in mind! Second, He winnowed the wheat from the chaff, allowing the nonbelievers' own bias to carry them away with the wind.

— 6:52 —

This is the sound of chaff: "How can this man give us His flesh to eat?"

— 6:53-58 —

Jesus didn't try to clarify their misconceptions. Their problem was not intellectual. Instead, He intensified their confusion. However, there was no danger of losing genuine believers. Despite His cryptic language and difficult teaching, He reassured authentic followers for a third time in His speech, "I will raise him up on the last day" (6:39-40, 44, 54).

— 6:59-65 —

By this time in His ministry, Jesus' disciples numbered in the tens of thousands with varying degrees of devotion. At least hundreds were serious enough to consider Him their rabbi and would have actively supported a movement to make Him king. But Jesus knew theirs was the kind of fickle devotion that sprouts quickly and withers suddenly in the heat. The fickle disciples described Jesus' teaching as *sklēros* [4642], which literally means "dry," "hard," or "rough." Figuratively, the term describes something or someone as "unyielding" or "not received without discomfort." Distressing news or challenging concepts would be called "hard." Jesus' teaching wasn't difficult to *understand*, just difficult to *accept*.

Jesus perceived the men's difficulty and asked if the teaching had, literally, "trapped them in." The Greek term is *skandalizō* [4624].[6] The original and most literal meaning is "to spring back and forth" or "to slam closed," as with a spring-loaded animal trap. Therefore, the verb generally means "to close something in." The figurative use of this word is rare outside of Jewish and Christian writings, but not altogether absent. One Greek playwright describes an unjust accuser dragging innocent men into court and "laying traps" with his questions.[7] Paul frequently used the term to describe Jesus as an intellectual and moral trap for any who oppose God and think themselves righteous (Rom. 9:33; 11:9; 1 Cor. 1:23; Gal. 5:11).

Jesus challenged the grumblers with a question. In effect, He asked, "You find yourself unable to accept my claims that I came down from heaven and that you must eat my flesh and drink my blood, so what will you think when I tell you that I will ascend to heaven?" To put it another way, "If this teaching is impossible for you to accept, you have no capacity to understand anything else I have to say."

Jesus then reiterated His earlier statement, "No one can come to Me unless the Father who sent Me draws him" (John 6:44). What God has to teach is so utterly contrary to the sinful, selfish sensibilities of humanity that no one can understand divine teaching without divine help. The people interpreted the words of Jesus literally because they lacked the spiritual wisdom God gives those who commune with Him. What is more, people are so entangled in their sinful ignorance that no one can escape unless God draws them toward Himself.

— 6:66-69 —

According to the other Gospels, Jesus made Capernaum His temporary home (Matt. 4:13-16; Mark 2:1), where multitudes sought Him for healing and instruction (Mark 1:28-29; 2:2, 13). It is likely that Jesus' teaching in Capernaum took place over a period of time through repeated discourses and extended dialogue. As a result of His teaching, many of his "disciples," which included multitudes of followers besides the "twelve," stopped following Him. Jesus already knew the answer to His own question; He challenged the "twelve" in order to reinforce His teaching on the true nature of salvation.

When the Twelve were asked if they, too, would stop following Him, Peter spoke for the group. He answered with a question that revealed his motivation for staying: "To whom shall we go?" The implied answer is, "To no one, for Jesus is our only option." His guileless response distinguishes him from the nonbelieving defectors. Whereas they thought they understood Jesus and rejected Him, Peter believed in Jesus while admitting He didn't completely understand His teaching. His qualification, "You have words of eternal life," merely parroted the Lord's (John 6:63). The nature of salvation and belief is not merely an intellectual problem; it's primarily volitional. The men wanted to see and then believe (6:30); the disciples believed and eventually began to see (14:16-19; 17:24; 20:29).

— 6:70-71 —

Jesus used this interchange to highlight another truth. From Peter's perspective, the Twelve chose to believe and follow Christ. Jesus didn't reject Peter's claim; He merely topped it: "I chose you." However, not all was as it appeared. One commentary paraphrased Jesus' closing remark this way: "Well said, Simon-Barjonas, but that 'we' embraces not so wide a circle as in the simplicity of thine heart thou thinkest; for though I have chosen you but twelve, one even of these is a 'devil.'"[8]

At least in this case, the "choosing" of Christ does not refer to salvation, but to His call, "follow me." Not all who are called and who appear to believe have been "chosen" in the sense of salvation (Matt. 22:14).

• • •

Most people admit to wanting a savior; however, just what kind of savior they desire depends upon what kind of crisis they hope to escape. People struggling with loneliness want a companion. People suffering an identity crisis want someone to give them meaning. The hungry want a provider; the oppressed want a champion; the discontented, a revolutionary; the hopeless, an inspiration. The proud? Why, they need no savior at all!

The multitude in the wilderness thought they needed a savior to bring them into a land flowing with milk and honey, someone to fill their bellies and rout their enemies. One day, Jesus will be that kind of savior. The Old Testament promises of physical abundance and a kingdom ruled by the Messiah will be fulfilled. Israel will indeed have its golden age, but not until the Savior has finished meeting the most crucial need of all: the need for salvation from the crisis of sin. Yet only those who recognize their need will seek the Son of God.

APPLICATION: JOHN 6:22-71

Three Responses to the Call of Truth

The term "gospel" comes from the Old English word "*gōdspel*," where *gōd* is "good" and *spel* means "story." The gospel is indeed a good story; however, this goodness has a sharp edge to it. The narrowness of the gospel is difficult to accept; its exclusivity is offensive. Jesus said, "I am the way . . . no one comes to the Father but through Me" (John 14:6). And Jesus did nothing to soften His message, especially among the Jews. To an audience that took great care to remove blood from any meat they consumed, He said, "Truly, truly, I say to you, unless you eat the flesh of the Son of Man and drink His blood, you have no life in yourselves" (6:53). It would seem that Jesus deliberately made the gospel difficult to accept rather than easy . . . something today's "seeker friendly" approach would find strange.

The purpose of the gospel message is not to convince detractors or to turn the hearts of rebels; that's the role of the Holy Spirit. The gospel message is the means by which prepared hearts respond to their Creator. The good news is the call of God; belief is the response of "His own" (see 5:25; 10:14). This truth is illustrated well in the events after the feeding of the multitude. As Jesus proclaimed the gospel, presenting Himself as the sole means of salvation, we see three responses on the part of His audience.

1. Open Defection (6:66)

Many years ago, I cultivated a close friendship with a brilliant medical doctor. He had earned more than one PhD and an MD and had spent many years in training, including an internship at the Mayo Clinic. To say he was smart would be a gross understatement.

For a long time, we enjoyed talking about life, work, family—anything and everything. I really liked the man and I wanted to share with him the most important decision of my own life, but I waited for a natural opening. One day it came. He asked me where I stood on this or that, which quickly led to the gospel. I took a napkin and drew a man on one side of a great chasm and God on the other. I labeled the gap "sin," and explained how our sinfulness separates us from God. Then I drew a cross bridging the vast gap, and explained how the sacrifice of God's Son allows us to come to the Father. When I finished perhaps the clearest explanation of the good news I think I have ever given, my friend picked up the napkin, turned it over, and said, "In a million years, I could *never* believe that." Many will reject the gospel openly and permanently. No amount of explaining or pleading will change anything.

2. Firm Determination (6:67-69)

While Peter is often the most criticized of the disciples, his response to Jesus' "hard teaching" illustrates genuine belief. He didn't pretend to understand everything Jesus taught, yet he tenaciously held on to his Master. He said, in effect, "Lord, we have no other options; You have the words of eternal life, even if we can't understand them fully." He got the order right: belief first, understanding later.

Belief like that is supernatural and it will persevere until the end of days. Don't wait for every question to be answered. Don't delay trusting in Christ because you cannot resolve every theological conundrum. God has called you to belief; respond in faith. In time, He will unravel mysteries as you walk through life with Him. And when you stand in His presence in eternity, all will be made clear.

3. Subtle Deception (6:70-71)

The third response unnerves me. Judas illustrates this type of response. He numbered himself among the faithful, he said and did everything necessary to appear genuine, and he even risked his life with the other disciples, yet Judas never truly believed. He fooled others and perhaps even himself, but his subtle deception eventually resulted in tragedy.

Not every pretend believer is a Judas. Many are well-meaning churchgoers who behave like their Christian peers, motivated by any number of reasons, none of which is authentic faith. Sadly, they will one day stand before the Savior to hear a rebuke instead of a welcome (Matt. 7:21-23). They expect to be rewarded for their good service, but we are saved by grace, not by works (Eph. 2:8-9).

Seeing how Jesus presented the gospel and how each individual responded according to the leaning of his or her heart gives me great comfort when I share the gospel. I used to worry that if my presentation wasn't clear and compelling, a soul might be lost . . . because of my failure. What unbelievable pressure for a mere man! Fortunately, this is not the case. Another person's soul is not yours or mine to win or lose. We have been charged with the responsibility to tell the "good story" as best we can; an individual's response is a private matter with God. Only the two of them know for sure whether it is authentic or mere pretense.

Jesus in the Lions' Den
JOHN 7:1-52

NASB

[1] After these things Jesus was walking in Galilee, for He was unwilling to walk in Judea because the Jews were seeking to kill Him. [2] Now the feast of the Jews, the Feast of Booths, was near. [3] Therefore His brothers said to Him, "Leave here and go into Judea, so that Your disciples also may see Your works which You are doing. [4] For no one does anything in secret [a]when he himself seeks to be *known* publicly. If You do these things, show Yourself to the world." [5] For not even His brothers were believing in Him. [6] So Jesus said to them, "My time is not yet here, but your time is always opportune. [7] The world cannot hate you, but it hates Me because I testify of it, that its deeds are evil. [8] Go up to the feast yourselves; I do not go up to this feast because My time has not yet fully come." [9] Having said these things to them, He stayed in Galilee.

[10] But when His brothers had gone up to the feast, then He Himself also went up, not publicly, but as if, in secret. [11] So the Jews were seeking Him at the feast and were saying, "Where is He?" [12] There was much grumbling among the crowds concerning Him; some were saying, "He is a good man"; others were saying, "No, on the contrary, He leads the people astray." [13] Yet no one was speaking openly of Him for fear of the Jews.

[14] But when it was now the midst of the feast Jesus went up into the temple, and *began to* teach. [15] The Jews then were astonished, saying, "How has this man become learned, having never been educated?" [16] So Jesus answered them and said, "My teaching is not Mine, but His who sent Me. [17] If anyone is willing to do His will, he will know of the

NLT

[1] After this, Jesus traveled around Galilee. He wanted to stay out of Judea, where the Jewish leaders were plotting his death. [2] But soon it was time for the Jewish Festival of Shelters, [3] and Jesus' brothers said to him, "Leave here and go to Judea, where your followers can see your miracles! [4] You can't become famous if you hide like this! If you can do such wonderful things, show yourself to the world!" [5] For even his brothers didn't believe in him.

[6] Jesus replied, "Now is not the right time for me to go, but you can go anytime. [7] The world can't hate you, but it does hate me because I accuse it of doing evil. [8] You go on. I'm not going* to this festival, because my time has not yet come." [9] After saying these things, Jesus remained in Galilee.

[10] But after his brothers left for the festival, Jesus also went, though secretly, staying out of public view. [11] The Jewish leaders tried to find him at the festival and kept asking if anyone had seen him. [12] There was a lot of grumbling about him among the crowds. Some argued, "He's a good man," but others said, "He's nothing but a fraud who deceives the people." [13] But no one had the courage to speak favorably about him in public, for they were afraid of getting in trouble with the Jewish leaders.

[14] Then, midway through the festival, Jesus went up to the Temple and began to teach. [15] The people* were surprised when they heard him. "How does he know so much when he hasn't been trained?" they asked.

[16] So Jesus told them, "My message is not my own; it comes from God who sent me. [17] Anyone who wants to do the will of God will know whether

NASB

teaching, whether it is of God or *whether* I speak from Myself. ¹⁸ He who speaks from himself seeks his own glory; but He who is seeking the glory of the One who sent Him, He is true, and there is no unrighteousness in Him.

¹⁹ "Did not Moses give you the Law, and *yet* none of you carries out the Law? Why do you seek to kill Me?" ²⁰ The crowd answered, "You have a demon! Who seeks to kill You?" ²¹ Jesus answered them, "I did one ᵃdeed, and you all marvel. ²² For this reason Moses has given you circumcision (not because it is from Moses, but from the fathers), and on *the* Sabbath you circumcise a man. ²³ If a man receives circumcision on *the* Sabbath so that the Law of Moses will not be broken, are you angry with Me because I made an entire man well on *the* Sabbath? ²⁴ Do not judge according to appearance, but ᵃjudge with righteous judgment."

²⁵ So some of the people of Jerusalem were saying, "Is this not the man whom they are seeking to kill? ²⁶ Look, He is speaking publicly, and they are saying nothing to Him. The rulers do not really know that this is ᵃthe Christ, do they? ²⁷ However, we know where this man is from; but whenever the Christ may come, no one knows where He is from." ²⁸ Then Jesus cried out in the temple, teaching and saying, "You both know Me and know where I am from; and I have not come of Myself, but He who sent Me is true, whom you do not know. ²⁹ I know Him, because I am from Him, and He sent Me." ³⁰ So they were seeking to seize Him; and no man laid his hand on Him, because His hour had not yet come. ³¹ But many of the crowd believed in Him; and they were saying, "When

NLT

my teaching is from God or is merely my own. ¹⁸ Those who speak for themselves want glory only for themselves, but a person who seeks to honor the one who sent him speaks truth, not lies. ¹⁹ Moses gave you the law, but none of you obeys it! In fact, you are trying to kill me."

²⁰ The crowd replied, "You're demon possessed! Who's trying to kill you?"

²¹ Jesus replied, "I did one miracle on the Sabbath, and you were amazed. ²² But you work on the Sabbath, too, when you obey Moses' law of circumcision. (Actually, this tradition of circumcision began with the patriarchs, long before the law of Moses.) ²³ For if the correct time for circumcising your son falls on the Sabbath, you go ahead and do it so as not to break the law of Moses. So why should you be angry with me for healing a man on the Sabbath? ²⁴ Look beneath the surface so you can judge correctly."

²⁵ Some of the people who lived in Jerusalem started to ask each other, "Isn't this the man they are trying to kill? ²⁶ But here he is, speaking in public, and they say nothing to him. Could our leaders possibly believe that he is the Messiah? ²⁷ But how could he be? For we know where this man comes from. When the Messiah comes, he will simply appear; no one will know where he comes from."

²⁸ While Jesus was teaching in the Temple, he called out, "Yes, you know me, and you know where I come from. But I'm not here on my own. The one who sent me is true, and you don't know him. ²⁹ But I know him because I come from him, and he sent me to you." ³⁰ Then the leaders tried to arrest him; but no one laid a hand on him, because his time* had not yet come.

³¹ Many among the crowds at the Temple believed in him. "After all,"

[a]the Christ comes, He will not perform more [b]signs than those which this man has, will He?"

³²The Pharisees heard the crowd muttering these things about Him, and the chief priests and the Pharisees sent officers to seize Him. ³³Therefore Jesus said, "For a little while longer I am with you, then I go to Him who sent Me. ³⁴You will seek Me, and will not find Me; and where I am, you cannot come." ³⁵The Jews then said to one another, "Where does this man intend to go that we will not find Him? He is not intending to go to the Dispersion among the Greeks, and teach the Greeks, is He? ³⁶What is this statement that He said, 'You will seek Me, and will not find Me; and where I am, you cannot come'?"

³⁷Now on the last day, the great *day* of the feast, Jesus stood and cried out, saying, "[a]If anyone is thirsty, [b]let him come to Me and drink. ³⁸He who believes in Me, as the Scripture said, 'From [a]his innermost being will flow rivers of living water.'" ³⁹But this He spoke of the Spirit, whom those who believed in Him were to receive; for the Spirit was not yet *given*, because Jesus was not yet glorified.

⁴⁰*Some* of the people therefore, when they heard these words, were saying, "This certainly is the Prophet." ⁴¹Others were saying, "This is [a]the Christ." Still others were saying, "Surely [a]the Christ is not going to come from Galilee, is He? ⁴²Has not the Scripture said that the Christ comes from the descendants of David, and from Bethlehem, the village where David was?" ⁴³So a division occurred in the crowd because of Him. ⁴⁴Some of them wanted to seize Him, but no one laid hands on Him.

⁴⁵The officers then came to the chief priests and Pharisees, and they said, "would you expect the Messiah to do more miraculous signs than this man has done?"

³²When the Pharisees heard that the crowds were whispering such things, they and the leading priests sent Temple guards to arrest Jesus. ³³But Jesus told them, "I will be with you only a little longer. Then I will return to the one who sent me. ³⁴You will search for me but not find me. And you cannot go where I am going."

³⁵The Jewish leaders were puzzled by this statement. "Where is he planning to go?" they asked. "Is he thinking of leaving the country and going to the Jews in other lands?* Maybe he will even teach the Greeks! ³⁶What does he mean when he says, 'You will search for me but not find me,' and 'You cannot go where I am going'?"

³⁷On the last day, the climax of the festival, Jesus stood and shouted to the crowds, "Anyone who is thirsty may come to me! ³⁸Anyone who believes in me may come and drink! For the Scriptures declare, 'Rivers of living water will flow from his heart.'"* ³⁹(When he said "living water," he was speaking of the Spirit, who would be given to everyone believing in him. But the Spirit had not yet been given,* because Jesus had not yet entered into his glory.)

⁴⁰When the crowds heard him say this, some of them declared, "Surely this man is the Prophet we've been expecting."* ⁴¹Others said, "He is the Messiah." Still others said, "But he can't be! Will the Messiah come from Galilee? ⁴²For the Scriptures clearly state that the Messiah will be born of the royal line of David, in Bethlehem, the village where King David was born."* ⁴³So the crowd was divided about him. ⁴⁴Some even wanted him arrested, but no one laid a hand on him.

⁴⁵When the Temple guards returned without having arrested

NASB

said to them, "Why did you not bring Him?" ⁴⁶ The officers answered, "Never has a man spoken the way this man speaks." ⁴⁷ The Pharisees then answered them, "You have not also been led astray, have you? ⁴⁸ No one of the rulers or Pharisees has believed in Him, has he? ⁴⁹ But this crowd which does not know the Law is accursed." ⁵⁰ Nicodemus (he who came to Him before, being one of them) said to them, ⁵¹ "Our Law does not judge a man unless it first hears from him and knows what he is doing, does it?" ⁵² They answered him, "You are not also from Galilee, are you? Search, and see that no prophet arises out of Galilee."

7:4 ªLit *and*   7:21 ªOr *work*   7:24 ªLit *judge the righteous judgment*   7:26 ªI.e. the Messiah   7:31 ªI.e. the Messiah   ᵇOr *attesting miracles*   7:37 ªVv 37-38 may also be read: *If anyone is thirsty,...let him come..., he who believes in me as...*   ᵇOr *let him keep coming to Me and let him keep drinking*   7:38 ªLit *out of his belly*   7:41 ªI.e. the Messiah

NLT

Jesus, the leading priests and Pharisees demanded, "Why didn't you bring him in?"

⁴⁶ "We have never heard anyone speak like this!" the guards responded.

⁴⁷ "Have you been led astray, too?" the Pharisees mocked. ⁴⁸ "Is there a single one of us rulers or Pharisees who believes in him? ⁴⁹ This foolish crowd follows him, but they are ignorant of the law. God's curse is on them!"

⁵⁰ Then Nicodemus, the leader who had met with Jesus earlier, spoke up. ⁵¹ "Is it legal to convict a man before he is given a hearing?" he asked.

⁵² They replied, "Are you from Galilee, too? Search the Scriptures and see for yourself—no prophet ever comes* from Galilee!"

7:8 Some manuscripts read *not yet going.*   7:15 Greek *Jewish people.*   7:30 Greek *his hour.*   7:35 Or *the Jews who live among the Greeks?*   7:37-38 Or *"Let anyone who is thirsty come to me and drink.* ³⁸*For the Scriptures declare, 'Rivers of living water will flow from the heart of anyone who believes in me.'"*   7:39 Several early manuscripts read *But as yet there was no Spirit.* Still others read *But as yet there was no Holy Spirit.*   7:40 See Deut 18:15, 18; Mal 4:5-6.   7:42 See Mic 5:2.   7:52 Some manuscripts read *the prophet does not come.*

As a child, one of my favorite Bible stories was "Daniel in the Lions' Den." You may have heard this familiar story. An eighty-some-year-old prophet, a faithful man of integrity, had won the friendship of King Darius. But some other men grew jealous of the old man's trusted status and schemed to have him killed. Through a complex chain of events, Darius was forced to send Daniel to an almost certain death. He was to be cast into the lions' den, presumably to be eaten right away. After the aged prophet was pushed through the entrance, "a stone was brought and laid over the mouth of the den; and the king sealed it with his own signet ring and with the signet rings of his nobles, so that nothing would be changed in regard to Daniel" (Dan. 6:17).

I remember my Sunday school teacher had a good memory and a vivid imagination. I could see the hungry lions pacing and hear the echoes of their roaring in a cavernous stone dungeon. Then, before hearing the end of the story, I cringed as I imagined the frightened old man screaming as the lions tore him limb from limb. And I remember when, to my relief and surprise, the lions never touched him. Neither tooth nor claw so much as grazed his skin. The Lord had graciously delivered Daniel from the killer instinct of these wild beasts.

> Then the king arose at dawn, at the break of day, and went in haste to the lions' den. When he had come near the den to Daniel, he cried out with a troubled voice. The king spoke and said to Daniel, "Daniel, servant of the living God, has your God, whom you constantly serve, been able to deliver you from the lions?" Then Daniel spoke to the king, "O king, live forever! My God sent His angel and shut the lions' mouths and they have not harmed me, inasmuch as I was found innocent before Him; and also toward you, O king, I have committed no crime." (Dan. 6:19-22)

Once Daniel had been lifted unharmed from the lions' pit, the men who had orchestrated the scheme were made to suffer the sentence they had intended for Daniel. They fell into the open mouths of the lions and were crushed before they hit the floor.

Years later, I decided the story should be called "The Lions in Daniel's Den." Life is the Lord's to give or take, and there is no lion in all of creation that He cannot tame. Daniel's enemies may have thought they were in charge, but they were gravely mistaken.

The lions of Jesus' day did not prowl about on four feet. They stood tall and proud, robed in the resplendent vestments of man-made righteousness, empowered by a hypocritical religion. The temple authorities in Jerusalem desired the assassination of Jesus because He continually exposed their jealousy and greed. He healed, and He fulfilled prophecy, and He forgave sins, and He gave glory to the Father while keeping none for Himself. He was unlike any rabbi or any political leader anyone had ever seen. He threatened their power and they wanted Him dead. Jesus was about to enter the lions' den.

— 7:1-2 —

The events in Capernaum took place shortly before Passover (John 6:4) in March or April and the Feast of Booths (September/October) was approaching. For six months or more, Jesus had been ministering in Galilee, where His "hard" teaching in the synagogue had squelched any talk of making Him king. Even after that winnowing, though, multitudes continued to follow in Galilee. Meanwhile, a growing underground of messianic hopefuls kept Jerusalem on edge.

Zev Radovan/BibleLandPictures.com

In fulfillment of God's commandment (Lev. 23:34-44), Jewish families continued to celebrate a weeklong autumn harvest festival in temporary houses constructed for the occasion. These "tabernacles" or "tents" reminded God's covenant people of His protection in the wilderness as they celebrated His continued provision through the harvest of produce from the Promised Land. Today Jews continue observing this festival in the celebration of Sukkot.

— 7:3-5 —

The Jews celebrated three festivals that all males in Israel were required to attend (Exod. 23:17; 34:23): Passover, Pentecost, and Tabernacles ("Booths"). Each festival served to remind the Jewish people of something their forebears had learned about the Lord through a particular experience. The Feast of Tabernacles, held during harvest time, reminded the Hebrew people of their ancestors' exodus from Egypt, their wilderness wandering, and their "ingathering" into the Promised Land. This celebration held even more meaning after the Exile, and looked forward to the time the Messiah would gather all the descendants of Abraham in a revived Hebrew nation.

Jesus' brothers taunted Him, suggesting He should go to Jerusalem and perform some magic tricks in order to rally the world behind Him. They had certainly seen His miraculous "signs" and probably wanted to make Him king for selfish reasons. Their taunt suggested that if He were the genuine article, He wouldn't mind meeting their challenge.

— 7:6-9 —

Several times throughout John's narrative, Jesus speaks of His "hour" or His "time," which refers to the moment His glory would be revealed to the world. The means of His glory would be suffering, which most of His followers did not understand, even on the eve of His arrest and crucifixion. In every instance except this one, the term He used was *hōra* [5610], "hour." Here, however, the Greek term translated "time" is *kairos* [2540], "season." Secular Greek literature and the Greek translation of the Old Testament use this term to indicate a decisive moment in which one era gives way to another. For example, one might say, "When the South declared war, Lincoln's *moment* had arrived." He or she means to say, "From that *instant*, the bumpkin from Springfield would be transformed into a national treasure."

As in 6:26-71 and the parables, Jesus spoke in such a way as to be understood on two levels. A person's interpretation naturally followed his or her chosen understanding of who Jesus is, and He allowed each person to be carried away by his or her willful misconception. On the surface, Jesus appeared to answer His brothers at face value. They taunted Him with the suggestion that He should publicize His identity as the conquering Messiah-king Israel longed to see. In response, He spoke truthfully, saying in effect, "The deciding moment for me to announce myself has not yet come, but the present is always the right time for you to do so." He then stated the reason His brothers' testimony would be welcomed by a world dedicated to evil: they were part of it!

Of course, the deeper meaning of Jesus' words referred to His mission. The Feast of Tabernacles was a harvest celebration, to be enjoyed when the harvest was complete. Jesus had more work to do in Galilee before going up to Jerusalem (4:35-38).

Many manuscripts and translations include the word "yet" in Jesus' declaration, "I do not go up to this feast [yet] because . . . ," but the original most likely omits this particular "yet." Some have suggested that Jesus lied to His brothers, but He didn't. His statement doesn't preclude His going later, which was His intention all along. He simply didn't want to accompany His arrogant brothers, who would have used His attendance to advance their own agenda. Instead, Jesus would journey more discreetly with His disciples and then address the Judeans in the time and manner of His own choosing.

— 7:10-11 —

It is noteworthy that Jesus recognized the mortal danger presented by the temple officials. He was in constant danger of assassination in Judea. While the Messiah had come to sacrifice His life, He would not leave the timing and circumstances of His death in the hands of His enemies. He would dictate the terms of His execution to accomplish

His mission. As long as He remained hidden where no enemy could find Him or appeared in front of a crowd where the religious authorities dared not touch Him, Jesus could minister in Jerusalem. So, He entered the city without attracting attention, perhaps even blending in with the crowds. Meanwhile, a hushed anticipation stirred debate among the common people in Jerusalem. Some favored Jesus; others condemned Him. None affirmed His true identity as the Christ and the Son of God.

— 7:14-19 —

The Feast of Tabernacles is a weeklong celebration (Deut. 16:13-15). On the third or fourth day of the celebration, Jesus stood in the temple to teach, which was not unusual for a rabbi. However, the teacher's credibility depended heavily upon his educational pedigree. Who trained him? With which school is he associated? The school of Hillel? Of Shammai? Of John the Baptizer? The religious authorities (not the common Jews) were astonished. Not because He could read and write—most Jewish men could. Nor did they object to His having the hubris to teach without a degree. What they could not understand was how He could have been so knowledgeable without having been to seminary, as it were (Matt. 7:28-29; Mark 1:22).

Jesus responded with a stinging rebuke based on elementary logic. Those who are intimately knowledgeable with the ultimate source of truth (God), will have no trouble spotting other truth-tellers. Moreover, people who care about the truth do not care about credentials as long as the truth is taught. He then offered another standard by which to judge the qualifications of a teacher: his obedience to previously revealed truth, the Law.

This is an ironic turn. The religious officials were angry with Jesus and had rebuked Him for breaking with tradition, man-made rules they had substituted for the Law of Moses (Matt. 15:3, 7-9; Mark 7:8). With this statement, Jesus turned the tables. He accused them of seeking to kill Him despite their own violation of the Law.

— 7:20-24 —

In response to Jesus' rebuke of the religious officials, the multitude, which had been generally split despite their spiritual ignorance, rebuked the Lord as a demon-possessed man. To say someone "has a demon" could be taken literally or figuratively. In this case, it was the ancient equivalent of someone saying, "You're a raving, paranoid lunatic!" They obviously didn't know of the religious leaders' desire to have Him killed. After all, the temple authorities were God's official representatives, custodians of the Almighty's house.

Jesus ignored the insult and continued His indictment, referring to the healing of the invalid by the pool of Bethesda (John 5:18). The antecedent of the plural pronoun "them" is unclear. The content of His rebuke appears to have been directed against the religious officials rather than the "crowd." However, throughout the rest of the speech, He freely directs His rebukes to either and both, thus placing the crowd and the officials in the same category.

To continue His earlier argument (7:16-19), Jesus appealed to the specific precedent of Moses (the human author of divine Law), circumcision (their most treasured rite), and the Sabbath (the institution perverted by man-made tradition). Circumcision was to take place on the eighth day of life for every male born to Hebrew parents, regardless of the day. This meant that some part of the man-made Sabbath traditions would have to be broken. If the rite of circumcision could override the Sabbath rules, why wouldn't the miraculous, God-orchestrated healing of a desperately infirmed man? No later than AD 100, rabbinic Judaism came to this same conclusion:

> The Rabbis counted 248 parts to a man's body. In the Talmud (b. Yoma 85b) R. Eleazar ben Azariah (ca. A.D. 100) states: "If circumcision, which attaches to one only of the 248 members of the human body, suspends the Sabbath, how much more shall the saving of the whole body suspend the Sabbath?" So absolutely binding did rabbinic Judaism regard the command of Lev 12:3 to circumcise on the eighth day, that in the Mishnah m. Shabbat 18.3; 19.1, 2; and m. Nedarim 3.11 all hold that the command to circumcise overrides the command to observe the Sabbath.[9]

The "appearance" to which Jesus referred was the symbolic show of righteousness that was undoubtedly impressive in the temple. Jesus called for Jews to ignore fancy robes and big hats in order to discern who was telling the truth by comparing his or her deeds to the commands of Scripture. The deeds of Jesus reflected the grace of God and did not violate the Sabbath. The religious officials condemned this act of mercy because it violated their man-made rules, which they themselves violated each time they circumcised a newborn on the Sabbath.

— 7:25-31 —

The religious leaders were unable to do anything to squelch Jesus or to eliminate Him. To seize Him publicly would divide the crowd or perhaps incite them to riot. And they certainly couldn't defeat His reasoning. This paralysis left the common Jews wondering if the leaders were undecided about Jesus, or if perhaps their silence was tacit approval of Jesus as the Messiah.

Apparently, another tradition in Jewish theology (which is still common today) interpreted "suddenly" in Malachi 3:1 to mean the Messiah would appear mysteriously and perhaps magically (cf. John 6:41-42). Their complaint is ironic in view of John 9:29, where they complain, "We do not know where he is from." Nevertheless, many began to believe, although they found it difficult to overcome the traditional evidences of the Messiah they had come to expect.

— 7:32-36 —

Jesus again spoke in multiple layers. He predicted His ascension to the Father's side and declared that the religious leaders would not even see heaven. Their eternal fate was vastly different from that of the disciples (13:36; 14:4). But as John had illustrated with the multitude in Galilee (6:26-54), the spiritual blindness of the nonbelievers limited them to a strictly literal understanding. They wondered if He might leave Israel altogether in order to win converts among Jews dispersed throughout the Roman Empire.

— 7:37-39 —

One ritual observed each day of the Feast of Tabernacles involved a solemn procession in which a priest carried a goblet of water from the Pool of Siloam (which was fed by the Gihon Spring), through the water gate, and into the inner temple court. As the congregation sang a hymn based on Isaiah 12:3, the priest poured the water on the altar, commemorating the Lord's provision of water in the wilderness (Num. 20:8-11).

The Feast of Tabernacles built toward a climactic convocation (Lev. 23:36), during which Jesus stood to address the throngs of people in the temple. Perhaps just before or even during the priest's procession from the pool of Siloam, Jesus called all people to receive from Him "living water," not unlike his offer to the Samaritan woman (4:13-14). John's editorial comment clarifies for the reader that the "living water" is indeed the Holy Spirit, which would not be given to believers until after Jesus' resurrection and ascension.

— 7:40-44 —

The crowd remained divided. Note their distinction between "the Prophet" and "the Christ," whom first century theologians thought to be two distinct individuals. They are in fact one person, and He was addressing them in the temple. Nevertheless, many were confused by Jesus' apparent origins in the region of Galilee, when prophecy had proclaimed the Messiah would come from Judah (Mic. 5:2).

As often occurred with Jesus, the audience split in two based upon their reaction to the truth. Some believed, while others sought His destruction. However, no one dared touch Him in public while opinions remained divided.

— 7:45-52 —

The "officers" here are the same men commissioned by the Pharisees to seize Jesus by force and charge Him with a crime (7:32). But Jesus was unlike other men who challenged the religious leaders' authority. The others had been quacks and false messiahs. No one could refute the truth Jesus was preaching in the temple.

The Pharisees didn't judge the truth based on Scripture or any other godly standard. To defend their assertion that Jesus was a heretic, they offered as evidence the fact that they were unanimous against Him (7:48) and their self-proclaimed expertise in the Law (7:49). They determined right from wrong in terms of power, not on the basis of divine truth. When they were challenged, they pointed to their diplomas rather than pointing to the Scriptures.

One of their number, however, was not so certain. Nicodemus had not openly believed, yet he could not easily dismiss Jesus or ignore His teaching. Therefore, he offered a reasonable defense for Jesus without exposing his true leanings. The rebuke by his fellow Pharisees included a statement that was patently untrue: "No prophet arises out of Galilee." Elijah, Jonah, and perhaps Nahum were from the region known in the first century as Galilee (1 Kgs. 17:1; 2 Kgs. 14:25).

• • •

Jerusalem was a lions' den for Jesus. He entered willingly, then He deftly moved between the security of seclusion and the safety of the public arena while relying upon His Father to close the angry jaws of His enemies. His "hour" was still months away and there was work to do in the meantime . . . much of it in Judea.

APPLICATION: JOHN 7:1-52

Walking with Lions

No one understood the danger presented by enemies of the gospel more than Jesus. Long before the Feast of Tabernacles, the religious authorities wanted Him dead (John 5:18; 7:1, 19, 25). Although He knew they wanted to kill Him, He refused to shrink from the task the Father had given Him. This is not to say the Lord carried out His purpose with foolhardy abandon. While He had come to earth to die for the sins of the world, His was not a suicide mission. He didn't seek the first available opportunity to be arrested. On the contrary, He repeatedly eluded capture until His "hour" had come. To recognize danger as a possible consequence of service to God doesn't require one to pursue a death wish. Rather, it's a matter of setting priorities. Which is more important? The purposes of God or one's own safety? Risk is a part of one's calling.

As a believer, you will undoubtedly face circumstances in which doing what is right necessarily involves danger. During such times, you must balance three primary issues: trust in God, danger from enemies, and dedication to mission. As the Lord walked among the lions in Jerusalem, He perfectly balanced all three. Here's how.

First, *He assessed the danger (7:1, 7)*. Jesus did not naively stroll into the lions' den. He knew the religious establishment in Jerusalem wanted Him dead. They had people scouting for His arrival so they might seize Him without attracting attention and then dispose of Him without anyone knowing how He came to His end. Always aware of the danger, Jesus walked wisely.

Second, *He devised a strategy to nullify the danger (7:10, 14)*. Jesus recognized that the religious authorities could not seize Him if they didn't know His whereabouts and that they dared not seize Him in front of witnesses. Seizing Jesus in public and then killing Him would have turned popular support against the religious elite, and nothing meant more to them than human approval (12:43). Therefore, Jesus used this to His advantage. He blended in with the multitude when entering or exiting the temple and then addressed the religious leaders only in the presence of great numbers.

Third, *He risked safety only when His mission put danger in His path (7:8, 14)*. Jesus' brothers chided Him by suggesting He boldly stride into the temple, stand before the multitudes, and proclaim Himself the Christ. But the Lord's mission was to *be* the Christ, not simply proclaim Himself the Christ. He came to embody divine truth and to proclaim it to God's covenant people. To accomplish this, He traveled the length and breadth of Judea, Samaria, and Galilee. Now, He had to confront the temple leaders directly.

Fourth, *He chose to do only what brought glory to God and avoided seeking glory for himself (7:18).* The Son of God came to earth to be our Savior, not to become a martyr. The death of a popular leader can become the catalyst for revolution; Jesus did not come for that. He spoke and acted on behalf of the Father and He did only what was necessary to complete His mission.

Fifth, *He trusted the Father to guard His safety until His "hour" had come (7:30, 32-33).* The Lord didn't adopt a fatalistic "I die when I die" attitude, but He did entrust His destiny to the Father's timing. He knew that death awaited Him and that the religious authorities would be the means of His death, but He also recognized that nothing occurs unless God permits it.

Sixth, *He stayed at His task until it was complete and then He retreated from danger (7:37-39; 8:59).* The Lord didn't retreat from the temple because danger mounted. He attended the feast until the closing convocation (see comments on 8:12), at which time He gave His most provocative speech yet in the temple. After engaging His enemies in debate and having accomplished the Father's purpose, He retreated from the lions' den until His mission required Him to return (8:59; 9:35).

The world system hated Jesus and it continues to hate those who follow Him (15:18-19; 17:13-14). More often than not, we can serve Christ and avoid danger; but sometimes, obedience and danger come as a combined package. No amount of planning will separate them. However, when confronted with such circumstances, we need not throw caution to the wind or adopt a cavalier attitude toward risk. Let us instead fervently pray, assess the danger, plan our approach, remain focused on the goal, seek to glorify God in all our actions, trust Him to accomplish His will, complete the task at hand without reluctance, and then retreat to safety when the time is right.

Letters in the Sand
JOHN 7:53–8:11

NASB

⁵³ [ᵃEveryone went to his home.

8:1 But Jesus went to the Mount of Olives. ²Early in the morning He came again into the temple, and all the people were coming to Him; and He sat down and *began* to teach them. ³The scribes and the Pharisees brought a woman caught in adultery, and having set her in the center *of the court*, ⁴they said to Him, "Teacher, this woman has been caught in adultery, in the very act. ⁵Now in the Law Moses commanded us to stone such women; what then do You say?" ⁶They were saying this, testing Him, so that they might have grounds for accusing Him. But Jesus stooped down and with His finger wrote on the ground. ⁷But when they persisted in asking Him, He straightened up, and said to them, "He who is without sin among you, let him *be the* first to throw a stone at her." ⁸Again He stooped down and wrote on the ground. ⁹When they heard it, they *began* to go out one by one, beginning with the older ones, and He was left alone, and the woman, where she was, in the center *of the court*. ¹⁰Straightening up, Jesus said to her, "Woman, where are they? Did no one condemn you?" ¹¹She said, "No one, ᵃLord." And Jesus said, "I do not condemn you, either. Go. From now on sin no more."]

7:53 ᵃLater mss add the story of the adulterous woman, numbering it as John 7:53-8:11
8:11 ᵃOr *Sir*

NLT

[*The most ancient Greek manuscripts do not include John 7:53–8:11.*]

⁵³ Then the meeting broke up, and everybody went home.

8:1 Jesus returned to the Mount of Olives, ²but early the next morning he was back again at the Temple. A crowd soon gathered, and he sat down and taught them. ³As he was speaking, the teachers of religious law and the Pharisees brought a woman who had been caught in the act of adultery. They put her in front of the crowd.

⁴"Teacher," they said to Jesus, "this woman was caught in the act of adultery. ⁵The law of Moses says to stone her. What do you say?"

⁶They were trying to trap him into saying something they could use against him, but Jesus stooped down and wrote in the dust with his finger. ⁷They kept demanding an answer, so he stood up again and said, "All right, but let the one who has never sinned throw the first stone!" ⁸Then he stooped down again and wrote in the dust.

⁹When the accusers heard this, they slipped away one by one, beginning with the oldest, until only Jesus was left in the middle of the crowd with the woman. ¹⁰Then Jesus stood up again and said to the woman, "Where are your accusers? Didn't even one of them condemn you?"

¹¹"No, Lord," she said.

And Jesus said, "Neither do I. Go and sin no more."

I have always disliked the term "textual criticism." It suggests that experts in the field have dedicated their lives to criticizing the Bible until the text of Scripture is either meaningless or untrustworthy. Undoubtedly, some scholars have attempted to do just that. But there are many fine men and women who pursue the true intent of "textual criticism": to ascertain which of the thousands of ancient manuscripts contain the original words the New Testament writers dutifully penned under the inspiration of the Holy Spirit.

As Paul, Luke, James, Peter, John, and other men in first-century Christianity wrote, the Holy Spirit prompted them to include all the information we would need to believe and obey God, and He kept them from error as they wrote. What emerged was divine truth, preserved in ink on papyrus. And because these words were immediately recognized as inerrant, divine truth, copyists made duplicates by hand for distribution to the other churches. Then, copies were made of these copies, and more copies were later produced from those copies. Before long, hundreds of copies were circulating among the churches. Meanwhile, the papyrus of the original texts deteriorated.

The original scrolls are long gone now, and unfortunately, the process of copying was not perfect. An added word here, a dropped word there, some letters confused with others . . . Then those small errors in one manuscript would become a part of every copy created from it. Occasionally, a scribe would inadvertently create an error trying to correct an earlier mistake—or what he thought to be a mistake—thus propagating another "variant." Many centuries later, there are more than five thousand manuscripts or fragments of manuscripts, all of them containing some portion of the original words of the New Testament.

A good example of this phenomenon showed up years ago on bulletin boards all over the United States. Someone copied what I had written in a piece I entitled "Attitudes." They typed it onto a sheet of paper in order to produce a rudimentary poster. Someone else liked it and copied it for a couple friends, who displayed it on their bulletin boards. Later on, copies of those copies were handwritten and/or faxed and copied again. Before long, my original piece had been copied and faxed so many times, it was barely legible—the letters were blotched and smeared and faded. Yet very few people had difficulty reading the quote, even with missing letters and words.

The original manuscripts went through a similar process, only with much greater care. Scribes were famously diligent; nevertheless, after hundreds of copies, some errors were propagated. Not to worry, though. It's not as bad as it sounds. While this manual copying system was far less than perfect, it nevertheless preserved divine truth as written by the original hands nearly two thousand years ago. The vast majority of errors are small, so the meanings of the original text have not been affected. In cases where the meanings have been impacted, the sheer number of manuscripts makes it relatively easy to spot the mistake and correct it. And because most variants involve *additions* to the original text, the original wording is usually easy to determine. Fortunately, we have the dedication and expertise of "textual critics" to analyze and compare thousands of ancient copies in order to recover the original text of Scripture. The Bibles we have today are extremely reliable copies of the original texts—as close to accurate as any church would have had back then—and all thanks to the efforts of godly scholars.

As we come to the eighth chapter of John's account of Jesus' earthly ministry, I face a dilemma—one that scholars have wrestled with for more than a century. It doesn't help matters that it involves one of the most beloved stories in all of the New Testament, the story of the woman caught in adultery. In Bibles printed today, the text of this episode begins with 7:53 and continues through 8:11; however, it does not appear at all in the earliest manuscripts of John, while later copies include the text in a variety of places. One family of manuscripts places the story after Luke 21:38. Complicating things even more, the vocabulary and style in this passage do not match the rest of John's Gospel.

So, what is to be done? The story is clearly not original to John's narrative. It is possible that this incident actually occurred and was preserved in some form outside of Scripture, only to be included much later. However, the likelihood of this is questionable considering the length of time between the first century and the sixth century, when it appears in manuscripts with a special notation indicating the scribes' doubt. Many fine Christian scholars consider the story authentic because the general consensus of church history has judged it worthy and because nothing in the story contradicts other teaching. In fact, the passage fits very well theologically with Jesus' teaching and reflects His attitude toward nonhypocritical sinners at other times in His ministry—his encounter with the Samaritan woman especially.

While I personally do not accept this segment of text as original to John, and I consider it neither inspired nor free from error, I certainly do not consider it worthless. Therefore, I have preached sermons from this passage (while cross-checking my theology and principles with Scripture) and I believe it worthy of our consideration here.

The story begins early one morning as Jesus taught in the outer courts of the temple. In good rabbinical fashion, He sat while giving instruction. Then a group of angry scribes and Pharisees—rigid technicians of Scripture—interrupted the Lord's lesson, thrusting a woman before Him and His listeners. She had been caught in the very act of adultery. Because of that, she was the perfect bait for their trap.

Having asserted His authority on matters of the Law and having declared all of His actions the will of the Father, Jesus was put on the spot when the scribes and Pharisees wanted to know what He would do with the woman. Of course, they didn't really care about His opinion. As on many occasions, they merely hoped to find some means of trapping Jesus with His own words (Matt. 22:15; Mark 12:13; Luke 20:20). Admittedly, theirs was a thorny question. The Law of Moses condemned adulterers to be stoned publically (Lev. 20:10; Deut. 22:22-24), but Roman law reserved execution for Roman courts. The Jews did not have the authority to stone the woman without Roman permission. It was a perfect setup. To honor God's law, Jesus would incur the wrath of Rome. To submit to Roman law, Jesus would have to ignore the law of God.

Before the men had finished their little speech, Jesus stooped over and began writing something in the sand with His finger. Since we're not told, we're left to speculate what He wrote. Whoever preserved the story obviously thought the content of His writing was not as important as the act of writing.

Whatever He wrote, it had little effect on the frowning accusers. They were single-minded in their desire to see Jesus trapped by His own words. They pressed Him for an answer, perhaps thinking that avoiding providing a verdict would be too awkward for Jesus in front of His learners. (Pharisees cared about image more than anything.) Eventually, Jesus stood to His feet and issued a challenge. He said, in effect, "The only worthy judge is one who cannot be condemned by the Law he supposedly upholds; therefore, let the perfectly qualified judge among you be the first to execute justice." Then He resumed His writing.

One by one, oldest to youngest, the hypocritical judges slithered away, leaving only the woman in the center of the court. The worthless judges could not condemn, and the sovereign Judge refused to condemn, even though He has that prerogative. True to His word, He did not come to condemn the lost, but to save us (John 3:16-17).

Reasons for Rejection
JOHN 8:12-59

¹²Then Jesus again spoke to them, saying, "I am the Light of the world; he who follows Me will not walk in the darkness, but will have the Light of life." ¹³So the Pharisees said to Him, "You are testifying about Yourself; Your testimony is not ªtrue." ¹⁴Jesus answered and said to them, "Even if I testify about Myself, My testimony is ªtrue, for I know where I came from and where I am going; but you do not know where I come from or where I am going. ¹⁵You judge ªaccording to the flesh; I am not judging anyone. ¹⁶But even if I do judge, My judgment is true; for I am not alone *in it,* but I and the Father who sent Me. ¹⁷Even in your law it has been written that the testimony of two men is ªtrue. ¹⁸I am He who testifies about Myself, and the Father who sent Me testifies about Me." ¹⁹So they were saying to Him, "Where is Your Father?" Jesus answered, "You know neither Me nor My Father; if you knew Me, you would know My Father also." ²⁰These words He spoke in the treasury, as He taught in the temple; and no one seized Him, because His hour had not yet come.

²¹Then He said again to them, "I go away, and you will seek Me, and will die in your sin; where I am going, you cannot come." ²²So the Jews were saying, "Surely He will not kill Himself, will He, since He says, 'Where I am going, you cannot come'?" ²³And He was saying to them, "You are from below, I am from above; you are of this world, I am not of this world. ²⁴Therefore I

¹²Jesus spoke to the people once more and said, "I am the light of the world. If you follow me, you won't have to walk in darkness, because you will have the light that leads to life."

¹³The Pharisees replied, "You are making those claims about yourself! Such testimony is not valid."

¹⁴Jesus told them, "These claims are valid even though I make them about myself. For I know where I came from and where I am going, but you don't know this about me. ¹⁵You judge me by human standards, but I do not judge anyone. ¹⁶And if I did, my judgment would be correct in every respect because I am not alone. The Father* who sent me is with me. ¹⁷Your own law says that if two people agree about something, their witness is accepted as fact.* ¹⁸I am one witness, and my Father who sent me is the other."

¹⁹"Where is your father?" they asked.

Jesus answered, "Since you don't know who I am, you don't know who my Father is. If you knew me, you would also know my Father." ²⁰Jesus made these statements while he was teaching in the section of the Temple known as the Treasury. But he was not arrested, because his time* had not yet come.

²¹Later Jesus said to them again, "I am going away. You will search for me but will die in your sin. You cannot come where I am going."

²²The people* asked, "Is he planning to commit suicide? What does he mean, 'You cannot come where I am going'?"

²³Jesus continued, "You are from below; I am from above. You belong to this world; I do not. ²⁴That is why

said to you that you will die in your sins; for unless you believe that ªI am *He,* you will die in your sins." ²⁵So they were saying to Him, "Who are You?" Jesus said to them, "ªWhat have I been saying to you *from* the beginning? ²⁶I have many things to speak and to judge concerning you, but He who sent Me is true; and the things which I heard from Him, these I speak to the world." ²⁷They did not realize that He had been speaking to them about the Father. ²⁸So Jesus said, "When you lift up the Son of Man, then you will know that ªI am *He,* and I do nothing on My own initiative, but I speak these things as the Father taught Me. ²⁹And He who sent Me is with Me; He ªhas not left Me alone, for I always do the things that are pleasing to Him." ³⁰As He spoke these things, many came to believe in Him.

³¹So Jesus was saying to those Jews who had believed Him, "If you continue in My word, *then* you are truly disciples of Mine; ³²and you will know the truth, and the truth will make you free." ³³They answered Him, "We are Abraham's descendants and have never yet been enslaved to anyone; how is it that You say, 'You will become free'?"

³⁴Jesus answered them, "Truly, truly, I say to you, everyone who commits sin is the slave of sin. ³⁵The slave does not remain in the house forever; the son does remain forever. ³⁶So if the Son makes you free, you will be free indeed. ³⁷I know that you are Abraham's descendants; yet you seek to kill Me, because My word ªhas no place in you. ³⁸I speak the things which I have seen ªwith *My* Father; therefore you also do the things which you heard from *your* father."

³⁹They answered and said to Him, "Abraham is our father." Jesus said to them, "If you are Abraham's

I said that you will die in your sins; for unless you believe that I Am who I claim to be,* you will die in your sins."

²⁵"Who are you?" they demanded.

Jesus replied, "The one I have always claimed to be.* ²⁶I have much to say about you and much to condemn, but I won't. For I say only what I have heard from the one who sent me, and he is completely truthful." ²⁷But they still didn't understand that he was talking about his Father.

²⁸So Jesus said, "When you have lifted up the Son of Man on the cross, then you will understand that I Am he.* I do nothing on my own but say only what the Father taught me. ²⁹And the one who sent me is with me—he has not deserted me. For I always do what pleases him." ³⁰Then many who heard him say these things believed in him.

³¹Jesus said to the people who believed in him, "You are truly my disciples if you remain faithful to my teachings. ³²And you will know the truth, and the truth will set you free."

³³"But we are descendants of Abraham," they said. "We have never been slaves to anyone. What do you mean, 'You will be set free'?"

³⁴Jesus replied, "I tell you the truth, everyone who sins is a slave of sin. ³⁵A slave is not a permanent member of the family, but a son is part of the family forever. ³⁶So if the Son sets you free, you are truly free. ³⁷Yes, I realize that you are descendants of Abraham. And yet some of you are trying to kill me because there's no room in your hearts for my message. ³⁸I am telling you what I saw when I was with my Father. But you are following the advice of your father."

³⁹"Our father is Abraham!" they declared.

"No," Jesus replied, "for if you

NASB

children, do the deeds of Abraham. ⁴⁰But as it is, you are seeking to kill Me, a man who has told you the truth, which I heard from God; this Abraham did not do. ⁴¹You are doing the deeds of your father." They said to Him, "We were not born of fornication; we have one Father: God." ⁴²Jesus said to them, "If God were your Father, you would love Me, for I proceeded forth and have come from God, for I have not even come on My own initiative, but ªHe sent Me. ⁴³Why do you not understand ªwhat I am saying? *It is* because you cannot hear My word. ⁴⁴You are of *your* father the devil, and you want to do the desires of your father. He was a murderer from the beginning, and does not stand in the truth because there is no truth in him. Whenever he speaks ªa lie, he speaks from his own *nature,* for he is a liar and the father of ᵇlies. ⁴⁵But because I speak the truth, you do not believe Me. ⁴⁶Which one of you convicts Me of sin? If I speak truth, why do you not believe Me? ⁴⁷He who is of God hears the words of God; for this reason you do not hear *them,* because you are not of God."

⁴⁸The Jews answered and said to Him, "Do we not say rightly that You are a Samaritan and have a demon?" ⁴⁹Jesus answered, "I do not have a demon; but I honor My Father, and you dishonor Me. ⁵⁰But I do not seek My glory; there is One who seeks and judges. ⁵¹Truly, truly, I say to you, if anyone keeps My word he will never see death." ⁵²The Jews said to Him, "Now we know that You have a demon. Abraham died, and the prophets *also;* and You say, 'If anyone keeps My word, he will never taste of death.' ⁵³Surely You are not greater than our father Abraham,

NLT

were really the children of Abraham, you would follow his example.* ⁴⁰Instead, you are trying to kill me because I told you the truth, which I heard from God. Abraham never did such a thing. ⁴¹No, you are imitating your real father."

They replied, "We aren't illegitimate children! God himself is our true Father."

⁴²Jesus told them, "If God were your Father, you would love me, because I have come to you from God. I am not here on my own, but he sent me. ⁴³Why can't you understand what I am saying? It's because you can't even hear me! ⁴⁴For you are the children of your father the devil, and you love to do the evil things he does. He was a murderer from the beginning. He has always hated the truth, because there is no truth in him. When he lies, it is consistent with his character; for he is a liar and the father of lies. ⁴⁵So when I tell the truth, you just naturally don't believe me! ⁴⁶Which of you can truthfully accuse me of sin? And since I am telling you the truth, why don't you believe me? ⁴⁷Anyone who belongs to God listens gladly to the words of God. But you don't listen because you don't belong to God."

⁴⁸The people retorted, "You Samaritan devil! Didn't we say all along that you were possessed by a demon?"

⁴⁹"No," Jesus said, "I have no demon in me. For I honor my Father—and you dishonor me. ⁵⁰And though I have no wish to glorify myself, God is going to glorify me. He is the true judge. ⁵¹I tell you the truth, anyone who obeys my teaching will never die!"

⁵²The people said, "Now we know you are possessed by a demon. Even Abraham and the prophets died, but you say, 'Anyone who obeys my teaching will never die!' ⁵³Are you greater than our father Abraham? He

who died? The prophets died too; whom do You make Yourself out *to be?*" ⁵⁴Jesus answered, "If I glorify Myself, My glory is nothing; it is My Father who glorifies Me, of whom you say, 'He is our God'; ⁵⁵and you have not come to know Him, but I know Him; and if I say that I do not know Him, I will be a liar like you, but I do know Him and keep His word. ⁵⁶Your father Abraham rejoiced ᵃto see My day, and he saw *it* and was glad." ⁵⁷So the Jews said to Him, "You are not yet fifty years old, and have You seen Abraham?" ⁵⁸Jesus said to them, "Truly, truly, I say to you, before Abraham ᵃwas born, I am." ⁵⁹Therefore they picked up stones to throw at Him, but Jesus ᵃhid Himself and went out of the temple.

died, and so did the prophets. Who do you think you are?"

⁵⁴Jesus answered, "If I want glory for myself, it doesn't count. But it is my Father who will glorify me. You say, 'He is our God,'* ⁵⁵but you don't even know him. I know him. If I said otherwise, I would be as great a liar as you! But I do know him and obey him. ⁵⁶Your father Abraham rejoiced as he looked forward to my coming. He saw it and was glad."

⁵⁷The people said, "You aren't even fifty years old. How can you say you have seen Abraham?*"

⁵⁸Jesus answered, "I tell you the truth, before Abraham was even born, I Am!*" ⁵⁹At that point they picked up stones to throw at him. But Jesus was hidden from them and left the Temple.

8:13 ᵃOr *valid* 8:14 ᵃOr *valid* 8:15 ᵃI.e. by a carnal standard 8:17 ᵃI.e. valid or admissible 8:24 ᵃMost authorities associate this with Ex 3:14, *I AM WHO I AM* 8:25 ᵃOr *That which I have been saying to you from the beginning* 8:28 ᵃLit *I AM* (v 24 note) 8:29 ᵃOr *did not leave* 8:37 ᵃOr *makes no progress* 8:38 ᵃOr *in the presence of* 8:42 ᵃLit *that One* 8:43 ᵃOr *My way of speaking* 8:44 ᵃLit *the lie* ᵇLit *it* 8:56 ᵃLit *in order that he might see* 8:58 ᵃLit *came into being* 8:59 ᵃLit *was hidden*

8:16 Some manuscripts read *The One.* 8:17 See Deut 19:15. 8:20 Greek *his hour.* 8:22 Greek *Jewish people;* also in 8:31, 48, 52, 57. 8:24 Greek *unless you believe that I am.* See Exod 3:14. 8:25 Or *Why do I speak to you at all?* 8:28 Greek *When you have lifted up the Son of Man, then you will know that I am.* "Son of Man" is a title Jesus used for himself. 8:39 Some manuscripts read *if you are really the children of Abraham, follow his example.* 8:54 Some manuscripts read *You say he is your God.* 8:57 Some manuscripts read *How can you say Abraham has seen you?* 8:58 Or *before Abraham was even born, I have always been alive;* Greek reads *before Abraham was, I am.* See Exod 3:14.

I once heard someone describe the ideal Christian as "one who is completely fearless, continually joyful, and constantly in trouble." Perhaps the theology could be refined, but that makes good, practical sense. Unquestionably, Christians could stand to be a little less fearful and a lot more joyful, but "in trouble"? Yes. In constant trouble.

That's not to suggest we are supposed to go out seeking trouble or inviting it. However, if we are faithfully standing for and proclaiming the truth, trouble will become our constant companion. We know this on an instinctive level and too frequently choose to keep the truth hidden away. Let's face it; we'd rather be liked than risk rejection by simply stating what we know to be true.

Jesus was a radical individual, a most imposing personality. Not intimidating, not frightening. Imposing. Formidable. Unafraid. He entered the temple to find people groping about in spiritual darkness and thirsting for divine truth, and He boldly stated, "If anyone is thirsty, let him come to Me and drink. He who believes in Me, as the Scripture said, 'From his innermost being will flow rivers of living water'" (John 7:37-38). "I am the Light of the world; he who follows Me will not walk in the darkness, but will have the Light of life" (8:12). He fearlessly spoke the truth without apology, He joyously walked in the truth with His Father, and therefore, He was constantly in trouble for His uninhibited love of truth.

Jesus understood better than any the price to be paid for speaking and living the truth because He is divine truth incarnate, the Light made flesh. Matthew recalled a particularly shocking statement by Jesus: "Do not think that I came to bring peace on the earth; I did not come to bring peace, but a sword" (Matt. 10:34). The purpose of a sword is to divide. Physically, it separates one part of a body from the rest. Figuratively, the sword of truth is so sharp that it can slide between the soul and spirit to lay the intentions of humankind open for all to see (Heb. 4:12). And socially, the sword separates groups into two categories; it attracts those who will surrender and incites to violence those who will not. There is no room for compromise before the gleaming sword of truth. Surrender or fight.

Jesus brought a sword into the temple during the Feast of Tabernacles. Some surrendered. Others began a futile, exhausting, self-destructive fight. Their response is a study in the stages of rejection:

Stages of Rejection

Contradiction	Cynicism	Denial	Insult	Sarcasm	Violence
"Your testimony is not true" [8:13]	"Where is Your Father?" "We were not born of fornication" [8:19, 41]	"We . . . have never yet been enslaved to anyone" [8:33]	"You are a Samaritan and have a demon" [8:48]	"Whom do You make Yourself out to be?" [8:53]	They picked up stones to throw at Him [8:59]

REASONS FOR REJECTION | JOHN 8:12-59

— 8:12-18 —

This discourse continues where 7:52 left off. The text should read:

> ⁷:⁵²They answered him, "You are not also from Galilee, are you? Search, and see that no prophet arises out of Galilee."
>
> ⁸:¹²Then Jesus again spoke to them, saying, "I am the Light of the world; he who follows Me will not walk in the darkness, but will have the Light of life."

However, John indicates a change of scene with the word "again," which is typical of him. These particular discourses took place over several days—not necessarily on the last day of the festival—and were undoubtedly repeated several times as visitors to the temple came and went. As Jesus began this address with the words, "I am the Light of the world," He stood near the temple treasury (8:20).

According to the Mishnah, the written record of Jewish oral tradition, priests erected four giant lampstands in the Court of Women during the Feast of Tabernacles. Each evening at sundown, young men climbed ladders to light these enormous oil lamps, which, according to Mishnah tractate Sukkah 5:3, reflected in every courtyard in Jerusalem.

The temple treasury was located in the Court of Women and, according to some historians, consisted of thirteen large, trumpet-shaped, bronze receptacles. The small mouth of each trumpet bore a sign to indicate the specific purpose for the money collected. Naturally, the size of each person's offering could be heard as dropped coins clattered against the bronze. Every evening during the Feast of Tabernacles, just after the evening sacrifice and before sunset, priests entered the Court of Women to light two (some historians say four) giant chandelier-like lampstands. Perhaps as the priests began to set each hanging lamp aflame, Jesus declared, "I am the Light of the world; he who follows Me will not walk in the darkness." Note how the statement is exclusive. He didn't say "I'm *a* light"—one among many—but *the* Light, the one and only source of truth. Later, He would invite a crowd of listeners to become children of the Light through belief (12:36) and He once predicted the future of His disciples saying, "You are the light of the world" (Matt. 5:14).

The Pharisees immediately challenged Jesus, declaring His self-declaration invalid because it did not have any accompanying proof (cf. John 3:11-12). Based on the context of the sentence, the Greek term translated "true" in 8:13 could also be rendered "real." After all, people can claim anything about themselves; mere statement doesn't establish truth. Jesus took their challenge at face value and offered the testimony of God the Father.

— 8:19-20 —

The Pharisees responded cynically, "Where is Your Father?" They knew the apparent circumstances of His birth (8:41) and that Joseph was dead. The question was a backhanded slur, delivered at the level of an inside joke. Perhaps the insult came with a wink and a knowing look.

Jesus ignored the insult and responded with a rebuke having an ironic double meaning. Anyone who believed that Joseph had fathered Jesus clearly didn't know the identity of Jesus' real Father, nor did he or she personally know God. With His second statement, "if you knew Me, you would know My Father also," Jesus declared Himself to be the means of knowing God personally, because Jesus is the perfect representation of the Father.

— 8:21-27 —

Jesus repeated His indictment of the Pharisees from 7:33-36, saying they would never see heaven because they did not know God. And again the religious elite took Him literally. So, Jesus explained His meaning in simple language. "Below" is the realm of fallen creation. "Above" is the heavenly realm in which no sin can exist. Those born below are doomed to die in their sin and then suffer eternal punishment for their deeds (3:3). Those born from above are holy and, therefore, will not suffer judgment. Jesus is from above because He is God. His statement is rendered "I am He"; however, the Greek is simply *egō eimi* [1473, 1510], "I AM," the classic self-designation of God (see Exod. 3:14). Believers can be born from above through belief (John 3:16-17).

When asked, "Who are You?" Jesus replied, "What have I been saying to you from the beginning?" But because of their willful blindness, the Pharisees failed to understand Jesus' reference to the Father (cf. 3:13).

If you take time to review 3:3-21, you will find a striking resemblance between this discourse and the Lord's conversation with Nicodemus.

— 8:28-30 —

The "lifting up" is of course a reference to His crucifixion, a prediction He had made to Nicodemus perhaps as much as two years earlier (3:14-15). He then repeated His teaching from His encounter with the Pharisees after healing the invalid (5:19-47).

Jesus didn't whisper the truth once and then leave the scene. He taught the same lessons to many audiences several times each day in the temple. The discourses preserved by John are representative of numerous instances in which Jesus became a target for the religious leaders' wrath after proclaiming the truth. However, John inserted a subtle editorial note to reassure the reader: While Jesus' opponents remained steadfast in their rebellion, some people believed.

— 8:31-36 —

Verse 31 may indicate another change of scene in which the conversation resumes. As Jesus spoke, many believed. He then addressed them directly in the hearing of the Pharisees and other nonbelievers. He assured them that belief was not the end of something, as though they had arrived; belief is a beginning, a birth after which growth must follow. Believers are to continue in obedience. As believers order their lives after His truth, they will "know" the truth. The Greek word is *ginōskō* [1097], which is one of at least four terms John could have chosen that mean "know." Unlike the others, *ginōskō* stresses understanding rather than mere sensory observation. It is closely related to the Hebrew verb *yada* [H3045], which describes the most intimate kind of knowledge (Gen. 3:5; 4:1).

Moreover, as one "knows" the truth, he or she is "made free." The Greek term is suggestive of release from indentured servanthood. When someone became indebted beyond his or her means of paying, one solution was to exchange a term of slavery for relief from the debt.

Sometimes the length of service could be the rest of one's natural life. The indebtedness, of course, is the penalty for sin; the freedom is spiritual release from judgment and the free gift of eternal life.

Jesus' statement, "the truth will make you free," has become something of a truism, and rightly so. While His primary point was spiritual and eternal, it is a fact that truth leads to freedom in the physical, temporal realm. Any recovering alcoholic will affirm this by experience. Any drug addict who has been "clean and sober" for a number of years will say the same: As they came to terms with the truth of their cravings, the truth about the origins and influences of their cravings, and the truth of their personal responsibilities, they found freedom. In fact, any repentant sinner will affirm the power of truth to liberate . . . including the one writing these words!

As usual, Jesus spoke on multiple levels. As usual, the Pharisees zeroed in on the literal interpretation. And, being the self-centered men they were, they applied Jesus' statement to their condition as descendants of Abraham, by which they claimed racial, cultural, and moral superiority. Furthermore, they claimed to have never been enslaved to anyone!

Well, except Egypt. Assyria. Babylon. Persia. Macedonia. Syria. Rome.

What could they have possibly meant by this? Possibly that they were never compelled to worship a man as a god despite their many political masters. Despite Roman domination and occupation, the Jews were able to worship God with virtually no interference from their captors. There in the temple environs, the Pharisees perhaps gestured toward the sanctuary as if to ask, "What freedom do we need that we don't already have?"

Jesus clarified the purpose of His statement. The master is sin. Jesus' statement that a "slave does not remain in the house forever; the son does remain forever," is meant to highlight the inferior status of a slave. Old Master Sin uses people for its own evil purposes, and when the body of the slave is wasted from use, the slave is cast out. The Son has come to liberate sin-slaves from their old master, allowing them to become children of God.

— 8:37-42 —

Jesus affirmed the fact that His hearers were descendants of Abraham, at least in the physical sense. However, their shared heritage ended there. Abraham is the spiritual ancestor of all who place their trust in

God because he heard and obeyed God's word. Because Jesus is the Word of God in human flesh, to reject Him is to reject God. Therefore, the disbelieving Jews were descendants of Abraham in name only.

The pronouns "My" and "your" in 8:38 are italicized in the New American Standard Bible because they are missing in the oldest Greek manuscripts. The translators have supplied these pronouns based on their best interpretation, and the fact that God and Satan are the contrasted "fathers" in 8:41 and 8:44. If the pronouns were left out originally, Jesus' statement is an imperative. After rebuking the Pharisees for failing to heed God's Word, He invited them to be true Hebrews, commanding them, "I speak the things which I have seen with the Father; therefore you also must do the things which you heard from the Father" (8:38, my translation). This fits well with the exchange in 8:39.

But the Pharisees, by not doing the deeds of their father Abraham, were rejecting their God. This, Jesus implied, made them sons of Satan, the father of lies and ultimate rebel against God. Rather than prompt reflection and repentance, His indictment incited hatred, which the Pharisees expressed with a sneer in a thinly veiled epithet. The phrase "born of fornication" was clearly aimed at the presupposition that Mary conceived Jesus illegitimately.

The Lord bypassed this insult as He had the other (8:19) to reinforce His earlier teaching that He was on earth to do the Father's will.

— 8:43-47 —

Having invited the Pharisees to believe in God as their ancestor Abraham had done, and having felt the sting of their insult, Jesus laid bare the source of their unbelief: they wanted to do the desires of Satan, whom He called their "father."

A particular trait of John is his portrayal of the universe as sharply divided between light and dark, truth and lie, life and death, the kingdom of God and "the world." For John, there is no middle ground. And it is perhaps this discourse that set his perspective like concrete. Satan is everything that God is not, and to practice sin is to side with Satan against God (1 Jn. 1:5-7). The plain and simple reason for the Pharisees' rejection of Jesus, the Word of God, was their dedication to the father of lies.

— 8:48-57 —

The Pharisees responded to Jesus' indictment with typical venom, beginning with a racial slur and then a counterclaim that He was the one controlled by Satan, not them. With biting sarcasm, they responded to Jesus' claim, "If anyone keeps My word he will never see death," in typical fashion: disbelief based on a spiritually myopic interpretation. And Jesus responded as He always had: by allowing the enemies of truth to be carried away by their own rebellious predisposition.

By the end of the encounter, Jesus had laid His ax against the root of their rebellion: pride. Jesus, though equal with the Father, did not seek His own glory, but did everything to glorify the Father. The Pharisees, on the other hand, glorified themselves and dared to label God as the source of their glory.

— 8:58-59 —

Jesus concluded His confrontation with the Pharisees with another unambiguous claim to deity, preceded by a solemn double *amēn* [281]: "Before Abraham was born, I am." This prompted the Pharisees to start gathering stones for an immediate execution on the charge of blasphemy.

• • •

I find it tragically ironic that Jesus was surrounded by men who were masters of the manuscript, dedicated guardians of the Scriptures, but they failed to recognize the Living Word when He stared them in the face. The Lord had entrusted the Jewish people with the care and proclamation of His Word. They were exposed to the truth of God daily as they faithfully preserved the text with meticulous care, making sure that each successive generation received a purely transcribed copy of God's inerrant Word. But, preoccupied with "every jot and tittle," they were unable to connect the obvious dots.

As the Feast of Tabernacles, the great ingathering harvest celebration, came to a close, Jesus had fulfilled His mission. He had harvested more believers whose hearts had been prepared by the Father.

APPLICATION: JOHN 8:12-59

Five Reasons People Reject the Messiah

Why do people reject Jesus as the Messiah? His encounter with the religious experts in Jerusalem highlights at least five reasons.

First, *they lack knowledge* (8:14). People do not accept Jesus as the

Messiah because they do not have adequate information about Him; they haven't been told, or what they have been told is wrong.

My wife, Cynthia, and I were enjoying dinner with some friends of ours who were reared in another country. They told us of their growing up without any knowledge of the Bible because the Scriptures were the exclusive possession of the clergy, who alone read, interpreted, and applied the Word of God. Therefore, they lived in complete ignorance of Jesus. Once they moved to a culture that encouraged everyone to read the Bible, they were amazed by what they had missed. They both came to faith in Christ and couldn't get enough of His Word.

This is why we take the gospel around the world—to reach those who do not know.

Second, *they lack perception* (8:15, 23). The religious experts "judge[d] according to the flesh"—that is, they discerned only in natural, physical, empirical terms. They lacked a spiritual dimension to their thinking, which kept them from comprehending spiritual truths.

Some people reject Jesus as the Messiah because they refuse to accept as real anything that cannot be seen, touched, weighed, measured, or tested in a lab. Philosophers call them "materialists," not because they value money or possessions, but because they believe the universe consists of matter and energy only. To the materialist, nothing exists beyond the tangible, and everything can be reduced to a reasonable, rational, quantifiable, scientific explanation.

This is not a mere lack of knowledge. This is a choice to reject the reality of anything supernatural—"beyond natural." Therefore, spiritual truths have no more meaning to them than the color red to a person born without sight.

Third, *they lack appropriation* (8:37). The religious experts had been exposed to the Word of God because it was their job to copy the manuscripts, learn the principles they contained, and apply them to everyday life. The nation of Israel had been founded on the books of Moses like the United States was established by a constitution. However, the priests and scribes never allowed the print on the page to make a journey into their hearts. They failed to internalize what they supposedly cherished.

Here is a more recent illustration of how the truth of Jesus Christ can be studied yet never appropriated.

At the village church in Kalinovka, Russia, attendance at Sunday school picked up after the priest started handing out candy to the peasant children. One of the most faithful was a pug-nosed, pugnacious lad who recited his Scriptures with proper piety, pocketed his reward, then fled into the fields to munch on it. The priest took a liking to the boy, persuaded him to attend church school. This was preferable to doing household chores from which his devout parents excused him. By offering other inducements, the priest managed to teach the boy the four Gospels. In fact, he won a special prize for learning all four by heart and reciting them nonstop in church.[10]

Sixty years later, the boy still enjoyed reciting Scripture. Today, his soul is who-knows-where; his body lies cold in the ground under a marker bearing his name: Nikita Khrushchev. He knew the Gospels better than most genuine Russian believers, yet apparently without appropriating the truths they contain.

This is a particular danger for second- and third-generation Christians, who benefit from the Bible knowledge of others and enjoy the benefits of a Christian culture, yet can fail to make the truths of Scripture their own. It's even possible for children of godly parents to leave the home, live their lives, and then go to the grave having never appropriated the truths they heard.

Fourth, *they lack desire* (8:44). The religious experts followed the desires of their own fallen nature rather than setting aside self-interest to obey God.

I have encountered more than one individual who refused to accept the truth of Jesus Christ because he or she didn't want to give up a chosen lifestyle, regardless of how personally destructive it had become. Drug addicts will never choose sobriety as long as they love their drug of choice; only when they come to hate their dependence will they try to end it. The same is true of less destructive yet equally futile pursuits, such as wealth, entertainment, or illicit relationships.

Fifth, *they lack humility* (8:52-53). The religious experts rejected Jesus as the Messiah because they thought they had outgrown the need for a Savior. They thought their ancestry guaranteed them God's approval. Moreover, they believed their religious knowledge and religious activity gave them exclusive access to truth.

When a person begins to list a pedigree or recite a resume, I can be reasonably sure he or she will not accept the truth of Jesus Christ. Children of great, godly parents. Members of high standing in this Christian organization or that. Religious officials. Denominational authorities.

Graduates of fine institutions of higher learning. None will enter heaven without first setting aside pride long enough to receive God's grace. But to receive grace, one must first recognize one's hopelessness without it. It requires humility to acknowledge the sinfulness of one's own sin.

Throughout my years of ministry, I have wrestled with a fear that many people in our churches are regularly exposed to the preaching and teaching of God's Word, yet have not accepted Jesus as their own Messiah. Naturally, we cannot go around testing to see who is and who isn't a genuine believer; however, we shouldn't take for granted that every Christian-in-name in our congregations and classes is truly born again.

Blind Men's Bluff
JOHN 9:1-41

NASB

¹ As He passed by, He saw a man blind from birth. ² And His disciples asked Him, "Rabbi, who sinned, this man or his parents, that he would be born blind?" ³ Jesus answered, "*It was* neither *that* this man sinned, nor his parents; but *it was* so that the works of God might be displayed in him. ⁴ We must work the works of Him who sent Me as long as it is day; night is coming when no one can work. ⁵ While I am in the world, I am the Light of the world." ⁶ When He had said this, He spat on the ground, and made clay of the spittle, and applied the clay to his eyes, ⁷ and said to him, "Go, wash in the pool of Siloam" (which is translated, Sent). So he went away and washed, and came *back* seeing. ⁸ Therefore the neighbors, and those who previously saw him as a beggar, were saying, "Is not this the one who used to sit and beg?" ⁹ Others were saying, "This is he," *still* others were saying, "No, but he is like him." ª He kept saying,

NLT

¹ As Jesus was walking along, he saw a man who had been blind from birth. ² "Rabbi," his disciples asked him, "why was this man born blind? Was it because of his own sins or his parents' sins?"

³ "It was not because of his sins or his parents' sins," Jesus answered. "This happened so the power of God could be seen in him. ⁴ We must quickly carry out the tasks assigned us by the one who sent us.* The night is coming, and then no one can work. ⁵ But while I am here in the world, I am the light of the world."

⁶ Then he spit on the ground, made mud with the saliva, and spread the mud over the blind man's eyes. ⁷ He told him, "Go wash yourself in the pool of Siloam" (Siloam means "sent"). So the man went and washed and came back seeing!

⁸ His neighbors and others who knew him as a blind beggar asked each other, "Isn't this the man who used to sit and beg?" ⁹ Some said he was, and others said, "No, he just looks like him!"

But the beggar kept saying, "Yes, I am the same one!"

NASB

"I am the one." [10] So they were saying to him, "How then were your eyes opened?" [11] He answered, "The man who is called Jesus made clay, and anointed my eyes, and said to me, 'Go to Siloam and wash'; so I went away and washed, and I received sight." [12] They said to him, "Where is He?" He said, "I do not know."

[13] They brought to the Pharisees the man who was formerly blind. [14] Now it was a Sabbath on the day when Jesus made the clay and opened his eyes. [15] Then the Pharisees also were asking him again how he received his sight. And he said to them, "He applied clay to my eyes, and I washed, and I see." [16] Therefore some of the Pharisees were saying, "This man is not from God, because He does not keep the Sabbath." But others were saying, "How can a man who is a sinner perform such [a]signs?" And there was a division among them. [17] So they said to the blind man again, "What do you say about Him, since He opened your eyes?" And he said, "He is a prophet."

[18] The Jews then did not believe *it* of him, that he had been blind and had received sight, until they called the parents of the very one who had received his sight, [19] and questioned them, saying, "Is this your son, who you say was born blind? Then how does he now see?" [20] His parents answered them and said, "We know that this is our son, and that he was born blind; [21] but how he now sees, we do not know; or who opened his eyes, we do not know. Ask him; he is of age, he will speak for himself." [22] His parents said this because they were afraid of the Jews; for the Jews had already agreed that if anyone confessed Him to be [a]Christ, he was to be put out of the synagogue. [23] For this reason his parents said, "He is of age; ask him."

[24] So a second time they called the

NLT

[10] They asked, "Who healed you? What happened?"

[11] He told them, "The man they call Jesus made mud and spread it over my eyes and told me, 'Go to the pool of Siloam and wash yourself.' So I went and washed, and now I can see!"

[12] "Where is he now?" they asked.

"I don't know," he replied.

[13] Then they took the man who had been blind to the Pharisees, [14] because it was on the Sabbath that Jesus had made the mud and healed him. [15] The Pharisees asked the man all about it. So he told them, "He put the mud over my eyes, and when I washed it away, I could see!"

[16] Some of the Pharisees said, "This man Jesus is not from God, for he is working on the Sabbath." Others said, "But how could an ordinary sinner do such miraculous signs?" So there was a deep division of opinion among them.

[17] Then the Pharisees again questioned the man who had been blind and demanded, "What's your opinion about this man who healed you?"

The man replied, "I think he must be a prophet."

[18] The Jewish leaders still refused to believe the man had been blind and could now see, so they called in his parents. [19] They asked them, "Is this your son? Was he born blind? If so, how can he now see?"

[20] His parents replied, "We know this is our son and that he was born blind, [21] but we don't know how he can see or who healed him. Ask him. He is old enough to speak for himself." [22] His parents said this because they were afraid of the Jewish leaders, who had announced that anyone saying Jesus was the Messiah would be expelled from the synagogue. [23] That's why they said, "He is old enough. Ask him."

[24] So for the second time they

man who had been blind, and said to him, "Give glory to God; we know that this man is a sinner." 25 He then answered, "Whether He is a sinner, I do not know; one thing I do know, that though I was blind, now I see." 26 So they said to him, "What did He do to you? How did He open your eyes?" 27 He answered them, "I told you already and you did not listen; why do you want to hear *it* again? You do not want to become His disciples too, do you?" 28 They reviled him and said, "You are His disciple, but we are disciples of Moses. 29 We know that God has spoken to Moses, but as for this man, we do not know where He is from." 30 The man answered and said to them, "Well, here is an amazing thing, that you do not know where He is from, and *yet* He opened my eyes. 31 We know that God does not hear sinners; but if anyone is God-fearing and does His will, He hears him. 32 ªSince the beginning of time it has never been heard that anyone opened the eyes of a person born blind. 33 If this man were not from God, He could do nothing." 34 They answered him, "You were born entirely in sins, and are you teaching us?" So they put him out.

35 Jesus heard that they had put him out, and finding him, He said, "Do you believe in the Son of Man?" 36 He answered, "Who is He, ªLord, that I may believe in Him?" 37 Jesus said to him, "You have both seen Him, and He is the one who is talking with you." 38 And he said, "Lord, I believe." And he worshiped Him. 39 And Jesus said, "For judgment I came into this world, so that those who do not see may see, and that those who see may become blind." 40 Those of the Pharisees who were with Him heard these things and said to Him, "We are not blind too,

called in the man who had been blind and told him, "God should get the glory for this,* because we know this man Jesus is a sinner."

25 "I don't know whether he is a sinner," the man replied. "But I know this: I was blind, and now I can see!"

26 "But what did he do?" they asked. "How did he heal you?"

27 "Look!" the man exclaimed. "I told you once. Didn't you listen? Why do you want to hear it again? Do you want to become his disciples, too?"

28 Then they cursed him and said, "You are his disciple, but we are disciples of Moses! 29 We know God spoke to Moses, but we don't even know where this man comes from."

30 "Why, that's very strange!" the man replied. "He healed my eyes, and yet you don't know where he comes from? 31 We know that God doesn't listen to sinners, but he is ready to hear those who worship him and do his will. 32 Ever since the world began, no one has been able to open the eyes of someone born blind. 33 If this man were not from God, he couldn't have done it."

34 "You were born a total sinner!" they answered. "Are you trying to teach us?" And they threw him out of the synagogue.

35 When Jesus heard what had happened, he found the man and asked, "Do you believe in the Son of Man?*"

36 The man answered, "Who is he, sir? I want to believe in him."

37 "You have seen him," Jesus said, "and he is speaking to you!"

38 "Yes, Lord, I believe!" the man said. And he worshiped Jesus.

39 Then Jesus told him,* "I entered this world to render judgment—to give sight to the blind and to show those who think they see* that they are blind."

40 Some Pharisees who were standing nearby heard him and asked, "Are you saying we're blind?"

NASB

are we?" [41] Jesus said to them, "If you were blind, you would have no sin; but [a] since you say, 'We see,' your sin remains.

9:9 [a] Lit *That one*   9:16 [a] Or *attesting miracles*
9:22 [a] I.e. the Messiah   9:32 [a] Lit *From the age it was not heard*   9:36 [a] Or *Sir*   9:41 [a] Lit *now*

NLT

[41] "If you were blind, you wouldn't be guilty," Jesus replied. "But you remain guilty because you claim you can see.

9:4 Other manuscripts read *I must quickly carry out the tasks assigned me by the one who sent me;* still others read *We must quickly carry out the tasks assigned us by the one who sent me.*
9:24 Or *Give glory to God, not to Jesus;* Greek reads *Give glory to God.*   9:35 Some manuscripts read *the Son of God?* "Son of Man" is a title Jesus used for himself.   9:38-39a Some manuscripts do not include *"Yes, Lord, I believe!" the man said. And he worshiped Jesus. Then Jesus told him.*
9:39b Greek *those who see.*

Imagine what life would be like if you had been born without the ability to see. A person born blind can experience the warmth of sunlight on his face, but the beauty of a sunset can only be experienced with the eyes. She can inhale the aromas of a garden but the words *red, yellow, purple,* and *green* are meaningless to her. He can hear the crashing surf and even taste the salty air at a seaside resort, but the panorama of a briny, blue-green ocean with massive waves meeting gleaming white sand is beauty he will never know. These rich experiences would be lost or diminished without the ability to see, yet those who are born without sight literally don't know what they are missing. Their perspective is limited to what they can experience. And were it not for the testimony of sighted friends and loved ones, people born blind would never suspect they were missing much at all.

What a perfect metaphor to illustrate the plight of those living in the darkness of sin—you, me, every person born of a human father. We are all born spiritually blind, a legacy handed down through the generations of humanity. Furthermore, we are born into a world that has been twisted by sin and evil, so that even before a baby can draw a breath outside the womb, he or she suffers the consequences of human sin—the collective sin of humanity past and the individual sins of individuals in the present.

God created the world "good" (Gen. 1:31) and He gave humanity the dignity of stewarding creation as His vice-regents (Gen. 1:26-28) . . . *and we blew it!* The responsibility for the present state of the world is ours as humanity, the culpability is ours as humankind, and we daily add to the problem of evil as individuals by doing what we shouldn't and by failing to do what we should. Because of this sinful world system, we have been born spiritually blind into a world populated exclusively by people born spiritually blind; therefore, we would not know what we were missing were it not for a miraculous event in which the Light of God entered the world in the flesh and bone and blood of humanity for the purpose of giving us sight.

Sometime after the Feast of Tabernacles but before the Feast of the Dedication (Hanukkah; see John 10:22), somewhere in the old city of Jerusalem, Jesus and His disciples happened upon a man who was born without sight. As the story unfolds, we learn that their "chance" meeting had been scheduled since the beginning of time, and the man's "meaningless" affliction had been given divine purpose from the foundation of creation.

— 9:1 —

John provides very little detail about the time and place of this encounter because it is a logical continuation of Jesus' escalating clash with the religious elite in Jerusalem. We know it took place after the Feast of Tabernacles (September/October) and before Hanukkah (November/December), somewhere in the vicinity of Jerusalem, but outside the temple complex.

John presents the episode as spontaneous in the sense that Jesus did not have a meeting marked in His appointment calendar. In fact, the apostle gives the impression that the encounter was mere coincidence; but make no mistake, the air of randomness is intentional. John allows us to accept the incident as haphazard only to reveal the truth. Whereas sin has stirred the world into a chaotic mess, the Creator interjects order. Where the sinful world system randomly and capriciously causes affliction, the Lord gives purpose to misfortune—for His own glory *and* the good of those who believe. Some things never change.

— 9:2-4 —

People who had disabilities customarily claimed spots along a well-traveled street leading to the temple—and this is still a common sight near religious sites today. While the man born blind undoubtedly joined many others that day, he drew the disciples' attention more than his peers, probably because his condition was congenital rather than the result of disease or injury. His disability aroused their curiosity.

The disciples' question reflected a common understanding of sin in first-century Judaism, one that is sadly common today. The disciples saw the man's affliction as the just penalty of someone's sin, either his own or that of his parents. It's human nature to find someone to blame.

The Pharisees and Sadducees regarded any misfortune as the direct result of someone's sin. The religious world attempts to reduce life to easily quantifiable terms in which good earns blessing while affliction is the just penalty of wrongdoing. It's the basis of kings claiming "divine right" and an easy excuse to ignore those in need of mercy.

We mustn't be too hard on the disciples; they merely understood the world as it had been taught to them. Their theology was the result of generations of blind men leading other blind men. Their treatment of the man saddens me more than their ignorance. The disciples looked upon the man born blind as nothing more than an interesting theological case study, not a fellow human in need of compassion. Their lack of emotion disturbs me.

Jesus answered the question directly and then gave the disciples a theological principle that can be applied to any instance of affliction or hardship. God did not cause the man's affliction; the world did that. Nevertheless, the Lord gave the man's affliction a divine purpose before anything had been created. The blind man lay at the intersection of the world's affliction and God's preordained choice to turn his blindness into an occasion for rejoicing; he lay waiting for the preordained moment when Christ would "happen by" and then fulfill His Father's mission.

Take note of the Lord's use of pronouns in this literal translation of 9:4: "It is necessary for *us* to work the works of the one who sent *Me*." The "work of God" is to bring salvation to humanity in order to redeem those who will believe. Jesus came to complete the work of God through specific deeds in complete obedience, and He calls us to do the same. The Lord then used the images of day and night to warn that His time on earth would come to an end soon—which illustrates another theological truth: the time of grace is limited before the world suffers the ultimate judgment of God.

— 9:5-7 —

As soon as Jesus finished correcting the faulty theology of His disciples, He declared, "I am the Light of the world," and then He gave the man sight. He spat on the ground, mixed it with the substance of man's creation (Gen. 2:7), and then smeared the clay over the man's eyes. In this one act, Jesus asserted His authority over disabilities, sin, bad theology, religion, the temple, the Sabbath, even the religious authorities who opposed Him. And He had this opportunity because an infant came into the world decades earlier without the ability to see.

EXCURSUS: GOD DOES NOT DISGUISE HIS WRATH

JOHN 9:1-12

I have heard more than one parent of a disabled child ask, Did someone's sin cause my child's disability or abnormality? Am I to blame for this?

The answer is complicated because it involves two very distinct issues that we frequently combine: the issues of consequences and divine punishment. Let me state this clearly: They are not the same. God is involved, but not in the way we naturally think.

On the one hand, God usually allows our actions to produce the expected consequences. Before we act, He instructs, He warns, He frequently intervenes. He always puts us in the very best position to choose well and never allows us to be tempted beyond what we are able. Once we make our choice, however, He allows us to reap what we have sown. Using illicit drugs, abusing the use of alcohol, and smoking tobacco can damage a developing fetus, usually resulting in some kind of complication. Sins and poor choices produce unwanted consequences that can feel very much like punishment. However, these negative effects are not divine punishment, but divine grace. Reaping the unhappy fruit of what we have sown teaches us to be responsible managers of our own freedom. God, in His grace, uses the consequences of our sins and even the sins of the world to discipline and instruct us.

Divine punishment, on the other hand, is a very real product of sin. Nevertheless, it does not come by way of natural consequences, but by supernatural wrath. God doesn't disguise His wrath against sin; He doesn't hand down afflictions like a sulking, passive-aggressive adolescent with unlimited power. When He punishes

sin, He takes personal responsibility, He leaves no room for questioning, His punishment for sin is severe, and it is forever. Punishment for sin doesn't come indirectly through the world, but directly from God Himself.

Fortunately, punishment for sin has been delayed until the end of physical life for individuals or the "end of days" for the world. Until then, we have been given a gracious opportunity, a period of grace during which each of us has been given a choice.

When Christ died on the cross, He took our sins upon Himself and endured the wrath of God on our behalf. If you have accepted His gift of grace by believing in Him, you will never experience the wrath—the divine punishment—you deserve. In grace, Jesus took it all and left *none* for you. None.

If, however, you choose to trust in your own goodness or hope that your good deeds will somehow purify or counteract your bad behavior—if you reject His free gift—God's wrath waits for you. When you die, or if the Lord should return before then, you will surely suffer divine punishment for your sins. But not before. Even though you continue to live in rebellion, the Lord uses the consequences of your sins and poor choices to teach you—all the while extending the offer of fellowship with Him.

God does not cause sin or prompt temptation, and He does not participate in evil. But He will use the sad results of sin and poor choices for His own purposes. When Jesus and His disciples encountered a man born blind—a congenital defect—He took the opportunity to clarify this very issue.[11]

We can only speculate as to why the Lord used a mixture of saliva and clay to heal the man. The method is similar to the magical formula for healing in the *asklēpieion* (see photo caption on p. 111), and similar to His method for healing others (Mark 7:33; 8:23). We are never told why Jesus sent the man to wash in the pool. John adds an editorial note that the Hebrew name is based on the verb "to send," but we don't know for certain why he considered this important.

It would be idle speculation to guess about things we don't know. We do know this: Jesus was sent by the Father, the blind man was sent by Jesus to the pool with specific instructions, the man followed Jesus' instructions to the letter, and he received sight just as promised.

— **9:8-12** —

Try to imagine the scene. The man's community undoubtedly knew him well because his begging for alms had made him a fixture of the community for many years. The Pharisees pitied him for his sin-inflicted malady, the Sadducees tsked in condescending approval of God's justice, a few people showed compassion, and others silenced their jingling coins as they tiptoed by. Suddenly, one day, this same man bounded into the temple without his stick and beggar's basket, marveling at the splendor of God's house. Remarkably, worshipers noticed a familiar face yet failed to see the truth of what had occurred.

We see plenty of debate and hear lots of questions, but where is the excitement? Where is the joy on behalf of this man who had been miraculously healed? Instead of leading him to a celebration, they dragged him to an inquisition. He was made to stand before the Pharisees to answer for his healing as though he had done something wrong.

From the Pharisees' point of view, something was indeed very wrong. You will recall the disciples' original question, which began with the widely held assumption that physical affliction was proof positive that someone had sinned and was suffering God's judgment. The man's sudden and obviously miraculous healing threw everything the Pharisees knew about God, sin, and justice into doubt. *Did the Lord change His mind? Did He set aside justice? Was the man no longer guilty of sin?* So theological questions eclipsed joyous celebration.

— **9:13-17** —

John's narrative typically compresses time. Verse 14 suggests the man's inquisition took place some time after the Sabbath, perhaps a few days later. When asked how he had received his sight, he merely recounted the events, which established the pattern for the balance of their inter-action. The Pharisees wanted the man to answer theologically; how-ever, the man held tightly to the facts. While the Pharisees tried to spin the facts to fit their preconceived notions, the man wouldn't budge from his bottom-line perspective except to say that Jesus was a "prophet"—that is, one who is sent from God to proclaim His Word.

— 9:18-23 —

The Pharisees had a problem on their hands. They desperately needed to discredit Jesus in order to maintain moral superiority before the people. Yet, even according to their own tradition, only an authentic man of God can work miraculous "signs" (3:2; 9:16). Therefore, the miracle must be discredited. Because the man would not cooperate, the religious leaders summoned his parents, hoping to uncover some additional facts that would support their intentions.

This was not a search for truth. This was a deliberate sifting of facts, in which inconvenient evidence was set aside in favor of what would build a damning case against the Pharisees' enemy.

The Pharisees' campaign of fear and intimidation was by this time well-known, so the parents would offer nothing more than the barest facts, instead deferring to their son. They said, in effect, "He is not our responsibility; if someone is to be punished for his testimony, punish him."

— 9:24-29 —

The Pharisees struggled to build a case against Jesus, which drove them to desperation. Their opening statement at the man's second inquisition reveals their predetermined conclusion, despite the over-whelming evidence to the contrary. Take note of the exchange. The Pharisees tried to persuade the man to agree with their conclusion that Jesus was a "sinner," but he kept returning to the facts. So, the Pharisees attempted to sift through the facts again, perhaps to find an inconsistency in the man's testimony. The man's response (9:27) high-lighted the absurdity of the questioning. This angered the Pharisees, who then resorted to intimidation and personal attack.

— 9:30-34 —

At the beginning of the inquisition, the man maintained a neutral stance concerning Jesus. The question of Jesus' identity and whether or not He was a sinner didn't concern him. He knew only what his experience told him: once he was blind, now he could see. By the end, however, the Pharisees' absurd quest to condemn Jesus merely pushed the man closer to genuine belief. His final response to the Pharisees could not have been more different from that of the invalid by the Bethesda Pool (5:11-15).

The contrast between the man and the Pharisees could not have been more conspicuous either, a fact he highlighted in his final speech. The religious leaders knew the Scriptures better than anyone, and they had been trained in Hebrew history and theology, yet the man born blind (supposedly because of God's punishment for sin) had no difficulty putting the facts together to arrive at an obvious conclusion. His response rested upon the very theological traditions the Pharisees held most dear.

By the end of the inquisition, the Pharisees had no option but to set aside the facts and play their trump card: their superior position of power. In my experience, it is a clear admission of defeat when someone starts quoting from his or her resume in the midst of a debate. It's even clearer when that person resorts to the use of power to silence his or her opponent. The Pharisees essentially admitted, "We don't have an answer, so we'll excommunicate him."

— 9:35-38 —

The man's unwillingness to set aside the truth about Jesus closely parallels the miracle of sight. He wanted to see Jesus as He is, whereas the Pharisees wanted an excuse to reject Jesus. Yet, while the man demonstrated uncommon courage despite the grave consequences of excommunication, he did not know Christ as Savior. Therefore, Jesus "found" him (see 1:41-45; 5:14). By that time, his heart had been prepared for the Lord's invitation, so his immediate response was worship.

— 9:39-41 —

At first glance, Jesus' statement, "For judgment I came into this world," appears to contradict 3:17, but the slight difference between the Greek words *krisis* (3:17) and *krima* (9:39) is significant. *Krisis* [2920] is the act of judging; *krima* [2917] is the result. It was like saying, "I didn't come to the world in a judging capacity, but how you respond to Me could lead to your condemnation." In 3:17, Jesus declared that His purpose for coming to earth was not to hold people accountable for sin or to sit in judgment; He will do that upon His return (Dan. 7:13-14; Rev. 20:11-15). However, the point here is that each encounter with Jesus became a moment of truth in which the individual's response to the Light revealed his or her eternal destiny (John 3:19-21)—the true nature of good and evil are exposed when subjected to the light of Christ.

This point was not lost on the Pharisees, who challenged Jesus with the question, "We are not blind too, are we?" The structure of the question in the original language indicates that the person asking anticipates a negative response. In other words, the Pharisees expected Jesus to say, "Why, no, of course you are not blind." But Jesus didn't cooperate—He knew them to be spiritually blind.

Jesus' response forms a paradox. Those who are spiritually blind do not think they are missing anything and therefore deny their need. Those who "see" are those who admit their need for spiritual sight. Spiritually blind people conceal their sinfulness in order to bluff themselves and everyone else into thinking they have no need of salvation. People with spiritual sight readily recognize their own sinfulness and their desperate need for a Savior.

• • •

This story of the man born blind, who received sight, and the Pharisees, who bluffed their way through blindness, reminds me of an old saying I learned as a child: "There are none so blind as those who will not see." John warned of this in his prologue:

> There was the true Light which, coming into the world, enlightens every man. He was in the world, and the world was made through Him, and the world did not know Him. He came to His own, and those who were His own did not receive Him. But as many as received Him, to them He gave the right to become children of God, *even* to those who believe in His name, who were born, not of blood nor of the will of the flesh nor of the will of man, but of God. (John 1:9-13)

APPLICATION: JOHN 9:1-41

How to Respond to Intimidation

Some people insulate themselves from truth, and for the most part, they reap the consequences without affecting anyone around them. However, when these people occupy positions of authority, truth-tellers face an unpleasant dilemma: suppress the truth or be at odds with leadership. The man born blind encountered just such a dilemma after the Lord gave him sight. The religious experts who ruled over the temple could not deny the miracle, so they applied pressure to the man in order to silence his testimony and thus discredit Jesus. But the man refused to play their game.

I see in the man's response a worthy model to follow when someone in authority tries to silence truth through intimidation.

First, *the man appealed to undeniable facts (9:15, 25, 32)*. Authorities who silence the truth through intimidation hope to incite sinful behavior and then seek vindication by destroying or silencing their target. Appealing to facts shifts the focus of debate back to where it belongs: impersonal objectivity rather than personal opinion. It says, in effect, "The truth is your real threat, not me."

Second, *the man answered directly, yet briefly (9:17)*. Attempts to sidestep, minimize, or soften the truth never accomplish anything. Nor do attempts to convert enemies of truth. In fact, more words simply provide greater opportunity to turn the debate into a personal conflict, which is the goal of authorities who use intimidation. Answering directly and briefly leaves enemies of truth less ammunition with which to destroy their target.

Third, *the man refused to argue (9:26-27)*. Authorities who silence the truth through intimidation hope to find an inconsistency or some means of creating doubt by having their target rehash facts or restate opinions. Refusing to argue denies enemies of truth any opportunity to turn a debate into a personal matter.

Fourth, *the man remained fearless and resolved (9:30-33)*. As many theologians have taught us, "All truth is God's truth." To depart from truth is to be at odds with God. Yet authorities who silence the truth through intimidation try to convince their victims that *their* power is to be feared rather than God's. Resolving to hold tightly to the truth deprives enemies of truth of the power to intimidate.

By the end of this encounter, the religious elite made themselves look foolish when their tactics failed to accomplish anything. Having been defeated by truth, they fell back on their flimsy credentials and then abused their power (9:34). While the man suffered some negative consequences, he gained more than he lost. His separation from a corrupt religious institution allowed him to receive new life in Jesus Christ.

The Living Door
JOHN 10:1-42

[1] "Truly, truly, I say to you, he who does not enter by the door into the fold of the sheep, but climbs up some other way, he is a thief and a robber. [2] But he who enters by the door is a shepherd of the sheep. [3] To him the doorkeeper opens, and the sheep hear his voice, and he calls his own sheep by name and leads them out. [4] When he puts forth all his own, he goes ahead of them, and the sheep follow him because they know his voice. [5] A stranger they simply will not follow, but will flee from him, because they do not know the voice of strangers." [6] This figure of speech Jesus spoke to them, but they did not understand what those things were which He had been saying to them.

[7] So Jesus said to them again, "Truly, truly, I say to you, I am the door of the sheep. [8] All who came before Me are thieves and robbers, but the sheep did not hear them. [9] I am the door; if anyone enters through Me, he will be saved, and will go in and out and find pasture. [10] The thief comes only to steal and kill and destroy; I came that they may have life, and [a]have *it* abundantly.

[11] "I am the good shepherd; the good shepherd lays down His life for the sheep. [12] He who is a hired hand, and not a shepherd, who is not the owner of the sheep, sees the wolf coming, and leaves the sheep and flees, and the wolf snatches them and scatters *them*. [13] *He flees* because he is a hired hand and is not concerned about the sheep. [14] I am the good shepherd, and I know My own and My own know Me, [15] even as the Father knows Me and I know the Father; and I lay down My life for the sheep. [16] I have other sheep,

[1] "I tell you the truth, anyone who sneaks over the wall of a sheepfold, rather than going through the gate, must surely be a thief and a robber! [2] But the one who enters through the gate is the shepherd of the sheep. [3] The gatekeeper opens the gate for him, and the sheep recognize his voice and come to him. He calls his own sheep by name and leads them out. [4] After he has gathered his own flock, he walks ahead of them, and they follow him because they know his voice. [5] They won't follow a stranger; they will run from him because they don't know his voice."

[6] Those who heard Jesus use this illustration didn't understand what he meant, [7] so he explained it to them: "I tell you the truth, I am the gate for the sheep. [8] All who came before me* were thieves and robbers. But the true sheep did not listen to them. [9] Yes, I am the gate. Those who come in through me will be saved.* They will come and go freely and will find good pastures. [10] The thief's purpose is to steal and kill and destroy. My purpose is to give them a rich and satisfying life.

[11] "I am the good shepherd. The good shepherd sacrifices his life for the sheep. [12] A hired hand will run when he sees a wolf coming. He will abandon the sheep because they don't belong to him and he isn't their shepherd. And so the wolf attacks them and scatters the flock. [13] The hired hand runs away because he's working only for the money and doesn't really care about the sheep.

[14] "I am the good shepherd; I know my own sheep, and they know me, [15] just as my Father knows me and I know the Father. So I sacrifice my life for the sheep. [16] I have other sheep,

which are not of this fold; I must bring them also, and they will hear My voice; and they will become one flock *with* one shepherd. ¹⁷For this reason the Father loves Me, because I lay down My life so that I may take it again. ¹⁸No one has taken it away from Me, but I lay it down on My own initiative. I have authority to lay it down, and I have authority to take it up again. This commandment I received from My Father."

¹⁹A division occurred again among the Jews because of these words. ²⁰Many of them were saying, "He has a demon and is insane. Why do you listen to Him?" ²¹Others were saying, "These are not the sayings of one demon-possessed. A demon cannot open the eyes of the blind, can he?"

²²At that time the Feast of the Dedication took place at Jerusalem; ²³it was winter, and Jesus was walking in the temple in the portico of Solomon. ²⁴The Jews then gathered around Him, and were saying to Him, "How long ᵃwill You keep us in suspense? If You are ᵇthe Christ, tell us plainly." ²⁵Jesus answered them, "I told you, and you do not believe; the works that I do in My Father's name, these testify of Me. ²⁶But you do not believe because you are not of My sheep. ²⁷My sheep hear My voice, and I know them, and they follow Me; ²⁸and I give eternal life to them, and they will never perish; and no one will snatch them out of My hand. ²⁹ᵃMy Father, who has given *them* to Me, is greater than all; and no one is able to snatch *them* out of the Father's hand. ³⁰I and the Father are ᵃone."

³¹The Jews picked up stones again to stone Him. ³²Jesus answered them, "I showed you many good works from the Father; for which of them are you stoning Me?" ³³The Jews answered Him, "For a good

too, that are not in this sheepfold. I must bring them also. They will listen to my voice, and there will be one flock with one shepherd.

¹⁷"The Father loves me because I sacrifice my life so I may take it back again. ¹⁸No one can take my life from me. I sacrifice it voluntarily. For I have the authority to lay it down when I want to and also to take it up again. For this is what my Father has commanded."

¹⁹When he said these things, the people* were again divided in their opinions about him. ²⁰Some said, "He's demon possessed and out of his mind. Why listen to a man like that?" ²¹Others said, "This doesn't sound like a man possessed by a demon! Can a demon open the eyes of the blind?"

²²It was now winter, and Jesus was in Jerusalem at the time of Hanukkah, the Festival of Dedication. ²³He was in the Temple, walking through the section known as Solomon's Colonnade. ²⁴The people surrounded him and asked, "How long are you going to keep us in suspense? If you are the Messiah, tell us plainly."

²⁵Jesus replied, "I have already told you, and you don't believe me. The proof is the work I do in my Father's name. ²⁶But you don't believe me because you are not my sheep. ²⁷My sheep listen to my voice; I know them, and they follow me. ²⁸I give them eternal life, and they will never perish. No one can snatch them away from me, ²⁹for my Father has given them to me, and he is more powerful than anyone else.* No one can snatch them from the Father's hand. ³⁰The Father and I are one."

³¹Once again the people picked up stones to kill him. ³²Jesus said, "At my Father's direction I have done many good works. For which one are you going to stone me?"

³³They replied, "We're stoning you

work we do not stone You, but for blasphemy; and because You, being a man, make Yourself out *to be* God." ³⁴Jesus answered them, "Has it not been written in your Law, 'I SAID, YOU ARE GODS'? ³⁵If he called them gods, to whom the word of God came (and the Scripture cannot be broken), ³⁶do you say of Him, whom the Father sanctified and sent into the world, 'You are blaspheming,' because I said, 'I am the Son of God'? ³⁷If I do not do the works of My Father, do not believe Me; ³⁸but if I do them, though you do not believe Me, believe the works, so that you may ᵃknow and understand that the Father is in Me, and I in the Father." ³⁹Therefore they were seeking again to seize Him, and He eluded their grasp.

⁴⁰And He went away again beyond the Jordan to the place where John was first baptizing, and He was staying there. ⁴¹Many came to Him and were saying, "While John performed no sign, yet everything John said about this man was true." ⁴²Many believed in Him there.

10:10 ᵃOr *have abundance* 10:24 ᵃLit *do You lift up our soul* ᵇI.e. the Messiah 10:29 ᵃOne early ms reads *What My Father has given Me is greater than all* 10:30 ᵃOr *a unity;* or *one essence* 10:38 ᵃLit *know and continue knowing*

not for any good work, but for blasphemy! You, a mere man, claim to be God."

³⁴Jesus replied, "It is written in your own Scriptures* that God said to certain leaders of the people, 'I say, you are gods!'* ³⁵And you know that the Scriptures cannot be altered. So if those people who received God's message were called 'gods,' ³⁶why do you call it blasphemy when I say, 'I am the Son of God'? After all, the Father set me apart and sent me into the world. ³⁷Don't believe me unless I carry out my Father's work. ³⁸But if I do his work, believe in the evidence of the miraculous works I have done, even if you don't believe me. Then you will know and understand that the Father is in me, and I am in the Father."

³⁹Once again they tried to arrest him, but he got away and left them. ⁴⁰He went beyond the Jordan River near the place where John was first baptizing and stayed there awhile. ⁴¹And many followed him. "John didn't perform miraculous signs," they remarked to one another, "but everything he said about this man has come true." ⁴²And many who were there believed in Jesus.

10:8 Some manuscripts do not include *before me.* 10:9 Or *will find safety.* 10:19 Greek *Jewish people;* also in 10:24, 31. 10:29 Other manuscripts read *for what my Father has given me is more powerful than anything;* still others read *for regarding that which my Father has given me, he is greater than all.* 10:34a Greek *your own law.* 10:34b Ps 82:6.

If a picture is worth a thousand words, then a symbol is worth a thousand lectures. Jesus understood the power of a familiar image to unlock the mysteries of heaven. And no sight was more common in first-century Judea than that of a shepherd leading his sheep. With some historical and cultural background, we can learn a great deal from the symbols Jesus used to describe Himself. To the lost sheep of Israel, He was the living door and the good shepherd.

Unlike many farmers in Europe, who raise sheep for food, shepherds in first-century Judea tended sheep for their wool. The animals grazed and grew thick mats of fleece, which could be sheared off and sold for significant sums of money. Naturally, the larger a shepherd's flock, the greater his income, so the loss of just one animal cost him not only a few pounds of fleece each season, but the ability to make more sheep. Therefore, he faithfully nurtured and protected each animal throughout its life. He sacrificed his own comfort to provide safe grazing during the day and risked his own safety to guard the flock against thieves and predators during the night. Consequently, it was not uncommon for a shepherd to know each of his animals individually and to call each one by name.

A good shepherd never allowed his flock to remain in the field as night fell; thieves and wild animals took advantage of darkness to steal and to kill. If the pasture was close enough to the village, the sheep would be driven from the field to a communal pen, which was guarded by a designated keeper. In the morning, shepherds led their sheep out to pasture again. During temperate months, shepherds frequently drove their flocks into the wilderness to find adequate grazing. They always remained with them, camping out under the stars for weeks at a time. As darkness fell each evening, they corralled the flock into a cave or some other natural enclosure and slept at the entrance.

Shepherds frequently worked together and even shared the same enclosure during the night. The following morning the flocks could be easily separated simply by calling them in opposite directions. Author H. V. Morton watched this firsthand during his travels in Israel back in 1934.

> Early one morning I saw an extraordinary sight not far from Bethlehem. Two shepherds had evidently spent the night with their flocks in a cave. The sheep were all mixed together and the time had come for the shepherds to go in different directions. One of the shepherds stood some distance from the sheep and began to call. First one, then another, then four or five animals ran towards him; and so on until he had counted his whole flock.[12]

John's account is unique among the Gospels in that he doesn't recount any of the Lord's parables; he does, however, recall His use of figurative language and extended metaphors. This self-portrait as "the good shepherd" draws upon a familiar image painted in Old Testament prophecy (Jer. 23; Ezek. 34; Zech. 11) in which the Lord warns Israel's unfaithful spiritual leaders that He will come to do the job of shepherding Himself. Jesus claimed to be the fulfillment of that long-standing promise. The religious authorities were slow to pick up on the implications, but they understood in time.

— 10:1-6 —

John presents the next discourse as a logical continuation of the last, providing no information about the time and place of the event. This is not uncommon for him. Unless details about the setting can provide additional insight, John leaves it out. It's very likely this discourse took place several weeks later as part of an extended conversation with multiple audiences of Pharisees (cf. 10:22).

The primary point of His metaphor has to do with the role of truth in the world. Jesus rarely presented truth in order to turn nonbelievers into believers; most often, the truth became His means of drawing believers out of the world. Beginning with the feeding of the multitude in the wilderness (chapter 6) and the discourses that followed, Jesus merely taught the unvarnished truth about His identity, and His flock began to divide. Genuine believers followed the voice of their Master, while those who were not "his own" rejected Him (6:44, 65; 8:43, 47; 10:14). H. V. Morton's observations near Jericho are especially helpful.

[The Near Eastern shepherd] never drives [his flock] as our own shepherds drive their sheep. He always walks at their head, leading them along the roads and over hills to new pasture: and, as he goes, he sometimes talks to them in a loud sing-song voice, using a weird language unlike anything I have ever heard in my life. The first time I heard this sheep and goat language I was on the hills at the back of Jericho. A goat-herd had descended into a valley and was mounting a slope of an opposite hill when, turning around, he saw his goats had remained behind to devour a rich patch of scrub. Lifting his voice, he spoke to the goats in a language that Pan must have spoken on the mountains of Greece. . . . No sooner than he had spoken than an answering bleat shivered over the herd, and one or two of the animals turned their heads in his direction. But they did not obey him. The goat-herd then called out one word and gave a laughing kind of whinny. Immediately a goat with a bell round its neck stopped eating and, leaving the herd, trotted down the hill, across the valley and up the opposite slopes. . . . Very soon a panic spread among the herd. They forgot to eat. They looked up for the shepherd. He was not to be seen. . . . From the distance came the strange laughing call of the shepherd, and at the sound of it the entire herd stampeded into the hollow and leapt up the hill after him.[13]

John's editorial comment at the end of Jesus' illustration is ironic. Their failure to "hear" merely validated the Lord's point.

To protect their livestock from predators and thieves, shepherds herded their animals into a natural enclosure, such as this cave, and then stretched their bodies across the entrance for a good night's sleep. Jesus drew on this familiar imagery when He said, "I am the door of the sheep" (John 10:7-9).

— 10:7-10 —

Jesus followed His first double *amēn* (10:1) with another, which interprets the first. Jesus' predecessors are the priests, scribes, and Pharisees who presently ruled over the Jews. By identifying them as "thieves and robbers," He cast them in the role prophesied by Jeremiah (Jer. 23), Ezekiel (Ezek. 34), and Zechariah (Zech. 11). Whereas the Annas Bazaar left the people of Israel physically and spiritually impoverished (see commentary on John 2:13-14), Jesus came to bring genuine abundance.

People in the West (especially the false prophets of the "Word of Faith" movement) interpret "abundance" to mean prosperity, an abundance of money and possessions, creature comforts, a fat wallet, a prestigious job, the nicest house in town, and the sleekest car in the driveway. Yet I see no indication that Jesus offered His followers anything by way of material wealth. No stack of shekels. No pension. No insurance coverage. Not even a guarantee of safety. In fact, He promised them quite the opposite (Luke 9:22-25).

Jesus was not preaching against wealth, per se. As far as Jesus was concerned, money and possessions are morally neutral and have no relation whatsoever to the new kingdom, except that they might distract us from what He considers important. So if abundance is not cash, possessions, or comfort, what is it? Given that Jesus' inner circle of followers suffered persecution and died as martyrs, what kind of abundance did they receive? The abundance Jesus offers is a spiritual abundance that transcends circumstances like income, health, living conditions, and even death.

The abundant life is life that never ends, yet we don't have to wait until the end of our physical life to receive this abundance and to enjoy it. Abundant life includes peace, purpose, destiny, a genuine purpose for living, the joy of facing any adversity—including the grave—without fear, and the ability to endure hardship with confident assurance.

— 10:11-18 —

Jesus' statement is a strong "I AM" (*egō eimi* [1473, 1510]) paired with the phrase "good shepherd," which is particularly emphatic in Greek. What follows is a clear foreshadowing of the persecution He will suffer and a strong affirmation of His substitutionary death on behalf of His believers. Just as important is His acknowledgement that truth has always been a lightning rod for evil; nevertheless, He will not flinch as evil strikes Him with all the power of hell. As the Creator, He cannot be overpowered by anything. Yet He will voluntarily suffer and die to carry out the Father's redemptive plan.

This sets Jesus apart from the religious leaders who supposedly shepherd the people of God. Whereas He is selfless, they are selfish. Whereas He would lay down His life for the sheep, they would abandon all to save themselves. Whereas Jesus lived in complete obedience to the Father, they obeyed their own lusts.

In the middle of His dialogue, Jesus mentioned "other sheep." This is almost certainly non-Jews, such as Samaritans (like the people of Sychar in 4:7-45) and Gentiles yet to hear the good news.

— 10:19-21 —

Jesus had declared earlier that His sword of truth divides people; His voice of truth summons His own. Just as expected, the dividing of "the Jews" (the religious officials) that occurred in 7:43 and 9:16 continued as a result of this discourse.

— 10:22-24 —

The Feast of the Dedication, now known as Hanukkah, is usually celebrated in December, roughly two months after Sukkot, the Feast of Tabernacles (7:1–8:30). The Feast of the Dedication celebrates the re-dedication of the temple in 165 BC, three years after the altar had been desecrated by Antiochus Epiphanes. It was the crowning moment of the Maccabean revolt, which essentially gave Israel its independence for a short time. During Jesus' time, Jewish resentment for Roman occupation ran especially high during this festival, and their desire for the Messiah was felt more acutely than usual.

John's mention of winter would be redundant after mentioning Hanukkah were it not for his using the season to set the literary tone. The winter of Jesus' life was approaching. As He walked along the eastern portico of the temple, presumably after entering the eastern gate, the temple officials surrounded Jesus. They appeared willing to consider the possibility that Jesus had been telling the truth all along, that He was indeed the Messiah (cf. 1:19-34), perhaps driven to eagerness by the holiday. But make no mistake; they wanted a messiah tailor-made to fit their own desires.

— 10:25-31 —

Some scholars have objected that Jesus had not, in fact, "told" them He is the Christ. But I can think of a strong reason for His avoiding the exact phrase, "I am the Christ" (in addition to the reason He gave here). By the first century, Jewish theologians had attached so much misinformation to the title that the people would have expected of Jesus what God had never intended. They expected a kind of "super-David" warrior king who would lead them to regain independence and restore their economy (6:15). At His second coming, Jesus will become Israel's warrior king, but He first came to save people from their sin. Jewish theologians had attached outlandish myths to the Messiah's arrival; to claim the title "Christ" would have been to adopt a mythic identity.

Instead, Jesus produced all of the "signs" predicted by the Old Testament, which clearly identified Him as the Messiah. Moreover, He freely quoted, paraphrased, and alluded to messianic passages in Scripture, identifying Himself using the vocabulary of prophets. Anyone willing to set aside their biased expectations long enough to compare His words and deeds to the image set forth by Scripture did not have trouble recognizing Him.

Jesus made His earlier indictment plain again. The religious leaders refused to hear the Word of God in the flesh because they had rejected God's written Word long ago. Their rejection of the true Christ was nothing more than a continuation of their rejecting God all along (5:17, 37-38; 6:45; 7:27-28; 8:42-45; 9:29-34). Genuine believers, however, heed the voice of truth and are eternally safe in the care of the Good Shepherd, who will lay down His life to save them and wield His divine power to keep them secure. Belief is the authenticating response of a believer to his or her Savior. It is the Savior who does the saving, not the saved. Therefore, it is the faithfulness of Christ that seals the believer's salvation, not the faithfulness of the believer. Plain and simple: those who believe in Christ will never be lost.

Jesus concluded this portion of His discourse with a statement that was even bolder and more provocative than "I am the Christ." He said, "I and the Father are one," an allusion to the chief doctrinal statement of the Hebrew faith: "The LORD is one" (Deut. 6:4). However, John recorded Jesus' statement using a slightly different form of the Greek word for "one" from the Septuagint, the Greek translation of the Old Testament.[14] The "neuter" form that John uses (as opposed to the "masculine" form in the Septuagint) indicates singleness in essence. Therefore, a more literal rendering would be, "We (I and the Father) are one being." This had been established numerous times through His many "signs," including dramatic, authentic healings.

While the English language cannot pick up on the subtle yet profound nuance in Jesus' statement, it was obviously plain to Jesus' audience. Clearly, they connected the dots. As a result, they prepared to stone Him for identifying Himself as God.

— 10:32-39 —

In response to the Jews' intention to stone Him, Jesus employed a complex bit of irony common to rabbinic argument. He turned the accusation around with a quote from Psalm 82, which reads:

> God takes His stand in His own congregation;
> He judges in the midst of the rulers [literally "gods"].
> How long will you judge unjustly
> And show partiality to the wicked?   Selah.
> Vindicate the weak and fatherless;
> Do justice to the afflicted and destitute.
> Rescue the weak and needy;
> Deliver them out of the hand of the wicked.
> They do not know nor do they understand;

They walk about in darkness;
All the foundations of the earth are shaken.
I said, "You are gods,
And all of you are sons of the Most High.
Nevertheless you will die like men
And fall like any one of the princes."
Arise, O God, judge the earth!
For it is You who possesses all the nations.

The psalmist reminded Israel's appointed judges that they were like little gods in that they had been appointed by the Supreme Judge to rule in His stead; therefore, they were accountable to Him. Jesus identified the worthless judges in the psalm as the religious leaders standing before Him and declared Himself to be the fulfillment of the poem's opening line: "God takes His stand in His own congregation; He judges in the midst of the [gods]" (Ps. 82:1). For these apostate rulers of Israel to judge the Supreme Judge was nothing short of blasphemy. In reality, it is *they* who should be stoned.

Jesus then pointed to the impossibility of overcoming their self-willed doubt. When He behaved in God-like fashion—cleansing the temple, feeding the hungry, healing the sick, fulfilling the promises of Scripture—He was rejected as one opposed to God (John 7:20; 8:48-52; 10:20). Yet they clamored for a "sign" (2:18; 4:48; 6:30). He then invited them to evaluate His deeds, the quintessential proof of goodness according to Hebrew wisdom.

The religious leaders reacted in typical religious fashion toward those they couldn't control: they sought to seize Jesus in order to execute Him. But He escaped.

— 10:40-42 —

Jesus left Jerusalem to minister in the wilderness east of the Jordan River, where John the Baptizer had proclaimed the coming of Messiah. By now, Herod Antipas had killed the Forerunner (Matt. 14:3-12), leaving his disciples without a leader. Unlike the little "gods" in the temple, these disciples compared the Baptizer's predictions to the works of Jesus and responded with belief.

• • •

As the ministry of Jesus continued, the spiritual distance between His sheep—"His own"—and the unbelieving world grew wider. The truth He proclaimed about Himself and His mission was the Shepherd's voice calling His sheep to follow; however, this same truth not only identified His enemies; it incited them to violence. Later, He would tell His disciples that the purpose for His confronting the apostate religious authorities with the truth was to give them an occasion to consummate their sin (John 15:22-25).

As the Feast of Dedication came to a close, Jesus retreated from Jerusalem. He had important work to do elsewhere. Nevertheless, this would not be His last confrontation with the religious leaders. The division between believers and nonbelievers grew steadily wider, though not yet to the point of breaking. That would happen soon enough.

APPLICATION: JOHN 10:1-42

Four Qualities of the Good Shepherd's Flock

Are you a part of the Good Shepherd's flock? At some point in your past, you should be able to recall a time when you repented of your sin, acknowledged your utter helplessness to save yourself, and then received from God the gift of eternal life through the atoning sacrifice of Jesus Christ on your behalf. The Bible teaches that this decision is the beginning of a lifelong process of transformation. As the years pass, the sheep faithfully follow their Shepherd and they become more and more like Him.

In His discourse with the religious experts, Jesus described four qualities of God's sheep. His purpose was to show that none of the religious experts bore any evidence of these qualities and therefore should be regarded as outsiders.

First, *God's sheep are sensitive to His leading (10:27a)*. If you were to travel the world and hold an informal conversation with Christians in different countries and from different cultures, you will eventually hear them describe a common experience: the inner prompting of the Holy Spirit leading them to do certain things or to go certain places. I'm amazed by the similarities in the descriptions of people living on opposite sides of the globe.

Second, *God's sheep are eager to obey His commands (10:27b)*. Sheep follow their shepherd because sheep without a shepherd die; they fall prey to wild animals, they wander into danger, they fail to find food and water, and they succumb to the elements. Obedient sheep live.

A genuine believer wants to obey; he or she is motivated by love, not fear. Furthermore, genuine believers soon learn that obedience allows them to enjoy life to its fullest.

Third, *God's sheep are confident (10:28)*. Domestic sheep and sheep in the wild behave very differently while grazing. Wild sheep remain ever vigilant against predators; they chew with their heads up, constantly scanning their surroundings for danger. Domestic sheep graze with their heads down, popping up only when a noise draws their attention. When sheep have a good shepherd, they feel secure; they don't live in constant fear.

Believers rest in the confidence that Christ has done everything to secure their eternal safety for them. Because He is completely faithful, we may rest in the confident assurance that we will be preserved from evil until evil no longer exists.

Fourth, *God's sheep are secure (10:29)*. This is a fact, not a feeling. Regardless of how insensitive, how disobedient, or how fearful the sheep choose to be, their place in the flock is secure. This is not to suggest the believer's behavior is irrelevant or unimportant. People who willfully resist spiritual growth and who evidence no change in their values or behavior need to seriously question their spiritual condition. However, eternal security—like salvation itself—is not based upon the goodness of the believer. We are just as incapable of holding onto salvation as we were of earning it in the first place.

While holding tightly to the fourth quality, let me encourage you to cultivate the first three as you continue following the Lord. Remain sensitive to His leading, obey Him with all diligence and without hesitation, and rest in the confidence of His power to protect you from all evil. After all, He's the Good Shepherd, so following Him is for your own good.

Back from Beyond
JOHN 11:1-46

NASB

¹Now a certain man was sick, Lazarus of Bethany, the village of Mary and her sister Martha. ²It was the Mary who anointed the Lord with ointment, and wiped His feet with her hair, whose brother Lazarus was sick. ³So the sisters sent *word* to Him,

NLT

¹A man named Lazarus was sick. He lived in Bethany with his sisters, Mary and Martha. ²This is the Mary who later poured the expensive perfume on the Lord's feet and wiped them with her hair.* Her brother, Lazarus, was sick. ³So the two sisters

saying, "Lord, behold, he whom You love is sick." 4But when Jesus heard *this*, He said, "This sickness is not to end in death, but for the glory of God, so that the Son of God may be glorified by it." 5Now Jesus loved Martha and her sister and Lazarus. 6So when He heard that he was sick, He then stayed two days *longer* in the place where He was. 7Then after this He said to the disciples, "Let us go to Judea again." 8The disciples said to Him, "Rabbi, the Jews were just now seeking to stone You, and are You going there again?" 9Jesus answered, "Are there not twelve hours in the day? If anyone walks in the day, he does not stumble, because he sees the light of this world. 10But if anyone walks in the night, he stumbles, because the light is not in him." 11This He said, and after that He said to them, "Our friend Lazarus has fallen asleep; but I go, so that I may awaken him out of sleep." 12The disciples then said to Him, "Lord, if he has fallen asleep, he will ªrecover." 13Now Jesus had spoken of his death, but they thought that He was speaking of ªliteral sleep. 14So Jesus then said to them plainly, "Lazarus is dead, 15and I am glad for your sakes that I was not there, so that you may believe; but let us go to him." 16Therefore Thomas, who is called ªDidymus, said to *his* fellow disciples, "Let us also go, so that we may die with Him."

17So when Jesus came, He found that he had already been in the tomb four days. 18Now Bethany was near Jerusalem, about ªtwo miles off; 19and many of the Jews had come to Martha and Mary, to console them concerning *their* brother. 20Martha therefore, when she heard that Jesus was coming, went to meet Him, but Mary ªstayed at the house. 21Martha then said to Jesus, "Lord, if You had been here, my brother would not have died. 22Even now I

sent a message to Jesus telling him, "Lord, your dear friend is very sick."

4But when Jesus heard about it he said, "Lazarus's sickness will not end in death. No, it happened for the glory of God so that the Son of God will receive glory from this." 5So although Jesus loved Martha, Mary, and Lazarus, 6he stayed where he was for the next two days. 7Finally, he said to his disciples, "Let's go back to Judea."

8But his disciples objected. "Rabbi," they said, "only a few days ago the people* in Judea were trying to stone you. Are you going there again?"

9Jesus replied, "There are twelve hours of daylight every day. During the day people can walk safely. They can see because they have the light of this world. 10But at night there is danger of stumbling because they have no light." 11Then he said, "Our friend Lazarus has fallen asleep, but now I will go and wake him up."

12The disciples said, "Lord, if he is sleeping, he will soon get better!" 13They thought Jesus meant Lazarus was simply sleeping, but Jesus meant Lazarus had died.

14So he told them plainly, "Lazarus is dead. 15And for your sakes, I'm glad I wasn't there, for now you will really believe. Come, let's go see him."

16Thomas, nicknamed the Twin,* said to his fellow disciples, "Let's go, too—and die with Jesus."

17When Jesus arrived at Bethany, he was told that Lazarus had already been in his grave for four days. 18Bethany was only a few miles* down the road from Jerusalem, 19and many of the people had come to console Martha and Mary in their loss. 20When Martha got word that Jesus was coming, she went to meet him. But Mary stayed in the house. 21Martha said to Jesus, "Lord, if only you had been here, my brother would not have died. 22But even now I know

NASB

know that whatever You ask of God, God will give You." ²³ Jesus said to her, "Your brother will rise again." ²⁴ Martha said to Him, "I know that he will rise again in the resurrection on the last day." ²⁵ Jesus said to her, "I am the resurrection and the life; he who believes in Me will live even if he dies, ²⁶ and everyone who lives and believes in Me will never die. Do you believe this?" ²⁷ She said to Him, "Yes, Lord; I have believed that You are ªthe Christ, the Son of God, *even* ᵇHe who comes into the world."

²⁸ When she had said this, she went away and called Mary her sister, saying secretly, "The Teacher is here and is calling for you." ²⁹ And when she heard it, she got up quickly and was coming to Him.

³⁰ Now Jesus had not yet come into the village, but was still in the place where Martha met Him. ³¹ Then the Jews who were with her in the house, and consoling her, when they saw that Mary got up quickly and went out, they followed her, supposing that she was going to the tomb to weep there. ³² Therefore, when Mary came where Jesus was, she saw Him, and fell at His feet, saying to Him, "Lord, if You had been here, my brother would not have died." ³³ When Jesus therefore saw her weeping, and the Jews who came with her *also* weeping, He was deeply moved in spirit and ªwas troubled, ³⁴ and said, "Where have you laid him?" They said to Him, "Lord, come and see." ³⁵ Jesus wept. ³⁶ So the Jews were saying, "See how He loved him!" ³⁷ But some of them said, "Could not this man, who opened the eyes of the blind man, ªhave kept this man also from dying?"

³⁸ So Jesus, again being deeply moved within, came to the tomb. Now it was a cave, and a stone was lying against it. ³⁹ Jesus said, "Remove

NLT

that God will give you whatever you ask."

²³ Jesus told her, "Your brother will rise again."

²⁴ "Yes," Martha said, "he will rise when everyone else rises, at the last day."

²⁵ Jesus told her, "I am the resurrection and the life.* Anyone who believes in me will live, even after dying. ²⁶ Everyone who lives in me and believes in me will never ever die. Do you believe this, Martha?"

²⁷ "Yes, Lord," she told him. "I have always believed you are the Messiah, the Son of God, the one who has come into the world from God." ²⁸ Then she returned to Mary. She called Mary aside from the mourners and told her, "The Teacher is here and wants to see you." ²⁹ So Mary immediately went to him.

³⁰ Jesus had stayed outside the village, at the place where Martha met him. ³¹ When the people who were at the house consoling Mary saw her leave so hastily, they assumed she was going to Lazarus's grave to weep. So they followed her there. ³² When Mary arrived and saw Jesus, she fell at his feet and said, "Lord, if only you had been here, my brother would not have died."

³³ When Jesus saw her weeping and saw the other people wailing with her, a deep anger welled up within him,* and he was deeply troubled. ³⁴ "Where have you put him?" he asked them.

They told him, "Lord, come and see." ³⁵ Then Jesus wept. ³⁶ The people who were standing nearby said, "See how much he loved him!" ³⁷ But some said, "This man healed a blind man. Couldn't he have kept Lazarus from dying?"

³⁸ Jesus was still angry as he arrived at the tomb, a cave with a stone rolled across its entrance. ³⁹ "Roll the stone aside," Jesus told them.

the stone." Martha, the sister of the deceased, said to Him, "Lord, by this time ᵃthere will be a stench, for he has been *dead* four days." ⁴⁰Jesus said to her, "Did I not say to you that if you believe, you will see the glory of God?" ⁴¹So they removed the stone. Then Jesus raised His eyes, and said, "Father, I thank You that You have heard Me. ⁴²I knew that You always hear Me; but because of the ᵃpeople standing around I said it, so that they may believe that You sent Me." ⁴³When He had said these things, He cried out with a loud voice, "Lazarus, come forth." ⁴⁴The man who had died came forth, bound hand and foot with wrappings, and his face was wrapped around with a cloth. Jesus said to them, "Unbind him, and let him go."

⁴⁵Therefore many of the Jews who came to Mary, and saw what He had done, believed in Him. ⁴⁶But some of them went to the Pharisees and told them the things which Jesus had done.

11:12 ᵃLit *be saved* 11:13 ᵃLit *the slumber of sleep* 11:16 ᵃI.e. the Twin 11:18 ᵃLit *15 stadia* (9,090 ft) 11:20 ᵃLit *was sitting* 11:27 ᵃI.e. the Messiah ᵇThe Coming One was the Messianic title 11:33 ᵃLit *troubled Himself* 11:37 ᵃLit *have caused that this man also not die* 11:39 ᵃLit *he stinks* 11:42 ᵃLit *crowd*

But Martha, the dead man's sister, protested, "Lord, he has been dead for four days. The smell will be terrible."

⁴⁰Jesus responded, "Didn't I tell you that you would see God's glory if you believe?" ⁴¹So they rolled the stone aside. Then Jesus looked up to heaven and said, "Father, thank you for hearing me. ⁴²You always hear me, but I said it out loud for the sake of all these people standing here, so that they will believe you sent me." ⁴³Then Jesus shouted, "Lazarus, come out!" ⁴⁴And the dead man came out, his hands and feet bound in graveclothes, his face wrapped in a headcloth. Jesus told them, "Unwrap him and let him go!"

⁴⁵Many of the people who were with Mary believed in Jesus when they saw this happen. ⁴⁶But some went to the Pharisees and told them what Jesus had done.

11:2 This incident is recorded in chapter 12. 11:8 Greek *Jewish people;* also in 11:19, 31, 33, 36, 45, 54. 11:16 Greek *Thomas, who was called Didymus.* 11:18 Greek *was about 15 stadia* [about 2.8 kilometers]. 11:25 Some manuscripts do not include *and the life.* 11:33 Or *he was angry in his spirit.*

Death is an inescapable fact of life.

Death is ruthless; it frequently comes without warning and strikes without mercy. Death is unrelenting; it cannot be cheated, bribed, outwitted, overcome, or eluded. Death is indiscriminate; it takes young and old, poor and rich, sick and healthy, wicked and benevolent. And death is universal; all must ultimately succumb to its darkness.

Death is a harsh reality of life . . . but it was not always so, and it need not be the end.

— 11:1-2 —

After His last encounter with the religious elite in Jerusalem, Jesus took refuge in the same wilderness that had protected the Baptizer from their murderous intent. The Lord ministered to John's disciples there for an unknown length of time (though not more than three months) before traveling to Perea or perhaps Galilee (11:7). All we know for certain is that Jesus was more than a day's walk from Bethany, which was the home of His friends Lazarus, Martha, and Mary, just two miles east of Jerusalem.

John's editorial note about Mary's anointing Jesus demonstrates that he assumed his audience was familiar with the Synoptic Gospels (Matthew, Mark, and Luke). John doesn't tell this story until 12:1-8.

— 11:3-6 —

Lazarus was not one of the twelve disciples, but the Lord loved him. The man's sisters sent a messenger to inform Jesus that His friend was near death with a serious illness. However, Jesus purposely delayed His departure, confidently declaring, "This sickness is not to end in death." Depending on how far away Jesus was from Bethany, it is very likely He knew what the disciples did not know at the time: Lazarus was already dead. Consider a possible order of events:

The first day: The messenger arrived with the news that Lazarus was ill. Jesus decided to remain where He was for two days. (The NASB inserts the word "longer," but the Greek sentence reads simply, "He remained two days in the place where He was.") [11:1-5]

The second day: Jesus deliberately remained where He was. [11:6]

The third day: Jesus departed for Judea. (Eastern cultures include the present day when counting elapsed days, whereas Western cultures don't begin counting until the dawn of the following day.) [11:7-16]

The fourth day: Jesus continued His journey, taking His customary direct route through Samaria, and arrived in Bethany late in the day.[15] He was told that Lazarus had been dead four days. [11:17]

If my hypothetical timetable is anywhere close to accurate, Lazarus was dead by the time the messenger reached Jesus. Regardless, Jesus did not need to rush to Bethany; the extent of His power isn't cut short by death. John's remark, "Now Jesus loved Martha and her sister and Lazarus," assures us the Lord did not callously allow Martha and Mary to grieve the loss of their brother merely to prove a point. His righteousness and sovereignty are always undergirded by His love.

Take note of an important detail. Jesus didn't promise that Lazarus wouldn't die; He promised that his sickness would not end in death. His point? Death might claim the life of Lazarus, but death would not have the final say in the matter.

— 11:7-16 —

By now, Jerusalem had become a dangerous place for Jesus; the unvarnished truth He proclaimed made Him a lightning rod. However, Jesus didn't leave the region to avoid danger; He retreated because the time for His atoning death had not come. When the disciples reminded Jesus of the danger, He reminded them of His mission and the need for urgency (cf. 9:4). Naturally, they fretted over His safety because they didn't want to see their messianic hope assassinated before He had the opportunity to claim His throne and inaugurate the new kingdom. Of course, the disciples' perspective was limited. Death might claim the life of Jesus, but death would not have the final say in the matter. Jesus would use this opportunity to expand their vision.

Some have been unfairly critical of Thomas's gloomy outlook. He merely acknowledged the truth of Jesus' circumstances. The religious leaders wanted little more than to see Jesus dead, and they were willing to do almost anything to kill Him. Even so, Thomas grimly stood beside his Master in the face of what appeared to be certain death.

— 11:17-19 —

As John demonstrates the Lord's power over death in this portion of the narrative, he reminds his readers of the danger looming just 2 miles (3.2 kilometers) across the Kidron Valley. The amount of tension the reader feels depends entirely upon his or her trust in Jesus' power. The disciples undoubtedly saw murder in the eyes of every Pharisee they encountered and wondered how or when the plot would unfold.

Meanwhile, mourners had been gathering near the home of Lazarus. In keeping with ancient Near Eastern custom, the dead man had been wrapped in spice-soaked linens and placed inside a burial cave the same day he died. The climate did not tolerate any delay. Jesus arrived on the fourth day, which may have been significant in view of rabbinic teaching. Jewish literature from the third century AD teaches that the soul of a dead individual remains near the body for three days, hoping to reenter; then, upon seeing decay set in, it gives up hope and departs.[16] If this literature reflects established teaching, resurrection after the third day was unthinkable. Apparently death plus decay was more hopeless than death alone.

— 11:20-27 —

Mary and Martha responded to the death of their brother with the same kind of disillusionment and anger any one of us would. Yet Jesus dealt tenderly with them, offering no rebuke and expressing no disappointment. He listened. He empathized. He gave them calm reassurance. His care for them is a marvelous pattern for pastors caring for those who must grieve a loss.

I don't see any rebuke in Martha's remarks. I see regret, a sorrowful acceptance of events she hoped would be different. I also see a fledgling faith submerged in grief. In that moment of time, she failed to comprehend the full extent of the Lord's power. Jesus does not have to be present to heal someone (4:46-54). Her statement, "Even now I know that whatever You ask of God, God will give You," cannot mean that she expected Jesus to bring her brother back to life (cf. 11:24, 39). Instead, this is a confession of her faith in Christ despite her disappointment. His delay and apparent decision not to act didn't diminish her confidence in Him.

Jesus reassured Martha with a statement having double meaning: "Your brother will rise again." Martha had accepted Jesus' teaching that He would raise up those who believed in Him in the last day (6:39-40, 44, 54). This is the abundant life Jesus had promised His followers (10:10); it is eternal and incorruptible. However, we do not have to wait until the "last day" to begin receiving this abundant life. We can receive it and enjoy it now. That's because the "abundant life"—eternal, incorruptible, transforming life—is not a special kind of energy or a commodity that is somehow transferred from God to an individual. This resurrection-life is a person: Jesus.

Martha continued to express her faith in Jesus, declaring Him to be the Christ and the Son of God. She demonstrated remarkably mature theological understanding, even more than the Twelve! Yet she still did not understand the Lord's full meaning. She would before sunset.

— 11:28-34 —

Mary was not able to meet with the Lord privately. Sometimes the grief-stricken need solitude but fail to find it because well-meaning loved ones fear to leave them alone. So, Mary met Jesus with an entourage in tow. Her remarks reflected those of Martha, perhaps because they shared some measure of disillusionment.

When the group arrived, Jesus witnessed their sorrow and was "deeply moved in spirit" and "troubled." The key Greek terms are *embrimaomai* [1690], which describes sternness or anger (Matt. 9:30; Mark 1:43; 14:5), and *tarassō* [5015], which literally means "to stir up, to agitate" (John 5:7). Some have suggested the general state of unbelief among the people angered Jesus, but this seems out of place given His compassionate care for Martha, whose struggle was not so much with incomplete faith as with incomplete knowledge. Unlike the selfish gods of mythology, the triune God of the Bible empathizes with His creation. Furthermore, He is justifiably angry with the cruelty of evil, which oppresses His beloved creation. Death is the ultimate affront to His creative act; it tries to destroy what He intended to last forever.

— 11:35-37 —

Upon arriving at the burial cave of Lazarus, Jesus wept (literally, "shed tears"). And the observation of the people was spot-on. Jesus did indeed love Lazarus. While the Son of God is fully divine, He is completely human. Moreover, He is the perfect representation of the Father, who is Spirit, yet nonetheless emotionally connected to the creatures bearing His likeness. When we weep, our Creator weeps with us; not with the kind of hopelessness we endure through our ignorance, but with compassion. No one hates the devastating consequences of sin more than He.

However, some of the people reflected the same limited thinking that plagued Martha and Mary—the same ignorance we display when we underestimate the power of God.

— 11:38-42 —

As Jesus approached the cave, He was again moved to anger (*embrimaomai*). He commanded the men in the crowd to remove the stone from the grave entrance, an act forbidden by rabbinic tradition. The men who obeyed the Lord's command risked ritual defilement; nevertheless, they obeyed.

When Martha protested that the smell of her brother's decomposing body had certainly overpowered the burial spices, Jesus reminded her of their earlier conversation and promised that her belief would allow her to see "the glory of God" (11:4). Once the stone was removed, Jesus prayed aloud so that witnesses to the miracle would understand that He and the Father were united in the miracle. Death is not the will of the Father; He *hates* death. Therefore, Jesus was not overriding His Father's decision to "take" Lazarus; He was reclaiming Lazarus from the enemy of life.

— 11:43-44 —

In fulfillment of His earlier prediction (5:28), the dead man responded to Jesus' voice. I once heard a country preacher say that if Jesus hadn't called Lazarus by name, every grave within earshot would have rumbled open and their long-dead inhabitants would have answered His call. One day, "all who are in the tombs will hear His voice," but on this day, only Lazarus had been summoned.

He emerged from the tomb still wrapped in the spice-soaked linen strips of cloth, perhaps even struggling to move. Corpses were typically encased in 75 to 100 pounds (35 to 45 kilograms) of perfumed resins (19:39-40). The witnesses to the miracle had to help Lazarus out of the burial wrappings. John includes these details to clarify a crucial difference between Lazarus's experience and that of Jesus (20:5-7). Rather than being resurrected, Lazarus was *resuscitated*. His old body had been reanimated, but it was the same body that had fallen ill and stopped working. Sometime later, after Lazarus was summoned from beyond, he went there again. He fell ill or suffered a fatal injury or simply grew feeble with age, and he died. He was buried and his body decayed. It awaits its resurrection (1 Thes. 4:13-17).

One day yet future, Lazarus, along with everyone who has died "in Christ," will be summoned from beyond, not to resume life in bodies that will again die, but to enjoy eternal life in bodies that cannot suffer, cannot fall ill, cannot die, and cannot decay. This will not be mere resuscitation. This will be the glorious day of *resurrection!*

— 11:45-46 —

Many of the religious leaders who visited Martha and Mary during their bereavement witnessed Jesus' power over death and chose to believe. However, some did not. Not even raising the dead convinced them! John concludes the story as he opened it, with a reminder of the danger Jesus faced being so close to Jerusalem (11:8, 16, 18).

• • •

Whenever I conduct the funeral of a believer in Jesus Christ, the promises of Easter fill my mind. Death is not the end for that individual. We weep because we miss seeing our loved one's face, hearing that familiar voice, feeling that reassuring touch. But we weep with a confident assurance that the souls of the dead in Christ are living joyfully in the presence of their Maker, awaiting the resurrection of their bodies (2 Cor. 5:1-10). We weep in anticipation of seeing them again.

Not so for the nonbeliever. Their funerals are among the most dreadful experiences of my life. They remained willfully deaf to the voice of Christ during life, and when His voice rattles the earth upon His return, they will lie motionless as stones. No one on earth will ever see them again, and they will be forever alone, forever subject to the consequences of sin.

Don't let that be you! Pause right now and place your complete trust in the Son of God. I want to have the pleasure of meeting you—if not in this life, in the life beyond.

APPLICATION: JOHN 11:1-46

A Better Time, a Better Plan, a Better Future

I admit it; sometimes I become very frustrated with the Lord. My prayer requests are for the most part asked with a pure motive, rarely selfish, yet He frequently chooses to allow events to unfold in ways I do not comprehend. His timing is rarely what I would expect of a God who loves His people. The money needed for a critical ministry is too little or arrives too late. Evil people flourish financially while good people suffer with cancer. His ways and His timing challenge my trust far more often than I wish, so I find myself repeating the words in my mind like a mantra, "The Lord is right in all His ways."

When I read the story of Martha and Mary's loss, I take comfort in knowing that I am not alone in my experience. Here are two women who knew the Son of God as personally as I know my closest friends, yet struggled to understand His handling of Lazarus's illness. Why did He not rush to Bethany as soon as He heard the news? Did He not care? Why would He allow Lazarus to suffer his illness one moment longer than necessary? Yet each woman—to her credit—expressed continued devotion to the Lord; neither lashed out in bitterness or questioned His goodness. They merely expressed disappointment, laced ever so subtly with bewilderment.

The Lord empathized with the sorrow of His friends and shared their anger at the ruthless oppression of death. Death, after all, is not the invention of God; it's the consequence of sin. How He responded to this latest expression of evil illustrates two truths that weave together like warp and woof to create a beautiful tapestry of grace.

First, *when events don't go as we think they should, God has a better time and a better way.* I have learned through the years never to fret over a missed flight. A friend of mine was flying from Florida to Dallas with a connection in New Orleans. He made the connection in plenty of time and felt very fortunate to have a seat on the overbooked plane. Unfortunately, there had been an error. Another gentleman had reserved that seat more than a month earlier, so my friend was forced to take another, much later flight.

This occurred long before cell phones and the Internet, computer-generated boarding passes, or even answering machines; communication was expensive and not nearly so instantaneous. By the time he called home, his wife was frantic. The plane he was forced to leave had experienced a midair collision. Needless to say, my friend felt very grateful for what he had thought a terrible inconvenience. The Lord had a better time and a better way to get him home.

When something difficult occurs, we rarely know what alternative circumstance the Lord saves us from experiencing. But one thing is certain: we would always be grateful if we saw everything from His viewpoint. God knows what He's about.

Second, *God's perspective is eternal, not temporal.*

If the Lord were to answer every prayer for healing by restoring health, no one would ever die, but we would be stuck in bodies that feel pain, fall ill, experience injury, grow tired, and wear out . . . forever. We would be forced to ride a perpetual roller coaster of illness and health, injury and repair, until we finally wearied of living and then wished for death! Thank God, He has a better way. He brought Lazarus back from the dead for the greater good of all, but eventually, the man joyfully traded his failing flesh for the hope of a body that cannot be touched by evil.

We tend to view our existence as limited to the seventy or eighty years we have before our bodies can stand no more and then cease to function. The Bible assures us that this part of our existence is nothing compared to what we will receive after death.

I admit, the words I sometimes speak to myself while in distress, "The Lord is right in all His ways," feel empty, like mere words. But they keep me calm until, eventually, the Lord breaks through and vindicates the trust I place in Him, although rarely by giving me the explanations I desire. Instead, His Spirit speaks to my spirit in a place deeper than mere words can penetrate, and then I find rest in the goodness of His blameless character and perfect plan.

The Breaking Point
JOHN 11:47-57

NASB

47 Therefore the chief priests and the Pharisees convened a council, and were saying, "What are we doing? For this man is performing many ᵃsigns. 48 If we let Him *go on* like this, all men will believe in Him, and the Romans will come and take away both our place and our nation." 49 But one of them, Caiaphas, who was high priest that year, said to them, "You know nothing at all, 50 nor do you take into account that it is expedient for you that one man die for the people, and that the whole nation not perish." 51 Now he did not say this ᵃon his own initiative, but being high priest that year, he prophesied that Jesus was going to die for the nation, 52 and not for the nation only, but in order that He might also gather together into one the children of God who are scattered abroad. 53 So from that day on they planned together to kill Him.

54 Therefore Jesus no longer continued to walk publicly among the Jews, but went away from there to the country near the wilderness, into a city called Ephraim; and there He stayed with the disciples.

55 Now the Passover of the Jews was near, and many went up to Jerusalem out of the country before the Passover to purify themselves. 56 So they were seeking for Jesus, and were saying to one another as they stood in the temple, "What do you think; that He will not come to the feast at all?" 57 Now the chief priests and the Pharisees had given orders that if anyone knew where He was,

NLT

47 Then the leading priests and Pharisees called the high council* together. "What are we going to do?" they asked each other. "This man certainly performs many miraculous signs. 48 If we allow him to go on like this, soon everyone will believe in him. Then the Roman army will come and destroy both our Temple* and our nation."

49 Caiaphas, who was high priest at that time,* said, "You don't know what you're talking about! 50 You don't realize that it's better for you that one man should die for the people than for the whole nation to be destroyed."

51 He did not say this on his own; as high priest at that time he was led to prophesy that Jesus would die for the entire nation. 52 And not only for that nation, but to bring together and unite all the children of God scattered around the world.

53 So from that time on, the Jewish leaders began to plot Jesus' death. 54 As a result, Jesus stopped his public ministry among the people and left Jerusalem. He went to a place near the wilderness, to the village of Ephraim, and stayed there with his disciples.

55 It was now almost time for the Jewish Passover celebration, and many people from all over the country arrived in Jerusalem several days early so they could go through the purification ceremony before Passover began. 56 They kept looking for Jesus, but as they stood around in the Temple, they said to each other, "What do you think? He won't come for Passover, will he?" 57 Meanwhile, the leading priests and Pharisees had publicly ordered that anyone

NASB

he was to report it, so that they might seize Him.

11:47 ᵃOr *attesting miracles* 11:51 ᵃLit *from himself*

NLT

seeing Jesus must report it immediately so they could arrest him.

11:47 Greek *the Sanhedrin.* 11:48 Or *our position;* Greek reads *our place.* 11:49 Greek *that year;* also in 11:51.

If you have lived very long at all, you have experienced at least one "moment of truth"—that sweet and terrible instant when the truth about some particular matter can no longer be denied, or minimized, or rationalized, or disguised. There it is, in all its stark, unforgiving glory, demanding a choice. You can bury the truth and then live in manic, strained denial for the rest of your days, or you can submit to that truth and then rest in its freedom. If you have faced such a moment, you know—try as you might to find it—there's no compromising middle way that will allow you to avoid the distressing consequences of either choice. Denial is a slippery slope leading to a quagmire of pretending and deception. Acceptance requires life-altering choices that will cause intense pain for everyone involved. At least with truth, the pain is the healing kind. But that doesn't make the choice any easier.

King David experienced his moment of truth when the prophet Nathan stuck a bony finger in his face and said, "You are the man!" (2 Sam. 12:7). By this act, the prophet exposed the king's secret sin and called him to account.

> "Thus says the LORD God of Israel, 'It is I who anointed you king over Israel and it is I who delivered you from the hand of Saul. I also gave you your master's house and your master's wives into your care, and I gave you the house of Israel and Judah; and if that had been too little, I would have added to you many more things like these! Why have you despised the word of the LORD by doing evil in His sight? You have struck down Uriah the Hittite with the sword, have taken his wife to be your wife, and have killed him with the sword of the sons of Ammon.'" (2 Sam. 12:7-9)

David's moment of truth offered him two choices, and only two: silence the prophet permanently, or else repent. It was a choice between power and truth. He could have become like his predecessor, Saul, who jealously clutched his power and wielded it to hunt down the Lord's anointed one (1 Sam. 16:13), hoping to murder him. Instead, David proved to be very different from Saul; David was a man after God's own heart (1 Sam. 13:14) despite his awful sins. He chose to submit to the truth and then rest in its inevitable reward: release from turmoil, freedom from fear, and eventually, peace with God (Pss. 32; 51).

The public ministry of Jesus was a three-year moment of truth for the religious leaders of first-century Israel. The Word of God, who had been promised for centuries, now stood before them in flesh and blood, truth incarnate. They denied the truth, disputed the truth, marginalized the truth, and even tried to silence the truth, but Jesus will not be set aside or put off. He leaves no compromising middle way. Each individual must decide what to do with Him. Deny or submit? Reject or believe? Embrace Him and experience freedom, or kill Him and preserve the illusion of power?

After Jesus exercised power over death, many religious leaders began to break ranks and believe in the Son of God (John 11:45). Therefore, the custodians of religious power in Jerusalem (see commentary on 10:32-39) could no longer put off the question of Jesus.

— 11:47-48 —

By the time of Jesus, the Jews had instituted what may be considered a provisional government in anticipation of the Messiah, who would rule as king. Until then, they vested the high priest with all the rights and privileges of a monarch (1 Maccabees 14:35-49) with the understanding that he should step aside when the Christ came to claim His rightful place on the throne of Israel. Except during the reign of Herod the Great, who had himself named "King of the Jews" by Rome, the high priest traditionally guided the nation as its provisional leader. Throughout its history, Israel also looked to a body of elders for day-to-day leadership, a council known as the Sanhedrin, which served as both parliament and supreme court. This ruling council of seventy learned men set Jewish policy (within limits established by Rome) and ruled on civil and criminal court cases.

The Sanhedrin placed a high priority on maintaining the uneasy balance between Rome's desire to dominate its subjects and the yearning of the Jewish people for independence. Normally the high priest (who was appointed by Rome) and the Sanhedrin (who advocated for independent-minded Jews) engaged in a kind of public rivalry, each pretending to work against the other, yet neither really wanting anything different. Change of any kind would threaten to strip everyone of their power.

The council met in order to decide what they should do with Jesus; He bore all the scriptural credentials and produced all the right "signs" of the Messiah, yet He lacked an army. To side with Jesus (as they understood the role of the Christ) was to defy Rome. But to defy Rome without an army was to invite the worst kind of death. Roman generals were known to line the roads of rebel cities with the crucified bodies of its men and women and to sell their children into slavery.

— 11:48-53 —

Throughout much of its history, the high priest presided over the Sanhedrin, acting as its moderator and official voice, but that ended around 200 BC when the council felt the need for a balance of powers. At that time, they created the office of *Nasi* to preside over the council and the office of *Av Bet Din,* "Head of the House of Law," to preside over matters involving the law. At the time of Jesus, the *Nasi* was a descendant of the legendary Jewish teacher Hillel.[17]

For the high priest to attend a special meeting of the Sanhedrin was not unprecedented, but it did suggest something extraordinary was occurring, much like the President of the United States attending a special meeting of Congress.

The high priest "that year" was Caiaphas, the corrupt son-in-law and figurehead of the true power in the temple, Annas. When Caiaphas heard the debate, he issued an unwitting prophecy. While he was not a genuine man of God, he ironically spoke a profound truth. He merely suggested they make Jesus the fall guy if Rome should seek someone to blame for the agitation of the crowds. John points to the theological truth of Jesus' substitutionary death for the sins of believers in Israel and of Gentile nations abroad.

By the end of the meeting, the religious leaders had decided upon their official disposition concerning Jesus. Submitting to the truth would require them to cede their power, which they refused to do. Therefore, because they wouldn't accept the truth that Jesus is the Messiah, they officially decided to kill Him.

— 11:54-57 —

Jesus avoided contact with the religious officials for the time being, though not out of fear. He simply had no need for further discussion. The die had been cast. The breaking point had been reached, the point of no return. Each man associated with the official powers of the nation had made up his mind, one way or another. The next time He would encounter the religious authorities of the temple, it would be in an official capacity. Soon He would enter Jerusalem as King Jesus, the Messiah, arriving to claim the throne of Israel and to assume command of His temple.

The exact location of the town "Ephraim" has been lost to history; however, the name may refer to Ephron, an ancient site near present-day et-Taiyibeh, about a day's walk northeast of Jerusalem.

APPLICATION: JOHN 11:47-57

To Thine Own Self Be Truthful

When I was a young man, I listened to sermons and lessons on the life of Jesus and the conspiracy to kill Him with great confusion. I couldn't understand why anyone would murder the Son of God, unless genuine ignorance or out-and-out insanity had clouded his or her vision. I even wondered whether, if the Lord could have spoken to them just one more time, maybe—just maybe—they would have seen their error. Perhaps one more miracle might have helped them see the truth; a great, collective "ah-ha" would have preceded their profound apologies and complete acceptance of Him as their long-awaited Messiah.

When I outgrew the callow innocence of youth, I accepted a sad, yet all-too-common reality: some people don't want the truth. The lies they tell themselves make the world theirs to control. At least that's what they've worked hard to believe. And they will destroy anyone who threatens to tear their fantasy worlds apart, because they are terrified to face the truth that we are, in fact, powerless.

Can there be a more senseless lie than one we tell ourselves?

In describing the last days of Jesus' public ministry in Jerusalem, John's matter-of-fact tone underscores a terrifying reality. The religious leaders had willfully rejected the truth of Jesus Christ, so He gave them over to their self-delusion. Theologians call this "judicial abandonment."[18] This tough-love decision on the part of God is not a passive releasing, but an active "giving over" for the purpose of redemption. When the Lord hands someone over to his or her sin, you can be sure of this: the consequences are grave. It is a defining moment in which a person will either break down in repentance or remain stubbornly rebellious, even in the face of damnation.

By way of application, I have only one point: *Seek the truths you most fear to find; they hold the greatest promise of freedom and the gravest threat of destruction.* This prompts several searching questions. Ponder each one seriously.

- What truths have you been resisting?
- What voice have you been silencing or keeping at a distance to avoid hearing what you instinctively know to be true?
- How has the Lord confronted you lately?
- Have you drowned out your own conscience with activity, or work, or relationships, or some other kind of escape?
- Do you ignore the inner voice of reason warning you to stop some behavior you know to be wrong?

I urge you to answer each question—honestly. Heed the truth; choose the freedom it brings, or unimaginable destruction will certainly follow.

Seeking before Hiding
JOHN 12:1-50

NASB

¹Jesus, therefore, six days before the Passover, came to Bethany where Lazarus was, whom Jesus had raised from the dead. ²So they made Him a supper there, and Martha was serving; but Lazarus was one of those reclining *at the table* with Him. ³Mary then took a ªpound of very costly perfume of pure nard, and anointed the feet of Jesus and wiped His feet with her hair; and the house was filled with the fragrance of the perfume. ⁴But Judas Iscariot, one of His disciples, who was intending to ªbetray Him, said, ⁵"Why was this perfume not sold for ªthree hundred denarii and given to poor *people?*" ⁶Now he said this, not because he was concerned about the poor, but because he was a thief, and as he had the money box, he used to pilfer what was put into it. ⁷Therefore Jesus said, "Let her alone, so that she may keep ªit for the day of My burial. ⁸For you

NLT

¹Six days before the Passover celebration began, Jesus arrived in Bethany, the home of Lazarus—the man he had raised from the dead. ²A dinner was prepared in Jesus' honor. Martha served, and Lazarus was among those who ate* with him. ³Then Mary took a twelve-ounce jar* of expensive perfume made from essence of nard, and she anointed Jesus' feet with it, wiping his feet with her hair. The house was filled with the fragrance.

⁴But Judas Iscariot, the disciple who would soon betray him, said, ⁵"That perfume was worth a year's wages.* It should have been sold and the money given to the poor." ⁶Not that he cared for the poor—he was a thief, and since he was in charge of the disciples' money, he often stole some for himself.

⁷Jesus replied, "Leave her alone. She did this in preparation for my burial. ⁸You will always have the

always have the poor with you, but you do not always have Me."

⁹ The large crowd of the Jews then learned that He was there; and they came, not for Jesus' sake only, but that they might also see Lazarus, whom He raised from the dead. ¹⁰ But the chief priests planned to put Lazarus to death also; ¹¹ because on account of him many of the Jews were going away and were believing in Jesus.

¹² On the next day the large crowd who had come to the feast, when they heard that Jesus was coming to Jerusalem, ¹³ took the branches of the palm trees and went out to meet Him, and *began* to shout, "Hosanna! BLESSED IS HE WHO COMES IN THE NAME OF THE LORD, even the King of Israel." ¹⁴ Jesus, finding a young donkey, sat on it; as it is written, ¹⁵ "FEAR NOT, DAUGHTER OF ZION; BEHOLD, YOUR KING IS COMING, SEATED ON A DONKEY'S COLT." ¹⁶ These things His disciples did not understand at the first; but when Jesus was glorified, then they remembered that these things were written of Him, and that they had done these things to Him. ¹⁷ So the ᵃpeople, who were with Him when He called Lazarus out of the tomb and raised him from the dead, continued to testify *about Him*. ¹⁸ For this reason also the ᵃpeople went and met Him, because they heard that He had performed this ᵇsign. ¹⁹ So the Pharisees said to one another, "You see that you are not doing any good; look, the world has gone after Him."

²⁰ Now there were some Greeks among those who were going up to worship at the feast; ²¹ these then came to Philip, who was from

poor among you, but you will not always have me."

⁹ When all the people* heard of Jesus' arrival, they flocked to see him and also to see Lazarus, the man Jesus had raised from the dead. ¹⁰ Then the leading priests decided to kill Lazarus, too, ¹¹ for it was because of him that many of the people had deserted them* and believed in Jesus.

¹² The next day, the news that Jesus was on the way to Jerusalem swept through the city. A large crowd of Passover visitors ¹³ took palm branches and went down the road to meet him. They shouted,

"Praise God!*
Blessings on the one who comes
   in the name of the LORD!
Hail to the King of Israel!"*

¹⁴ Jesus found a young donkey and rode on it, fulfilling the prophecy that said:

¹⁵ "Don't be afraid, people of
   Jerusalem.*
Look, your King is coming,
   riding on a donkey's colt."*

¹⁶ His disciples didn't understand at the time that this was a fulfillment of prophecy. But after Jesus entered into his glory, they remembered what had happened and realized that these things had been written about him.

¹⁷ Many in the crowd had seen Jesus call Lazarus from the tomb, raising him from the dead, and they were telling others* about it. ¹⁸ That was the reason so many went out to meet him—because they had heard about this miraculous sign. ¹⁹ Then the Pharisees said to each other, "There's nothing we can do. Look, everyone* has gone after him!"

²⁰ Some Greeks who had come to Jerusalem for the Passover celebration ²¹ paid a visit to Philip, who was

NASB

Bethsaida of Galilee, and *began to ask him*, saying, "Sir, we wish to see Jesus." 22 Philip came and told Andrew; Andrew and Philip came and told Jesus. 23 And Jesus answered them, saying, "The hour has come for the Son of Man to be glorified. 24 Truly, truly, I say to you, unless a grain of wheat falls into the earth and dies, it remains alone; but if it dies, it bears much fruit. 25 He who loves his ªlife loses it, and he who hates his ªlife in this world will keep it to life eternal. 26 If anyone ªserves Me, he must follow Me; and where I am, there My servant will be also; if anyone ªserves Me, the Father will honor him.

27 "Now My soul has become troubled; and what shall I say, 'Father, save Me from this hour'? But for this purpose I came to this hour. 28 Father, glorify Your name." Then a voice came out of heaven: "I have both glorified it, and will glorify it again." 29 So the crowd *of people* who stood by and heard it were saying that it had thundered; others were saying, "An angel has spoken to Him." 30 Jesus answered and said, "This voice has not come for My sake, but for your sakes. 31 Now judgment is upon this world; now the ruler of this world will be cast out. 32 And I, if I am lifted up from the earth, will draw all men to Myself." 33 But He was saying this to indicate the kind of death by which He was to die. 34 The crowd then answered Him, "We have heard out of the Law that ªthe Christ is to remain forever; and how can You say, 'The Son of Man must be lifted up'? Who is this Son of Man?" 35 So Jesus said to them, "For a little while longer the Light is among you. Walk while you have the Light, so that darkness will not overtake you; he who walks in the darkness does not know where he goes. 36 While you have the Light,

NLT

from Bethsaida in Galilee. They said, "Sir, we want to meet Jesus." 22 Philip told Andrew about it, and they went together to ask Jesus.

23 Jesus replied, "Now the time has come for the Son of Man* to enter into his glory. 24 I tell you the truth, unless a kernel of wheat is planted in the soil and dies, it remains alone. But its death will produce many new kernels—a plentiful harvest of new lives. 25 Those who love their life in this world will lose it. Those who care nothing for their life in this world will keep it for eternity. 26 Anyone who wants to serve me must follow me, because my servants must be where I am. And the Father will honor anyone who serves me.

27 "Now my soul is deeply troubled. Should I pray, 'Father, save me from this hour'? But this is the very reason I came! 28 Father, bring glory to your name."

Then a voice spoke from heaven, saying, "I have already brought glory to my name, and I will do so again." 29 When the crowd heard the voice, some thought it was thunder, while others declared an angel had spoken to him.

30 Then Jesus told them, "The voice was for your benefit, not mine. 31 The time for judging this world has come, when Satan, the ruler of this world, will be cast out. 32 And when I am lifted up from the earth, I will draw everyone to myself." 33 He said this to indicate how he was going to die.

34 The crowd responded, "We understood from Scripture* that the Messiah would live forever. How can you say the Son of Man will die? Just who is this Son of Man, anyway?"

35 Jesus replied, "My light will shine for you just a little longer. Walk in the light while you can, so the darkness will not overtake you. Those who walk in the darkness cannot see where they are going. 36 Put

believe in the Light, so that you may become sons of Light."

These things Jesus spoke, and He went away and ªhid Himself from them. 37 But though He had performed so many ªsigns before them, *yet* they were not believing in Him. 38 *This was* to fulfill the word of Isaiah the prophet which he spoke: "LORD, WHO HAS BELIEVED OUR REPORT? AND TO WHOM HAS THE ARM OF THE LORD BEEN REVEALED?" 39 For this reason they could not believe, for Isaiah said again, 40 "HE HAS BLINDED THEIR EYES AND HE HARDENED THEIR HEART, SO THAT THEY WOULD NOT SEE WITH THEIR EYES AND PERCEIVE WITH THEIR HEART, AND ªBE CONVERTED AND I HEAL THEM." 41 These things Isaiah said because he saw His glory, and he spoke of Him. 42 Nevertheless many even of the rulers believed in Him, but because of the Pharisees they were not confessing *Him,* for fear that they would be ªput out of the synagogue; 43 for they loved the ªapproval of men rather than the ªapproval of God.

44 And Jesus cried out and said, "He who believes in Me, does not believe in Me but in Him who sent Me. 45 He who sees Me sees the One who sent Me. 46 I have come *as* Light into the world, so that everyone who believes in Me will not remain in darkness. 47 If anyone hears My sayings and does not keep them, I do not judge him; for I did not come to judge the world, but to save the world. 48 He who rejects Me and does not receive My sayings, has one who judges him; the word I spoke is what

your trust in the light while there is still time; then you will become children of the light."

After saying these things, Jesus went away and was hidden from them.

37 But despite all the miraculous signs Jesus had done, most of the people still did not believe in him. 38 This is exactly what Isaiah the prophet had predicted:

"LORD, who has believed our
    message?
To whom has the LORD
    revealed his powerful arm?"*

39 But the people couldn't believe, for as Isaiah also said,

40 "The Lord has blinded their eyes
    and hardened their hearts—
so that their eyes cannot see,
    and their hearts cannot
      understand,
and they cannot turn to me
    and have me heal them."*

41 Isaiah was referring to Jesus when he said this, because he saw the future and spoke of the Messiah's glory. 42 Many people did believe in him, however, including some of the Jewish leaders. But they wouldn't admit it for fear that the Pharisees would expel them from the synagogue. 43 For they loved human praise more than the praise of God.

44 Jesus shouted to the crowds, "If you trust me, you are trusting not only me, but also God who sent me. 45 For when you see me, you are seeing the one who sent me. 46 I have come as a light to shine in this dark world, so that all who put their trust in me will no longer remain in the dark. 47 I will not judge those who hear me but don't obey me, for I have come to save the world and not to judge it. 48 But all who reject me and my message will be judged on the day of judgment by the truth I have

NASB

will judge him at the last day. ⁴⁹For I did not speak ᵃon My own initiative, but the Father Himself who sent Me has given Me a commandment *as to* what to say and what to speak. ⁵⁰I know that His commandment is eternal life; therefore the things I speak, I speak just as the Father has told Me."

12:3 ᵃI.e. a Roman pound, equaling 12 oz   12:4 ᵃOr *hand Him over*   12:5 ᵃEquivalent to 11 months' wages   12:7 ᵃI.e. the custom of preparing the body for burial   12:17 ᵃLit *crowd*   12:18 ᵃLit *crowd*   ᵇOr *attesting miracle*   12:25 ᵃLit *soul*   12:26 ᵃOr *is serving*   12:34 ᵃI.e. the Messiah   12:36 ᵃLit *was hidden*   12:37 ᵃOr *attesting signs*   12:40 ᵃLit *be turned*; i.e. turn about   12:42 ᵃI.e. excommunicated   12:43 ᵃOr *glory*   12:49 ᵃLit *of Myself*

NLT

spoken. ⁴⁹I don't speak on my own authority. The Father who sent me has commanded me what to say and how to say it. ⁵⁰And I know his commands lead to eternal life; so I say whatever the Father tells me to say."

12:2 Or *who reclined.*   12:3 Greek *took 1 litra* [327 grams].   12:5 Greek *worth 300 denarii.* A denarius was equivalent to a laborer's full day's wage.   12:9 Greek *Jewish people*; also in 12:11.   12:11 Or *had deserted their traditions*; Greek reads *had deserted.*   12:13a Greek *Hosanna,* an exclamation of praise adapted from a Hebrew expression that means "save now."   12:13b Ps 118:25-26; Zeph 3:15.   12:15a Greek *daughter of Zion.*   12:15b Zech 9:9.   12:17 Greek *were testifying.*   12:19 Greek *the world.*   12:23 "Son of Man" is a title Jesus used for himself.   12:34 Greek *from the law.*   12:38 Isa 53:1.   12:40 Isa 6:10.

Chapter 12 of John's narrative marks a significant transition in Jesus' life. While no less than three years elapsed in the first eleven chapters, John slows the pace of his narrative to cover less than a week in this chapter, and then three days in chapters thirteen to twenty. This segment also marks a sudden shift from public ministry to private mentoring. Chapters 1–11 saw Jesus traveling up and down that narrow strip of land that is Israel, conducting a widely public ministry, healing and teaching multiple thousands of followers. His immense popularity commanded the attention of the chief priests and Pharisees and at the same time protected Him from assassination, most notably during His Triumphal Entry. This gave Him ample opportunity to proclaim the

Final Week: From Public to Private

according to the Gospel of John

BETHANY	EPHRAIM	BETHANY	JERUSALEM		
PUBLIC				PRIVATE	
John 11:1-45	John 11:46-57	John 12:1-11	John 12:12-19	John 12:20-50	John 13–17
Miracle	**Escape**	**Supper**	**Entry**	**Greeks**	**Conference**
	The Breaking Point	Mary's Worship vs. Judas's Greed	Worship of People vs. "Jews'" Envy		"He went away and hid Himself" (12:36b)
		6 days before	*5 days before*	*4 days before*	*The night before*

Word of God in the temple, to confront the religious leaders about their abuse of power, to correct their theology concerning sin and salvation, and to set straight their crooked messianic expectations. His ministry of presenting the truth of God (of which He was the literal embodiment) attracted believers, whose hearts had been prepared to respond to Him. However, this very same truth also repulsed nonbelievers, pushing them to the breaking point.

As the appointed "hour" of Jesus' glory approached—the time of His suffering, death, burial, resurrection, and ascension—the work of preparation had been completed. His final week on earth would be spent in the company of His closest friends as He prepared His disciples for what lay ahead, all while walking the path to the cross His Father had prepared beforehand.

— 12:1-2 —

Six days before His crucifixion, Jesus returned to Bethany, just two miles from the hornets' nest of conspiratorial enemies in Jerusalem. John 11:45 tells us that when Jesus brought Lazarus back from the beyond, a number of "Jews"—chief priests, scribes, and Pharisees—believed in the Son of God. The parallel account of this in the Synoptic Gospels tells us that a Pharisee named Simon hosted a supper in honor of Jesus (Matt. 26:6-13; Mark 14:3-9; Luke 7:36-50).

Some commentators object to the suggestion that the account in Luke 7 is the same as that in John 12, primarily for two reasons. First, they assume Jesus was in Galilee at the time; however, a close reading reveals that although Jesus was in the Galilean towns of Capernaum (Luke 7:1) and Nain (where he raised another man from the dead; Luke 7:11) prior to dining with the Pharisee, Luke says nothing about the location of the meal itself. Nothing in the text precludes the possibility of the banquet taking place in Judea.

A second objection points to the characterization of the woman as "immoral" or "a sinner" (Luke 7:37, 39), while Mary of Bethany is described as a very devout, godly follower of Christ. If Mary had been a particularly notorious woman of questionable morals before encountering Jesus, there is even greater reason to believe she became a particularly notable woman of God after believing in Him. It would be just like Luke to stress the sinfulness of her former life while telling the story of her unrestrained worship of Jesus in the presence of a legalist.

If the four accounts describe the same event, the banquet took place in the home of a Pharisee named Simon, who would not have been welcome in the temple because of his leprosy—or, more likely because of Jesus, leprosy that had been healed.[19] Jesus and Lazarus reclined at the table with the other guests, while Martha helped to serve. Jesus would have been reclining on one side with His feet pulled away from the table behind Him.

— 12:3-6 —

Mary may not have been invited to the banquet by the Pharisaic leper, who may not have left his hypocritical ways far behind. Or, Mary may have elected to abandon her serving duties to express her devotion to Jesus (cf. Luke 10:38-42). Regardless, sometime during the meal, she opened an alabaster jar of expensive perfume and anointed Jesus' head (Matt. 26:7; Mark 14:3). Then, moved by her enormous gratitude for grace, or overtaken by grief for the ordeal He was about to suffer, Mary knelt over His feet, broke the alabaster jar, and emptied the perfume on Jesus' feet in a lavish gesture of worship. She drenched His feet with her tears and dried them with her hair. The fragrance of her spontaneous devotion filled the room.

In doing this, Mary violated several cultural norms. First, her society expected her to be serving. Second, touching the feet of another person was considered degrading; Mary's wiping the feet of Jesus with her hair—the crown and glory of a woman—left her with no public dignity whatsoever. Third, a woman was never to take her hair down in public—ever. Fourth, the perfume she collected was a typical treasure kept by women for their dowry, which she emptied on Jesus. Her lavish act of worship left her without a dowry, thus reducing her prospects for a favorable marriage.

Simon silently protested, "If this man were a prophet He would know who and what sort of person this woman is who is touching Him, that she is a sinner" (Luke 7:39). Judas objected for another reason. He watched in horror as he witnessed nearly one year's wage for a common laborer seep through the cracks in the floor. John, writing more than sixty years later, knew the true reason for Judas's objection. The trusted treasurer had been embezzling the group's funds for some time. The man was greedy to the core, despite his pious-sounding suggestion.

Judas had been cultivating a double life for months or quite possibly years. Truth, like a sharp blade, divides whatever stands before it, separating even soul from spirit to reveal the heart of a man (Heb. 4:12). In the case of Judas, it created a gaping chasm between his public persona and his private self. His charming religious facade kept a seething resentment carefully hidden from anyone he hoped to impress.

— 12:7-8 —

We cannot know for certain what was in Mary's mind as she worshiped the Lord with her aromatic treasure, but the Lord gave it profound theological purpose. The first step in preparing a body for burial was to rinse it with water and anoint it with perfumed oil. Jesus used her expression of devotion to signal the coming of His own death.

Jesus' public rebuke of Judas finally brought the duplicitous disciple to his breaking point. According to Matthew and Mark, it was after this event he decided to betray the Lord.

— 12:9-11 —

Despite His winnowing the multitudes, Jesus remained immensely popular. Undoubtedly, genuine believers could be found among the crowds, but in this case, the motivation appears to be mere curiosity. And their presence revealed Jesus' location, which He had previously kept discreet. Once the religious leaders learned of Jesus' presence and gained the help of a spy within Jesus' inner circle, a plot to kill Him began to form and accelerate.

— 12:12-19 —

John's narrative suddenly shifts from the fragrant banquet room in Bethany to a bustling street leading into Jerusalem, where thronging worshipers had come in anticipation of the Passover feast. As with other feasts, worshipers wondered if Jesus would attend and eagerly watched for His arrival (see John 7:11; 11:56). Upon His arrival, they lined His path to the city with palm branches and clothes, shouting "Hosanna!" which means, "Save us." Their shouts included words from a messianic psalm (Ps. 118:26).

Jesus had entered the city of Jerusalem many times during His ministry, but this "triumphal entry" to the capital of the Hebrew nation differed in one primary respect. He no longer visited as a worshiper; this day He claimed it as King. However, unlike a conquering warrior king, He entered the city on a symbol of peace. He rode on a humble donkey rather than sitting high in the saddle of a prancing white steed or riding in a stately chariot behind a team of horses. John quotes Zechariah 9:9 to stress the fact that Jesus fulfilled a well-known messianic prophecy.

"Daughter of Zion" is a tender expression for the citizens of Jerusalem.

The events of this day wouldn't make any sense to the disciples until after Jesus ascended to heaven and they received the Holy Spirit.

The Pharisees, on the other hand, understood the meaning of the event all too well. Their reaction belies their true motive. They prized the approval of men above all else—above truth, above the Law, above even the welfare of Israel. Because the arrival of the Messiah would shift the loyalty of the people away from them, leaving them powerless, they had no other option but to eliminate Jesus.

— 12:20-22 —

These "Greeks" may have been "God-fearers," Gentiles interested in converting but, for whatever reason, unable. For example, eunuchs were not eligible. More likely, however, these were proselytes. Full participation in the Passover feast was open to any Gentiles who joined themselves to God's covenant with Abraham through circumcision and, by the first century, water baptism. Why they approached Philip and not one of the other disciples is a matter of conjecture. Perhaps they were drawn to his Greek name, which means "lover of horses." Philip then took them to Andrew (another Greek name, meaning "manliness"), and the pair took the proselytes to see Jesus.

— 12:23-26 —

Somehow, the curiosity of the Gentiles signaled to Jesus that His "hour" had arrived. Throughout His ministry, Jesus had been anticipating the time when He would be "glorified" (2:4; 7:6, 8, 30; 8:20), which He defined as suffering death, rising again, and then ascending to heaven (7:39; 12:16, 23; 13:32). The Lord appears to direct His response to the wider audience, while ignoring the proselytes completely. It's likely that Jesus met with the "Greeks" in private, and that John chose to highlight the significance of their coming to Him rather than the details of their conversation.

Jesus had come to the Jews with the gospel and it had accomplished its purpose; it attracted "His own" while repelling nonbelievers. If Jesus' path to the cross consisted of a series of gates, only one remained. When the Gentiles came to see Him and perhaps even believed, a prophecy was fulfilled. It was a prediction quoted by Jesus during the second temple cleansing (Matt. 21:13; Mark 11:17; Luke 19:46):

"Also the foreigners who join themselves to the LORD,
To minister to Him, and to love the name of the LORD,
To be His servants, every one who keeps from profaning the
sabbath
And holds fast My covenant;
Even those I will bring to My holy mountain
And make them joyful in My house of prayer.
Their burnt offerings and their sacrifices will be acceptable
on My altar;
For My house will be called a house of prayer for all the
peoples."
The Lord GOD, who gathers the dispersed of Israel, declares,
"Yet others I will gather to them, to those already gathered."
(Isa. 56:6-8)

Jesus knew that once this final element of the Father's plan had fallen into place, nothing stood between Him and the cross. His dreadful hour had arrived. In celebration of that moment, Jesus outlined the rest of Christian history in just three sentences: He explained the theological basis of His substitutionary death on behalf of sinners (John 12:24), articulated a primary principle of the kingdom that He would apply personally (12:25), and called for believers to follow His example through discipleship (12:26).

— 12:27-30 —
The realization that nothing stood between Jesus and the cross led to a poignant glimpse of His humanity. In a particularly transparent moment, we see the Lord overcome by dread; He knew He would face agony on a cosmic scale, far more than the physical pain of crucifixion. Nevertheless, it was for this agony He came to earth, a fact the Father verified in a voice heard from heaven.

Some understood words while others heard only thunder.

— 12:31-33 —
Jesus reaffirmed His earlier teaching that the proclamation of truth is a form of judgment by which individuals decide their own fate through either belief or unbelief (3:18-19; 5:24; 9:39; 12:48). His use of the phrase "lifted up from the earth" is another instance of an intentional double meaning. In the literal sense, the phrase was a familiar idiom for crucifixion, a death He would endure on behalf of all. He calls "all men" to die with Him by proxy (Rom. 6:3-8). In other words, anyone may

appropriate His atoning death (which paid the complete penalty of sin) to their own account through belief. Those who choose not to believe will not benefit from this gift of grace, thus judging and condemning themselves. Yet, in a figurative sense, the phrase "lifted up from the earth" also describes His rising from the dead, ascending to heaven, and then calling "all men" to join Him there.

Jesus declared that His substitutionary death—which is appropriated through belief—is the fatal blow to evil. Evil obviously lingers for a time, but its demise is inevitable. However, the death of evil can be a present reality for the believer, who finds he or she is no longer a slave to sin through faith in Christ (Rom. 6:8-9).

— 12:34-36 —

The crowd immediately understood the literal portion of Jesus' assertion that He, the Christ, would be "lifted up from the earth." Their challenge reflects a theological problem concerning the Messiah, which persists among Jews today. The Messiah described in the Old Testament is a warrior king who will vanquish Israel's foes, lead them into prosperity, and rule from the throne of David forever. Yet He is also a suffering servant who will die on behalf of His people. How can a dead man vanquish any foe and rule from any throne?

To solve the conundrum, many Jews theorized—as many do today— that the Messiah would be *two* individuals acting in concert. The Jews in Jesus' day hadn't considered the possibility that a single individual might die on behalf of His people and then rise from the grave to become their everlasting King. Clearly, the people in Jesus' audience didn't pick up on the figurative aspect of His statement.

After Jesus completed His revelation, He retreated to the safety of seclusion, not to avoid death—He came to earth to die—but to spend His final hours preparing His disciples.

— 12:37-43 —

The remaining verses in chapter 12 are a two-part postscript to the end of this section of John's narrative. The first part (12:36-43) consists of John's editorial comments regarding the state of belief among the people of Israel. The second part (12:44-50) is a summary of Jesus' teaching throughout His ministry of three-plus years.

John quoted two passages from Isaiah to explain the unbelieving response on the part of Israel's religious leaders. Both support his explanation that the nonbelievers were "blinded" and "hardened"

EXCURSUS: A TALE OF TWO HEARTS

When the Bible states that the Lord "hardened" someone's heart, what exactly does it mean? At first glance, it would appear unjust. How can the Lord justify punishing someone for rejecting Him when the person's heart had been "hardened" by God? Perhaps the best example of divine hardening can be seen in the contrast between Moses and Pharaoh.

These two men began their lives under similar circumstances. Both grew up in the household of the Egyptian sovereign. Both received an education in the schools of idolatrous priests. Both enjoyed a standard of living far above that of the mud-pit existence of slaves. Both became heir to all the privileges of royalty. However, their paths diverged when God intervened in the life of one. Though Moses was guilty of murder, the Lord hid him on the other side of nowhere and devoted the next forty years to transforming his character.

Pharaoh, on the other hand, continued his privileged existence in the palace of Egypt and eventually became its sovereign. He did not suffer the humiliation of becoming a fugitive; he did not endure the hardscrabble existence of an itinerant shepherd in the wilderness. He spent forty years living just as he had before.

When the proper time arrived for the next stage in God's redemptive plan, He brought the two men face to face. Moses demanded the release of the Israelites, but Pharaoh refused, claiming the right of sovereignty over them. At that moment, the Lord could have batted an eyelash and reduced Egypt to a piece of lint on the page of history. Instead, He responded with a series of afflictions, which gradually increased in severity. His stated purpose: "To show you My power and in order to proclaim My name through all the earth" (Exod. 9:16).

Pharaoh stubbornly dedicated *himself* to evil in direct opposition to God's redemptive plan. This was Pharaoh's personal choice. He chose evil; God did not choose it for him. However, the Lord did "harden" him; that is, *God solidified his resolve to pursue the evil that was deeply embedded in his heart.* And the Lord was completely righteous in doing so. He does not *owe* grace to anyone. Therefore, He was no less just to allow Pharaoh to remain in his chosen evil and to suffer the consequences of it. Moreover, the Lord turned Pharaoh's evil into an opportunity to assert His own sovereign claim over the Israelites and to demonstrate His power to triumph over evil.

In Romans, Paul recounts the divergent paths taken by Moses and Pharaoh to vindicate the righteous character of God (Rom. 9:14-18). Their story does this in two ways. First, it demonstrates God's grace; He intervened in the life of both men, giving both ample opportunity to humble themselves and to accept His right of sovereignty. Second, it demonstrates God's justice; He responded to each man according to his own choice.

By the end of Jesus' ministry, He successfully divided believers from nonbelievers, willing hearts from rebellious hearts, and He confirmed each individual in his or her choice. He received willing hearts with grace while "hardening" others (John 12:37-43). And by hardening, Scripture declares He solidified the resolve of each rebellious man or woman to pursue the evil that was deeply embedded in his or her heart.[20]

by God and therefore could not believe. While this sounds patently unfair—How can someone be prevented from believing and then be justly punished for unbelief?—one must understand the nature of divine "hardening." In the case of Jesus, truth became the means by which hearts were either softened to the point of surrender or hardened in their chosen state of rebellion.

John qualified his indictment of the Jewish leaders by noting that some believed secretly and remained silent for fear of losing favor with their peers.

— 12:44-50 —

This series of seven declarations by Jesus is a summary of His teaching throughout His public ministry. I find five timeless truths in His summary:

1. Jesus is one with the Father; to believe in one is to believe in the other (12:44-45).
2. Jesus is the personal representation, the literal embodiment, of all truth; therefore, to believe divine truth is not to accept a certain set of facts, but to believe in the person named Jesus (12:46).
3. Jesus did not come to condemn anyone, but to present Himself as truth to be believed; those who fail to believe in Him condemn themselves (12:47-48).
4. Everything Jesus does is necessarily the will of the Father because they are of the same essence (12:49).
5. The reason the Father sent the Son to earth was to provide humanity the ability to receive eternal life by grace alone, through faith alone (12:50).

• • •

Once Jesus had proclaimed the good news to the world and had fulfilled all of the Old Testament prophecies concerning the Messiah, He concluded His public ministry. In the next section, Jesus will prepare His disciples in seclusion for His departure and their future work of evangelism and disciple-making.

APPLICATION: JOHN 12:1-50

Freedom of Worship

When God established Israel in the land promised to Abraham and his descendants, He directed them to construct a place of worship and gave them detailed procedures to follow. In the beginning, Israel worshiped God in a tent, a "tabernacle." Later, Solomon erected a temple in Jerusalem. And for many generations thereafter, followers of God traveled to this mountaintop location to offer their sacrifices, to seek God's forgiveness, and to worship Him.

When the Son of God arrived, however, He brought with Him a change in the worship order.

In His dialogue with the Samaritan woman at the well, Jesus said, "Believe me, dear woman, the time is coming when it will no longer matter whether you worship the Father on this mountain or in Jerusalem. . . . But the time is coming—indeed it's here now—when true worshipers will worship the Father in spirit and in truth. The Father is looking for those who will worship him that way. For God is Spirit, so those who worship him must worship in spirit and in truth" (John 4:21-24, NLT).

When God walked the earth in human flesh, no one needed a temple or a priest to interact with the Almighty; people could meet with God face-to-face. Worshipers didn't have to travel to a fixed location; God came to them in the person of His Son. Worship didn't follow a prescribed form; God welcomed any expression of worship offered with sincerity. From the moment the Son of God arrived on earth, He released worship from the temple—which had been an early necessity—so that all might worship freely.

This chapter of John's Gospel highlights this momentous paradigm shift by describing several acts of worship, beginning with Mary's spontaneous and extravagant adoration. From her we learn that worship should be an outpouring of complete devotion, holding back nothing, expressed by a sincere heart. Too often, however, we enter the church sanctuary at the appointed time, go through motions at the direction of a worship leader, sing without feeling, and then leave the building as empty as we came. How often we hear the complaint, "I didn't get anything out of worship this week."

In the days you have before next Sunday, prepare yourself for worship with three simple activities.

1. Begin a list of blessings on a notepad—all the ways God has protected you from harm or provided for your needs. Keep it somewhere handy, like your desk at work, the refrigerator door, or the kitchen counter. Expand the list as things occur to you. Worship flows naturally from a grateful heart.

2. For each of the next few days, print on a small card one of God's attributes, such as omniscience, omnipotence, sovereignty, compassion, love, steadfastness . . . Then, keep it in your pocket or someplace you'll contact it often. Throughout the day, meditate on how this attribute makes God worthy of worship. Consider how this attribute benefits you personally.

3. Make a point to tell at least one person each of the next few days how God has changed your life, and why you take time each week to worship Him.

Complete these three simple exercises, and see how your preparation affects your worship on Sunday.

CONFIRMATION OF THE WORD (JOHN 13:1–17:26)

I was ten years old when my father spoke to me what we both thought would be his final words before dying.

He was too old to serve in the military when the United States entered World War II. But he wanted to do his part, so we moved to Houston, Texas, where he took a job in a defense plant. He worked long and hard to help manufacture parts for the tanks and aircraft used to subdue the tyranny of Nazi Germany and Imperialist Japan. But he worked too long and too hard—Swindolls are not known for doing anything halfway. As a result, he suffered a physical breakdown. Doctors puzzled over how to cure my father as he steadily grew weaker. Before long, he lay close to death's door as everyone prayed for a miracle. I will never forget the special kind of silence that falls upon a house during a deathwatch.

One night, my father called me into his room. He could barely talk above a whisper, so I bent down close as he counseled me on life—how I should live as a man and how I should conduct myself as his son. After just a few minutes, he finished. He didn't have the strength to talk for long. I left his room and went across the hall to the little bedroom I shared with my older brother. All alone, I closed the door, collapsed on the bed, and sobbed, convinced I would never see him alive again. I couldn't imagine life without him.

That experience haunted me for a long time after that. Thankfully, my father recovered fully and went on to live for many years. As a matter of fact, after my mother passed away, he came to live with us in Fullerton, California. Sometimes, just before going to bed, I would check on him, only to find him asleep. Seeing his slumbering form in the quiet of his room often took me back to that awful night in Houston and to the moments I thought would be his last.

Final words are powerful things. As the "hour" of Jesus' Passion approached, He took the opportunity to spend a final evening with His disciples. He knew they were unprepared for the difficult and confusing time they were about to face. Like most people in first-century Israel, the disciples expected the Messiah to claim the throne, rout their enemies, lead Israel to unprecedented power and prosperity, and bring the entire world under His dominion. He had predicted His own death and resurrection beforehand; nevertheless, His arrest, trials, torture, crucifixion, burial, resurrection, and departure from earth would come as a terrible shock, like a perfect dream turning into a nightmare.

As the evening passed, Jesus spoke of life and ministry on earth without His physical presence. The disciples quickly began to understand the gravity of these moments. And their "troubled" hearts were soon gripped by the same forsaken dread orphans feel once they realize they are alone in the world.

They couldn't imagine life without Him.

KEY TERMS IN JOHN 13:1–17:26

doxazō **(δοξάζω)** [1392] "to glorify," "to make glorious," "to render excellent," "to reveal the worth of something"

In the Greek translation of the Old Testament, God's *doxa* [1391] is usually a physical manifestation of His holy, righteous nature. In the vocabulary of heaven, *doxa* is righteousness made visible. In the Gospel of John, glorification occurs when God's righteous nature is revealed. Therefore, a body is glorified when it again reflects the full image of God, which was distorted by the Fall. Eventually, believers will share the glory of Christ (Rom. 8:17; Col. 1:27; 3:4) when they receive a resurrected body like His (Phil. 3:21). *See John 12:28; 13:31; 16:14; 17:1.*

ginōskō **(γινώσκω)** [1097] "to know," "to understand," "to comprehend"

This term and its close cousin, *oida* [1492], both refer to intelligent comprehension with emphasis on the process or act of knowing. Throughout John's literature, "knowing" and "obeying" are inseparable (as they are in Old Testament literature). In the upper room, Jesus placed great emphasis on His followers knowing the mind of God so they might become integral to His redemptive plan. Unfortunately, the disciples struggled with lack of understanding until they received the Holy Spirit. *See John 10:14; 14:7, 17; 17:3.*

***menō* (μένω)** [3306] "abide," "remain," "stay," "live"

The normal, casual use of this verb has its subject "remaining" in one place for a period of time, such as in a residence, an occupation, or a state of being. One "abides" in his or her home, "remains" in his or her occupation for a number of years, or "stays" married. John—drawing his influence from Jesus—gives the term a deeply significant theological meaning throughout his literature. In "abiding," the believer has access to all the promises of heaven, his or her only limitation being the effects of sin. One "abides" by "knowing" God, which necessarily includes obedience. *See John 14:16; 15:4, 7, 10.*

***miseō* (μισέω)** [3404] "to hate," "to detest," "to treat with disdain," "to neglect"

In Semitic cultures, there are two categories of "hate," unlike modern Western cultures, which have only one. I will call them "comparative hate" and "ontological hate." Semitic cultures often use "hate" in the context of comparison (e.g., Matt. 6:24; Luke 14:26), which involves little or no emotion. A preferred object is said to be "loved" while another is "hated." Comparative hate expresses preference or priority. Ontological hate, on the other hand, is the kind most familiar in Western cultures; it expresses malicious feelings and/or actions toward its object (e.g., Matt. 24:10; Luke 6:22). The world's hatred of Christ is ontological hate. *See John 15:18, 19, 23; 17:14.*

***paraklētos* (παράκλητος)** [3875] "helper," "advocate," "comforter," "encourager"

This term, like *agapē* [26], was not widely used outside the New Testament; therefore, it became an ideal loanword for John to describe the ministry of the Holy Spirit. (We don't know which Aramaic term Jesus Himself used in the upper room.) Secular Greeks used the term to describe the actions of an attorney "advocating" on behalf of his client—providing guidance, advice, and even speaking on his or her behalf before the judge. Jewish philosophers who were heavily influenced by the Greeks expanded the advocate idea to personify wisdom. The Christian idea of the *Paraklētos* comes largely from John's writings. *See John 14:16, 26; 15:26; 16:7.*

Humility Personified
JOHN 13:1-17

NASB

¹ Now before the Feast of the Passover, Jesus knowing that His hour had come that He would depart out of this world to the Father, having loved His own who were in the world, He loved them ᵃto the end. ² During supper, the devil having already put into the heart of Judas Iscariot, *the son* of Simon, to betray Him, ³ *Jesus,* knowing that the Father had given all things into His hands, and that He had come forth from God and was going back to God, ⁴ got up from supper, and laid aside His garments; and taking a towel, He girded Himself.

⁵ Then He poured water into the basin, and began to wash the disciples' feet and to wipe them with the towel with which He was girded. ⁶ So He came to Simon Peter. He said to Him, "Lord, do You wash my feet?" ⁷ Jesus answered and said to him, "What I do you do not realize now, but you will understand hereafter." ⁸ Peter said to Him, "Never shall You wash my feet!" Jesus answered him, "If I do not wash you, you have no part with Me." ⁹ Simon Peter said to Him, "Lord, *then wash* not only my feet, but also my hands and my head." ¹⁰ Jesus said to him, "He who has bathed needs only to wash his feet, but is completely clean; and you are clean, but not all *of you.*" ¹¹ For He knew the one who was betraying Him; for this reason He said, "Not all of you are clean."

¹² So when He had washed their feet, and taken His garments and reclined *at the table* again, He said to them, "Do you know what I have done to you? ¹³ You call Me Teacher and Lord; and ᵃyou are right, for *so* I am. ¹⁴ If I then, the Lord and the Teacher, washed your feet, you also

NLT

¹ Before the Passover celebration, Jesus knew that his hour had come to leave this world and return to his Father. He had loved his disciples during his ministry on earth, and now he loved them to the very end.* ² It was time for supper, and the devil had already prompted Judas,* son of Simon Iscariot, to betray Jesus. ³ Jesus knew that the Father had given him authority over everything and that he had come from God and would return to God. ⁴ So he got up from the table, took off his robe, wrapped a towel around his waist, ⁵ and poured water into a basin. Then he began to wash the disciples' feet, drying them with the towel he had around him.

⁶ When Jesus came to Simon Peter, Peter said to him, "Lord, are you going to wash my feet?" ⁷ Jesus replied, "You don't understand now what I am doing, but someday you will." ⁸ "No," Peter protested, "you will never ever wash my feet!" Jesus replied, "Unless I wash you, you won't belong to me." ⁹ Simon Peter exclaimed, "Then wash my hands and head as well, Lord, not just my feet!" ¹⁰ Jesus replied, "A person who has bathed all over does not need to wash, except for the feet,* to be entirely clean. And you disciples are clean, but not all of you." ¹¹ For Jesus knew who would betray him. That is what he meant when he said, "Not all of you are clean."

¹² After washing their feet, he put on his robe again and sat down and asked, "Do you understand what I was doing? ¹³ You call me 'Teacher' and 'Lord,' and you are right, because that's what I am. ¹⁴ And since I, your Lord and Teacher, have washed

ought to wash one another's feet. ¹⁵ For I gave you an example that you also should do as I did to you. ¹⁶ Truly, truly, I say to you, a slave is not greater than his master, nor *is* one who is sent greater than the one who sent him. ¹⁷ If you know these things, you are blessed if you do them.

13:1 ^aOr *to the uttermost;* or *eternally* **13:13** ^aLit *you say well*

your feet, you ought to wash each other's feet. ¹⁵ I have given you an example to follow. Do as I have done to you. ¹⁶ I tell you the truth, slaves are not greater than their master. Nor is the messenger more important than the one who sends the message. ¹⁷ Now that you know these things, God will bless you for doing them.

13:1 Or *he showed them the full extent of his love.* **13:2** Or *the devil had already intended for Judas.* **13:10** Some manuscripts do not include *except for the feet.*

Jesus often stated His identity and even used vivid metaphors to describe His relationship with humanity (John 6:35; 8:12; 9:5; 10:9, 11; 11:25), but He rarely spoke of Himself directly. Only once in all of Scripture did He describe His inner self. That occurred as a congregation of Jews gathered to hear Him preach: He invited all who were weary of trying to satisfy the impossible demands of religion to find rest in Him, "for," He said, "I am gentle and humble in heart" (Matt. 11:29). The Greek adjective translated "humble" derives from a verb that means "to make low" or "to make small or insignificant." Humility was expressed physically by bowing the head, kneeling down, or even prostrating oneself. Isn't it significant that He used *this* term to describe Himself?

Humility is the quintessential posture of the believer. It does not mean being bowed down in defeat or shame. Our pattern is Jesus. The humble Son of God cannot be defeated and He has no reason for shame. Though he was "gentle and humble," the omnipotence He laid aside for the sake of becoming like us could be taken up again in a moment. Humility is not for the down-and-out. On the contrary, authentic humility is only possible for victorious men and women!

As evening fell upon the upper room, Jesus had many lessons to teach; but before anything else, He would teach them the all-important, noble art of bowing low.

— 13:1 —

John opens this section of his narrative with a summary statement of Jesus' ministry among the disciples. While His "hour" was at hand, He had loved "His own" *eis telos* [1519, 5056]—literally, "to the final goal." He had loved them to completion, to the fullest, all the way to the end. He had completed their training. During this final evening with the

Twelve, He needed only to review their most important lessons and reveal their immediate future.

John takes great care to note the timing of Jesus' last meal with His disciples and His subsequent ordeal. Before the end of this section, he establishes a clear connection between the Passover lamb and Jesus, "the Lamb of God who takes away the sin of the world" (1:29).

— 13:2-5 —

Verses 2-4 form one very long compound sentence. The simple form can be seen by pasting together the first phrase of each verse: "During supper . . . Jesus . . . got up from supper." The supporting clauses establish the timing and describe Jesus' inner thoughts so we will understand the full significance of His next act.

Verse 2 reveals that Judas had already determined to betray the Lord as he reclined at table with the other disciples. According to Luke, he had already received the money (Luke 22:3-6) and was looking for a good opportunity to hand Jesus over to the temple authorities.

Verse 3 reveals that Jesus knew He was about to endure great suffering, die, rise from the grave, and then receive glory as the ruler of all creation (see Dan. 7:13-14).

Verse 4 tells us that, despite His knowing all of that, Jesus slipped away from the table and silently traded His robes for the attire of a slave. But not just any slave, the lowest rank of slave, a slave who washes road grime from the feet of houseguests. When a host family invited someone to dine in their home in those days, they customarily stationed a servant by the door with basin, pitcher, and towel. As each guest arrived, the servant removed his or her sandals (see John 1:27), rinsed each foot, and then wiped away the dirt and water with a clean towel. John most likely assumed his readers were familiar with the other three accounts of this final evening. We know from Luke 22:24 that the disciples had been quarrelling again over who among them was best suited for the most prominent positions in the Lord's new government. Even on the eve of the Lord's crucifixion, they still expected Jesus to topple the Romans and establish a new monarchy, which would lead to their promotion. But Jesus came to establish a new kind of kingdom. In the kingdom of God, one receives greater authority through humble service. If anyone in the room deserved to be treated like a king, it was Jesus. If anyone was worthy of devotion, it was the Lord. Yet He took it upon Himself to become the servant of all. Jesus washed the feet of the disciples . . . all of them . . . all twelve . . . including Judas!

— 13:6-11 —

Jesus had already washed the feet of several disciples before coming to Peter. The brash disciple protested, saying, literally, "Lord, You? Washing my feet?!" The Lord reassured His pupil that the significance of the washing—and the whole evening, for that matter—would become clear in time. But Peter protested again, "You will absolutely not wash my feet into eternity!" Today we might say, "Never! Not in a million years!"

At first glance, Peter appears very humble, as if to say, "Oh, Lord, I should be washing Your feet instead!" But this was not his meaning. This was self-assertive pride that refuses to accept grace from another, the kind that will not be vulnerable in front of others. If Peter had dirty feet, he would take care of washing them himself! "No charity needed here, thank you very much!"

Jesus reminded Peter that eternity is not his to enjoy apart from grace. Peter, not being a man of moderation, ran to the other extreme, requesting a complete bath! But Jesus rejected his interpretation of the foot washing. Because Peter believed in the Son of God and had received salvation from sin by grace, he was already clean. (Perhaps we could say, "Once bathed, always bathed!") However, the grace of God continues throughout the life of the believer, whose feet collect dust from the world.

Jesus' predominant themes throughout the evening were the need for continual communion with God, the help of the Holy Spirit, love and unity within the body of believers, and the danger posed by the world. His opening illustration brought these themes together. While the believer has been cleansed of sin in the legal sense—past, present, and future sins will not be counted against him or her in eternity—the believer will continually struggle to remain clean experientially before entering eternity.

John's editorial comment reminds us that Jesus knew Judas was looking for an opportunity to betray his Master, even as he received this poignant act of grace.

— 13:12-17 —

Once Jesus finished His opening act of humility, He began to teach. First, he explained His purpose. In classic didactic fashion, He posed a carefully crafted question to His students. He asked them to interpret the meaning of His washing their feet. I suspect He entertained some creative responses, some of which were undoubtedly funny. Then He established two principles of humility that were to become foundational to His kingdom.

First, *humility doesn't discriminate; humility is expressed equally to all.* Jesus didn't ask His students to wash His feet in return, but to wash the feet of one another. Let's face it; most of us would stand in line to wash the Savior's feet because *He's worthy!* But how many are ready to wash the feet of another person in the church, particularly someone we don't like very much? This lesson would hit the disciples even harder later on when they recalled that Jesus bowed before Judas to wash his feet along with the others.

Second, *humility turns the structure of authority upside down.* Earlier in His ministry, Jesus stated flatly, "If anyone wants to be first, he shall be last of all and servant of all" (Mark 9:35; cf. Matt. 18:4; 19:30; 20:16; Mark 10:31; Luke 9:48; 13:30). Jesus, as the King of the new kingdom, reduced Himself to become the least of humanity, taking on Himself the sin of the world—*becoming* sin, as it were (2 Cor. 5:21)—and then suffering the most humiliating death ever devised by man. While no other human can possibly match His humility, we have been summoned to imitate our Master.

We do not become "great" in the new kingdom by suffering crucifixion; the need for sacrificial death has been completely satisfied by Christ. We become "great" in the new kingdom by bowing low to serve one another.

• • •

Let me be completely transparent with you. I find the idea of foot washing—both literal and figurative—much easier to teach than to practice. But Jesus didn't promise to release blessing upon those who teach foot washing, but to those who *do* it. Humility isn't learned in a classroom or even a Bible study. Humility is a behavior one chooses to make habitual, even to the point he or she forgets about "greatness" or becoming lowly. The people I remember as genuinely humble rarely thought about themselves at all. They didn't need to. The blessing they received in the process of serving others provided all the contentment any man or woman could desire.

Jesus taught humility through His example; He personified humility. Let us resolve to learn humility as He taught it.

APPLICATION: JOHN 13:1-17

Cultivating the Noble Art of Bowing Low

When Jesus laid aside His outer garment, dressed Himself like a slave, and bowed low to wash His disciples' feet, He taught the men several important lessons about humility, not the least of which is that humility is an action, not simply an attitude. One does not feel humble or think humble thoughts. In fact, a person of genuine humility has no thought of self at all. Humility is a behavior, and in its purest form, involves little emotion, except perhaps affection.

With that in mind, allow me to draw a few principles from Jesus' lesson on humility.

First, *humility is unannounced.* Jesus didn't rise from the table and boldly announce, "I am now going to demonstrate humility." He simply began washing feet. Once someone calls attention to his or her deed of service, it has become contaminated with pride (Matt. 23:1-12). One doesn't announce a humble deed, either before or after it is done. (Jesus broke this rule after washing the disciples' feet for the sake of instruction, but it was the only time He did.)

Second, *humility is being willing to receive service without embarrassment.* We usually feel embarrassed by deeds of service because we perceive that the normal "rules" of status or rank have been breached. In Peter's mind, the lesser should serve the greater. Jesus inverted this worldly norm. The "greatest" in the kingdom of God serves and receives service with no thought of status, worth, or rank.

Third, *humility is not a sign of weakness.* Jesus did not serve His disciples because He was weak, or needed their goodwill, or desired their approval, or coveted their loyalty. Jesus, none other than almighty God, bowed low to serve the people He loved. He washed those twenty-four feet because they were dirty and needed washing.

Fourth, *humility does not discriminate.* Jesus washed the feet of every man in the room, including those of Judas, the man He knew had already made plans to betray Him. Jesus didn't line up the disciples in order of closeness, or loyalty, or any other standard. He didn't wait for the traitor among them to depart on his evil mission before washing their feet. He washed the feet that needed washing without favoritism or prejudice.

By way of application, here are two additional principles to keep in mind.

First, *humility includes serving one another, not just the Lord.* Serving the Lord is the greatest delight in the world. Serving one another is not always as rewarding. The Lord is worthy of service and easy to love; our fellow soiled and sinful brothers and sisters, however, are not always lovely and frequently fail to express gratitude. Nevertheless, genuine humility doesn't seek reward other than the joy of service itself.

Second, *the joy of humility can only be experienced through humility in action.* Humility comes through *doing,* not merely reading about it, hearing others talk about it, or seeing others practice it. Jesus demonstrated humility and then urged His disciples to follow His example.

After hearing one of my sermons on this topic, someone remarked, "You know, I've got to learn to love so-and-so better, because I'm gonna spend eternity with him!" He's right. But I'd like to turn his thought around. If humility—serving and being served without regard for status or rank—will define our mutual experience in heaven, why wait? God has encouraged us to create a little bit of heaven on earth and He has given us the ability . . . so what are we waiting for?

How High Is Your A.Q.?
JOHN 13:18-30

NASB

18 I do not speak of all of you. I know the ones I have chosen; but *it is* that the Scripture may be fulfilled, 'HE WHO EATS MY BREAD HAS LIFTED UP HIS HEEL AGAINST ME.' 19 From now on I am telling you before *it* comes to pass, so that when it does occur, you may believe that I am *He.* 20 Truly, truly, I say to you, he who receives whomever I send receives Me; and he who receives Me receives Him who sent Me."

21 When Jesus had said this, He became troubled in spirit, and testified and said, "Truly, truly, I say to you, that one of you will ªbetray Me." 22 The disciples *began* looking at one another, at a loss *to know* of which one He was speaking. 23 There was reclining on Jesus' bosom one of His disciples, whom Jesus loved.

NLT

18 "I am not saying these things to all of you; I know the ones I have chosen. But this fulfills the Scripture that says, 'The one who eats my food has turned against me.'* 19 I tell you this beforehand, so that when it happens you will believe that I Am the Messiah.* 20 I tell you the truth, anyone who welcomes my messenger is welcoming me, and anyone who welcomes me is welcoming the Father who sent me."

21 Now Jesus was deeply troubled,* and he exclaimed, "I tell you the truth, one of you will betray me!"

22 The disciples looked at each other, wondering whom he could mean. 23 The disciple Jesus loved was sitting next to Jesus at the table.*

²⁴So Simon Peter gestured to him, and said to him, "Tell *us* who it is of whom He is speaking." ²⁵He, leaning back thus on Jesus' bosom, said to Him, "Lord, who is it?" ²⁶Jesus then answered, "That is the one for whom I shall dip the morsel and give it to him." So when He had dipped the morsel, He took and gave it to Judas, *the son* of Simon Iscariot. ²⁷After the morsel, Satan then entered into him. Therefore Jesus said to him, "What you do, do quickly." ²⁸Now no one of those reclining *at the table* knew for what purpose He had said this to him. ²⁹For some were supposing, because Judas had the money box, that Jesus was saying to him, "Buy the things we have need of for the feast"; or else, that he should give something to the poor. ³⁰So after receiving the morsel he went out immediately; and it was night.

13:21 ªOr *hand Me over*

²⁴Simon Peter motioned to him to ask, "Who's he talking about?" ²⁵So that disciple leaned over to Jesus and asked, "Lord, who is it?" ²⁶Jesus responded, "It is the one to whom I give the bread I dip in the bowl." And when he had dipped it, he gave it to Judas, son of Simon Iscariot. ²⁷When Judas had eaten the bread, Satan entered into him. Then Jesus told him, "Hurry and do what you're going to do." ²⁸None of the others at the table knew what Jesus meant. ²⁹Since Judas was their treasurer, some thought Jesus was telling him to go and pay for the food or to give some money to the poor. ³⁰So Judas left at once, going out into the night.

13:18 Ps 41:9. **13:19** Or *that the 'I AM' has come;* or *that I am the LORD;* Greek reads *that I am.* See Exod 3:14. **13:21** Greek *was troubled in his spirit.* **13:23** Greek *was reclining on Jesus' bosom.* The "disciple Jesus loved" was probably John.

For many years, educational systems around the world subjected students to a battery of tests to determine each individual's I.Q., "Intelligence Quotient." This quantified each person's ability to remember facts, to think imaginatively, to put information together logically, and ultimately to solve problems. The I.Q. became a means of identifying intellectually gifted students so they might be challenged to maximize their abilities; however, it also became a pretext for pushing a great many others to the fringes of education.

In 1983, Harvard University professor Howard Gardner proposed a new theory, suggesting that intelligence has many different forms. Someone can be a mathematical genius, yet have difficulty working his home entertainment system. Another may score the highest I.Q. ever recorded, yet fail to interact with others at the most basic level of competence. Dr. Gardner recognized the existence of "multiple intelligences" and reacted strongly against assigning worth to people based on a single, rather arbitrarily chosen kind of intelligence. There is more to a person than his or her ability to solve mental puzzles.

Jesus never placed supreme value on a person's I.Q.; He cared much more about developing the A.Q.—the "Acceptance Quotient"—of His disciples. Whereas the I.Q. quantifies an individual's mental capacity, the A.Q. measures one's capacity for relationship.

I define "acceptance" as one's ability to receive other people and recognize their worth without holding them to a predetermined standard or requiring any specific performance. Here is how one author describes this freedom, from the perspective of those we choose to accept:

> Acceptance. It means you are valuable just as you are. It allows you to be the *real* you. You aren't forced into someone else's idea of who you really are. It means your ideas are taken seriously since they reflect you. You can talk about how you feel inside and why you feel that way—and someone really cares.
>
> Acceptance means you can try out your ideas without being shot down. You can even express heretical thoughts and discuss them with intelligent questioning. You feel safe. No one will pronounce judgment on you, even though they don't agree with you. It doesn't mean you will never be corrected or shown to be wrong; it simply means it's safe to be *you* and no one will destroy *you* out of prejudice.[1]

This quality of acceptance, exemplified and encouraged by Jesus, requires some clarification, lest anyone misunderstand. First, acceptance does not negate discernment. Christian maturity requires discernment. To accept someone is not to be blinded to that person's weakness, but rather to overlook those weaknesses when choosing to show honor. It is to demonstrate love without regard for another's flaws.

Second, acceptance does not deny human sinfulness. On the contrary, acceptance takes sinfulness fully into account as one receives another into fellowship. If you're looking for perfect people with whom to share fellowship, you're destined to be lonely.

Third, acceptance does offer unlimited freedom for each individual to be openly authentic without fear of rejection. Each person can be at complete ease knowing that being himself or herself will not lead to condemnation or rejection.

After Jesus rose from washing the disciples' feet, He put on His robes and taught them about humility. However, He warned that not everyone around the table would understand the lesson, much less apply it. The fact that Jesus had just washed the feet of His betrayer would become the occasion of His next lesson. Humility not only bows low to serve others; humility also offers fellowship to lowly people.

— 13:18-20 —

Jesus announced that someone reclining at the table that evening would not be receiving any blessing. One among them ate the unleavened bread provided by the Son of God as a means of betraying Him, which the Lord noted by quoting Psalm 41:9. He said, in effect, "The betrayer may think he has cleverly remained incognito, but his treachery was revealed long before he was born." Make no mistake; this was a final warning.

Imagine yourself reclining at the table beside Jesus. How would you respond if Jesus named your secret sin and then predicted your doom? I don't know about you, but I would repent! "No, Lord! Save me from my own sinfulness!" But not Judas. From before the beginning of the supper (John 13:2; see Luke 22:3-6), Judas had determined to betray Jesus to the religious authorities; he simply needed to determine the most opportune time.

Jesus knew that Judas's betrayal would soon shake the faith of the other disciples down to its foundation. So He reassured them in advance. To "receive" one sent by Christ is to receive Christ, and to receive Christ is to receive the Father. A better English translation of the Greek term is "accept." He assured His disciples that their acceptance had divine backing.

— 13:21-22 —

John described Jesus' inner state as "troubled." It's the same Greek word used in 11:33, 12:27, 14:1, and 14:27. It means "agitated," presumably by deep distress or sometimes anger. I believe the Lord genuinely grieved the loss of Judas. I believe the love He held for His betrayer nearly broke His heart.

Jesus stunned the table with a revelation of divine truth: one of the disciples would betray Him. As the disciples exchanged inquisitive looks and expressed their alarm, I have no doubt Judas feigned disbelief as credibly as the others.

— 13:22-26 —

Apparently Peter sat opposite Jesus at the table, too far away to have a private conversation. So, he motioned for John to ask Jesus the identity of the traitor. The customary posture for dining was to lie on one's left side, propped on one elbow, with the feet angled away from the table. John reclined on Jesus' right. Rather than turn his head, he merely leaned back on Jesus' chest and looked up. Someone would only do

CHART: THE DOUBLE *AMĒN* ("TRULY, TRULY") IN JOHN

1:51	And He said to him, "Truly, truly, I say to you, you will see the heavens opened and the angels of God ascending and descending on the Son of Man."
3:3	Jesus answered and said to him, "Truly, truly, I say to you, unless one is born again he cannot see the kingdom of God."
3:5	Jesus answered, "Truly, truly, I say to you, unless one is born of water and the Spirit he cannot enter into the kingdom of God."
3:11	"Truly, truly, I say to you, we speak of what we know and testify of what we have seen, and you do not accept our testimony."
5:19	Therefore Jesus answered and was saying to them, "Truly, truly, I say to you, the Son can do nothing of Himself, unless it is something He sees the Father doing; for whatever the Father does, these things the Son also does in like manner."
5:24	"Truly, truly, I say to you, he who hears My word, and believes Him who sent Me, has eternal life, and does not come into judgment, but has passed out of death into life."
5:25	"Truly, truly, I say to you, an hour is coming and now is, when the dead will hear the voice of the Son of God, and those who hear will live."
6:26	Jesus answered them and said, "Truly, truly, I say to you, you seek Me, not because you saw signs, but because you ate of the loaves and were filled."
6:32	Jesus then said to them, "Truly, truly, I say to you, it is not Moses who has given you the bread out of heaven, but it is My Father who gives you the true bread out of heaven."
6:47	"Truly, truly, I say to you, he who believes has eternal life."
6:53	So Jesus said to them, "Truly, truly, I say to you, unless you eat the flesh of the Son of Man and drink His blood, you have no life in yourselves."
8:34	Jesus answered them, "Truly, truly, I say to you, everyone who commits sin is the slave of sin."
8:51	"Truly, truly, I say to you, if anyone keeps My word he will never see death."
8:58	Jesus said to them, "Truly, truly, I say to you, before Abraham was born, I am."
10:1	"Truly, truly, I say to you, he who does not enter by the door into the fold of the sheep, but climbs up some other way, he is a thief and a robber."
10:7	So Jesus said to them again, "Truly, truly, I say to you, I am the door of the sheep."
12:24	"Truly, truly, I say to you, unless a grain of wheat falls into the earth and dies, it remains alone; but if it dies, it bears much fruit."
13:16	"Truly, truly, I say to you, a slave is not greater than his master, nor is one who is sent greater than the one who sent him."
13:20	"Truly, truly, I say to you, he who receives whomever I send receives Me; and he who receives Me receives Him who sent Me."
13:21	When Jesus had said this, He became troubled in spirit, and testified and said, "Truly, truly, I say to you, that one of you will betray Me."
13:38	Jesus answered, "Will you lay down your life for Me? Truly, truly, I say to you, a rooster will not crow until you deny Me three times."
14:12	"Truly, truly, I say to you, he who believes in Me, the works that I do, he will do also; and greater works than these he will do; because I go to the Father."
16:20	"Truly, truly, I say to you, that you will weep and lament, but the world will rejoice; you will grieve, but your grief will be turned into joy."
16:23	"In that day you will not question Me about anything. Truly, truly, I say to you, if you ask the Father for anything in My name, He will give it to you."
21:18	"Truly, truly, I say to you, when you were younger, you used to gird yourself and walk wherever you wished; but when you grow old, you will stretch out your hands and someone else will gird you, and bring you where you do not wish to go."

this with a very close friend or relative, but it would not have been an unusual sight around an ancient Near Eastern supper table.

Jesus revealed to John the identity of the traitor with a familiar gesture of friendship. Jesus dipped a piece of unleavened bread into one of the bowls containing a paste made from bitter herbs, or perhaps lamb stew, and gave it to Judas. Apparently, Judas reclined within easy reach, suggesting he may have been lying to Jesus' left, the honored position at a banquet.

This was Jesus' final act of grace to Judas. He had washed the man's feet and given him the place of honor by His side; then, despite the sin in the traitor's heart, the Lord offered him fellowship.

— 13:27-30 —

Verse 27 is one of the most chilling verses in all of Scripture. Just as willing hearts receive Christ, willing hearts receive Satan.

Secret sin inevitably warps the mind and twists one's values. Embezzlers like Judas rarely steal very much at first. But as the pilfering becomes habitual, and then ritualized, the thief must learn to rationalize his sin or face the awful prospect of repentance. Driven by shame, he must keep his sin a secret. Meanwhile, the cycle of compulsion and shame drives a wedge between his private thoughts and a fastidiously maintained—and often pious—public persona. Eventually, the sinner accepts his public facade as his true self in a desperate attempt to escape the relentless pursuit of shame. When caught in sin, an embezzler almost always appears shocked. And in some ways he is surprised by the accusations because he has convinced himself that no one can see the true person he had long ago concealed.

Judas had been cultivating a double life for months or quite possibly years (6:70-71). His charming religious facade kept a seething resentment safely concealed from others. No one suspected his secret sin, much less wondered about his loyalty. Even as he received the morsel from Jesus and departed into the night without explanation, no one suspected anything.

• • •

John wrote of these events some sixty years after they had occurred, which gave him ample time to reflect. Moreover, the Holy Spirit directed the spotlight of his mind to certain details in order to communicate deep spiritual truths. Jesus' living lessons on humility and acceptance took place while Judas was present. The Lord washed his feet, gave him the seat of honor at the table, and even offered him fellowship. Because Jesus was fully human, experiencing all of the emotions, weaknesses, and temptations we endure, we can be certain the gestures of acceptance did not come easily. Grace is often a costly gift to give.

APPLICATION: JOHN 13:18-30

How to Spot a Falling A.Q.

If grace is our defining doctrine as genuine believers, then our ability to accept others is certainly a visible test of our belief. I am unreservedly conservative in my theology and I find the greatest affinity among my fellow conservative theologians, so I appreciate their uncompromising desire for pure doctrine and their rapid identification and occasional reproof of false teachers. And I join their courageous stand against the world's encroaching evil. However, must we lower our A.Q. to maintain a high theological I.Q.?

Here are three signs of a falling Acceptance Quotient, three indications that grace has not bridged the gap between one's head and heart.

First, *people with a falling A.Q. are unwilling to accept people without maintaining partiality.* Accept people while remaining partial? It happens all the time. The apostle James refers to this when admonishing church leaders:

> My brethren, do not hold your faith in our glorious Lord Jesus Christ with an attitude of personal favoritism. For if a man comes into your assembly with a gold ring and dressed in fine clothes, and there also comes in a poor man in dirty clothes, and you pay special attention to the one who is wearing the fine clothes, and say, "You sit here in a good place," and you say to the poor man, "You stand over there, or sit down by my footstool," have you not made distinctions among yourselves, and become judges with evil motives? (Jas. 2:1-4)

No one outright rejected the man with dirty clothes; however, they expected him to know his place.

Similarly today, we are often partial in the way we treat people. Deep pockets get the good seats and positions in leadership; people with suspicious backgrounds are welcome, as long as they dutifully wear the appropriate scarlet letter: *A* for *adultery, E* for *emotional trauma, S* for *single,* or *D* for (God forbid!) *divorce.* Once they prove their worth or patiently dispel our suspicions, we might grant them greater access to the privileged inner circle of the fully accepted. How wrong! How unlike Christ!

Second, *people with a falling A.Q. are unwilling to accept another's personal style without criticism.* I'm not referring to matters of morality or doctrine, but one's choice of personal expression. In some churches, the pastor wears a robe. In others, a flashy suit. In still others, business attire. In a great many, jeans and a T-shirt. If Christ is preached and souls are added to the kingdom, who cares about attire!

Churches divide over differing taste in music. Some Christians are unwilling to sit through even one service in which music fits another style. They grouse and complain because others dared to enjoy a worship service they didn't personally care for. Oh, they are willing to accept others who prefer a different style, as long as they attend the *other* service.

Third, *people with a falling A.Q. are unwilling to suffer offenses without holding a grudge.* People who hold grudges reject others who do not meet their expectations and accept only those who do. That attitude is more characteristic of nonbelievers than genuine members of Christ's body. I've heard more than one nonbeliever reject the notion of going to church because "it's full of a bunch of hypocrites." To which, I say, "Come on in; there's room for one more!"

Let's face it; relationships would go a lot smoother in churches if they were filled with perfect people. But the key to acceptance is not perfection, so we must learn to set aside offenses and accept one another, not in spite of our flaws—that's conditional love—but *with* our flaws.

Acceptance doesn't mean we have to lower the biblical standard of righteousness, or become like other people, or even adopt their personal styles as our own. Acceptance merely honors the value of other people as the unique workmanship of a delightfully creative God. Acceptance is having the grace to let others be.

Intellectually, you are probably very bright, perhaps above average. But how high is your A.Q.? In the kingdom of God, that's what really matters.

Agapē: Authentic Love
JOHN 13:31-38

NASB

31 Therefore when he had gone out, Jesus said, "Now ªis the Son of Man glorified, and God ªis glorified in Him; 32 ªif God is glorified in Him, God will also glorify Him in Himself, and will glorify Him immediately. 33 Little children, I am with you a little while longer. You will seek Me; and as I said to the Jews, now I also say to you, 'Where I am going, you cannot come.' 34 A new commandment I give to you, that you love one another, even as I have loved you, that you also love one another. 35 By this all men will know that you are My disciples, if you have love for one another."

36 Simon Peter said to Him, "Lord, where are You going?" Jesus answered, "Where I go, you cannot follow Me now; but you will follow later." 37 Peter said to Him, "Lord, why can I not follow You right now? I will lay down my life for You." 38 Jesus answered, "Will you lay down your life for Me? Truly, truly, I say to you, a rooster will not crow until you deny Me three times.

13:31 ªOr *was* **13:32** ªMost early mss do not contain this phrase

NLT

31 As soon as Judas left the room, Jesus said, "The time has come for the Son of Man* to enter into his glory, and God will be glorified because of him. 32 And since God receives glory because of the Son,* he will give his own glory to the Son, and he will do so at once. 33 Dear children, I will be with you only a little longer. And as I told the Jewish leaders, you will search for me, but you can't come where I am going. 34 So now I am giving you a new commandment: Love each other. Just as I have loved you, you should love each other. 35 Your love for one another will prove to the world that you are my disciples."

36 Simon Peter asked, "Lord, where are you going?"

And Jesus replied, "You can't go with me now, but you will follow me later."

37 "But why can't I come now, Lord?" he asked. "I'm ready to die for you."

38 Jesus answered, "Die for me? I tell you the truth, Peter—before the rooster crows tomorrow morning, you will deny three times that you even know me.

13:31 "Son of Man" is a title Jesus used for himself. **13:32** Several early manuscripts do not include *And since God receives glory because of the Son.*

In 1970, Francis Schaeffer wrote *The Mark of the Christian,* a tiny volume with a weighty message. If you have the courage to read it, you will not find anything written about bumper stickers, fish emblems, lapel crosses, or cleverly marketed bracelets. For that matter, you won't read a word about biblical doctrine or church membership. The book is about the true mark of a Christian: love.

John 13 is a penetrating, challenging chapter to read. Jesus taught His disciples about humility and acceptance—lessons that would not impact them completely until the truth of Judas's betrayal became a matter of history. Once Judas had disappeared into the darkness, Jesus continued His review of fundamental Christian teaching, which begins with love.

— 13:31-32 —

Throughout John's narrative, Jesus has spoken of a coming "hour" in which the Son of God would be "glorified." Jesus announced the arrival of His hour using a form of the Greek term *doxa* [1391] five times in two verses. *Doxa* derives from the verb *dokeō* [1380], which means "to believe, to think." To be glorified is to be revealed in such a way as to be thought good. To be glorified is to be vindicated in the eyes of all witnesses. Therefore, the concept of glory in Jesus' vocabulary meant that the truth He had been teaching and the truth of His identity would be vindicated in the eyes of all humanity. His identity as the Word in human flesh would be confirmed by his going to the cross, rising from the dead, and ascending to heaven.

With the departure of Judas to betray Him, the process of glorification had begun.

— 13:33-35 —

Jesus understood that the betrayal of one disciple would ultimately end in His conquering death for all of humanity. However, the remaining eleven knew nothing. While Jesus had often predicted His own death and had promised many times to rise from the dead (Matt. 12:40; 16:21; 17:23; 20:19; Mark 9:9; 10:34; 14:28; Luke 9:22; 24:7; John 2:19-22), His closest followers failed to connect the dots. As far as they were concerned, Judas's betrayal and Jesus' death represented the end of all their messianic hopes. Therefore, He reassured them in simpler, more direct terms. He wanted them to know that God's plan had not been thwarted; His impending ordeal was a necessary part of it.

To reassure His disciples, Jesus revealed three facts: His leaving was imminent. People would look for Him. No one could come with Him. And the announcement stunned them. Jesus had been the center of their world for no less than three and a half years. They never expected that to change.

As the men sat in bewildered silence, Jesus issued a completely new command. While He would no longer be among them physically, part of their support would come from one another. Just as He had loved them, they were to love one another. The men had finally learned to love their Master and had grown accustomed to His faithful love for them. He now

A NEW KIND OF LOVE

JOHN 13:33-35

The Greek word *agapē* is rarely found outside the Bible. The Greek language celebrated *erōs*, an intoxicating, impulsive love between men and women, and honored *philia*, the warm, noble affection of deep friendship. But *agapē* remained pitifully undeveloped as a term. The human authors of the New Testament needed a Greek word to express the kind of love taught by Christ and commanded by Him in the upper room, but the most common Greek terms wouldn't suffice. Fortunately, *agapē* was relatively unknown and largely undefined, so it perfectly suited their purposes. Like an empty wineskin, it waited to be filled with distinctly Christian meaning.

While believers began to adopt this new kind of love, their secular contemporaries decried the steady loss of virtue in Roman society. More and more, their peers exchanged venerable *philia* for fleeting *erōs*. As the two cultures moved in opposite directions, the contrast could not have been more absolute.

ERŌS[2]	AGAPĒ
a general love of the world seeking satisfaction wherever it can	a love which makes distinctions, choosing and keeping to its object
determined by a more or less indefinite impulsion towards its object [him or her]	a free and decisive act determined by its subject [us]
in its highest sense is used of the upward impulsion of man, of his love for the divine	relates for the most part to the love of God, to the love of the higher lifting up the lower, elevating the lower above others
seeks in others the fulfillment of its own life's hunger	must often be translated "to show love"; it is a giving, active love on the other's behalf

Based on John's rendering of Christ's teaching, the Lord predicted, "By this all men will know that you are My disciples, if you have [*agapē*] for one another" (John 13:35). Given the contrast with *erōs*, it's no wonder!

expected each man among the remaining eleven to cultivate that same relationship with the other ten.

While Jesus walked among them on earth, no one doubted whose disciples the men were. Once He returned to heaven, however, their mutual love should be strong enough to maintain their identity before the watching world. With Jesus physically gone, their love should sustain them. In a very real sense, the love between Master and disciple would be multiplied by ten upon His leaving the earth.

The kind of love Jesus called his men to express is called *agapē* [26]— the kind that seeks the highest, greatest good of another. If the men had any trouble understanding the meaning of this term and how to express it, all they had to do was recall their time with Jesus. He had been their living illustration for more than three years.

— 13:36-38 —

When Jesus completed His exhortation for the disciples to love one another in His absence, Peter reacted to the Lord's announced departure. We can only imagine what he was thinking, although it certainly didn't involve love for his fellow disciples. His passion cannot be denied; however, his motivation was suspect. Jesus commanded His followers to love one another, yet Peter declared supreme love for Jesus, even to the point of dying by His side in battle. Clearly, the impulsive disciple was ready to defend his Lord . . . but where was his obedience?

Jesus would save the lesson on love and obedience for another time (21:15-22). For now, He simply stated the simple truth that Peter's love was just as fickle as his zeal. The kind of battle Jesus envisioned for the disciples cannot be fought with the kind of sword that has a steel blade. He wanted soldiers wielding a sword of truth, obedient to the end, and united in *agapē.*

• • •

Some time ago, a lady had lost her husband and requested that I conduct his funeral. He was an exceptionally good man and he was matched well with this woman. They were the rare sort of couple who constantly thought of ways to bring family, friends, and neighbors to faith in Jesus Christ. As she expressed her desires for the funeral service, she said, "I know if my husband were sitting right here, he would agree. I want this funeral service to honor Jesus Christ. And I have one neighbor in mind especially. We have tried different ways to reach her. We've had her over for dinner and we've given her cassettes, booklets, and other little gifts, but we have never been able to get through to her."

So I said, "Okay, let's pray right now that she'll be reached in some way through this whole process." So we did.

The morning of the funeral, I stopped by to see how the woman was doing. I was surprised to see her neighbor sitting with her and a steady stream of church members coming and going. Some brought food. Others helped clean the house and did chores left by her husband. One couple offered to drive her anywhere she needed to go and even offered to loan her their car. Most just stopped by to share her sorrow and to cry with her.

A few days later, my phone rang. It was the widow. Sorrow and joy mingled in her voice as she spoke. "Do you remember the neighbor I told you about?"

"Sure," I said.

"She stayed until everybody else had gone, and she said to me, 'My, what love. Were all those people members of your family?'"

Her remark became a perfect opportunity for the widow to say, "Yes. In a different way than you're thinking, we're all from the same family."

If you have a fish symbol on your car, that's fine. People will associate you with a movement. Do you display a cross? Nothing bad about that. People will link you to a religion. If you carry a Bible everywhere you go, people will assume you attend a particular kind of church. If, on the other hand, you display love that is authentic to the core—observable love—then people will know you are a follower of Jesus Christ.

APPLICATION: JOHN 13:31-38

It Isn't Love Until You Give It Away

The world struggles to understand love. Most people think mainly of romantic love, that mysterious sickness that overtakes someone like a delightful case of the flu—can't eat, can't sleep, can't concentrate on anything except one's lover—a disease for which time is the only cure. That kind of love comes and goes as it pleases and trumps all logic. No one knows its cause.

Many accept the existence of family love, but it's usually conflicted. In many families, love is something to be endured on special holidays and for no longer than absolutely necessary. Loyalty is the primary word for this kind of love; kindness is entirely optional.

Authentic love—*agapē*—embodies the finest qualities of romantic love and family love, but it is permanent and always characterized by kindness. Moreover, *agapē* bears three distinct qualities that set it apart as distinctly heaven-made.

First, *authentic love is unconditional in its expression.* Throughout the Gospels, Jesus expressed love for all kinds of "undesirable" people, including Roman collaborators, prostitutes, thieves, religious zealots, rich rulers, working-class people, unredeemed lawyers, and the desperately down-and-out. He turned away no one who desired His love and even wept for those who did not. Authentic love gives without conditions.

Second, *authentic love is unselfish in its motive. Agapē* expects nothing in return for kindness and gives without regard for self-interest. It's easy to love those who express gratitude and who respond with love in return. But authentic love gives kindness to others regardless of their ability to return it, including those who are simply unwilling. Loving the unlovely for their sake is the essence of *agapē.*

Third, *authentic love is unlimited in its benefits.* Because *agapē* is its own reward, it always benefits the giver. The satisfaction of authentic love never fades, but only if it's unconditional and unselfish. In fact, many acts of authentic love often leave the giver feeling like they received the most joy from their deeds!

Unlike the elation of romantic love and the loyalty of family love, which live as emotions hidden within the heart, *agapē* cannot exist apart from action. At least one anonymous poet understood what is meant by authentic love:

A bell isn't a bell till it's rung,
A song isn't a song till it's sung,
Love isn't put in your heart to stay,
Love isn't love till it's given away.[3]

Tranquil Words for Troubled Hearts
JOHN 14:1-24

NASB

[1] "Do not let your heart be troubled; [a]believe in God, believe also in Me. [2] In My Father's house are many dwelling places; if it were not so,

NLT

[1] "Don't let your hearts be troubled. Trust in God, and trust also in me. [2] There is more than enough room in my Father's home.* If this were not

NASB

I would have told you; for I go to prepare a place for you. ³If I go and prepare a place for you, I will come again and receive you to Myself, that where I am, *there* you may be also. ⁴And you know the way where I am going." ⁵Thomas said to Him, "Lord, we do not know where You are going, how do we know the way?" ⁶Jesus said to him, "I am the way, and the truth, and the life; no one comes to the Father but through Me.

⁷If you had known Me, you would have known My Father also; from now on you know Him, and have seen Him."

⁸Philip said to Him, "Lord, show us the Father, and it is enough for us." ⁹Jesus said to him, "Have I been so long with you, and *yet* you have not come to know Me, Philip? He who has seen Me has seen the Father; how *can* you say, 'Show us the Father'? ¹⁰Do you not believe that I am in the Father, and the Father is in Me? The words that I say to you I do not speak on My own initiative, but the Father abiding in Me does His works. ¹¹Believe Me that I am in the Father and the Father is in Me; otherwise believe because of the works themselves. ¹²Truly, truly, I say to you, he who believes in Me, the works that I do, he will do also; and greater *works* than these he will do; because I go to the Father. ¹³Whatever you ask in My name, that will I do, so that the Father may be glorified in the Son. ¹⁴If you ask Me anything in My name, I will do *it*.

¹⁵"If you love Me, you will keep My commandments.

¹⁶I will ask the Father, and He will give you another ªHelper, that He may be with you forever; ¹⁷*that is* the Spirit of truth, whom the world cannot receive, because it does not see Him or know Him, *but* you know Him

NLT

so, would I have told you that I am going to prepare a place for you?* ³When everything is ready, I will come and get you, so that you will always be with me where I am. ⁴And you know the way to where I am going."

⁵"No, we don't know, Lord," Thomas said. "We have no idea where you are going, so how can we know the way?"

⁶Jesus told him, "I am the way, the truth, and the life. No one can come to the Father except through me. ⁷If you had really known me, you would know who my Father is.* From now on, you do know him and have seen him!"

⁸Philip said, "Lord, show us the Father, and we will be satisfied."

⁹Jesus replied, "Have I been with you all this time, Philip, and yet you still don't know who I am? Anyone who has seen me has seen the Father! So why are you asking me to show him to you? ¹⁰Don't you believe that I am in the Father and the Father is in me? The words I speak are not my own, but my Father who lives in me does his work through me. ¹¹Just believe that I am in the Father and the Father is in me. Or at least believe because of the work you have seen me do.

¹²"I tell you the truth, anyone who believes in me will do the same works I have done, and even greater works, because I am going to be with the Father. ¹³You can ask for anything in my name, and I will do it, so that the Son can bring glory to the Father. ¹⁴Yes, ask me for anything in my name, and I will do it!

¹⁵"If you love me, obey* my commandments. ¹⁶And I will ask the Father, and he will give you another Advocate,* who will never leave you. ¹⁷He is the Holy Spirit, who leads into all truth. The world cannot receive him, because it isn't looking for him

because He abides with you and will be in you.

18 "I will not leave you as orphans; I will come to you. 19 aAfter a little while the world will no longer see Me, but you *will* see Me; because I live, you will live also. 20 In that day you will know that I am in My Father, and you in Me, and I in you. 21 He who has My commandments and keeps them is the one who loves Me; and he who loves Me will be loved by My Father, and I will love him and will disclose Myself to him." 22 Judas (not Iscariot) said to Him, "Lord, what then has happened that You are going to disclose Yourself to us and not to the world?" 23 Jesus answered and said to him, "If anyone loves Me, he will keep My word; and My Father will love him, and We will come to him and make Our abode with him. 24 He who does not love Me does not keep My words; and the word which you hear is not Mine, but the Father's who sent Me.

14:1 aOr *you believe in God* 14:16 aGr *Paracletos, one called alongside to help;* or *Comforter, Advocate, Intercessor* 14:19 aLit *Yet a little and the world*

and doesn't recognize him. But you know him, because he lives with you now and later will be in you.* 18 No, I will not abandon you as orphans— I will come to you. 19 Soon the world will no longer see me, but you will see me. Since I live, you also will live. 20 When I am raised to life again, you will know that I am in my Father, and you are in me, and I am in you. 21 Those who accept my commandments and obey them are the ones who love me. And because they love me, my Father will love them. And I will love them and reveal myself to each of them."

22 Judas (not Judas Iscariot, but the other disciple with that name) said to him, "Lord, why are you going to reveal yourself only to us and not to the world at large?"

23 Jesus replied, "All who love me will do what I say. My Father will love them, and we will come and make our home with each of them. 24 Anyone who doesn't love me will not obey me. And remember, my words are not my own. What I am telling you is from the Father who sent me.

14:2a Or *There are many rooms in my Father's house.* 14:2b Or *If this were not so, I would have told you that I am going to prepare a place for you.* Some manuscripts read *If this were not so, I would have told you. I am going to prepare a place for you.* 14:7 Some manuscripts read *If you have really known me, you will know who my Father is.* 14:15 Other manuscripts read *you will obey;* still others read *you should obey.* 14:16 Or *Comforter,* or *Encourager,* or *Counselor.* Greek reads *Paraclete;* also in 14:26. 14:17 Some manuscripts read *and is in you.*

This particular section of Scripture is good for those struggling with heart troubles. I don't mean the kind of troubles that can be treated with a glycerin pill or bypass surgery. In some ways, that kind of heart trouble is easier to cure. I'm referring to the kind of heart trouble that steals sleep and keeps the mind churning throughout the day. This kind of trouble induces stress and quashes joy. Some call it "worry," but we Christians have more acceptable terms, such as "concern," "interest," "lack of peace," or my very favorite, "burden." To be "burdened" over some situation we cannot control sounds so much more spiritual than simply admitting, "I'm worried sick."

The disciples were stunned to hear Jesus' announcement, "Little children, I am with you a little while longer. You will seek Me; and as I said to the Jews, now I also say to you, 'Where I am going, you cannot come'" (John 13:33). Just a few moments before, the obviously "troubled" Master had exclaimed, "Truly, truly, I say to you, that one of you will betray Me" (13:21). Only John knew that Judas was the culprit. The others undoubtedly wondered, *Have we caused such offense that the Lord must separate Himself from us?* Peter protested the Lord's need to withdraw from all of them, declaring himself loyal unto death, which prompted a prediction that he would indeed deny his Master three times before dawn.

Obviously Jesus didn't mean that He must leave them behind because some or all of them would be disloyal. Nevertheless, the disconnect between His perspective and the disciples' is dramatic. Despite Jesus' many predictions concerning His own death, burial, and resurrection, which He termed "glory," the men felt abandoned by Him, perhaps even resigned to the fact that they did not deserve His continued care for them. This is what prompted Jesus' reassurance in 14:1-24. Their separation had nothing to do with the behavior of the disciples; the Lord's leaving was part of God's plan to redeem the world, which He established before time began. Furthermore, Christ will be faithful to His followers regardless of their success or failure as disciples.

The Lord's reassurance to the remaining eleven disciples presents us with six truths that offer peace when our hearts are troubled:

1. Personal faith in a personal Lord brings personal relief (14:1).
2. Our long-term future is secure (14:2-3).
3. The sovereign hand of God is at work in each believer's life (14:8-11).
4. Greater results occur when we pray in Jesus' name and for the Father's glory (14:12-14).
5. We are not alone; we have been given an indwelling Helper (14:15-17).
6. We are inseparably linked to Christ (14:18-21).

— 14:1 —

Personal faith in a personal Lord brings personal relief.

The Lord's exhortation, "do not let your heart be troubled" (the same Greek term that was used in 13:21), could appear hypocritical if we

JESUS FORETELLS HIS DEATH AND RESURRECTION

Matthew 12:40	"For just as Jonah was three days and three nights in the belly of the sea monster, so will the Son of Man be three days and three nights in the heart of the earth."
Matthew 16:21	From that time Jesus began to show His disciples that He must go to Jerusalem, and suffer many things from the elders and chief priests and scribes, and be killed, and be raised up on the third day.
Matthew 17:22–23	And while they were gathering together in Galilee, Jesus said to them, "The Son of Man is going to be delivered into the hands of men; and they will kill Him, and He will be raised on the third day." And they were deeply grieved.
Matthew 20:18–19	"Behold, we are going up to Jerusalem; and the Son of Man will be delivered to the chief priests and scribes, and they will condemn Him to death, and will hand Him over to the Gentiles to mock and scourge and crucify Him, and on the third day He will be raised up."
Mark 8:31–32	And He began to teach them that the Son of Man must suffer many things and be rejected by the elders and the chief priests and the scribes, and be killed, and after three days rise again. And He was stating the matter plainly. And Peter took Him aside and began to rebuke Him.
Mark 9:31	For He was teaching His disciples and telling them, "The Son of Man is to be delivered into the hands of men, and they will kill Him; and when He has been killed, He will rise three days later."
Mark 10:33–34	"Behold, we are going up to Jerusalem, and the Son of Man will be delivered to the chief priests and the scribes; and they will condemn Him to death and will hand Him over to the Gentiles. They will mock Him and spit on Him, and scourge Him and kill Him, and three days later He will rise again."
Luke 9:22	"The Son of Man must suffer many things and be rejected by the elders and chief priests and scribes, and be killed and be raised up on the third day."
Luke 18:31–33	Then He took the twelve aside and said to them, "Behold, we are going up to Jerusalem, and all things which are written through the prophets about the Son of Man will be accomplished. For He will be handed over to the Gentiles, and will be mocked and mistreated and spit upon, and after they have scourged Him, they will kill Him; and the third day He will rise again."
John 2:19–21	Jesus answered them, "Destroy this temple, and in three days I will raise it up." The Jews then said, "It took forty-six years to build this temple, and will You raise it up in three days?" But He was speaking of the temple of His body.

fail to consider the context. Jesus did not condemn worry, per se; neither does the Bible for that matter.[4] Feelings of distress are common to humanity and the Lord shared that part of human nature. Clearly, He meant, "Do not let your hearts be troubled *by My going away.*"

He followed this by a second exhortation to believe in God and His Son. The imperfect tense of the verb implies continuous action: "Keep on believing . . ." To believe in someone is to rely upon or trust that person. In the case of God, we are encouraged to trust in His ability and willingness to care for His own.

Let's face it; when something terrible occurs in life, humanity immediately looks heavenward and asks one of two questions: "Why did God allow this to happen?" or "Where was God?" Both suggest the Lord was either unable or unwilling to prevent tragedy. When pressed by worldly affliction, we naturally begin to wonder if He has abandoned us; we doubt His goodness or power.

Jesus asked for His followers' trust in the midst of their confusion.

— 14:2-3 —

Our long-term future is secure.

Jesus reassured His disciples that His going away had nothing to do with any of their personal failures, past or future. His purpose for going away was to secure their eternal future. The metaphor of home construction refers to His going to the cross on behalf of all humanity in order to secure eternal life for those who believe. He declared that His leaving was necessary and His return is assured.

The phrase, "many dwelling places," has been rendered "mansions" in older translations, which has inspired some to dream of owning their own castle-like estate in heaven. They have simply transferred their frustrated materialism to the spiritual realm. We earthlings are good at that! However, the Greek term is *monai* [3438], a plural noun based on the verb *menō* [3306], which means "to abide" or "to remain." This verb will be central to Jesus' exhortation later (15:1-11).

Jesus used the metaphor of an "abode" to illustrate our future relationship with the Father rather than to reveal our prospects in real estate. In ancient Near Eastern cultures, once a groom was betrothed, he had a set period of time in which to add a new wing to his family home. Then, after the betrothal period, he returned to receive his bride. After the wedding feast, the new couple moved into their newly added "abode" and became an integral part of the family estate.

Jesus' promise to "come again" refers to both His resurrection and the rapture of the church in the end times.

— 14:4-7 —

Jesus reminded the disciples that they knew the way to heaven, although they undoubtedly failed to understand that heaven was His subject. (Much of what He said in the upper room was intended to become clear once the men had received the Holy Spirit.) However, the way Jesus would travel would not be the path taken by the disciples. Jesus would go to heaven by way of suffering: Gethsemane, the trials, scourging, the cross, death, burial, resurrection, and then ascension.

In response to Thomas's question, obviously based on a literal interpretation of Jesus' words, the Lord declared Himself to be the path to heaven. In calling Himself "the way, and the truth, and the life," Jesus united three predominant themes John has taken care to weave throughout his narrative. The images of light (truth) and water (life) can be seen in virtually every story leading up to the Last Supper. Now these were joined to one of the first images Jesus used in His ministry: that of the Son of Man becoming the means by which people enter heaven (1:51).

While verse 6 declares a cardinal truth of the gospel, verse 7 is a rebuke. This is not new teaching. The disciples had been watching and listening to Jesus for more than three years, yet some followers outside the Twelve understood His teaching better than they (cf. 11:24).

— 14:8-11 —

The sovereign hand of God is at work in each believer's life.
Jesus' response to Thomas led to a challenge by Philip, one commonly expressed by everyone at one time or another. We live under the illusion that the will of God would be easier to accept if only we could receive a personal visit from Him. Suffering would be more bearable if God were to appear with personal reassurance. Instructions would be easier to follow if He were to communicate them audibly. However, we do not fear or fail merely because of doubt; we fear or fail because our sinful nature is enslaved to sin (see Rom. 7).

Jesus reminded Philip and the others that He is the perfect representation of the Father. The Father cannot take a visible, audible form more suitable than the Son. Because they are the same being, everything the Son says or does is a reflection of the Father's words and deeds. Therefore, everything Jesus had said and done in the upper room was in obedience to the sovereign plan of God.

— 14:12-14 —

Greater results occur when we pray in Jesus' name and for the Father's glory.

Many have taken Jesus' promise to mean "Name it, and it's yours," but this reduces the Lord to little more than a genie in a bottle. He never intended this promise to mean that prayer is a means of uncorking wishes on command. (The "Word of Faith" movement usually substitutes the term "blessing" for "wish," but the intent is the same. This movement reduces the almighty, sovereign God to little more than a genie, whom they call upon to produce whatever they ask.)

Verse 12 establishes the context. When Christ goes to the Father, His disciples are to step into the ministry vacuum He leaves behind. Those who believe will pick up where Jesus left off and will extend His ministry even farther. Verse 13 flows right out of verse 12. Jesus declared that supplications offered in the continuation of the Son's ministry will be answered as if He had spoken the prayer Himself. Verse 14 clarifies an underlying condition to the promise. To speak or act in someone's name is to act on his behalf or in pursuit of his interests. In other words, the Lord will not grant requests that contradict His own nature or oppose His plan.

More often than not, we do not pray in the interests of Jesus' plans or for the glory of God. In our immaturity, we seek our own interests and for what will improve our own situations. Then, as we grow wiser in grace and stronger in faith, we learn to ask for what we *think* is good. However, we still struggle to know what that is. I can recall many requests I prayed for in earnest—noble, unselfish petitions—only to thank God later for denying my petitions! I prayed with limited knowledge and sometimes with a hint of presumption.

Jesus promised that as we discover the will of God and align our prayers to fulfill His purposes, our prayers will become as powerful as His own.

— 14:15-17 —

We are not alone; we have been given an indwelling Helper.

Jesus established an unbreakable connection between love for God and obedience to His commands. Whereas Peter wanted to express his love in a blaze of glory with sword in hand at Jesus' last stand, his Master asked for something far more difficult: daily, consistent obedience. However, the Lord knows the human heart; we are woefully incapable of obedience on our own. In partial fulfillment of the new

Witnessing Made Cheap and Easy

JOHN 14:12-14

Many years ago, I stuck a fish emblem—a silver ichthus—on the back of my Volkswagen. It cost me 39 cents and roughly 45 seconds to advertise myself as a Christian on the freeways of Southern California. Behaving like a Christian on those freeways took a lot more out of me!

I don't have anything against Christian T-shirts, or bumper stickers with an encouraging message, or plaques displaying Bible verses, or any other wholesome knickknacks people want to buy. Those are fine. But I wonder how many believers unconsciously hope to impact the world with Christian merchandise instead of allowing their conduct to make a difference. I admit that putting a fish on my car felt pretty good at the time, but it's not my preference today. I have since discovered that nonbelievers don't pay much attention to what we wear or what we display on our cars. They observe how we behave.

Are you up for a challenge? It won't be easy, but it's relatively uncomplicated. Why not place a silver fish emblem on the inside of the car? Right in the middle of the steering wheel. Then, see if you can behave on the road in such a way as to cause other drivers to think, Ah, that person must be a Christian!

Not so cheap and not so easy, but definitely more what Christ had in mind.

covenant promise (Jer. 31:31-33; 2 Cor. 1:22; Eph. 1:13-14), Jesus promised the Holy Spirit would come to dwell within the hearts of those who believe in Him.

If this news didn't stun those eleven men, it should have. Throughout the Old Testament, the Holy Spirit was a rare gift and almost always temporary. He came upon certain individuals for a brief time for a specific purpose and then departed. A very few individuals were granted the indwelling presence of the Holy Spirit for life, among them John the Baptizer (Luke 1:15). So, the announcement that each of them would be inhabited by the presence of God was astounding news.

With the promise of the indwelling Holy Spirit comes a dramatic shift in how Jesus views the relationship between believers and "the world." Throughout John's narrative, Jesus uses the term "world" to include all of humanity who are fundamentally and organically bound by its fallen system and therefore hostile to Him (John 1:10). As the narrative unfolds, we see a gradual differentiation between "His own" and "the world" (13:1). "His own" are somehow different. They remain somewhat intertwined with creation, yet they are no longer bound by its fallen ways. Jesus later acknowledges that "His own" must remain *in* the world but are not *of* the world (15:19). After the promise of the Holy Spirit, Jesus portrays believers and "the world" as mortal enemies. From this point forward, believers are associated with God, and the world opposes believers just as it opposes Him.

— 14:18-21 —

We are inseparably linked to Christ.

Jesus' promise to return involves a twofold prediction. He will indeed return through His own resurrection and the disciples will see Him. However, His own resurrection also makes possible the resurrection of all believers. We will also see Him in eternal life after death. In the meantime, we are not orphans, because He is still present through the Holy Spirit. Just as the Son and the Father are two persons and one being, so are the Son and the Spirit.

When Jesus can no longer be seen physically by the world, believers will continue to see Him because they have been given sight (9:39). The presence of the Holy Spirit is the means by which this promise is fulfilled, while obedience is the method. As we grow in obedience and our relationship with Him strengthens as a result, we "see" Him—not physically (until His return), but spiritually.

— 14:22-24 —

Judas (not the traitor, but another disciple) asked a question that gave the Lord another opportunity to emphasize the distinction between "His own" and "the world." He simply reworded His earlier statement that the means of "seeing" Him is the indwelling of the Holy Spirit and the method by which we view Christ is obedience. Those who do not believe are like people without eyes; they cannot see Christ if they do not have the means. Moreover, even if they did have eyes, they would refuse to open them through obedience. Jesus used this figurative language to unite several concepts. Obedience, love, the words of Christ, seeing Christ, and abiding are all facets of the same positive response to God, and all are made possible by the Holy Spirit.

• • •

We have the advantage of history as we read this story of the Last Supper. Because we know the disciples' future, we see their experience from a divine perspective; therefore, we remain calm while they despaired. Now the tables are turned. If indeed people in heaven watch events on earth, they remain calm while we despair. They see our experience from a divine perspective.

If only we could see from that perspective. According to Jesus, we can.

APPLICATION: JOHN 14:1-24

Medicine for the Heart

Based on my study of John 13:33-38, I find three sources of heart trouble that affected the disciples and continue to plague believers today. Jesus addressed these troubles in John 14.

Heart Trouble #1: *Death is near (13:33a)*. The Son of God faced imminent death. The disciples naturally worried that if Jesus could not escape His own demise, what hope did anyone have? Death is the ultimate fear; however, we're also deathly afraid of disease, sickness, accidents, crime, war, poverty, and a host of other mortal afflictions. We fear dying and we fear that someone we love will be taken in death.

Heart Trouble #2: *Daily problems (13:33b)*. The disciples wondered, *How are we going to handle daily life without Jesus?* Each day we roll out of bed and enter daily life, we risk damaging something valuable, suffering something painful, hurting or losing someone important, or failing something critical. People experience pressure, lose jobs, suffer pain, endure hardship, feel rejection, face bankruptcy, and fall ill. And sometimes those problems of daily life feel overwhelming.

Heart Trouble #3: *Disobedience (13:38)*. Because we are fundamentally sinful from birth and we will never be anywhere near sinless in this life, we continually battle the consequences of our own disobedience. Guilt, shame, regret, remorse, self-condemnation, fear of discovery, dread of repentance, avoidance of responsibility . . . Oh, how exhausting to walk around with unresolved sin hanging from our hearts like a huge stone!

Death produces fear. Daily problems cause anxiety. Disobedience generates shame. Each and every day of our existence, we run a gauntlet of fear, anxiety, and shame—the full array of dangers to humanity.

Jesus, though sinless, was truly human. Therefore, He personally experienced the complete range of human weaknesses and afflictions, so we have a high priest who ministers with complete understanding. Just before leaving the earth for heaven, He gave His disciples—and us—six truths to help them bear the struggles of life with hope (see the introduction discussion on 14:1-24).

I want to offer three practical techniques to counter the deadly effects of heart trouble.

Technique #1: *To dispel fear, meditate on truth*. For the believer, fear is the result of ignorance. People who are afraid of God do not know Christ. People who fear the future do not know prophecy. People who dread judgment for sin do not know the good news. And people who are terrified of death do not know the Lord's promises. Christians, on the other hand, have no reason to fear anything, including death. Granted, no one looks forward to dying and everyone wants to prolong life, but death itself loses its power to frighten because Christ has overcome it.

Divine truth dispels fear.

Technique #2: *To reduce anxiety, allow divine truth to guide every decision*. Jesus did not bring truth to the earth merely for the sake of education; He expects us to absorb the truth and to apply the truth so that our lives will be conformed to His way. When we know we're living in harmony with God's will, anxiety fades. Meditate on the truths Jesus articulated in the upper room and discover new ways to apply them to each situation in life.

Technique #3: *To release shame, choose to love Christ and serve His body.* Shame is self-condemnation, a self-centered pattern of thought that is inappropriate once repentance for sin has taken place and Christ has removed all guilt. However, some continue to struggle with guilt because they continue in disobedience. Many others struggle with shame because they remain self-focused. The solution is to turn one's attention outward, choosing to love and serve Christ by loving and serving each other.

Overcoming Fear
JOHN 14:25-31

NASB

25 "These things I have spoken to you while abiding with you. 26 But the Helper, the Holy Spirit, whom the Father will send in My name, He will teach you all things, and bring to your remembrance all that I said to you. 27 Peace I leave with you; My peace I give to you; not as the world gives do I give to you. Do not let your heart be troubled, nor let it be fearful. 28 You heard that I said to you, 'I go away, and I will come to you.' If you loved Me, you would have rejoiced because I go to the Father, for the Father is greater than I. 29 Now I have told you before it happens, so that when it happens, you may believe. 30 I will not speak much more with you, for the ruler of the world is coming, and he has nothing in Me; 31 but so that the world may know that I love the Father, ªI do exactly as the Father commanded Me. Get up, let us go from here.

14:31 ªLit *and as the Father...so I do*

NLT

25 I am telling you these things now while I am still with you. 26 But when the Father sends the Advocate as my representative—that is, the Holy Spirit—he will teach you everything and will remind you of everything I have told you.

27 "I am leaving you with a gift—peace of mind and heart. And the peace I give is a gift the world cannot give. So don't be troubled or afraid. 28 Remember what I told you: I am going away, but I will come back to you again. If you really loved me, you would be happy that I am going to the Father, who is greater than I am. 29 I have told you these things before they happen so that when they do happen, you will believe.

30 "I don't have much more time to talk to you, because the ruler of this world approaches. He has no power over me, 31 but I will do what the Father requires of me, so that the world will know that I love the Father. Come, let's be going.

While fear is a primal response, it is completely unnatural to humanity as God first created us. The first emotion recorded in the Bible is "not ashamed" (Gen. 2:25). Adam and Eve enjoyed perfect intimacy with God and one another, uninhibited by sin or the shame it brings. The second emotion specifically named in Scripture is fear. After trying to conceal his shame, Adam confessed that fear drove him into hiding when his Creator came to confront him (Gen. 3:10). Fear is a product of the Fall, and we have been trying to cope with it ever since. Fear of heights. Fear of crowds. Fear of open spaces. Fear of germs. Fear of death. I have even read articles in psychological journals about the fear of fear!

Fear can be debilitating. Fear strips the athlete of his prowess, drains creativity from the artist, muddies the leader's clarity, and drives the soldier deeper into his foxhole. I have seen people literally paralyzed with fear, unable to move a muscle in its grip. More commonly, fear keeps people from becoming everything God created them to be and prevents them from loving one another fully.

Jesus' announcement of His departure sent the disciples into an emotional tailspin. They couldn't imagine their future without Jesus and the prospect of going on alone terrified them . . . and rightfully so! I cannot imagine having to face life without Christ in my life. Those trembling eleven men needed courage, just as we do today. So, Jesus confronted their fears with four truths that, when applied, help provide believers with the power to overcome fear of any kind:[5]

1. We may be inadequate, but the Holy Spirit will make us competent and courageous (14:25-26).
2. We may be fearful, but the peace of Jesus Christ is ours for the taking (14:27).
3. Circumstances may be dire, but victory has been assured (14:28-29).
4. Circumstances may be difficult, but courage can be found in obedience (14:30-31).

— 14:25-26 —

We may be inadequate, but the Holy Spirit will make us competent and courageous.

"These things" refers to the Lord's teaching on obedience, love, and "abiding." He promised that everything He taught them would continue to be taught by the Holy Spirit living within them. The word translated "Helper" is *paraklētos* [3875], which we have transliterated to form the term "Paraclete."

The Greek term can also be translated "advocate," "encourager," or even "coach." In modern terms, the word carries the idea of a trainer running alongside someone in a race providing counsel, correction, hope, comfort, and positive perspective. A *paraklētos* helps another toward excellence. Like a coach encouraging and challenging an athlete to reach a particular goal, He trains believers to dedicate themselves, to discard hindrances, and to become obedient like Christ. The Helper does this supernaturally, in part by recalling the words of Christ to the mind and by applying them to the heart.

The disciples learned volumes of truth at Jesus' feet, far more than anyone could remember without supernatural help. After Jesus ascended to heaven, the men never saw Him again as they did during His earthly ministry. Their days of casual, face-to-face conversation came to an end. They had to depend upon the Holy Spirit to give them perfect recall and to help them pass on the Lord's teachings without error.

While we have not been tasked to write Scripture, we as believers have the same Holy Spirit abiding within us nonetheless. In the interim period while Jesus is away, before He returns, His Spirit rests within His followers to instruct and to remind us of previously revealed truth.

— 14:27 —

We may be fearful, but the peace of Jesus Christ is ours for the taking.

Jesus left His followers with a legacy, "Peace I leave with you," and a treasure, "My peace I give to you." The disciples were going to face uncertain days in the future, especially between the time of Jesus' death and the giving of the Holy Spirit nearly two months later. He wanted to focus their attention on the final victory.

Imagine watching a championship football game along with a group of friends. If the game had been previously recorded and you already knew the final score (but your friends didn't), you would experience the game very differently than your friends. They might gasp when their team fumbled or cringe when the opponents scored. But you would remain relatively unaffected because you would be viewing everything through the lens of an assured outcome. If any of your friends wanted peace in the midst of their doubt, all they would have to do is look to you. Your peace would become theirs.

A little later, Jesus would reassure His disciples, "These things I have spoken to you, so that in Me you may have peace. In the world you have tribulation, but take courage; I have overcome the world" (16:33).

— 14:28-29 —

Circumstances may be dire, but victory has been assured.

Jesus noted that His imminent death could be seen as either a calamity or a victory, depending upon one's perspective. He had predicted His death and resurrection many times, but the disciples failed to understand that they were taking part in something far greater than any of them imagined. If they accepted the fact that their Master's death was part of the Father's plan, they would be hopeful instead of fearful.

Note the Lord's use of "when" instead of "if" in 14:29. The Father's plan is not an "if" plan, it's a "when" plan. There are no contingencies to plan for. Nothing will stop Him. While the Lord has not rescinded His gift of self-determination to each individual, He has written the future, and it is no more changeable than the past. While the future will bring tribulation and our experiences will not always be pleasant, we can endure with hope—confident assurance—because the plans of God are assured of victory. No one understood this better than God's Son, who faced a deeper darkness than any other man or woman will ever endure.

— 14:30-31 —

Circumstances may be difficult, but courage can be found in obedience.

The "ruler of the world" is Satan. When the first man chose to disobey God, all of creation fell under the dominion of the author of sin, evil, death, and corruption. The incarnation of God in the person of Jesus Christ was an invasion, a liberation force of One. And He suffered the assault of the enemy in order to free humanity from the dominion of sin.

Jesus warned that the enemy planned to strike soon. At that very moment, Judas was making plans with the religious officials to organize a cohort of temple guards and Roman soldiers. The Lord assured His followers that the means of overcoming fear of the enemy is obedience. He declared, "I do exactly as the Father commanded me." While the prospect of suffering the penalty of sin on behalf of the whole world troubled Him deeply, obedience gave Him courage.

• • •

Jesus pulled His disciples aside before His arrest to equip them for ministry without His physical presence. He had called them to shine the light of truth in a world still ruled by evil and He had faithfully equipped them with all the information they would need; however, fear threatened to render them powerless. Why? For the same reason fear plagues Christians today: lack of *confidence* in the truth of His words. The disciples trusted in Christ, but they lacked confidence.

There is a profound difference between "trust" and "confidence."

Trust is the decision to accept as truth the words of Jesus and to make them the basis of all future decisions. Confidence is the growing feeling of peace as we apply the words of Christ and see them confirmed over and over again. Trust is a decision; confidence is a feeling.

In response to the disciples' fear, Jesus confirmed again the truth He had been teaching from the beginning. Believers no longer have reason to fear. Unlike Adam after his disobedience, we have peace with God because of Jesus' atoning sacrifice (Rom. 5:1); therefore, God's omnipotence is our ally against any conceivable enemy. But confidence in this truth does not occur the instant we believe in Him. Our decision to trust begins a process of growth in which we experience the truth of Christ's words personally through obedience. This, in turn, leaves less and less room for fear.

Jesus called this process of growing confidence through obedience "abiding."

APPLICATION: JOHN 14:25-31

Focus

Every waking moment, we choose to focus on one of five different facets of life. All of them are present and very real, so we cannot ignore them. However, only one should be our *focus*.

Self—When self becomes the focus of life, one becomes conceited and, inevitably, discouraged. When the world revolves around self, we interpret all of life in terms of how we view ourselves. When good or bad things happen, we assume they are somehow related to our innate goodness or badness. A healthy self-esteem becomes twisted into vanity, while a poor self-esteem spirals into depression.

Circumstances—The quickest way to become overwhelmed by fear or hopelessness is to focus on circumstances. In many ways, it is the opposite of focusing on self. People who focus on circumstances presume that nothing in the surrounding world can be affected by their own choices. They feel helpless and victimized by a world they feel powerless to change.

Possessions—People frequently substitute the acquisition and maintenance of things for what really satisfies. Relationships with other people—close, intimate bonds in which one is known and knows another—are frightening to some; they find relationships with things much easier to manage. This is especially true of one's relationship with God; therefore, great effort is spent trying to fill a Christ-shaped void with possessions.

People—We need people. God made us for relationships with others as well as with Himself. However, relationships are prime candidates for idolatry. We too easily allow the voices of those around us to overshadow the truth of Scripture and replace the internal prompting of the Holy Spirit. Some allow themselves to be tossed about on the waves of others' opinions.

The Lord—Jesus called for us to focus on the triune God, who is sovereign over self, circumstances, possessions, and other people. When these other four influences are subordinated to Him, everything finds the right balance. We see ourselves as we ought, circumstances become tools of God's providence, possessions become blessings, and people become our equals before Christ—equally unworthy of grace and equally worthy of love.

If you're like me, you are relentlessly pragmatic. You want to know how to turn these truths into actions that make a difference. How can we render fear obsolete? How can we put fear out of our daily experience? Here are some simple, direct suggestions that work well for me.

1. *Acknowledge your source of power.* If you have trusted in Christ, you have within you the presence and power of almighty God. The Holy Spirit lives within you. When confronted by something you fear, choose to turn your attention to the power of God residing within and consciously ask Him to take control of you.

2. *Begin each day with prayer.* This can quickly dissolve into meaningless routine with memorized prayers. There will be times when you do not know what to say. So, say that— "Lord, I have no idea what to say right now." If no specific worry or fear comes to mind, make your prayer one of thanksgiving. This may take two minutes or two hours. Either way, beginning the day with prayer is a means of consciously placing the Lord in charge of each new day. And for me, this is a crucial source of power and peace.

3. *Correct your habit of pessimism.* Our penchant to fear the worst as unpleasant events unfold is one of the primary reasons God gave us prophecy. It is virtually impossible to remain pessimistic when you know the future of God's plan. However dismal the present may appear,

however victorious evil appears to be, we are assured that God's redemptive plan *cannot* be defeated.

4. *Devote yourself to obedience.* When we are obedient, we give the Accuser less opportunity to frighten us. When bad circumstances surround us, Satan loves to tell us that we are to blame for displeasing the Lord and that further obedience is pointless. Nothing could be further from the truth—disobedience breeds fear. Obey the Lord out of love, and amazingly, fear will fade.

Abiding
JOHN 15:1-11

NASB

[1] "I am the true vine, and My Father is the vinedresser. [2] Every branch in Me that does not bear fruit, He takes away; and every *branch* that bears fruit, He [a]prunes it so that it may bear more fruit. [3] You are already [a]clean because of the word which I have spoken to you. [4] Abide in Me, and I in you. As the branch cannot bear fruit [a]of itself unless it abides in the vine, so neither *can* you unless you abide in Me. [5] I am the vine, you are the branches; he who abides in Me and I in him, he bears much fruit, for apart from Me you can do nothing. [6] If anyone does not abide in Me, he is thrown away as a branch and dries up; and they gather them, and cast them into the fire and they are burned. [7] If you abide in Me, and My words abide in you, ask whatever you wish, and it will be done for you. [8] My Father is glorified by this, that you bear much fruit, and *so* [a]prove to be My disciples. [9] Just as the Father has loved Me, I have also loved you; abide in My love. [10] If you keep My commandments, you will abide in My love; just as I have kept My Father's commandments and abide in His love. [11] These things I have

NLT

[1] "I am the true grapevine, and my Father is the gardener. [2] He cuts off every branch of mine that doesn't produce fruit, and he prunes the branches that do bear fruit so they will produce even more. [3] You have already been pruned and purified by the message I have given you. [4] Remain in me, and I will remain in you. For a branch cannot produce fruit if it is severed from the vine, and you cannot be fruitful unless you remain in me.

[5] "Yes, I am the vine; you are the branches. Those who remain in me, and I in them, will produce much fruit. For apart from me you can do nothing. [6] Anyone who does not remain in me is thrown away like a useless branch and withers. Such branches are gathered into a pile to be burned. [7] But if you remain in me and my words remain in you, you may ask for anything you want, and it will be granted! [8] When you produce much fruit, you are my true disciples. This brings great glory to my Father.

[9] "I have loved you even as the Father has loved me. Remain in my love. [10] When you obey my commandments, you remain in my love, just as I obey my Father's commandments and remain in his love. [11] I have told

NASB

spoken to you so that My joy may be in you, and *that* your joy may be made full.

NLT

you these things so that you will be filled with my joy. Yes, your joy will overflow!

15:2 ªLit *cleans;* used to describe pruning
15:3 ªI.e. pruned like a branch   15:4 ªLit *from*
15:8 ªOr *become My disciples*

After hearing of Jesus' imminent departure from the world on the eve of His crucifixion, fear gripped the disciples like a steel vice. How could they possibly go on without Jesus? What would come of His kingdom? Was the Lord challenging them to build a kingdom without a king? Not exactly. First, He promised that His going away played a crucial role in the plan of God to redeem the world and that He would return (John 14:1-15). Second, He promised that He would not leave them to fend for themselves; He would be present within them in the person of the Holy Spirit, whose role is to teach and provide courage (14:16-24). Third, He promised that confidence in the truth of His words and comfort in His continual presence would grow as they obeyed Him (14:25-31).

The disciples had placed their trust in Jesus Christ, but they lacked maturity. The Lord had taught them divine truth for three and a half years, but it had not yet been put to the test. The time had come for these infant Christians to begin walking on their own. Their only hope of overcoming fear was to allow confidence in the truth of Jesus Christ to grow and to gradually displace it.

In chapter 15, Jesus described three key relationships that every believer must manage if they are to cultivate confidence and rise above the consequences of the Fall, including fear:

SECTION	RELATIONSHIP	KEY TERM	EMPHASIS
John 15:1-11	Believer with Christ	"Abide" (10 times in 11 verses)	Union
John 15:12-17	Believer with Believer	"Love" (4 times in 6 verses)	Communion
John 15:18-27	Believer with the World	"Hate" (8 times in 10 verses)	Persecution

As we examine 15:1-11, four observations will help our interpretation.

First, this passage has meaning for believers only. Any nonbeliever trying to apply these truths will be hopelessly confused. Jesus was not describing how one becomes a Christian, but how one lives as a Christian after placing his or her trust in Him.

Second, Jesus draws heavily on the metaphor of a vineyard, a powerful symbol with roots running deep into the soil of Israel's history (Ps. 80:8-9; Isa. 5:1-7; Ezek. 15:1-5; Hos. 10:1). No illustration touched the Hebrew soul like the image of a vinedresser and his vineyard.

Third, the primary subject of Christ's teaching is abiding, not bearing fruit. At no point in the discourse is the believer *commanded* to produce fruit. Instead, we are promised that if we abide, fruit will result.

Fourth, the illustration Jesus chose would have been familiar to every disciple and virtually all of John's readers, but unfamiliar to most of us today. Therefore, we must be careful not to milk every detail for symbolic meaning. Illustrations allow us to see the big picture—that must be our focus here.

Cyuszko/iStockphoto

Vinedressers encourage healthy growth through a process called "training," in which new branches are lifted up and carefully tied to the horizontal wire of a trellis.

— 15:1-2 —

The image of a vine and vinedresser poignantly illustrated God's special care for the nation of Israel, which gave the prophets Isaiah and Ezekiel a perfect image for their stinging rebukes (Isa. 5:1-7; Ezek. 15:1-5). God had originally planted Israel in the Promised Land to be a means of revealing His Word to the world and for teaching all nations about His grace. Israel was to flourish as a living example of how obedience bears the fruit of righteousness. Moreover, the Lord promised to bless Israel as the nation's relationship of trust grew stronger. But Israel failed.

By declaring Himself the "true vine," Jesus took the place of Israel, claiming to be the authentic, healthy vineyard the nation had failed to become (Isa. 5:1-7). Just as the Father had tended the failed vineyard of Israel, He would tend the flourishing vineyard of the Son.

Jesus then summarized the care a vinedresser gives to a vine. The Greek verb *airō* [142], translated "takes away," has the primary definition of "to lift from the ground," although the term can and often does mean "to lift with a view to carrying, to carry off or put away."[6] John has used *airō* in both senses: "take away" (John 11:39, 48; 16:22; 17:15) and "to lift up" (5:8-12; 8:59). Therefore, a strong case for either definition can be made.

I favor the definition "to lift up" for a couple reasons. First, these two verses introduce the illustration in summary fashion, describing the general care of a vinedresser nurturing a vine. Vinedressers are rarely seen cutting off branches during the growing season. Instead, they carry a bundle of strings and a pair of pruning shears as they work their way down a row. They carefully lift sagging branches and tie them to the trellis—a procedure called "training." They also strategically snip smaller shoots from branches in order to maximize their yield of fruit, which is called "pruning."

I favor "to lift up" for a second reason. A combination of "takes away" and "prunes" places too great an emphasis on cutting the vine when Jesus appears to be highlighting the Father's care during the growing season. The image of carrying off dead branches is a detail that will appear later as He refines the illustration.

— 15:3-4 —

The Lord reassured the disciples that they had already been pruned. The adjective translated "clean" is based on the same verb for "prune" in 15:2. He followed this assurance with a command to "abide." The verb means "to remain" or "to stay in place," very often in reference to one's home. Upon meeting Jesus, Andrew and John asked Him, "where are You staying (or abiding)?" (1:38). "Abiding" in terms of this metaphor refers to the branch remaining connected to the vine. Branches that do not receive nourishing sap from the vine cannot produce fruit—or continue living, for that matter.

A key to understanding what Jesus meant by "abiding" is the expression "in Me," which reflects a theological concept called "positional truth" or "identification." Paul the apostle often described believers as being "in Christ." "Identification" describes the believer's relationship with Christ such that God treats him or her as He would Jesus.

Imagine driving to the front gate of Buckingham Palace in London. You won't get very far before having to turn around. Without the proper credentials, the guards will turn you away. However, if the Queen sent her official car to pick you up and drive you to the gate, you would receive the same treatment she does. Because you are in the Queen's official car, the guard will give you the same royal treatment due the monarch of Great Britain. Similarly, being "in Christ" allows the believer to share the Son's identity. Consequently, those who are "in Christ" enjoy all the benefits of His relationship, including unrestricted access to the Father.

Jesus didn't use this illustration to make any points about salvation. In 15:3, the Lord affirmed the disciples' salvation, assuring them that God had already done His part; they were "already clean." With the matter of salvation settled, Jesus used this illustration to discuss the Christian life after salvation. He turned from the issue of *position*—"in Me"—to that of *production*. Once an individual chooses to believe and receives the assurance of eternal life, what is our purpose? How then shall we live? Like branches on a vine, we live to bear fruit (15:2).

— 15:5 —

As we examine this illustration, it is vitally important to keep two points in focus: The subject is not salvation, but vitality as a believer. The image of "fruit" in biblical literature is a common metaphor for "evidence." Fruit proves the identity of a plant and reveals its state of health (15:8).

An expert horticulturist knows when he or she is looking at a pear tree instead of an apple tree just by examining its leaves and bark. Untrained observers will have difficulty identifying what kind of tree they're observing. If, however, the tree hangs heavy with fruit, then there's no chance of error. Furthermore, good quality fruit is a strong indication of good health. Even a novice in horticulture knows that lots of lush, delicious fruit can come only from a strong, vibrant plant. A seriously sick plant cannot accomplish its purpose.

Jesus clearly indicated that the branches are the disciples—not nonbelievers—and He promised that abiding would inevitably lead to bearing fruit. If they remain connected to Him, they will receive nourishing sap, grow strong, and eventually bear unmistakable evidence of their identity as members of the vine (15:8). Moreover, the presence of fruit will testify to their good health in Christ. On the other hand, branches that do not bear fruit do not cease to be grapevines; however, their health becomes suspect and their identity might be questioned. In fact, branches that do not remain connected to the vine wither away and become good for nothing.

Christians often assume that producing fruit is their responsibility, something they must do in gratitude for what Christ has done for them. They strive to produce fruit only to fail, pick themselves up, promise to do better, try again, and then continue this wretched cycle of failure. Jesus instructed His followers to focus their attention on abiding rather than production.

— 15:6 —

The interpretation of John 15:6 can be the cause of heated debate among believers. Some have suggested that those who "do not abide in Me" are believers who have been unfaithful and have lost their salvation, that the Vinedresser decided they should be cut off and thrown away. But Jesus said that no one can be saved and then unsaved (10:27-29). Others suggest that the non-abiding branches represent those who never genuinely believed—people who reject Jesus outright or those who merely profess to believe. However, Jesus' illustration applies only to believers. We know this because John 15:2 speaks of every branch "in Me," which presumes a relationship exists, and because 15:3 specifies Jesus' audience as those who are "already clean."

More likely, Jesus drew upon the imagery of Ezekiel's illustration:

> Then the word of the LORD came to me, saying, "Son of man, how is the wood of the vine better than any wood of a branch which is among the trees of the forest? Can wood be taken from it to make anything, or can men take a peg from it on which to hang any vessel? If it has been put into the fire for fuel, and the fire has consumed both of its ends and its middle part has been charred, is it then useful for anything? Behold, while it is intact, it is not made into anything. How much less, when the fire has consumed it and it is charred, can it still be made into anything!" (Ezek. 15:1-5)

The point is simply this: vinedressers toss disconnected branches aside because they are good for nothing. As Warren Wiersbe so succinctly states,

It is unwise to build a theological doctrine on a parable or allegory. Jesus was teaching one main truth—the fruitful life of the believer—and we must not press the details too much. Just as an unfruitful branch is useless, so an unfruitful believer is useless; and both must be dealt with. It is a tragic thing for a once-fruitful believer to backslide and lose his privilege of fellowship and service.[7]

Jesus drew upon Ezekiel's analogy to call believers who do not abide in Him good for nothing. We cannot produce fruit on our own. If, however, we abide in Christ, we will accomplish our created purpose and be easily identified as healthy members of God's family (John 15:8).

— 15:7-9 —

Jesus quickly turned from the negative to the positive. As the believer abides, or remains vitally connected to Jesus Christ, he or she begins to assume a Christlike character. The believer is transformed from the inside out. His or her mind dwells on the kinds of thoughts that God thinks. The believer's heart begins to reflect the values of God (Jer. 31:31-33). And as we think as God thinks, we ask for what is consistent with His plan, which results in His giving us what we ask.

— 15:10-11 —

So what does it mean to "abide"? We know the analogy only applies to believers, and that abiding produces something in the life of the believer such that others can easily identify him or her as connected to Christ (15:8). But how does one "abide in Christ"? According to Jesus, the question is answered in one word: obedience. "Keeping commandments" and "abiding in love" are synonymous.

Take note of the parallel relationships established by Jesus. His connection with the Father is the pattern for our connection with Him. He obeys and loves the Father; we obey and love Christ. Because our relationship with Christ is just like His with the Father, we will receive the same benefit, which He called "joy." The Greek word describes someone in a state of gladness, such as at harvesttime (4:36) or at a wedding feast (3:29). It's an emotive word intended to be the very opposite of fear.

• • •

As the dialogue opened, Jesus noted the disciples' fear at the announcement of His departure. He first assured them that His departure was not intended to punish their shortcomings; rather, His departure was necessary to bless them in spite of their failures (14:1-15). He then promised to be with them through the indwelling presence of the Holy Spirit and that they would sense His continuing presence through Him (14:16-31). In addition to that reassurance, He gave us a remedy against fear and a means to experience His ongoing presence despite His physical absence: obedience (15:1-11). When we obey, confidence displaces fear (1 Jn. 2:28), resulting in joy.

APPLICATION: JOHN 15:1-11

The Fruit of Abiding

If you have trusted in Christ, your eternal destiny has been set. You are chosen by God and nothing will pluck you from His hand. Your *position* in Christ is secure; however, your *production* is another matter. If you "abide" in Christ—that is, obey Him, primarily by loving others—you will enjoy four specific results.

First, *prayers are answered.* This is not to suggest that God will become our personal genie. The promise is conditional. If we are connected to the vine and we are becoming more and more like Jesus, our prayers will not be selfish, but the kind of requests *He* would make. Jesus received everything He requested because He and the Father are completely and consistently aligned in their thinking.

Second, *God is glorified.* As we model the character of Jesus, obeying His commands in the same way He obeyed those of the Father, the triune God receives all the credit. He delights to see us reflecting His character, and He looks for opportunities to pour out His blessings on His children in response.

Third, *love is stimulated.* Note the absence of struggle or exertion. As we abide in Christ, the character qualities that honor the Lord begin to emerge, like grapes naturally growing from a healthy, vine-connected branch. Because God is love (1 Jn. 4:8), others will notice this divine quality developing within us.

Fourth, *joy will overflow.* "Joy" doesn't refer to superficial happiness or shallow cheerfulness. Joy is a deeply felt contentment that transcends difficult circumstances and derives maximum enjoyment from every good experience. Although it isn't all about laughter, abiding in Christ inspires laughter like you've never experienced before. Deep, contented joy comes from a place of complete security and confidence—even in the midst of trial. As I once heard, "Joy is the flag that flies over the castle of our hearts, announcing that the King is in residence."

You know, it's possible to pastor a church without abiding in Christ. I've done that a few times in my life and it is miserable. It's the best way I know to get an ulcer. It's also possible to run a business as a Christian, to teach Bible classes, to be a wife or a husband, and even to counsel people, all without abiding in Christ. However, any good we do and any success we enjoy will not have a lasting impact. Conversely, when we obey, when we allow His strength to flow through us, the Lord produces results that defy natural explanation—powerfully effective prayers, God-honoring blessings, unbounded love, and inexplicable joy.

Qualities of a Friend
JOHN 15:12-17

NASB

12 "This is My commandment, that you love one another, just as I have loved you. 13 Greater love has no one than this, that one lay down his life for his friends. 14 You are My friends if you do what I command you. 15 No longer do I call you slaves, for the slave does not know what his master is doing; but I have called you friends, for all things that I have heard from My Father I have made known to you. 16 You did not choose Me but I chose you, and appointed you that you would go and bear fruit, and *that* your fruit would remain, so that whatever you ask of the Father in My name He may give to you. 17 This I command you, that you love one another.

NLT

12 This is my commandment: Love each other in the same way I have loved you. 13 There is no greater love than to lay down one's life for one's friends. 14 You are my friends if you do what I command. 15 I no longer call you slaves, because a master doesn't confide in his slaves. Now you are my friends, since I have told you everything the Father told me. 16 You didn't choose me. I chose you. I appointed you to go and produce lasting fruit, so that the Father will give you whatever you ask for, using my name. 17 This is my command: Love each other.

Samuel Taylor Coleridge was a lonely genius. Born to aging parents in Devonshire, England, the youngest of ten children, he did not receive the love most children are given and, therefore, never had the opportunity to cultivate close relationships. His father died before his tenth birthday, after which he was sent to a boarding school notorious for its harsh treatment, and then to live with various family members. Nevertheless, his caretakers did recognize his exceptional intellect and enrolled him at Cambridge, where he quickly distinguished himself as a scholar.

Coleridge became known for three notable habits in school: voracious reading, prolific writing, and radical thinking. Eventually, his philosophical pursuits led him away from the faith of his father, a notable clergyman before his death, and away from Cambridge before graduating. He accumulated a large debt, pursued French philosophy, attempted to found a utopian society in Pennsylvania, married, divorced, became hopelessly addicted to opium, and eventually managed to estrange himself from family and friends alike.

Then, he met William Wordsworth, who befriended the rootless genius. This led to his most productive period of writing and publishing, during which he wrote the poems "Remorse," "Love," "Kubla Khan," and his most famous work, "The Rime of the Ancient Mariner." The main character in this emotional autobiography laments,

> Alone, alone, all, all alone;
> Alone on a wide, wide sea!
> And never a saint took pity on
> My soul in agony.[8]

Eventually, Wordsworth discontinued his relationship with Coleridge, who became excessively dependent upon opium, separated from his second wife, abandoned his children, and could no longer sustain any meaningful workload. He moved into the home of an apothecary, James Gillman, hoping to reduce his dosage of opium, but quickly found a secondary source. Nevertheless, Gillman allowed Coleridge to remain in his family's care for the rest of his life.

A few years before his death, Coleridge acknowledged the value of his sole friend in his poem, "Youth and Age," which includes the line, "Friendship is a sheltering tree."[9]

How true that is. As a young man, I denied the need for close friendships, convinced that a need for others is a sign of emotional or spiritual weakness. I didn't like to be alone, so I sought playmates for companionship. But I didn't want close friends who would challenge me to become a better man. I had not yet suffered the sting of life in the real world. I had not yet experienced a tragedy that required the help of devoted friends. As I matured, however, I realized that seeking close friends is a sign of emotional and spiritual maturity. As I grew in wisdom, I began to see that Jesus, the most capable, mature man who ever lived, sought out the companionship of twelve men and cultivated close friendships with a few of them. Then, on the eve of His crucifixion, He retreated into seclusion with the Twelve, not only to share His wisdom but also to draw comfort and receive support.

During His discourse on how the men and subsequent generations of disciples should conduct themselves after His departure, the Lord highlighted the importance of close friends. These sheltering trees spread their protection with four branches:

- A disregard for personal sacrifice (15:13).
- A dedication to mutual aims (15:14).
- A mutual confidentiality (15:15).
- A shared desire for success (15:16).

— 15:12 —

The commandments Jesus referenced in 15:10 are embodied in this one "new" command (13:34; cf. Matt. 22:37-40; Mark 12:29-34). He commanded believers to love one another.

In the worldly sense of the term, the command sounds impossible to carry out. How can we possibly love someone we barely know and for whom we have no feelings? The world's concept of love is self-oriented, performance based, and driven by fickle sentiment. People fall into love and out of love as though it were a random, mysterious force that affects two minds for a season and may fade as quickly as it came.

The Greek word here is not fickle *erōs*, or even heartfelt *philia* [5373], but *agapē* [26]. (See the earlier discussion, "A New Kind of Love" on page 260.) *Agapē* quite often involves deep feeling, but it begins with a decision. *Agapē* doesn't consider merit and doesn't wait for inspiration. *Agapē* is the kind of love exemplified by God, especially in relationship with His Son. Moreover, the tense of the verb is "imperfect," which suggests repeated or ongoing action: "keep loving one another." And the quality of that love must be the same kind as the love we receive from Christ. He is our example and our standard.

The Lord then described this love in practical terms, giving four examples followed by a repetition of the command (John 15:17).

— 15:13 —

A disregard for personal sacrifice.
While this verse has in view the act of Jesus dying in the place of all humanity, His sacrifice illustrates an important principle. The ultimate

example of love for another is the willingness to give higher priority to that person's life than to one's own. Charles Dickens incorporated this in his novel *A Tale of Two Cities,* whose characters were caught up in the swirling insanity and rampant bloodshed of the French Revolution. In the final scene (spoiler alert!), the dissipated lawyer, Sydney Carton, took his friend's place on the guillotine to secure his safety. Onlookers recalled Carton's serene expression as he climbed the steps of the scaffold, saying in effect, "It is a far, far better thing that I do, than I have ever done; it is a far, far better rest that I go to than I have ever known."[10]

This ultimate sacrifice is the ultimate expression of love; however, we are unlikely to face such a choice. More often, we are asked to give up our lives in small measures, day by day, rather than in one grand gesture. And in many ways, this is more difficult. Love for a friend doesn't keep a record of sacrifice; this kind of love values the other more than self so that sacrifice becomes a matter of small significance.

— 15:14 —

A dedication to mutual aims.

This statement involves a condition. If we do as He commands, we are identified as His friends and recipients of His sacrifice (15:13). This is not to suggest we must obey perfectly; after all, we are not able. Instead, this speaks of our intent to pursue His aims by following His instructions.

A soldier on the battlefield supports the mission aim by following the orders given by the commanding officer—even if he dies before accomplishing his task. If he deliberately disobeys, then he undermines the mission. So it is with us. We are His friends when we support His aims.

— 15:15 —

A mutual confidentiality.

This use of *philos* [5384], "friend" or "comrade," is unusual with respect to Jesus, who is usually addressed as "Lord," "Master," "Rabbi," or "my God." *Philos* in this context suggests a peer relationship; however, we certainly cannot claim equality with Christ, even when we eventually see Him face to face and are made to be like Him (1 Jn. 3:2). The relationship is one in which Jesus elevates us to a higher standing than we deserve; nevertheless, His superiority is never compromised.

As a young boy, I enjoyed the company of older men who treated me like a man; and for a time, I felt like their equals. However, whenever we got into an automobile, I was reminded that I was not their peer.

They had a license to drive and I did not; they knew how to operate the vehicle while my feet could barely reach the pedals. So it is with Christ. He elevates us to the status of "friend," He shares with us the details of His redemptive plan for the world, and He calls us to stand beside Him in accomplishing it. Through the indwelling Holy Spirit, the Son of God allows us complete access to His mind, freely sharing His deepest thoughts and plans. He brings us into fellowship with the Trinity, even though we are not morally perfect and we do not possess divine attributes like omnipotence or omniscience. He treats us like equals even though we can never actually be His peers.

Genuine friendships are not founded upon superficiality. Intimacy between friends affords little room for secrets. And when friends share every detail of life, regardless of how embarrassing or scandalous, opportunities for recovery, healing, and growth abound. The almighty Creator of the universe has invited us to relate to Him as a friend, to enjoy peer status with our Maker!

— 15:16 —

A shared desire for success.

This verse makes it clear that the relationship the Lord calls us to share with Him is reciprocal. Believers are chosen and appointed for the purpose of obedience ("bearing fruit"). He commands us to love one another as He loves us and to join Him in building His kingdom. As we obey, we are transformed. As we are transformed, we begin to think with the mind of Christ and to pray for what God desires to accomplish. Consequently, we experience a growing oneness with God in mind and purpose.

— 15:17 —

The Lord's concluding command not only brackets His teaching on love in the kingdom of God; it also introduces a new concept. Jesus will begin to describe the contrast between the kingdom of God and "the world" (15:18-27). One is characterized by love, obedience, unity, and grace, the other by hatred, selfishness, rejection, and persecution. As we study the next passage, the importance of our love for one another will become as obvious as a light shining in the darkness.

• • •

The love relationship that characterizes the oneness of the Trinity is the same kind of love relationship the Lord desires for His own. Furthermore, our love for one another allows us to receive the love of God.

The opposite is also true. We cannot know the love of God if we do not love the people He sent His Son to save (1 Jn. 3:10). Failing to love one another makes us like the world, which is characterized by hate. Jesus leaves no middle ground between love and hate. We must choose one or the other.

APPLICATION: JOHN 15:12-17

Sheltering a Friend

By the end of his life, Samuel Taylor Coleridge entertained a steady stream of admirers, but years of addiction to opium left him with only one genuine friend. James Gillman became Coleridge's sheltering tree.

As noted above, we learn from the Lord's discussion on love that a sheltering friend spreads his or her protection with four branches.

1. *A disregard for personal sacrifice.* To sacrifice means to forfeit something without expectation of anything in return. The sole motivation for sacrifice must be the highest, greatest good of the other person. Therefore, do not sacrifice anything you are unwilling to lose. Do not sacrifice anything unless you are willing to receive nothing in return and to have your sacrifice taken for granted. After all, grace probably isn't grace without the possibility of its being abused. If you are unwilling to sacrifice without hard feelings, it is better not to offer that particular kindness and to admit that the trust shared in your friendship is not yet deep enough.

2. *A dedication to mutual aims.* Genuine friendships are founded upon shared values. Individual goals might be different for two friends; however, their objectives do not conflict and ultimately honor the same principles. For example, one woman might be wholeheartedly committed to missions abroad, while her closest friend feels compelled to evangelize near home. Each can encourage the aims of the other because they share the value of spreading the good news. A dedication to mutual aims does not require friends to pursue identical goals in the same manner. However, they do support one another.

3. *A mutual confidentiality.* Holding the confidence of another involves keeping private matters with absolute discretion. Moreover, sharing a confidence requires complete honesty between friends. There are a handful of men that I trust to give me honest counsel when sorting

through my plans. I depend upon them to share their honest thoughts, especially when they disagree with my approach. And, most difficult of all, I heed their advice, even when I am not yet convinced they are right. Let me restate that another way, because this is crucial: The greatest test of trust in my friendship with these men is when I heed their counsel *before* I am fully convinced myself. If they tell me a certain course of action is unwise or unjust, I avoid that approach regardless of how convinced I am. I don't mean to say that I make decisions by majority rule; however, I trust these few friends to steer me around my own blind spots.

4. *A shared desire for success.* Friends don't undermine one another's efforts. Friends want to see each other achieve the honorable desires of their hearts, and they help one another achieve those goals. Friends encourage, challenge, guide, critique, celebrate, and supplement one another.

Each of these four qualities should be applied to healthy relationships, in which each friend has earned and preserved the trust of the other. In some rare cases, selflessness, dedication, loyalty, and support can be twisted to cause more harm than good. If we are to be a genuine friend to others, we must understand what each element does and does not entail.

As a young man, I wanted to have as many companions as possible. I mistakenly called these casual companions "friends." But as I matured, I realized that being friendly is not the same as being a friend. We should be liberal with our kindnesses; however, genuine and deep friendship is costly. Therefore, I now choose my close friends wisely, because I realize that I do not have inexhaustible resources to sacrifice. I have only so much to give in support of another's endeavors. Furthermore, I cannot maintain the confidence of infinite friends. So, my list of genuine friends is manageably short, while I choose to enjoy camaraderie with many and offer kindness to all.

The Promise of Persecution
JOHN 15:18-16:4

NASB

18 "If the world hates you, ᵃyou know that it has hated Me before *it hated* you. 19 If you were of the world, the world would love its own; but because you are not of the world, but

NLT

18 "If the world hates you, remember that it hated me first. 19 The world would love you as one of its own if you belonged to it, but you are no longer part of the world. I chose you

NASB

I chose you out of the world, because of this the world hates you. [20] Remember the word that I said to you, 'A slave is not greater than his master.' If they persecuted Me, they will also persecute you; if they kept My word, they will keep yours also. [21] But all these things they will do to you for My name's sake, because they do not know the One who sent Me. [22] If I had not come and spoken to them, they would not have [a]sin, but now they have no excuse for their sin. [23] He who hates Me hates My Father also. [24] If I had not done among them the works which no one else did, they would not have [a]sin; but now they have both seen and hated Me and My Father as well. [25] But *they have done this* to fulfill the word that is written in their Law, 'THEY HATED ME WITHOUT A CAUSE.'

[26] "When the [a]Helper comes, whom I will send to you from the Father, *that is* the Spirit of truth who proceeds from the Father, He will testify about Me, [27] [a]and you *will* testify also, because you have been with Me from the beginning.

[16:1] "These things I have spoken to you so that you may be kept from stumbling. [2] [a]They will make you outcasts from the synagogue, but an hour is coming for everyone who kills you to think that he is offering service to God. [3] These things they will do because they have not known the Father or Me. [4] But these things I have spoken to you, so that when their hour comes, you [a]may remember that I told you of them. These things I did not say to you at the beginning, because I was with you.

15:18 [a]Or (imperative) *know that* 15:22 [a]I.e. guilt 15:24 [a]I.e. guilt 15:26 [a]Gr *Paracletos*, one called alongside to help; or *Comforter, Advocate, Intercessor* 15:27 [a]Or (imperative) *and bear witness* 16:2 [a]Or *They will have you excommunicated* 16:4 [a]Or *will remember them, that I told you*

NLT

to come out of the world, so it hates you. [20] Do you remember what I told you? 'A slave is not greater than the master.' Since they persecuted me, naturally they will persecute you. And if they had listened to me, they would listen to you. [21] They will do all this to you because of me, for they have rejected the one who sent me. [22] They would not be guilty if I had not come and spoken to them. But now they have no excuse for their sin. [23] Anyone who hates me also hates my Father. [24] If I hadn't done such miraculous signs among them that no one else could do, they would not be guilty. But as it is, they have seen everything I did, yet they still hate me and my Father. [25] This fulfills what is written in their Scriptures*: 'They hated me without cause.'

[26] "But I will send you the Advocate*—the Spirit of truth. He will come to you from the Father and will testify all about me. [27] And you must also testify about me because you have been with me from the beginning of my ministry.

[16:1] "I have told you these things so that you won't abandon your faith. [2] For you will be expelled from the synagogues, and the time is coming when those who kill you will think they are doing a holy service for God. [3] This is because they have never known the Father or me. [4] Yes, I'm telling you these things now, so that when they happen, you will remember my warning. I didn't tell you earlier because I was going to be with you for a while longer.

15:25 Greek *in their law.* Pss 35:19; 69:4.
15:26 Or *Comforter,* or *Encourager,* or *Counselor.* Greek reads *Paraclete.*

We in the United States of America no longer live in a Christian nation. I dare say we do not even live in a post-Christian nation. I am now convinced more than ever that we live in an anti-Christian nation. When did the tide shift? No one can say for certain, but when political correctness forbids humor at the expense of anyone except Christians and popular culture finds blasphemy entertaining, a flood of persecution will soon follow. History has taught us that much.

The words of Jesus should be particularly relevant for us. We, like the disciples, receive them during a time of relative peace and security. But our future is no less certain than theirs was on the eve of Jesus' arrest. As the Savior prepared the remaining eleven disciples for ministry after His physical departure from the world, He urged them to draw strength from God through obedience and to nurture one another in the same kind of love shared within the Trinity. But He also wanted to prepare them for reality. While victory is assured, the followers of Jesus are soldiers in a great conflict between two realms: the kingdom of God and the world system ruled by Satan—the forces of light and darkness (John 1:5; 3:19-21; 8:12; 12:36; 1 Jn. 1:5-7; 2:8-11; Rev. 21:23-24; 22:5). Furthermore, war brings hardship, suffering, gloom, and even death.

In this passage, we will discover answers to four questions concerning the nature of this conflict and our role as believers in the midst of it:

- Who will side with the world system against God's kingdom?
- What will the enemies of God's kingdom do?
- Why will this conflict take place?
- How shall we conduct ourselves during the conflict?

— 15:18-19 —

Jesus identified the enemy of God's kingdom as "the world." The construction of the Greek sentence and this particular use of the term translated "if" indicate that the condition is assumed to be true. This would be like a man saying, "If the sun comes up tomorrow, I'll be playing golf." In other words, the man is certain to be on the fairways the following day. Therefore, we can substitute the term "if" with "because."

"The world" does not mean the planet Earth, per se. The planet does not have a mind, so it cannot be evil. Nature has been twisted and corrupted by evil, but it is not evil in itself. In fact, Paul personified nature as an innocent bystander, suffering the ill effects of evil, groaning for redemption by its rightful Owner (see Rom. 8:20-22). Instead, "the world" represents the fallen world system, which operates according to Satan's values and is subject to the curse of sin (Gen. 3:14-19). "The world" also represents the portion of humanity that lives by this system's values and willingly serves its ends. Jesus originally came to redeem the world (John 3:17; 12:47), but He was rejected by the world (3:18; 12:48); therefore, He began to separate "His own" from the world (10:14, 26-27; 13:1; 15:19). His crucifixion would formally declare the dividing line between the kingdoms of God and Satan, and His resurrection would demand a choice from each individual.

The world either loves or hates; there is no neutral ground. The world loves or hates depending upon whether one is in agreement with it or not. The disposition of the world is completely conditional, which is one reason we know the conditional acceptance offered by legalistic religion is of the world, not Christ. The world system, of which religion is a part (16:2), clothes its hatred in sophistication, refinement, culture, and peace. But the world system is a boorish, slobbering, ignorant enemy of God and, therefore, despises any who dare side with Him.

If you are unsure of this, go to places of higher learning, or seek out captains of industry, or stand before political powers, and then present the gospel of Jesus Christ plainly. Watch as their "tolerance" fades. Observe as their cool, rational demeanor dissolves into petty disdain. I caution you to plan your escape route, for soon popular opinion will no longer give them reason to veil their hatred and they will give full vent to their anger. The chronicles of times past are proof that the cycle of history will come around again.

— 15:20-24 —

The fruit of hatred is persecution. Jesus promised His closest followers that persecution would be their reward in the world. The Greek term translated "persecute" means "to put to flight," "to pursue," or as A. T. Robertson defines it, "to chase like a wild beast."[11] In persecution, hatred becomes deliberate, not merely coincidental. The world will pursue Christians for the sake of venting its hatred.

Jesus stated that the world's hatred had always existed and was concentrated in the house of God under the guise of true devotion. Before He came to earth, the hatred of the world had little opportunity for expression. It had killed the Lord's prophets, polluted His words, ignored His warnings, and turned His house into a den of brigands, but a case could be made—however thin—for doubt or misunderstanding. But when God presented Himself in person, in the flesh of humanity and in fulfillment of every messianic expectation, He left all of humanity no excuse for rejecting Him. The flesh of God's Son became the occasion for "the world"—those who reject Christ—to expose their hatred for their Creator and, thus, consummate their sin.

— 15:25 —

Jesus explained the reason for the world's war on the kingdom of God: because believers are not of the world and the world hates what is not of it (15:19), and because the world does not acknowledge (or "know") God as its sovereign (15:21) and therefore rejects Christ as His emissary. Furthermore, the world persecutes believers in fulfillment of its destiny (15:25). The world is constitutionally predisposed to hate anything associated with God; therefore, it cannot behave any other way.

The earthly ministry of Jesus is one grand illustration of this truth, which John foreshadowed in the prologue of his narrative (1:5, 8-11).

THE *FILIOQUE* CONTROVERSY

JOHN 15:26-27

The clause "who proceeds from the Father" (John 15:26) has been at the center of a historic controversy between the Eastern and Western churches, primarily as it relates to the Nicene Creed. In affirming the Holy Spirit, the creed was amended in AD 381 to state, "[We believe] in the Holy Spirit, the Lord, the giver of life, who proceeds from the Father. With the Father and the Son he is worshiped and glorified . . ." And for more than two centuries all the churches were in agreement.

In the sixth century, the churches of Western Europe, which spoke Latin, amended the creed again to include the words, "and the Son" (called the *filioque*). Thus the creed stated, "[We believe] in the Holy Spirit, the Lord, the giver of life, who proceeds from the Father *and the Son*. With the Father and the Son he is worshiped and glorified . . ." The Western churches argued that the added phrase was necessary to preserve the equality of the Father and Son against heresy. However, the Eastern Church argued that the phrase was not included in John 15:26 and that Scripture should be definitive. Eventually, the Eastern and Western Churches split, in part because of this controversy.

In fact, Jesus did not utter this truth for the purpose of defining the nature of the Trinity, but to explain the role of the Holy Spirit in the lives of believers and in the plan of God to proclaim truth in the world. So, both sides of the debate have a strong point when trying to craft an official declaration of belief in the Trinity. Regardless, both the Western and Eastern Churches affirm the same truth: It is inappropriate to speak of the Father and Son as separate beings in relation to the Spirit. The Father, Son, and Spirit are three persons and one God.

— 15:26-27 —

The Lord's abrupt mentioning of the Holy Spirit was apparently purposeful. The Spirit's role in the life of the believer is to provide supernatural courage in the face of persecution. Suffering often brings doubt. The Holy Spirit will testify to the truth of Jesus Christ within believers, as well as through believers to their persecutors and others who witness their persecution.

— 16:1-3 —

When the human authors of Scripture prepared their manuscripts, they wrote in the style of the time, which did not include punctuation, breaks between words, or chapter/verse divisions. These were added by later editors and translators and are not considered inerrant like the original text. Ordinarily, the locations of chapter breaks make good, logical sense. However, the break between chapters 15 and 16 is unfortunate. John 16:1-4 belongs with chapter 15.

"These things" refers to everything Jesus had to say about the believer's relationship to the world, which is strained at best, hostile at other times, and can become deadly. Jesus revealed this to the disciples so they would not be startled and then stumble in their spiritual walk. However, as with many of Jesus' lessons, they did not take heed and all of them stumbled and fell. Upon His arrest, they fled. During His crucifixion, most hid. Before His resurrection, all despaired. After His resurrection, they doubted. And before the coming of the Holy Spirit, they faltered. Only after receiving the Holy Spirit did they act decisively and speak boldly.

Jesus predicted the scourge of religion upon the backs of genuine believers. Indeed, religious people would kill believers thinking they were pleasing the Lord. An example is Paul, who later became an apostle: He was among the crowd of religious authorities who murdered the first Christian martyr, Stephen (Acts 7:54–8:1).

— 16:4 —

This verse concludes the Lord's statement in 16:1 after the parenthetical aside in 16:2-3. It also transitions the conversation away from the inevitable persecution after Jesus' departure, toward the blessing of the Holy Spirit.

The Lord recognized that His words would have little meaning at the time; the disciples still did not understand what was about to happen or why. But at the appropriate time, His words would come to mind and help them make sense of the tribulation they faced. They wouldn't have to wonder, *Are we struggling through persecution because of some failure on our part?* No, persecution was expected, a normal consequence of living in hostile territory during the great conflict between good and evil, between the Lord and the ruler of this world, Satan.

• • •

I remember a time when I read the book of Revelation with secret skepticism. It seemed inconceivable to me that anyone would openly oppose the living God. That's because I was reared in an era when Hollywood filmmakers—few of whom professed belief in Jesus as the Messiah—avoided showing the face of an actor portraying Christ because it was considered irreverent. Such was the respect that nonbelievers had for Christianity. So, I reasoned that the blasphemy predicted through John's visions must be caused by ignorance. Who would oppose the Creator to His face? Who would be so foolish as to mock the One who holds the power of life and death over all of humanity?

Many decades later, any doubt I may have had in John's vision is gone. I have since traveled beyond the bubble of Christian culture around prewar Houston, Texas. I have seen the darkness of idolatry in non-Christian nations. I have felt the hatred born in the hearts of those who spread their religion through violence and terrorism. I have seen my own nation grow tolerant of every conceivable philosophy and religion *except* Christianity. And now, I need only turn on my television to hear crowds laugh uproariously as a comedian taunts the power of the Almighty, or to see late-night animated cartoons depicting Jesus and Satan as the main characters of a situation comedy.

Brace yourselves, Christians. The line between satire and spite is surprisingly thin. Humor at the expense of any particular group invites hatred, and hatred blazes a trail for persecution. If we are headed for such a time again, we should not be surprised. Jesus warned us.

APPLICATION: JOHN 15:18–16:4

Preparation for Persecution

Christians in the Western world have enjoyed a long period of relative peace and remarkable authority, particularly in the United States, which was founded upon Christian principles. But we must accept that this has been an anomaly in the greater scheme of world history. Our summer in the sun will soon give way to the dark of winter. In fact, autumn breezes have been unmistakably chilly of late.

This should not come as a surprise. John warned us in Revelation that evil will eventually become unimaginably powerful over the world and unspeakably cruel to genuine believers in Jesus Christ. There are many antichrists who will someday bow before the Antichrist. Many persecutions will ultimately give way to the Great Tribulation of the end times. This is prophecy, and it will come to pass. Therefore, we must prepare ourselves. Jesus explained how as He prepared His disciples for the difficult hours before them.

First, *rely upon the Holy Spirit to supply wisdom, abilities, and courage (15:26)*. "When the Helper comes, whom I will send to you from the Father, that is the Spirit of truth who proceeds from the Father, He will testify about Me, and you will testify also, because you have been with Me from the beginning" (15:26-27). He promised the Spirit would provide all that believers need to faithfully bear witness of Jesus Christ.

Second, *faithfully proclaim divine truth and stand firm (15:27)*. Note that while battling immorality and pursuing social justice is commendable, our primary mission is to "testify." The only effective weapon against evil is truth. The Holy Spirit will bring knowledge of Jesus Christ to mind and enable us to communicate His truth. And, because truth-tellers have been guaranteed persecution, He will supply supernatural courage to endure evil with dignity.

One New Testament scholar writes, "It is here that Christians fail most."[12] When we are persecuted, we back off. We run away. We change our stand. Don't change your stand. Stand firm. *Foxe's Book of Martyrs* is a weighty book, filled with the prayers of dying saints. Time and again the Holy Spirit was called upon for strength as flames consumed the bodies of faithful believers.

Third, *keep from being ensnared by evil (16:1)*. The Greek verb translated "stumble" is *skandalizō* [4624]. The main idea carried by the term is "closing on something,"[13] like a spring-loaded rabbit trap. It later became the word of choice for deliberately placing a trip hazard in the path of another to cause a fall. Jesus urged His disciples to abide—that is, obey His command to love one another—in order to avoid falling into the snare of the world. When we fail to love one another, we behave like the world, which serves self at the expense of others.

Fourth, *never forget that persecution and the rise of evil are inevitable (16:4)*. When evil triumphs over truth, we quickly begin to wonder if we have done something wrong, or if we neglected to do something we should have. Jesus warned His disciples that evil would appear to enjoy victory upon His death and burial, but that His suffering was part of the divine plan to redeem humanity from the beginning. He suffered and died to atone for the sin of humanity, not because of any specific failure on the part of the remaining eleven disciples.

We must never forget that evil will enjoy short-term victories, but that Christ has already conquered evil, sin, disease, suffering, death, and decay. Persecution is inevitable and, in many cases, fatal; however, death is not the end of life. The resurrection awaits, in which we will exist beyond the reach of the world and its affliction. We must never forget that, one day soon, Christ will return to silence the enemies of God through a crushing defeat. He was vindicated through His resurrection; we will be vindicated through ours.

Christians are notorious for remembering what we ought to forget and forgetting what we ought to remember! Forget your sin; Christ has conquered it. Remember that persecution is inevitable; anticipate His triumph.

As we prepare ourselves to endure persecution for proclaiming Christ, let me draw three helpful distinctions.

First, *there's a great difference between picking a fight and enduring persecution.* Jesus neither sought trouble nor invited persecution. He faithfully proclaimed divine truth and evil found Him—because evil always seeks to destroy truth.

Second, *there's a great difference between loving the world and becoming a part of it.* Jesus left us in the world in order to share His love with the lost; however, He cautioned us to avoid thinking and behaving like the world. The world has declared itself the enemy of all who believe, so it makes no sense to do as the world does.

Third, *there's a great difference between living in fear and exercising caution.* Jesus knew his destiny. He knew He would suffer the anguish of the cross to bear the penalty of all sin. Nevertheless, He took reasonable steps to avoid capture in public and He kept His location private at other times. No one needs to volunteer for persecution or martyrdom. If that is our destiny, persecutors will find us. Then we must face it with courage.

In his book *God Tells the Man Who Cares*, A. W. Tozer observes a dangerous perspective among Christians. "Men think of the world, not as a battleground but as a playground. We are not here to fight, we are here to frolic. We are not in a foreign land, we are at home. We are not getting ready to live, we are already living."[14] We cannot afford to think this way. The longer we live here, the more homesick we should become. Let our prayer be the amen to John's: "Come, Lord Jesus" (Rev. 22:20).

Functions of the Holy Spirit
JOHN 16:5-15

NASB

5 "But now I am going to Him who sent Me; and none of you asks Me, 'Where are You going?' 6 But because I have said these things to you, sorrow has filled your heart. 7 But I tell you the truth, it is to your advantage that I go away; for if I do not go away, the [a]Helper will not come to you; but if I go, I will send Him to you. 8 And He, when He comes, will convict the world concerning sin and righteousness and judgment; 9 concerning sin, because they do not believe in Me; 10 and concerning righteousness, because I go to the Father and you no longer see Me; 11 and concerning judgment, because the ruler of this world has been judged.

12 "I have many more things to say to you, but you cannot bear *them* now. 13 But when He, the Spirit of truth, comes, He will guide you into all the truth; for He will not speak on His own initiative, but whatever He hears, He will speak; and He will disclose to you what is to come. 14 He will glorify Me, for He will take of Mine and will disclose *it* to you. 15 All things that the Father has are Mine; therefore I said that He takes of Mine and will disclose *it* to you.

16:7 [a]Gr *Paracletos*, one called alongside to help; or *Comforter, Advocate, Intercessor*

NLT

5 "But now I am going away to the one who sent me, and not one of you is asking where I am going. 6 Instead, you grieve because of what I've told you. 7 But in fact, it is best for you that I go away, because if I don't, the Advocate* won't come. If I do go away, then I will send him to you. 8 And when he comes, he will convict the world of its sin, and of God's righteousness, and of the coming judgment. 9 The world's sin is that it refuses to believe in me. 10 Righteousness is available because I go to the Father, and you will see me no more. 11 Judgment will come because the ruler of this world has already been judged.

12 "There is so much more I want to tell you, but you can't bear it now. 13 When the Spirit of truth comes, he will guide you into all truth. He will not speak on his own but will tell you what he has heard. He will tell you about the future. 14 He will bring me glory by telling you whatever he receives from me. 15 All that belongs to the Father is mine; this is why I said, 'The Spirit will tell you whatever he receives from me.'

16:7 Or *Comforter*, or *Encourager*, or *Counselor*. Greek reads *Paraclete*.

Jesus' words must have sounded like a jumble of puzzle pieces to the bewildered disciples. After announcing His imminent departure from the earth (John 13:33; 14:1-6), He urged His followers to obey His commandments (14:12-15; 15:1-11), to love one another (15:12-17), and to beware the hostility of the world (15:18-27). While offering these pre-dictions, promises, and commands, Jesus alluded to the coming of the Holy Spirit to teach believers all they would need to know (14:16-17, 26; 15:26). But these passing references could only have been mystify-ing. In the Old Testament, the Holy Spirit was reserved for kings and prophets, and occasionally for regular folk when the Lord wanted to accomplish something extraordinary. The idea that the Spirit of God would indwell each believer was unthinkable—an unbelievable ex-travagance of which no one was worthy. The disciples' heads must have been spinning.

Although the disciples didn't ask about the Holy Spirit—they were too preoccupied with the thought of Jesus going away—the Lord re-turned to this particular promise in order to clarify His role in the lives of the disciples . . . and the lives of believers throughout all time.

— 16:5-7 —

Jesus lamented that the disciples were so preoccupied with their own security they were not the least bit curious about Jesus' immediate future. The next few days would see the most momentous events in human history, which would inaugurate the age of grace, the begin-ning of the universal church on earth, and the worldwide spread of the gospel. After His unspeakable suffering, Jesus would receive inexpress-ible glory. He wanted to share all of this with His companions, but more than that, He wanted them to be interested.

Nevertheless, Jesus attended their sorrow-filled hearts. The Greek term translated "sorrow" means "pain," which can be either physical or emotional. Pain filled the hearts of the disciples, who felt like spiri-tual orphans. All they could think of was losing Him.

Jesus soothed their pain with a wonderful truth. The Lord's physical presence would be replaced by something far superior. Whereas Jesus in the flesh could be in only one place at a time, the Holy Spirit can be everywhere at once. Limited access to the presence of God would give way to continual communion with Him. Teaching through physi-cal means would take place directly within the heart. Far from being abandoned, the disciples would experience the presence of God like never before.

The ministry of the Holy Spirit, the Master explained, would be two-fold: His ministry to the world (16:8-11) and His ministry to believers (16:13-15).

— 16:8-11 —

The Holy Spirit's Ministry to the World

The Greek verb translated "convict" has a wide range of meaning outside the New Testament, including "to scorn," "to bring into contempt," and "to rebuke." However, New Testament writers restricted the definition to one: "to show people their sins and summon them to repentance."[15] The Holy Spirit confronts the world concerning three primary topics: "sin" (people's guilt), "righteousness" (people's helplessness), and "judgment" (people's destiny). Of sin we are all guilty. As to righteousness, we are powerless to help ourselves. Consequently, our eternal destiny is dreadful without divine help.

"Sin" (*hamartia* [266]) refers to one's inability or unwillingness to do as God commands, resulting in guilt before Him. Jesus died to pay the penalty of sin for the whole world, but only those who believe in Him have appropriated His sacrifice and, therefore, stand guiltless before the Father. Those who do not believe in Christ remain in their sin and must answer for their choices (16:9).

"Righteousness" (*dikaiosunē* [1343]) refers to one's legal standing before God as "not guilty." In this context, Jesus relates the issue of righteousness to His "going to the Father." Throughout His ministry, Jesus claimed oneness with the Father, for which the world (the religious leaders) accused Him of sin, deceit, and blasphemy (5:18; 7:12; 9:16, 24; 10:33). His going to the Father is the ultimate vindication of Christ's righteousness over that of the world. The Holy Spirit will confront humanity with the righteousness of the Son (16:10).

"Judgment" (*krisis* [2920]) refers to one's life and character being sifted in order to determine one's moral worth. Jesus stated repeatedly that He did not come for the purpose of judging, but that individuals would reveal themselves by their response to truth incarnate (3:17-18; 5:22-23; 12:48). By virtue of Christ's vindication, Satan has been sifted and found wanting. The Holy Spirit will confront humanity concerning its choice for Satan instead of the Son (16:11).

Interestingly, the confrontation of the Holy Spirit does not appear to be directly within the hearts of nonbelievers. He may, in fact, do this; however, that is not what Jesus was teaching here. In 16:7-8, Jesus said, "I will send Him to you. And He, when He comes, will convict the world . . ." The context of 16:8-11 is the coming of the Holy Spirit "to you." In other words, the Holy Spirit will confront the world from within believers, through believers. Those who are of the world do not have the Holy Spirit active within them in this way.

The child of God living on this earth, empowered by the Spirit of God, is a living letter observed by the world. As the world witnesses the child of God being controlled by the Spirit, the world observes a life undergoing transformation. The world is confronted by the Holy Spirit via His activity in believers.

— 16:12 —

Jesus acknowledged the limitations of both time and ability for the disciples to receive more truth. Their concern for self prevented their absorbing more information concerning their mission after Jesus' departure. Furthermore, without the Holy Spirit, their minds could not comprehend the spiritual truths He wanted to impart. He promised further revelation of truth through the Holy Spirit.

— 16:13-15 —

The Holy Spirit's Ministry to Believers

One of many distinctions between "the world" and "His own" is the manner in which the Holy Spirit ministers. His ministry to the world convicts in order to bring about repentance. His ministry to believers, on the other hand, is to bring about obedience through transformation.

The Spirit accomplishes His mission of believer transformation by bringing divine truth to the minds of His own. Before Scripture had been written, He revealed truth directly to certain people: prophets in the Old Testament, prophets and apostles in the New Testament. Once John, the last living apostle, completed the final written communication from God, the book of Revelation, humanity had received all the divine truth needed to live obediently. Now the Spirit's ministry is to call Scripture to mind, illumine its meaning, couple it with experience, and apply it. We participate in the Holy Spirit's transformation process through the exercise of spiritual disciplines (such as prayer, worship, service, evangelism, etc.).

How were the disciples to know when the Spirit of God was bringing them new revelation? How were they to distinguish the thoughts of God from their own imaginations? According to Jesus, revelation from the Holy Spirit would always "glorify" the Son. As we discovered in our study of 13:31-38, the Greek word for "glory" is *doxa* [1391], which derives from the verb meaning "to believe, to think." To be glorified is to be revealed in such a way as to be considered good. To be glorified is to be vindicated in the eyes of all witnesses. Therefore, the concept of glory in Jesus' vocabulary means that the truth He had been teaching and the truth of His identity would be vindicated in the eyes of all humanity. He promised that the Holy Spirit would only bring new revelation consistent with what Jesus Himself had already taught, and that the Spirit's ministry would always serve to prove the Son genuine.

• • •

Jesus' promise of the Holy Spirit probably didn't do much to calm the troubled minds of the eleven disciples. The gift of the Holy Spirit would have been beyond their comprehension, not unlike it is for us—only in reverse. We cannot fathom life without Him, and therefore it is easy for us to take His indwelling wisdom for granted. If we want to know what life would be like as believers left on our own, all we need to do is observe the disciples after Jesus' resurrection and before Pentecost. They were dull of mind and weak of spirit; fearful, confused, doubting, despondent, aimless, and lethargic. Consequently, Jesus instructed them to wait upon the arrival of the Holy Spirit before attempting ministry (Acts 1:4). When the Spirit of God filled the believers, everything changed. The book of Acts describes the rise of the church as believers, filled with the Holy Spirit, began to change the world.

Thank God, He has not left us alone!

APPLICATION: JOHN 16:5-15

Changing the Channels

Jesus gave us the task of proclaiming the good news to a hostile world and sharing His love for the lost—an impossible mission without divine help! Fortunately, He did not leave us alone. He sent the Holy Spirit to convict the world of sin. I find in this section of Scripture two practical principles that help clarify our calling so we might more faithfully obey.

First, *in convicting the world, the Spirit desires to use a channel.* The Spirit of God doesn't use buildings, pulpits, or symbols to convict the world. He doesn't use nature, science, philosophy, or even theology to convict the world. In fact, Scripture indicates that He does not convict sinners directly. According to Jesus, *believers* convict the world! The Holy Spirit uses transformed Christians as the means of confronting the world.

This is not to say He has appointed us to be the world's conscience.

He has not called us to point out sins and take down names. Yes, there are times when we must stand against wrongdoing or declare that a certain activity is sin. However, He has not deputized us as His holy police force. Instead, He convicts the world of sin by sanctifying "His own." When people sin in groups, they cannot stand it when one of their number starts to do what is right. They try to pull the individual back into line and, when that fails, grow hostile toward him or her.

Second, *in communicating the Word, the Spirit desires to see changes.* When He teaches, He desires to see the lives of people transformed. In fact, He will often use unpleasant circumstances as the means of transforming believers, which often causes tension. Whereas we pray for God to change circumstances, He prefers to change *us!*

"Lament psalms" typically begin with the psalmist on his face, begging for change. Everything has broken loose, his life has fallen apart, he's surrounded and afflicted, and he has run out of options. Amazingly, by the end, he's praising God for His goodness. Nothing about the man's circumstances had changed from the time he began writing until he completed the composition. Instead, worshiping God changed the psalmist. *He* was changed deep within.

Many years ago, I received a letter from a church member who had endured the worst year imaginable. His wife left him and took their children with her. Challenges in his business brought pressures he had never known before. He was quickly running out of options. In his letter, he admitted, "With enemies all around, I suddenly discovered through the information I got from God's Word that I could love those who hate me and I didn't have to live with the acid of resentment eating away in me. I learned that I could, in fact, pray for my wife and love her just as I loved the little ones she has taken from me." He concluded by saying, "These have been the hardest circumstances I've ever known, but I am transformed. Praise God."

This man became an agent of divine change in his own sector of the world by allowing the Word and the Spirit to change him from within. When we are transformed, we become channels of God's transformation of the world. As we are changed, we become divine agents of change in the world.

Three Words That Keep Us Going
JOHN 16:16-33

16 "A little while, and you will no longer see Me; and again a little while, and you will see Me." 17 *Some* of His disciples then said to one another, "What is this thing He is telling us, 'A little while, and you will not see Me; and again a little while, and you will see Me'; and, 'because I go to the Father'?" 18 So they were saying, "What is this that He says, 'A little while'? We do not know what He is talking about." 19 Jesus knew that they wished to question Him, and He said to them, "Are you deliberating together about this, that I said, 'A little while, and you will not see Me, and again a little while, and you will see Me'? 20 Truly, truly, I say to you, that you will weep and lament, but the world will rejoice; you will grieve, but your grief will be turned into joy. 21 Whenever a woman is in labor she has ªpain, because her hour has come; but when she gives birth to the child, she no longer remembers the anguish because of the joy that a ᵇchild has been born into the world. 22 Therefore you too have grief now; but I will see you again, and your heart will rejoice, and no one *will* take your joy away from you. 23 In that day you will not question Me about anything. Truly, truly, I say to you, if you ask the Father for anything in My name, He will give it to you. 24 Until now you have asked for nothing in My name; ask and you will receive, so that your joy may be made full. 25 "These things I have spoken to you in ªfigurative language; an hour is coming when I will no longer speak to you in ªfigurative language, but will tell you plainly of the Father. 26 In that day you will ask in My name, and I do not say to you that

16 "In a little while you won't see me anymore. But a little while after that, you will see me again."

17 Some of the disciples asked each other, "What does he mean when he says, 'In a little while you won't see me, but then you will see me,' and 'I am going to the Father'? 18 And what does he mean by 'a little while'? We don't understand."

19 Jesus realized they wanted to ask him about it, so he said, "Are you asking yourselves what I meant? I said in a little while you won't see me, but a little while after that you will see me again. 20 I tell you the truth, you will weep and mourn over what is going to happen to me, but the world will rejoice. You will grieve, but your grief will suddenly turn to wonderful joy. 21 It will be like a woman suffering the pains of labor. When her child is born, her anguish gives way to joy because she has brought a new baby into the world. 22 So you have sorrow now, but I will see you again; then you will rejoice, and no one can rob you of that joy. 23 At that time you won't need to ask me for anything. I tell you the truth, you will ask the Father directly, and he will grant your request because you use my name. 24 You haven't done this before. Ask, using my name, and you will receive, and you will have abundant joy.

25 "I have spoken of these matters in figures of speech, but soon I will stop speaking figuratively and will tell you plainly all about the Father. 26 Then you will ask in my name. I'm

I will request of the Father on your behalf; 27for the Father Himself loves you, because you have loved Me and have believed that I came forth from the Father. 28I came forth from the Father and have come into the world; I am leaving the world again and going to the Father."

29His disciples said, "Lo, now You are speaking plainly and are not ausing a figure of speech. 30Now we know that You know all things, and have no need for anyone to question You; by this we believe that You came from God." 31Jesus answered them, "Do you now believe? 32Behold, an hour is coming, and has *already* come, for you to be scattered, each to his own *home,* and to leave Me alone; and *yet* I am not alone, because the Father is with Me. 33These things I have spoken to you, so that in Me you may have peace. In the world you have tribulation, but take courage; I have overcome the world."

16:21 aLit *grief* bLit *human being* **16:25** aLit *proverbs;* or *figures of speech* **16:29** aLit *saying a proverb*

not saying I will ask the Father on your behalf, 27for the Father himself loves you dearly because you love me and believe that I came from God.* 28Yes, I came from the Father into the world, and now I will leave the world and return to the Father."

29Then his disciples said, "At last you are speaking plainly and not figuratively. 30Now we understand that you know everything, and there's no need to question you. From this we believe that you came from God."

31Jesus asked, "Do you finally believe? 32But the time is coming—indeed it's here now—when you will be scattered, each one going his own way, leaving me alone. Yet I am not alone because the Father is with me. 33I have told you all this so that you may have peace in me. Here on earth you will have many trials and sorrows. But take heart, because I have overcome the world."

16:27 Some manuscripts read *from the Father.*

Jesus' last occasion for teaching the disciples was drawing to a close. These final moments of tranquility among friends would soon give way to anguish in Gethsemane, injustice during prosecution, cruel ridicule, and brutal scourging, followed by suffering and death through crucifixion. Yet, despite His own desire for comfort and encouragement, Jesus comforted and encouraged His followers. Selfless to the end, Jesus offered three promises to keep His disciples going as the looming shadow of the cross darkened their days. These promises can be reduced to three words that are no less helpful for us today:

- *Joy* (16:19-24)
- *Love* (16:25-28)
- *Peace* (16:31-33)

As we examine the promises of Jesus—joy, love, and peace—take note of the central place given to prayer in our claiming them.

— 16:16 —

In 16:16, Jesus offered His disciples a negative prediction followed by a positive promise. "You will no longer see me" predicts His imminent death on the cross, while "you will see me" promises His appearance through resurrection. The phrase "a little while" precludes the possibility of His talking about His Second Advent at the end of days.

This prediction-promise formula establishes a definable pattern for the balance of His discussion with the remaining eleven disciples. Their dialogue follows this pattern of discussion:

- A prediction and a promise—Resurrection! (16:16)
- The disciples react (16:17-18)
- A prediction and a promise—"Joy" (16:19-24)
- A prediction and a promise—"Love" (16:25-28)
- The disciples react (16:29-30)
- A prediction and a promise—"Peace" (16:31-33)

— 16:17-18 —

The disciples were not unlike a six-year-old child asking questions at a funeral; they could only handle so much detail. Therefore, Jesus prepared them for the difficult hours ahead as best He could without revealing too much specific information. Unfortunately, the disciples had become so agitated by the prospect of His going away that nothing would console them, not even the promise of the indwelling presence of God!

Jesus tried to keep the matter as bottom-line simple as possible: "In a little while, I am going away, and after a little while, you will see Me again" (my paraphrase). Yet even this stirred the disciples' anxiety.

— 16:19-24 —

Joy

Jesus predicted that the disciples would experience intense sorrow while the world would celebrate a perceived victory. Clearly, this is in reference to His imminent suffering, death, and burial; however, His ordeal illustrates a great principle for all those living between the time of the Lord's ascension and His return at the end of days. During this interval, during this great in-between time we call the "church age," or the "age of grace," Christians experience sorrow. Loved ones die. Bodies contract diseases. Innocent people suffer persecution. Meanwhile, malicious people prosper and evil appears to enjoy the spoils of victory.

Jesus followed His prediction with a promise: The world's victory celebration will come to an abrupt end. When the Son of God is vindicated through His resurrection, "His own" will be vindicated with Him. The sorrow of believers will be turned to joy (16:20, 22, 24).

The Lord illustrated His promise with the poignant image of a woman suffering the intense pain of childbirth—not coincidentally one of the curses of the Fall (Gen. 3:16). As the pain grows, the transition from sorrow to joy nears. Then, in an instant, the greatest of human suffering becomes the occasion of our greatest joy. The affliction of the curse yields new life.

"In that day" (John 16:23) refers to the era after His resurrection, the time in which the disciples could rejoice. While the reason for joy cannot be taken away, Jesus implied a condition. The means of experiencing this joy is prayer. Once the atoning sacrifice has been made, the barrier between humanity and God is removed. Believers are granted access to the Father because of the Son. Anything we ask that is in agreement with the will of God ("in My name") will be granted. The result of this intimacy of prayer is joy—joy to the fullest measure.

— 16:25-28 —

Love

Jesus then predicted that the need for His teaching them through "figurative language" would disappear. The Greek term John used to describe Jesus' obscure manner of speech literally means "byword." A byword, in this sense, is any term that has a complex technical meaning. For instance, I might say to someone, "The annuity of your lifestyle is about to mature." A financial planner, who is very familiar with the concept of an annuity, will instantly understand the metaphor and the point I would be making—that the results of the person's choices were about to come to fruition.

Jesus evidently regretted His having to be circumspect with the disciples, but it was for their good. His purpose for using technical terms—much like that of prophecy in general—was to give them hope for the coming tribulation and to equip them for obedience. The meaning of His words would become clear as events unfolded; the terms and their full meanings would spring to mind at crucial moments and the disciples would then know how to respond well.

"In that day" (16:26) refers to the same era as 16:23. Under the old covenant, people approached God through the priesthood, divinely appointed officials in the temple who mediated the relationship between a worshiper and God. During Jesus' ministry, He became the physical means of human-divine relations. People approached Jesus for miracles, for divine teaching, for revelation from God, and for forgiveness of sin. Jesus promised that, after His resurrection, He would be the permanent bridge between humanity and God. Through Him, "in His name," believers would be able to approach the Father directly.

He characterized this unrestricted access to the Father and His welcoming response as "love." Through prayer, believers enjoy a love relationship with the Father that is no longer hindered by unpunished sin. And the means of this free exchange of love is, again, prayer.

— 16:29-30 —

I find the response of the disciples charming, as I am sure the Lord did. Note their use of "now" in response to the Lord's "in that day." They gained but a small glimpse of the future and thought they understood Him fully. Their statements about the deity of Jesus and His exclusive claim to divine truth were absolutely spot on . . . if only they had understood them completely! Later, when the Holy Spirit filled them, the disciples would fully appreciate the mystery and wonder of God's incarnation. They were like toddlers at a performance of Handel's *Messiah*. They heard the sounds and saw the sights, but the breadth and depth of meaning would come only with maturity.

— 16:31-33 —

Peace

Jesus welcomed the disciples' breakthrough. Their dialogue had been a long series of fear-reassurance cycles. However, as the disciples stepped decisively away from their fear, Jesus checked their runaway excitement. They did not know nearly as much as they had assumed. He responded with another prediction and promise.

Jesus predicted the disciples would abandon Him, undoubtedly thinking of this as the fulfillment of Zechariah 13:7 (cf. Matt. 26:31; Mark 14:27). He said the "hour" was coming and indeed "has already come." At that moment, the mob gathered by Judas had already begun to light their torches. Soon, they would surround Gethsemane.

He followed this gloomy prediction with a promise. While all of humanity would soon abandon Jesus, including His beloved disciples, the Father would remain faithful. While Jesus did later cry out from the cross, "My God, My God, why have You forsaken Me?" (Matt. 27:46), this was not to implicate the Father for abandoning Him. Jesus uttered this to call everyone's attention to David's prophetic Psalm 22. While the emotional anguish of the cross was accurately reflected in the Lord's lament, He, like

David, knew the Father had not, in fact, forsaken Him (see Ps. 22:24). The Father and the Son are one; nothing can possibly divide the triune God.

Jesus further promised that "in Him" we may have peace. This peace is not only peace with God (Rom. 5:1), but the subjective kind as well. Despite the chaos of living in a hostile world, we may experience tranquility. However, this too is conditional. Like joy, peace is available, but we must choose it. We choose peace when we choose to believe that Christ has "overcome" the world.

You may recall John's statement in the prologue: "The Light shines in the darkness, and the darkness did not comprehend it" (John 1:5). The Greek term for "comprehend" is deliberately ambiguous and can also mean "overpower" (see note on 1:4-8). In this context, however, John chose the unambiguous verb *nikaō* [3528], "to conquer." As if to summarize Jesus' entire ministry on earth, John opened his narrative with, "The Light shines in the darkness, and the darkness did not comprehend [or overpower] it" (1:5), and he concluded the Lord's teaching ministry with, "I have overcome the world."

• • •

Jesus challenged His disciples—and us by extension—to "take courage." The Greek term means "to dare," "to be bold," "to be of good courage," "to be cheerful or confident."[16] The definition includes two other nuanced meanings. First, "to trust in," "rely on," and, second, "to be bold against someone or something," "to go out bravely to."[17] The entire range of meanings is appropriate to the Lord's exhortation. His victory over the world—sin, evil, Satan, death, the twisted manner by which the world operates—gives us reason to throw ourselves headlong into the conflict. We have nothing to fear. For even if we die, we live.

Joy, love, and peace are ours, if only we will believe in Him.

Do you?

APPLICATION: JOHN 16:16-33

Three Words to Keep Us Going

If I could somehow put myself inside the skin of those disciples and relive what it must have been like to get up from the table and have the Lord lead in prayer as He did in John 17, and then walk down those steps and find my way to Gethsemane, I believe two thoughts would have settled over me. First, *His life may not have been long, but His death is not a mistake.* Second, *my life may not be easy, but I can go on.*

By the end of His discourse, Jesus had said, in effect, "I promise you, life in this world is going to be difficult, but I've overcome the world. Nevertheless, you can be more than conquerors because of My power." He showed them how to persevere with joy, triumph in love, and live in peace.

Do you have a joy that cannot be taken away? Do you have confidence in God's love? Are you confident in the truth that He is *for* you? Can you rest confidently in His wisdom and say to Him, "Lord, You know everything, so I'm not questioning You any longer"? When life comes crashing down, the qualities of joy, love, and peace are God's gift to keep us going. But like a full bank account, they do us no good if we fail to draw upon them. The gifts of joy, love, and peace require faith. Failing to trust in the promise of God leads to lack of joy, failing love, and unsteady peace.

Lack of Joy

We lack joy when evil gains the upper hand and we worry it will become permanent. But what if we knew for certain each trial would become the means of receiving a great blessing? Suppose you lived in a world in which each lost job led to a better, higher-paying job; each illness led to increased health and a longer life; each financial setback eventually resulted in a higher salary. How would you regard each affliction? With dread or anticipation? With gloom or joy? How would your belief affect your ability to persevere?

While the world I just imagined does not exist—the Lord has not promised to make us healthy and wealthy in this life—God has promised that He has overcome evil and we will receive far greater blessing than we can imagine in the life to come. Affliction here on earth will eventually give way to eternal life. In the meantime, the blessing we gain from affliction is healing for our souls, increased spiritual health.

When we trust that we will ultimately prevail over suffering, we persevere with joy. The difference is faith.

Failing Love

The kind of love Jesus taught is selfless. We cannot obey His command to love one another if we are primarily concerned with our own needs and wants.

When the Sadducees sought to trap Jesus with a silly question concerning marriage in heaven, He stunned them with His answer. Marriage will be obsolete "in the resurrection" (Matt. 22:29-40; Mark 12:24-31). In heaven, intimate, selfless, caring love will be shared among *all* who live there. Here on earth, however, we struggle to maintain that kind of love relationship with just one person! How many marriages are strained by individuals manipulating one another to get their needs met? They resort to manipulation, control, sulking, yelling, blame, and any other imaginable means because they don't trust their own mate to care for them.

Let's face it; we don't love others because we don't trust them to return our love. We live under the false notion that if we don't take care of ourselves, no one will . . . not even God. Consequently, the majority of our energies go to taking care of ourselves rather than trusting the Lord as we give priority to the needs of others.

It all comes back to faith. When we fail to trust the Lord to care for us, we fail to obey His most basic command: "love one another" (John 15:17).

Unsteady Peace

Jesus contrasted His peace with the world's tribulation (16:33). To have Christ's peace is to have the ultimate fulfillment of Hebrew *shalom*—life and fulfillment in abundance. This peace with Christ will certainly result in estrangement and, therefore, persecution from the world; nevertheless, tribulation will ultimately give way to overwhelming blessing.

While we have this peace as a byproduct of God's grace, our ability to experience inner peace depends entirely upon our trust in His sovereign care and steadfast goodness. He has promised tribulation; however, He also promised that the victories of the world are short-lived. He has overcome the world; therefore, we may peacefully endure short-term suffering with the certain expectation of His ultimate triumph.

Divine Intercession
JOHN 17:1-19

NASB

¹Jesus spoke these things; and lifting up His eyes to heaven, He said, "Father, the hour has come; glorify Your Son, that the Son may glorify You, ²even as You gave Him authority over all flesh, that to ªall whom You have

NLT

¹After saying all these things, Jesus looked up to heaven and said, "Father, the hour has come. Glorify your Son so he can give glory back to you. ²For you have given him authority over everyone. He gives eternal life

given Him, He may give eternal life. ³This is eternal life, that they may know You, the only true God, and Jesus Christ whom You have sent. ⁴I glorified You on the earth, ᵃhaving accomplished the work which You have given Me to do. ⁵Now, Father, glorify Me together with Yourself, with the glory which I had with You before the world was.

⁶"I have manifested Your name to the men whom You gave Me out of the world; they were Yours and You gave them to Me, and they have kept Your word. ⁷Now they have come to know that everything You have given Me is from You; ⁸for the words which You gave Me I have given to them; and they received *them* and truly understood that I came forth from You, and they believed that You sent Me. ⁹I ask on their behalf; I do not ask on behalf of the world, but of those whom You have given Me; for they are Yours; ¹⁰and all things that are Mine are Yours, and Yours are Mine; and I have been glorified in them. ¹¹I am no longer in the world; and *yet* they themselves are in the world, and I come to You. Holy Father, keep them in Your name, *the name* which You have given Me, that they may be one even as We *are*. ¹²While I was with them, I was keeping them in Your name which You have given Me; and I guarded them and not one of them perished but the ᵃson of perdition, so that the Scripture would be fulfilled.

¹³But now I come to You; and these things I speak in the world so that they may have My joy made full in themselves. ¹⁴I have given them Your word; and the world has hated them, because they are not of the world, even as I am not of the world. ¹⁵I do not ask You to take them out of the world, but to keep them ᵃfrom ᵇthe evil *one*. ¹⁶They are not of the world, even as I am not of the world. ¹⁷Sanctify them in the truth; Your

to each one you have given him. ³And this is the way to have eternal life—to know you, the only true God, and Jesus Christ, the one you sent to earth. ⁴I brought glory to you here on earth by completing the work you gave me to do. ⁵Now, Father, bring me into the glory we shared before the world began.

⁶"I have revealed you* to the ones you gave me from this world. They were always yours. You gave them to me, and they have kept your word. ⁷Now they know that everything I have is a gift from you, ⁸for I have passed on to them the message you gave me. They accepted it and know that I came from you, and they believe you sent me.

⁹"My prayer is not for the world, but for those you have given me, because they belong to you. ¹⁰All who are mine belong to you, and you have given them to me, so they bring me glory. ¹¹Now I am departing from the world; they are staying in this world, but I am coming to you. Holy Father, you have given me your name;* now protect them by the power of your name so that they will be united just as we are. ¹²During my time here, I protected them by the power of the name you gave me.* I guarded them so that not one was lost, except the one headed for destruction, as the Scriptures foretold.

¹³"Now I am coming to you. I told them many things while I was with them in this world so they would be filled with my joy. ¹⁴I have given them your word. And the world hates them because they do not belong to the world, just as I do not belong to the world. ¹⁵I'm not asking you to take them out of the world, but to keep them safe from the evil one. ¹⁶They do not belong to this world any more than I do. ¹⁷Make them holy by your truth; teach them your

word is truth. ¹⁸As You sent Me into the world, I also have sent them into the world. ¹⁹For their sakes I sanctify Myself, that they themselves also may be sanctified in truth.

17:2 ªLit *everything that You have given Him, to them He may*   **17:4** ªOr *by accomplishing*   **17:12** ªHeb idiom for one destined to perish   **17:15** ªOr *out of* the power of   ᵇOr *evil*

word, which is truth. ¹⁸Just as you sent me into the world, I am sending them into the world. ¹⁹And I give myself as a holy sacrifice for them so they can be made holy by your truth.

17:6 Greek *have revealed your name;* also in 17:26.   **17:11** Some manuscripts read *you have given me these [disciples].*   **17:12** Some manuscripts read *I protected those you gave me, by the power of your name.*

The time was probably around midnight. Jesus and the remaining eleven had already left the place where they had eaten supper together for another location, perhaps outside in the courtyard (John 14:31). After declaring, "In the world you have tribulation, but take courage; I have overcome the world" (16:33), I imagine Jesus allowed a long silence to seal the moment. As the warnings and promises of the Lord began to sink in, I can only imagine the disciples' feeling of helplessness as they stared into the vast expanse of stars above them. How vulnerable they must have felt, knowing they would soon be without their Master, who had led them and protected them. Doubtless, few among them could remember the time before He entered their lives, summoned them to follow, and gave them purpose.

After a time of silent reflection, I imagine the words of Jesus—quiet, yet resonant—washing over the despairing disciples, enveloping them for a moment before rising into the heavens. The words of the Son addressing His Father reminded the men that the void of space is filled with the presence of the Almighty. And He would never leave them alone.

Scholars have named this prayer of Jesus His "High Priestly Prayer," but I prefer another name. This is truly the "Lord's Prayer," more so than the example by which He taught the disciples (Matt. 6:9-13; Luke 11:2-4). Furthermore, "high priestly" sounds cold to me, like the rote prayer of a robed and very bored church official. This is the prayer of a man who loved His followers and cared enough to summon the protection of God around them. With great passion, He prayed first for Himself and the success of His mission (John 17:1-12), then for the protection of His disciples as they fulfilled their purpose (17:13-19), and finally for the generations of believers who would follow Him as a result of the disciples' ministry (17:20-26).

— 17:1-3 —

The Greek term translated "heaven" is the same word for "sky." Context usually clarifies which the author intended. In this case, either "heaven" or "sky" is appropriate; however, Jesus' exhortation in 14:31 suggests the men departed the room and may have been making their way out of Jerusalem for Gethsemane.

The terms "hour" and "glory" have been significant throughout John's narrative. "Glory" refers to the Lord's crucifixion, resurrection, and ascension, which would vindicate the truth of His teaching and His identity as the Son of God. The "hour" had been appointed before the beginning of time; it was the destiny to which Jesus had been born (Dan. 7:13-14). However, Jesus didn't focus on the suffering He was about to endure. Instead, He called attention to the fulfillment of God's plan, the glory the Father would receive, and the gift of eternal life to all of "His own."

Jesus defined eternal life as having a relationship with God and His Son, the Messiah, Jesus. The word "know" comes from a Greek term meaning "to understand" rather than merely to perceive or to recognize. The term implies an exchange of ideas and values between two people, such that they share complete familiarity with each other. It is the term that describes the relationship of close friends and even married couples. Eternal life is not only long life but abundant life (John 10:10); its quantity is matched by quality. And this satisfaction can be enjoyed only when an individual fulfills his or her created purpose: to glorify God and to enjoy Him fully.

— 17:4-5 —

Jesus reflected the truth of His identity, recalling how He had come from glory to reflect the glory of the Father on earth. Having completed His task, He looked forward to His return to glory. However, this is not to say that Jesus shook off His humanity; rather, He returned to heaven in a glorified resurrection body—the very kind we will receive when believers are resurrected in the end times.

These words reflect the deep longing Jesus felt for heaven. (Would we dare to call it homesickness?) We too easily forget that while Jesus became a man and placed Himself in the world through a miraculous birth, He is not of this world. We tend to see everything from an earthly perspective, so we recall His earthly life, appreciate His greatness as a man, and imagine what a joyful experience it must have been to work and live and minister with Him. But think of what He gave up to take on human flesh and suffer the very worst of human afflictions. Think of what He left behind when He departed heaven to enter the world in Bethlehem and to depart the world less than ten miles away in Jerusalem—to be born under such humbling circumstances and to suffer such humiliation in death.

To God be all glory—Jesus did not depart the earth in humiliation! Instead, He completed His task and then conquered death to depart in glory.

— 17:6-8 —

Even the Lord's petitions for Himself were brief and selfless. He quickly turned the focus of His prayer to the needs of the eleven gathered around Him and the disciples they would soon lead. While He prayed specifically for them, the principles of His prayer apply to all believers since that time.

Jesus stated that He had "manifested" the Father's "name" to the world. One's name represented his or her character and attributes. The Greek term translated "manifested" means "to reveal" or "to display." The Son not only taught divine truth, He represented divine truth in His very presence. To see the Son was to see the Father.

The Lord identified His followers as those whom God gave to Him "out of the world" and who "kept" His word. This "word" is Old Testament Scripture; God's own were those who remained sensitive to His written words and who obeyed Him. When Jesus, the Word of God in human flesh, presented Himself to the world, "His own" received Him in faith. Jesus, in turn, received them and, through this prayer, officially presented them to the Father while personally vouching for their authenticity.

— 17:9-11 —

Jesus' request begins with the phrase, "I ask on their behalf," and then abruptly shifts to a parenthetical aside before resuming in 17:11 with, "keep them in Your name." His parenthetical aside specifies who Jesus intends the Lord to "keep." The world at large is not in view here, but "His own"—men and women who had responded to the Word in belief, who were no longer identified with the world. Once Jesus ascended to join His Father, believers would be citizens of heaven living in hostile territory, as it were, among citizens of the world. He petitioned His Father to "keep" them and to unify them.

The verb translated "keep" is a term that describes the primary duty of a shepherd; it means "to guard" or "to protect." The idea is to keep them separated from the dangers of the world even as they continue to live among their hostile neighbors. Furthermore, the Lord asked the

Father to bind believers together so that they would enjoy the same kind of oneness shared by the persons of the Trinity.

— 17:12-13 —

Jesus lamented leaving His disciples in the world, yet also acknowledged that the Father's plan was best for all. He had carefully and faithfully kept them from evil and preserved them to this point; now He placed them in the capable hands of His Father.

Only the "son of perdition" had succumbed to Satan. The phrase "son of perdition" or "son of destruction" is a Semitic expression for one who is destined for damnation. Of course, Jesus was referring to Judas, whom He called "a devil" (6:70), who welcomed the idea of Satan to betray the Lord (13:2), and into whom Satan entered (13:27). Judas had not been "lost," because he never truly believed. He merely occupied a place among the faithful, a circumstance predicted by prophecy and utilized by God to accomplish His purposes (cf. Ps. 41:9; John 13:18).

Much of the Lord's teaching on this final evening with the disciples would not have meaning for them at the time. However, once the difficult hours of His suffering had passed and He again stood before them in the glory of His resurrection body, the disciples would find immeasurable hope in these words. More than sixty years later, John gave preeminence to this final discourse, to which he devoted five of twenty-one chapters in his narrative.

— 17:14-16 —

Take note of the sharp distinction between genuine believers and "the world." The Word of God is the cause of this division, drawing a battle line between those who heed the Word and those who hate the Lord and "His own." The Greek verb *miseō* [3404] means "to hate" or "to detest," and describes one's choice to give priority to one thing over another (12:25). *Miseō* may or may not involve intense emotion.

The universe John describes is dualistic, meaning that a sharp division exists between good and evil. God created the world and pronounced it "good" (Gen. 1:31). Sin entered the world and brought with it evil, suffering, and death. As a result, the world operates according to Satan's values, which are entirely opposed to God's way at every level. Consequently, neither side can tolerate the other. John illustrates this division using the opposite images of light and darkness. Where there is light, darkness cannot exist; darkness cannot abide the light. Similarly, people cannot live in both simultaneously. People who prefer darkness will not tolerate anyone who threatens their existence by bringing light.

Interestingly, Jesus did not ask the Father to remove believers from the darkness-oriented world. Instead, He asked the Father to preserve believers from Satan. He asked for unity (John 17:11) and for preservation from evil (17:15), and I cannot help but see the relationship between the two. In fact, John established this connection between unity and preservation from evil in his letter to the churches in Asia Minor. "[The apostates] went out from us, but they were not really of us; for if they had been of us, they would have remained with us; but they went out, so that it would be shown that they all are not of us" (1 Jn. 2:19). He then braided the concepts of light (belief in the truth of Christ), love (unity among the believers), and obedience (proof of genuine belief) in order to lash Christians to the mast of sanctification so that all would be preserved to the end, or "overcome the world" (1 Jn. 5:1-12).

Verse 15 is a clear description of Jesus' strategy. Jesus never encourages believers to cloister themselves within the walls of a monastery— either physically or spiritually. He wants the darkness of the world to be illumined, not only from heaven by the Son, but by multitudes of smaller lights. He asked His Father to give us insulation, not isolation. He asked, in effect, "Insulate believers so they can move in the midst of evil without being burned by the evil one."

— 17:17-19 —

Jesus expressed the means by which believers remain unified and preserved from the evil one: sanctification. The Greek verb is *hagiazō* [37], which means "to dedicate for specific use." This was a common word in pagan worship, describing the process of making something clean and then setting it aside for special use in worship. Something that had been sanctified was considered ceremonially pure. The Jews used the term in reference to anything reserved for God's use, including His covenant people, the Hebrew race. Paul gave the term an even greater personal application. Because the Holy Spirit dwells within the believer, the believer is a temple and, therefore, no less consecrated than the most holy place (see Exod. 26:33-34; Lev. 16:2; 1 Cor. 6:19-20).

Jesus used the term even more specifically in reference to the truth— the divine truth expressed through the Old Testament prophets, who faithfully recorded God's revelation, the divine truth the world had forsaken through Adam's sin and continues to reject through ongoing sin, the divine truth literally embodied by the Son of God. Jesus prayed that His followers would not merely perceive divine truth or simply acknowledge the truth, but that they would be made clean by it and be set apart from the world for God's special use.

This is not something that will occur overnight. Positionally, we have been sanctified; experientially, we must become sanctified as the Holy Spirit conforms us to the truth.

• • •

I can think of few experiences more humbling and encouraging than hearing the prayers of another on my behalf. When earthly concerns bear down on my shoulders and squeeze my temples, hearing someone carry my burdens to heaven is relief I can barely describe.

I feel understood. I know that someone empathizes with my struggle and takes it seriously enough to unite his spirit with mine in seeking God's intervention.

I receive confidence. Hearing the intercession of another gives me reasonable assurance that my own prayers are consistent with God's values.

I grow wiser. The prayer of another offers perspectives I had not considered.

I find courage. Someone with more objectivity can pray with greater confidence in the power and goodness of God, which is always infectious.

I gain perspective. People who aren't caught up in my suffering are better able to see my struggle from an eternal perspective, and that is always helpful.

It's too bad we don't do this for one another more often.

Now imagine hearing the Son of God approach His Father on your behalf. Imagine the encouragement, confidence, wisdom, courage, and perspective you would gain by hearing Him intercede for you. A perfect prayer from the lips of the perfect man.

What a marvelous gift the Lord gave His disciples on the eve of His torment! Their preparation for ministry was complete; having consecrated them for ministry, Jesus turned His prayer toward the generations of believers these eleven disciples had been charged to lead.

APPLICATION: JOHN 17:1-19

Prayer and the Work of God

Jesus' prayer for Himself, His disciples, and the generations of believers to follow underscores three fundamental truths about the relationship between prayer and any God-honoring endeavor.

First, *prayer helps us keep God's glory as the first priority in every endeavor.* Jesus began His prayer by acknowledging the primary purpose of His mission on earth. As the Son of God, He asked to be glorified—to be vindicated in the sight of all humanity as the embodiment of divine truth—not for His own sake, but that He might reflect this glory back to the Father.

When we go to the Father, through the Son, asking for anything to be accomplished, we are wise to acknowledge God's glory as the primary goal in every human endeavor, whether directly associated with ministry or not. When asking for success in business, let it be for the glory of God—and let it be genuinely so, not merely lip service. When asking for ministry to expand, lead off your prayer by submitting all things to the glory of God. I would even go so far as to include the following: "And, Lord, if this does not bring glory to you, please deny our request and then guide us to accomplish Your will in Your way."

Second, *prayer helps us remember that any God-honoring endeavor will succeed because of His power, not ours.* Jesus acknowledged that people came to Him because they belonged to God. The Father drew them; Jesus kept them (John 6:37, 39, 65; 12:32; 17:2, 6, 9, 24). Of course, it's silly to ask whether the Father or the Son was responsible for success because they are the same in essence—the Father and Son are two persons and one God. However, the Son's prayer is our example.

When we pray, let us subordinate our desires to the greater design of God. After all, we are part of *His* redemptive plan, not the other way around!

Third, *prayer causes us to look to God for success rather than to the world.* Jesus acknowledged in His prayer that the desires of the world are opposed to those of the Father (17:9, 11). Jesus prayed, in effect, "Lord, unify them, preserve them, set them apart, and work through them." He said, "Lord, may the world assist in accomplishing Your plan."

The world is not a friend to grace; therefore, we should expect resistance, not help in proclaiming the good news. Prayer helps us remember whom to thank for success, even when the world appears to be cooperative.

I cannot imagine trying to accomplish the task the Lord has given us apart from prayer. How discouraging to think He would charge us to change the world and then leave us to do it on our own. He might as well have asked us to dip the oceans dry with a teaspoon. Thankfully, He did not leave us to accomplish this God-sized task without divine power. Rather, He has promised to accomplish the work Himself. He has called us to join Him so we might enjoy the spoils of victory with Him when the work is complete. Therefore, let every goal we pursue and every prayer we offer reflect this transforming truth.

When Jesus Prayed for You
JOHN 17:20-26

NASB

20 "I do not ask on behalf of these alone, but for those also who believe in Me through their word; 21 that they may all be one; even as You, Father, *are* in Me and I in You, that they also may be in Us, so that the world may ᵃbelieve that You sent Me.

22 The glory which You have given Me I have given to them, that they may be one, just as We are one; 23 I in them and You in Me, that they may be perfected ᵃin unity, so that the world may ᵇknow that You sent Me, and loved them, even as You have loved Me. 24 Father, I desire that they also, whom You have given Me, be with Me where I am, so that they may see My glory which You have given Me, for You loved Me before the foundation of the world.

25 "O righteous Father, ᵃalthough the world has not known You, yet I have known You; and these have known that You sent Me; 26 and I have made Your name known to them, and will make it known, so that the love with which You loved Me may be in them, and I in them."

17:21 ᵃGr tense indicates *continually believe*
17:23 ᵃLit *into one*   ᵇGr tense indicates *continually know*   17:25 ᵃLit *even the world*

NLT

20 "I am praying not only for these disciples but also for all who will ever believe in me through their message. 21 I pray that they will all be one, just as you and I are one—as you are in me, Father, and I am in you. And may they be in us so that the world will believe you sent me.

22 "I have given them the glory you gave me, so they may be one as we are one. 23 I am in them and you are in me. May they experience such perfect unity that the world will know that you sent me and that you love them as much as you love me. 24 Father, I want these whom you have given me to be with me where I am. Then they can see all the glory you gave me because you loved me even before the world began!

25 "O righteous Father, the world doesn't know you, but I do; and these disciples know you sent me. 26 I have revealed you to them, and I will continue to do so. Then your love for me will be in them, and I will be in them."

Josephus, the Jewish historian, records a marvelous story that may or may not be true.[18] In his great campaign for world domination in the 330s BC, Alexander the Great moved from the Hellespont to Egypt, laying siege to walled cities and conquering land in between. His path to Egypt took him down the narrow land bridge between the Mediterranean Sea and the Arabian Desert, a land ruled by Jerusalem. Israel was a choice piece of land for anyone wanting to control trade with Egypt. No one knew that better than the citizens of Jerusalem who trembled at the sound of hoof beats and chariots racing south to plunder their beloved Zion. The people of Jerusalem rallied around the high priest, Jaddua, who fell to his knees before God for answers. How would he defend the defenseless people of Israel? The walls of the city were crumbling with age and no one dared stand against the seasoned warriors of Greece. The Lord led him to decorate the city and open the gates. He was to have each person greeting Alexander's army dress in white, while the priests wore the vestments of their order.

As Alexander's army moved closer to Jerusalem, Jaddua led the procession of priests and greeters north to meet him. The high priest wore purple and scarlet garments and his decorative headpiece, which bore a golden plate engraved with the name of God. He stood his ground as the dust from hoof and chariot billowed up and darkened the sky. When the Greeks came within sight of the Jewish procession, Alexander stopped his march, dismounted, stood before the high priest, and then worshiped the name of God—something he had never done before. According to Josephus, the conqueror had previously seen a vision of white-clad people, the priests, and the name of God engraved in gold.

Upon his arrival in Jerusalem, Alexander offered sacrifice to God per Jaddua's instructions, and he treated the Jews with great kindness. Then Jaddua opened an ancient scroll to the prophecy of Daniel, probably chapters 7 and 8. He showed Alexander a two-hundred-year-old prophecy, predicting Greek dominion over the Western world (Dan. 8:21). Suddenly, Alexander was overjoyed. Although a man of dark moods, he suddenly rejoiced, promising to put a perimeter of protection around Zion and to allow the Jews to retain their own law.

Alexander had seen himself in Scripture and was deeply affected by the experience.

We have that opportunity today. John faithfully recorded the Lord's prayer on the eve of His arrest, in which He interceded for you and me. He went to His Father on our behalf, knowing our needs ahead of time and asking that each of them be filled in abundance. Think of it! He prayed for us! In fact, He prayed specifically for three crucial needs:

- Our spiritual unity (17:21-23)
- Our eternal destiny (17:24)
- Our mutual love (17:25-26)

— 17:20 —

See the words "those also"? That's where your name belongs. If you have believed in Jesus Christ, He prayed for you. Having prayed for Himself and the success of His mission, and having interceded for the disciples' protection and success in ministry, the Lord petitioned His Father for the generations of believers who would come to faith either directly or indirectly through the disciples' ministry. This included believing Jews in Jerusalem as well as believing Gentiles (John 10:16). To be sure, this act of divine intercession included every believer who has ever lived or will live before the old creation is superseded by the new (Rev. 21:1).

Note the expression "through their word." No longer just the "Word of God" or even "My word"—the disciples now possessed the truth and could rightfully claim it as their own. By identification with Christ, believers are one with Him and are therefore light bearers. This truth is ours, in that He has filled us with divine truth in the person of the Holy Spirit.

— 17:21-23 —

The Lord first asked for unity among the body of believers. He repeated the term three times in three verses, expressing His desire for our unity in faith (17:20b-21), our unity in glory (17:22), and our unity in obedience (17:23). We cannot ignore the significance of the Lord's thinking of all the needs of all believers throughout all time, and then asking for unity among all of them. There will be all manner of circumstances and all sorts of "isms," but there can be only one body of Christ, bound together in one faith.

When all have their identity in Christ, then all share the same spiritual DNA. Furthermore, believers will share the glory the Father gave to the Son. The destiny of all believers is to follow Christ into eternity. Just as Jesus was vindicated upon His resurrection, received a resurrection body, and went to be with the Father, so shall all believers!

To be "perfected" means to be made mature or complete. He desired all Christians to be completely unified in obedience, so that the truth of Christ would be impossible for the world to ignore. However, this unity of faith, glory, and obedience needs clarification, lest anyone misunderstand.

Unity is not uniformity. Training for the military strips each recruit of his or her individuality in order to create a uniform kind of unity. All new recruits are given the same haircut and required to wear the same uniform. At graduation from boot camp, all emerge looking the same, sounding the same, behaving the same, and prepared for the same kind of duty. But the body of Christ is not uniform (1 Cor. 12).

Here's just a brief sampling of Christ's body: Saul of Tarsus, who became Paul, a Jew who became an apostle of Christ. Luke, the physician, a Gentile believer and careful historian. Tertullian, a church father, passionate, fiery, zealous, yet logical. Bernard of Clairvaux, the French monk who wrote fine hymns from a cloister. John Wycliffe, the morning star of the Reformation, who devoted his life to the translation of the text into English. William Tyndale, who defied laws against translating the Scriptures into English and then paid the ultimate price for his service to the church. George Whitefield, the Calvinistic, Church of England evangelist. John Wesley, founder of the Methodists and tireless itinerant preacher. Charles Haddon Spurgeon, the Baptist Calvinist, known as the "prince of preachers." Dwight L. Moody, the uneducated evangelist who founded a college and a publishing house.

Unity is not unanimity. Unanimity requires absolute agreement on every matter, including matters of conscience and matters of opinion. While we must agree on certain crucial matters of absolute truth, we have the freedom to disagree on many matters without having to forfeit love or acceptance. And thank goodness we don't have to agree on everything, or many of the great advances in Christian ministry would never have occurred—not the least of which is the rebirth of foreign missions through a passionate, young idealist named William Carey.

Unity is not unification. I don't think Jesus Christ is half as disturbed as many people are by the existence of various denominations. The manner in which some believers broke away from others might not have been admirable, and the doctrines of some are not as pure as others; however, the concept of churches differing on nonessential matters and maintaining distinct identities is not necessarily dangerous to unity. It is quite possible to differ amicably while fulfilling a common purpose. On the other hand, some extremists seek reasons to separate. Some believers are unable to distinguish between essential and nonessential matters of doctrine and behave arrogantly toward those who disagree, perceiving more divisions than there are.

— 17:24 —

The Lord's second request was for believers to enjoy eternity in heaven with their Savior. Our eternal destiny is an answer to Jesus' prayer on our behalf, and we can be certain the Son's requests from the Father will be faithfully answered.

The reason He gave was that we might see His glory. The older rendering of the Greek verb translated "see" is "behold," which better captures the nuance of the original term. "Behold" carries the nuance of observing with wonder and deep appreciation. In translating Jesus' Aramaic into Greek, John could have chosen any one of five different Greek terms, but he chose *theōreō* [2334]. This term typically describes spectators at a religious festival, who view with wonder, curiosity, or contemplation.[19] The object of this beholding will be His "glory" in heaven, where the *shekinah* will not be shrouded in mortal flesh. In the book of Revelation, John described the glory of the Son as the source of all light in the new creation (Rev. 21:22-24). In His presence, there will be no night, no darkness at all (cf. John 1:5; 1 Jn. 1:5).

— 17:25-26 —

Jesus' final request of the Father was for our mutual love—the same kind of love shared within the Trinity and demonstrated by the Father for the world in sending His Son.

At the time of Jesus' earthly ministry, Judaism had pushed God to the periphery of worship. They had come to see their Creator as so transcendent, so ineffably unapproachable, that they feared to speak His name out loud. And they had so venerated the Law above the Lawgiver that they failed to recognize His great love for them. Jesus reintroduced the true character and attributes of God to the disciples so that all people might know the overwhelming love the Creator has for His creatures. At least one reason for leaving believers in the world is so the world will know the love of the Father by observing His people.

• • •

It occurs to me as I reflect on this last request of Jesus that we have within us the ability to join the Father in answering the prayer of our Savior. He desired unity in faith, unity in destiny, and unity in love. He has guaranteed unity in destiny—He will preserve His believers until the end. Unity in faith and unity in love, however, are within our reach because of the indwelling Holy Spirit.

If only we would yield to His control.

After Jesus concluded His prayer, the men departed, walking silently toward the garden of Gethsemane. He wanted to tell them much more, but His words would be wasted as long as the disciples continued to worry about living without their Master. No matter. He had given them all the information they would need to carry on. He trusted the Holy Spirit to help them recall His words, glean wisdom from them, and then grow confident in ministry. However, before receiving this gift of indwelling light, the eleven men would have to walk through a terrible darkness. For a time, it would seem to them that the darkness of the world had overpowered the Light.

APPLICATION: JOHN 17:20-26

Answering the Prayer of Jesus

As the prayer of Jesus closes, I find in His words a challenge each of us must answer. I find three specific applications. They're simple, but they speak to the heart.

First, *to grow in unity requires giving in.* If you plan to be a person of unity, you'll have to give in. And I use that expression in its best sense. By "give in," I mean we should be flexible in terms of style. Be open. Be accommodating. Be gracious. Don't give an inch in terms of absolute biblical truth, but for heaven's sake, relax! As the years of pastoral ministry have rounded off my rough edges, I've come to see that so many of the issues that used to keep me awake at night actually made the church better and stronger. I think God uses people who have a wide tolerance level to keep His church flexible in style yet firm on truth.

Second, *to know our destiny requires giving up.* You cannot keep your way and get to heaven. If you're going to get to heaven, you have to go God's way. You'll have to give up your plan and get yourself on the Lord's agenda. I'm not talking about cleaning up your act or reforming your behavior. You undoubtedly know from experience how that will work out.

I'm talking about believing in Jesus Christ, receiving the gift of eternal life, and trusting that He will do a marvelous work of transformation within you. Give up your belief in your own ability to reform or in humanity's gradual improvement. Take on Christ's divine plan, the gift of eternal life.

Third, *to show His love means giving out*. Please don't think for a moment that you really have Christian love if it's not expressed. There's no such thing as repressed Christian love. Christian love is, by definition, active. That doesn't mean you're always effervescing or perpetually in motion. It does mean, however, that your love relationship with other believers is characterized by tangible or observable expressions of love. It also means that you take the time to demonstrate kindness and compassion to people outside the church—including your enemies.

VINDICATION OF THE WORD
(JOHN 18:1–21:25)

Jesus entered the world in controversy and lived much of His life under the shadow of doubt. His mother received an angelic visit informing her that she would be the mother of the Messiah, and that His birth would be in literal fulfillment of an ancient prophecy: "Behold, a *virgin* will be with child and bear a son, and she will call His name Immanuel" (Isa. 7:14, emphasis mine; cf. Matt. 1:23). In other words, her baby would be conceived without a human father. Unfortunately, her wonderful secret would soon become a neighborhood scandal. Her betrothed was prevented from filing a quiet divorce by another angelic vision, but we have no indication the Lord supernaturally revealed the truth regarding the conception to anyone other than Joseph. No one else in Nazareth received an angelic visit telling them the truth. In other words, everyone else thought what you would think: that Jesus was illegitimate.

From the very beginning and throughout His public ministry, belief in the Christ would be a matter of choice. Which evidence would people trust? Scripture, or their own prejudices and presuppositions? Which authority would people accept? The Word of God, or their own desires?

As Jesus proclaimed divine truth, His critics relished every opportunity to question His origins (John 6:42; 7:27, 41; 8:19, 41; 9:29), taking great care to avoid the overwhelming prophetic evidence of His divine identity. As we have observed, most people persistently ignored the "signs" He miraculously performed (9:16; 11:47-48; 12:37)—ironically, while demanding He prove Himself by performing miraculous signs (2:18; 4:48; 6:30). Nevertheless, many others were attracted to His obvious divine power. Ultimately, "His own" moved beyond the need for miraculous signs to accept the *Man* as the Word of God, their Messiah, the Son of God.

By the end of His public ministry, Jesus had polarized the nation. On one side stood the unbelieving temple authorities in all their religious finery; on the other, a ragtag collection of a few hundred committed believers. Between them stood a vast multitude, whose souls hung in the balance. And each side—the minions of evil and the followers of Jesus—had been tasked to claim them.

As the sun set one evening before Passover, each side retreated to

KEY TERMS IN JOHN 18:1–21:25

***akoloutheō* (ἀκολουθέω)** [190] "to follow," "to go the same way," "to go after"

Literally, this verb means "to go the same way," which of course carries the metaphorical connotation of imitating the thoughts, beliefs, actions, or lifestyle of another. Similarly, we might say of a boy adopting his father's occupation, "He's following in the footsteps of his father." The Old Testament doesn't prefer this metaphor for following God's ways. It becomes a favored term in the New Testament, however, perhaps because the example of Christ is more accessible. *See John 1:43; 10:27; 21:19, 22.*

***tetelestai* (τετέλεσται)** [5055] "completed," "brought to fulfillment," "paid in full"

This is the perfect passive form of the verb "to complete" or "to fulfill." A verb in the passive voice indicates that the object is acted upon by some external influence (e.g., "The ball *was thrown*"). The perfect tense places the action in the past, while emphasizing ongoing results. This Greek term declares that something has been brought to a state of completion and therefore needs no more involvement. It was also an accounting term, meaning "paid in full." *See John 19:28, 30.*

***phaneroō* (φανερόω)** [5319] "to manifest," "to make visible," "to reveal," "to shine"

Classical Greek made very little use of this term, which means "to make visible what was invisible."[1] It is a causative verb, meaning that the subject causes the action of the verb. The term also places particular emphasis on the prior state of being unseen. Therefore, it finds wide use in the New Testament, which records a remarkable time of divine revelation. Jesus perfectly manifested God in the sense that humankind experienced God in ways not possible before. Jesus manifested truth as only a "God-man" could. And then Jesus manifested Himself in a state never before seen—a glorified, incorruptible form of humanity. *See John 2:11; 17:6; 21:1, 14.*

prepare for the first real battle of an invisible war, a cosmic campaign for the souls of humanity. Both claimed to be the sole guardian of divine truth, but the religious leaders hoped to settle the matter quickly. Before the end of the Passover festival, they intended to prove their case by killing Jesus. They would put Him on trial for openly opposing the temple authorities—and God by extension—and then crucify Him as a blasphemer. By sundown on "the day of preparation," they hoped to bury His body and, with it, any notion that He was the promised Messiah, the Son of God, the Word incarnate, the Savior of humanity. With the good news—salvation by grace alone, by faith alone, in Christ alone—lying cold in a tomb, their proud religion of works could again reign supreme, with the temple authorities back in control.

But, as Jesus had promised His disciples, the victory gained by the evildoers would be short-lived. They would destroy themselves by the very weapons they wielded against their Creator. The incarnate Word would rise from the grave in a glorious resurrection body, triumphant over disease, disaster, death, and decay, victorious over sin and evil. By the break of light on Sunday morning, divine truth would emerge from the grave completely vindicated in the eyes of all humanity. His words of reassurance were clearly and repeatedly stated. His disciples heard them . . . but quickly forgot them as the tide of public opinion and official decisions turned against Him. In a few hours, they would all walk away.

Truth on Trial
JOHN 18:1-27

NASB

¹ When Jesus had spoken these words, He went forth with His disciples over the ᵃravine of the Kidron, where there was a garden, in which He entered ᵇwith His disciples. ²Now Judas also, who was ᵃbetraying Him, knew the place, for Jesus had often met there with His disciples. ³Judas then, having received the *Roman* ᵃcohort and officers from the chief priests and the Pharisees, came there with lanterns and torches and weapons. ⁴So Jesus, knowing all the things that were coming upon Him,

NLT

¹After saying these things, Jesus crossed the Kidron Valley with his disciples and entered a grove of olive trees. ²Judas, the betrayer, knew this place, because Jesus had often gone there with his disciples. ³The leading priests and Pharisees had given Judas a contingent of Roman soldiers and Temple guards to accompany him. Now with blazing torches, lanterns, and weapons, they arrived at the olive grove.

⁴ Jesus fully realized all that was going to happen to him, so he

went forth and said to them, "Whom do you seek?" 5They answered Him, "Jesus the Nazarene." He said to them, "I am *He*." And Judas also, who was betraying Him, was standing with them. 6So when He said to them, "I am *He*," they drew back and fell to the ground. 7Therefore He again asked them, "Whom do you seek?" And they said, "Jesus the Nazarene." 8Jesus answered, "I told you that I am *He*; so if you seek Me, let these go their way," 9to fulfill the word which He spoke, "Of those whom You have given Me I lost not one." 10Simon Peter then, having a sword, drew it and struck the high priest's slave, and cut off his right ear; and the slave's name was Malchus. 11So Jesus said to Peter, "Put the sword into the sheath; the cup which the Father has given Me, shall I not drink it?"

12So the *Roman* ᵃcohort and the ᵇcommander and the officers of the Jews, arrested Jesus and bound Him, 13and led Him to Annas first; for he was father-in-law of Caiaphas, who was high priest that year. 14Now Caiaphas was the one who had advised the Jews that it was expedient for one man to die on behalf of the people.

15Simon Peter was following Jesus, and *so was* another disciple. Now that disciple was known to the high priest, and entered with Jesus into the court of the high priest, 16but Peter was standing at the door outside. So the other disciple, who was known to the high priest, went out and spoke to the doorkeeper, and brought Peter in. 17Then the slave-girl who kept the door said to Peter, "You are not also *one* of this man's disciples, are you?" He said, "I am not." 18Now the slaves and the officers were standing *there,* having made a charcoal fire, for it was cold and they were warming themselves;

stepped forward to meet them. "Who are you looking for?" he asked.

5"Jesus the Nazarene,"* they replied.

"I Am he,"* Jesus said. (Judas, who betrayed him, was standing with them.) 6As Jesus said "I Am he," they all drew back and fell to the ground! 7Once more he asked them, "Who are you looking for?"

And again they replied, "Jesus the Nazarene."

8"I told you that I Am he," Jesus said. "And since I am the one you want, let these others go." 9He did this to fulfill his own statement: "I did not lose a single one of those you have given me."*

10Then Simon Peter drew a sword and slashed off the right ear of Malchus, the high priest's slave. 11But Jesus said to Peter, "Put your sword back into its sheath. Shall I not drink from the cup of suffering the Father has given me?"

12So the soldiers, their commanding officer, and the Temple guards arrested Jesus and tied him up. 13First they took him to Annas, since he was the father-in-law of Caiaphas, the high priest at that time.* 14Caiaphas was the one who had told the other Jewish leaders, "It's better that one man should die for the people."

15Simon Peter followed Jesus, as did another of the disciples. That other disciple was acquainted with the high priest, so he was allowed to enter the high priest's courtyard with Jesus. 16Peter had to stay outside the gate. Then the disciple who knew the high priest spoke to the woman watching at the gate, and she let Peter in. 17The woman asked Peter, "You're not one of that man's disciples, are you?"

"No," he said, "I am not."

18Because it was cold, the household servants and the guards had made a charcoal fire. They stood around it, warming themselves, and

and Peter was also with them, standing and warming himself.

¹⁹The high priest then questioned Jesus about His disciples, and about His teaching. ²⁰Jesus answered him, "I have spoken openly to the world; I always taught in ᵃsynagogues and in the temple, where all the Jews come together; and I spoke nothing in secret. ²¹Why do you question Me? Question those who have heard what I spoke to them; they know what I said." ²²When He had said this, one of the officers standing nearby struck Jesus, saying, "Is that the way You answer the high priest?" ²³Jesus answered him, "If I have spoken wrongly, testify of the wrong; but if rightly, why do you strike Me?" ²⁴So Annas sent Him bound to Caiaphas the high priest.

²⁵Now Simon Peter was standing and warming himself. So they said to him, "You are not also *one* of His disciples, are you?" He denied *it,* and said, "I am not." ²⁶One of the slaves of the high priest, being a relative of the one whose ear Peter cut off, said, "Did I not see you in the garden with Him?" ²⁷Peter then denied *it* again, and immediately a rooster crowed.

18:1 ᵃLit *winter-torrent* ᵇLit *and* **18:2** ᵃOr *handing Him over* **18:3** ᵃNormally 600 men; *a battalion* **18:12** ᵃOr *battalion* ᵇI.e. chiliarch, in command of a thousand troops **18:20** ᵃLit *a synagogue*

Peter stood with them, warming himself.

¹⁹Inside, the high priest began asking Jesus about his followers and what he had been teaching them. ²⁰Jesus replied, "Everyone knows what I teach. I have preached regularly in the synagogues and the Temple, where the people* gather. I have not spoken in secret. ²¹Why are you asking me this question? Ask those who heard me. They know what I said."

²²Then one of the Temple guards standing nearby slapped Jesus across the face. "Is that the way to answer the high priest?" he demanded.

²³Jesus replied, "If I said anything wrong, you must prove it. But if I'm speaking the truth, why are you beating me?"

²⁴Then Annas bound Jesus and sent him to Caiaphas, the high priest.

²⁵Meanwhile, as Simon Peter was standing by the fire warming himself, they asked him again, "You're not one of his disciples, are you?"

He denied it, saying, "No, I am not."

²⁶But one of the household slaves of the high priest, a relative of the man whose ear Peter had cut off, asked, "Didn't I see you out there in the olive grove with Jesus?" ²⁷Again Peter denied it. And immediately a rooster crowed.

18:5a Or *Jesus of Nazareth;* also in 18:7. **18:5b** Or *"The 'I AM' is here";* or *"I am the LORD";* Greek reads *I am;* also in 18:6, 8. See Exod 3:14. **18:9** See John 6:39 and 17:12. **18:13** Greek *that year.* **18:20** Greek *Jewish people;* also in 18:38.

Injustice is an inevitable fact of life in a fallen world. Sooner or later, everyone will be misunderstood, misquoted, falsely accused, slandered, gossiped about, or openly maligned. It's an experience we all share, but that doesn't make it any easier to endure. We bear the image of God, who loves justice as much as He loves mercy, and that aspect of our nature longs for right to prevail over wrong . . . especially when our own well-being is at stake.

Jesus was the only person to live His entire life without failing morally, yet He was arrested, tried, convicted, and condemned to suffer a criminal's punishment. His arrest was a betrayal, His trials a farce, His conviction illegal, and His punishment a travesty of justice. Yet throughout the ordeal, He remained calm, He answered sincere questions directly, He spoke the truth with dignity, and He calmly resolved to allow the Father to vindicate Him at the proper time.

— 18:1 —

As Jesus concluded His prayer (17:1-26), His words undoubtedly felt like a warm blanket around the disciples as they came to terms with His imminent departure. They were indeed eternally secure in the sovereign care of God, but they scarcely realized the horrific evil mounting against the Lord that very moment. Even as the remaining eleven men trusted their Master to fulfill His promises, one had slipped into the dark of night to betray Him. The temple officials were organizing a raiding party of combined Roman and Jewish troops, soon to surround Jesus and haul Him before six criminal hearings.

The Passover feast begins at twilight on the fourteenth day of Nisan on the Jewish calendar. Because the Jews reckoned the year by the lunar cycle, it's almost impossible to pinpoint the exact date of Jesus' crucifixion. The day could have occurred anytime between late March and early April. Probably around midnight, the men started out for Gethsemane. Some expositors interpret 14:31 to mean they departed the upper room for the garden as Jesus continued His discourse en route (15:1–17:26). However, I find it difficult to imagine Jesus concluding this intimate discussion with such a solemn prayer while walking through the city or down the slope of the Kidron Valley. The construction of this sentence (literally, "Having said these things, Jesus departed . . .") suggests that although the men had left the upper room, they did not set out for the garden until Jesus had finished praying. Perhaps Jesus concluded His "farewell discourse" in a courtyard outside the residence where they had eaten . . . or under torchlight on the southern steps of Herod's temple.

The men most likely exited Jerusalem through an eastern gate, traveled northeast along the outer perimeter of the wall past the temple mount, and then crossed the Kidron ravine. The literal Greek description is "the winter-flowing of Kidron," meaning a narrow valley that is swollen with runoff in winter but relatively dry at other times. David also crossed this valley when put to flight by Absalom's revolt, during which one of his trusted advisors had betrayed him (2 Sam. 15:23-31).

	THE TRIALS OF JESUS					
Trial	Officiating Authority	Scripture	Accusations	Legality	Type	Result
1	Annas, former high priest from AD 6–15	John 18:12-23	No specific charges brought.	Illegal: • No jurisdiction • Held at night • No charges • No witnesses • Abused during trial	Jewish and Religious	Found "guilty" of irreverence and sent to Caiaphas.
2	Caiaphas, high priest from AD 18–36, and the Sanhedrin	Matthew 26:57-68 Mark 14:53-65 John 18:24	Claimed to be the Messiah, the Son of God, which they deemed blasphemy.	Illegal: • Held at night • False witnesses • No formal charge • Abused during trial	Jewish and Religious	Declared "guilty" of blasphemy and held for sentencing until morning.
3	Sanhedrin	Mark 15:1 Luke 22:66-71	As a continuation of the earlier trial before the Sanhedrin, the charges remained the same.	Illegal: • Accusation changed • No witnesses • Improper vote	Jewish and Religious	Sentenced to be turned over to Romans for execution.
4	Pilate, governor of Judea from AD 26–36	Matthew 27:11-14 Mark 15:2-5 Luke 23:1-7 John 18:28-38	Charged with treason and sedition against Rome.	Illegal: • Found "not guilty," yet kept in custody • No defense representation • Abused during trial	Roman and Civil	Declared "not guilty" and pawned off on Herod Antipas to find a loophole.
5	Herod Antipas, governor of Galilee from 4 BC–AD 39	Luke 23:8-12	No specific charges brought. Questioned at length by Herod.	Illegal: • No jurisdiction • No specific charges • Abused during trial	Roman and Civil	Mistreated, mocked, falsely accused, and returned to Pilate without a decision made.
6	Pilate	Matthew 27:15-26 Mark 15:6-15 Luke 23:13-25 John 18:39–19:16	As a continuation of the earlier trial before Pilate, the charges remained the same.	Illegal: • Declared "not guilty," yet condemned.	Roman and Civil	Declared "not guilty" but sentenced to be crucified to mollify the angry mob. Simultaneously, a man guilty of murder, treason, and sedition was released.

339

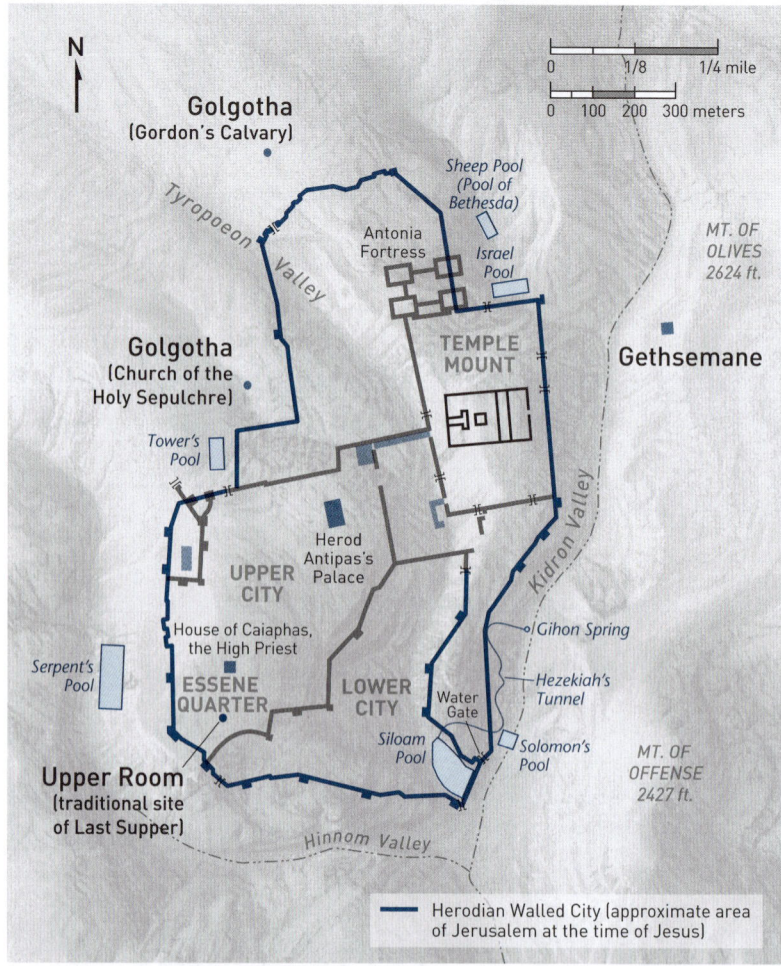

After supper, Jesus led His disciples past the great temple, across the Kidron Valley, and up the western slope of the Mount of Olives to a familiar retreat. Although John does not name the place, we know from Matthew 26:36 and Mark 14:32 that the garden was called Gethsemane.

John may have mentioned the Kidron Valley detail as a deliberate allusion to this well-known event from Israel's history, much like someone today alluding to the beaches of Normandy. Immediately, visions of D-Day spring to mind.

— 18:2-3 —

Their destination was their customary retreat (18:2), a walled garden on the Mount of Olives, perhaps on the western slope overlooking the Holy City. The other Gospels tell us that He went there to pray and to prepare Himself for the awful ordeal He was about to endure (Matt. 26:36-46; Mark 14:32-42; Luke 22:39-46). John's readers knew this part of the story well, so he probably didn't see any added benefit to including it in his narrative.

The name *Gethsemane* means "olive press." This olive grove is the traditional site of Christ's last anguished night before His arrest. Because many such gardens occupied the Mount of Olives, no one can be certain. Regardless, Gethsemane undoubtedly looked very similar to this picture.

According to Matthew, Jesus prayed for approximately three hours (Matt. 26:40, 42, 44). When Jesus finished praying, Judas arrived with a small army of Roman soldiers and temple guards. At the time of Jesus, a Roman "cohort" consisted of 480 fighting men, not including officers and support personnel. The fact that they came with lanterns and torches tells us the mountain was shrouded in darkness, perhaps around three or four in the morning.

Naturally, they never would have known His whereabouts were it not for Judas. The temple officials had tried to seize Jesus on several other occasions, but He eluded their grasp in the temple, or multitudes of witnesses discouraged His would-be abductors, or He kept His movements a secret. However, once they found an inside man willing to betray Jesus, they could seize Him privately.

Had they been successful earlier, the temple authorities might have simply ambushed and murdered Jesus and few would have noticed Him missing. But just days earlier, Jesus had entered the city with multitudes shouting, "King of Israel!" and "Hosanna!" which means "Save [us] now!" To murder Him would clearly implicate them in wrongdoing and turn Jesus into a martyr. He had become too popular. So now they would first need to discredit Him and turn the common man against Him. A carefully chosen accusation and the appearance of propriety would turn the public to their side against Jesus. The scheme had the added benefit of solidifying the Sadducees' hold on political power. Caiaphas saw killing Jesus as a means of demonstrating goodwill toward Rome, saying in effect, "See how well we keep the peace? You can trust us to keep a lid on Jewish uprisings!" (John 11:49-51; 18:14).

— 18:4-9 —

The soldiers undoubtedly surrounded the garden perimeter wall to prevent any from escaping, but Jesus wasn't running; He knew they were coming for Him long before they arrived. He called into the darkness the simple question, "Whom do you seek?" When the commander answered, "Jesus the Nazarene," the Lord confirmed that He was indeed present. At this, the soldiers "drew back and fell to the ground" (18:6). This could mean that they anticipated a counterassault (hence their bringing nearly six hundred men to the fight) and took up defensive positions. However, there is another possibility. John rarely includes details unless they have theological significance. Jesus again employed the highly significant self-designation *egō eimi* [1473, 1510], "I AM" (4:26; 8:24, 28, 58; 13:19; cf. Exod. 3:14). He used this culturally and biblically loaded terminology to identify Himself as deity. John then uses "drew back and fell to the ground" to describe the men's response, which is also culturally and biblically significant. At Gethsemane, the enemies of God shrank before the presence of the Almighty, foreshadowing their posture at the end of time (Isa. 45:23; Rom. 14:11; Phil. 2:10-11; Rev. 3:9). Either way, the initial reaction of the cohort offers a little comic relief: Six hundred well-armed men terrified of a single rabbi and his eleven followers, only one of whom carried a weapon!

Jesus, always the selfless leader, asked for the release of His disciples, which John noted was a literal fulfillment of the Lord's earlier statement to the Father (John 17:12; see also 6:39).

— 18:10-11 —

Peter had earlier stated that he was ready to go into battle with the Lord and to give his life in the fight (13:37; cf. Matt. 26:33-35). He obviously meant what he said. He was ready to wield a sword of metal in order to help Jesus take the throne by force and then institute His new kingdom. One man with a short sword against six hundred! That's Peter. Brash, impulsive, passionate, brave . . . but earthly-minded.

John includes the detail that Peter cut off the right ear of the high priest's servant, Malchus ("kingly one"). Some expositors—including me in the recent past—have suggested Peter intended to kill the man by splitting his head open, and that Malchus dodged at the last moment, thus losing his ear. However, after reconsidering several details, I prefer another explanation. First, the downward motion of a blade by a right-handed man would not likely strike a right ear unless the victim was attacked from behind and a left-handed Peter would be an odd detail to omit. Furthermore, a hard blow that sliced off an ear would likely have caused more damage, but John mentions none.

Because John typically includes details for their symbolic value, it's more likely Peter aimed for the man's right ear for the express purpose of leaving an insulting injury. Malchus was an emissary of the high priest, and therefore represented his authority. Cutting off an ear or a nose was considered particularly humiliating, especially since Jews barred maimed individuals from serving in the temple. Moreover, Jewish tradition prescribed higher restitution for organs and extremities on the right side of the body.

Jesus rebuked Peter for behaving like a nonbeliever and for failing to see the plan of God unfolding, despite Jesus' many predictions. The "cup" of which Jesus spoke was a well-known expression for His crucifixion in the other Gospels (Matt. 20:22; 26:39; Mark 14:36; Luke 22:42).

— 18:12-14 —

To arrest Jesus, the soldiers undoubtedly followed Roman procedure by pulling His arms behind His back and placing them in irons or binding them tightly with rope. We may assume He remained bound with a noose around His neck throughout His ordeal. Then Jesus was taken to the highest Jewish power in Israel, Annas.

Although Caiaphas officially held the office of high priest, many recognized his father-in-law, Annas, as the true authority in Jerusalem and the final voice in every matter concerning the temple.

— 18:15-18 —

The disciples scattered immediately after the arrest in the garden (Matt. 26:56); however, Peter and John returned to follow the Lord's movements from a safe distance. When the soldiers had taken Jesus to the

ANNAS, THE "GODFATHER" OF JERUSALEM

JOHN 18:12-24

During the first century, the office of high priest in Israel was essentially the same as king; however, his appointment had to be approved by Rome and he governed under the authority of the Roman procurator. Though Caiaphas officially held the office, many recognized his father-in-law, Annas, as the true power behind the throne.

Annas was originally appointed high priest in AD 6 by Quirinius, but was later deposed by Valerius Gratus in AD 15. Nevertheless, he remained the head of a vast empire of organized corruption in Jerusalem. "He and his family were proverbial for their rapacity and greed."[2] After his removal from office, he wielded power through his son, Eleazar, and then his son-in-law, Caiaphas. In fact, his family held a virtually unbroken line of succession after Caiaphas through four more sons and a grandson.

In addition to the benefits of Sadducean aristocracy, he held a monopoly on animals deemed acceptable for sacrifice in the temple, which he sold "in the four famous 'booths of the sons of Annas' on the Mount of Olives, with a branch within the precincts of the temple itself."[3] According to the Law of Moses, the priests were to determine which animals were of sufficient quality for sacrifice. And, of course, Annas controlled the priests.

When Jesus cleansed the temple of what He called "robbers" (Matt. 21:13), several religious authorities demanded to know, "By what authority are You doing these things, and who gave You this authority?" (Matt. 21:23). Understandably, they could not imagine one man challenging the Annas crime family without the backing of someone immensely powerful. When they discovered Him to be acting alone, the plot to seize Him began.

A casual observer at the second trial might have been impressed by the religious zeal of Caiaphas, who "tore his robes and said, 'He has blasphemed!'" (Matt. 26:65) when Jesus claimed to be the Messiah. In reality, though, he and Annas wanted Jesus dead for two other reasons. First, He dared to defy the high priest's sovereign control over the temple. Second—and more importantly—He was bad for business.

residence of Annas—around three or four o'clock in the morning—John was permitted inside. His acquaintance with Annas most likely came by way of his family's wealth and social status.

As Peter entered the great hall of Annas's residence, the doorkeeper recognized him as a disciple. His denial of Jesus would be the first of three the Lord had predicted earlier (John 13:38).

Take note of John's detail concerning the fire—it was a *charcoal* fire.

John includes this seemingly insignificant feature to imprint on the readers' minds the image of Peter looking across a fire and denying His Master. Later, John will recall this image around another charcoal fire (21:9).

— 18:19-21 —

Some experts have called into question the historicity of the Gospel accounts, noting that the trials of Jesus before the Jewish authorities didn't fit the established protocol. However, the illegality of the trials is precisely the point in the Gospels. Jewish tradition carefully regulated the conduct of criminal trials, even more so than civil cases. No trial was to be held in secret or at night, and the only proper place to hear criminal cases was the "Hall of Judgment" in the temple. Furthermore, when hearing evidence, the accused could not be compelled to testify in his own case. All charges had to be substantiated by multiple corroborating witnesses.

Annas broke Sanhedrin rules by asking Jesus directly about His followers and His teaching, hoping to hear something incriminating. At first blush, Jesus' response appears insolent; however, He was merely pointing out the proper procedure. In a present-day American courtroom, council for the defense might have said, "Objection! According to *Mishnah: Sanhedrin* 3:3-4, the accused may not be compelled to present evidence against himself; furthermore, the presiding judge may not examine a witness (or the accused)."

Jesus then called for witnesses to testify. Everything He had said and done took place in the presence of multitudes. According to Jewish custom, conflicting testimonies could not condemn the accused, only acquit him. Jesus knew that a fair polling of witnesses would either exonerate Him of all charges or cancel the false testimony of the religious leaders.

— 18:22-24 —

Brutality was not permitted in the courtroom, yet one of the guards stepped in front of Jesus and punched His face. Jesus maintained perfect composure and responded with a reasonable request. He said, in effect, "If My objection should be overruled, state the legal precedent. If it should be sustained, I should not be punished for being right."

Having established the fact that no one had testified against Him and that He wasn't guilty of anything more than allowing Annas to make a fool of himself, the old high priest had nothing more to say. Clearly,

THE MIS-TRIALS OF JESUS

	Rule	Primary Source
#1	No trials were to occur during the night hours (before the morning sacrifice).	Mishnah: Sanhedrin 4:1
#2	Trials were not to occur on the eve of a Sabbath or during festivals.	Mishnah: Sanhedrin 4:1
#3	All trials were to be public; secret trials were forbidden.	Mishnah: Sanhedrin 1:6
#4	All trials were to be held in the Hall of Judgment in the temple area.	Mishnah: Sanhedrin 11:2
#5	Capital cases required a minimum of twenty-three judges.	Mishnah: Sanhedrin 4:1
#6	An accused person could not testify against himself.	Mishnah: Sanhedrin 3:3-4
#7	Someone was required to speak on behalf of the accused.	
#8	Conviction required the testimony of two or three witnesses to be in perfect alignment.	Deuteronomy 17:6-7; 19:15-20
#9	Witnesses for the prosecution were to be examined and cross-examined extensively.	Mishnah: Sanhedrin 4:1
#10	Capital cases were to follow a strict order, beginning with arguments by the defense, then arguments for conviction.	Mishnah: Sanhedrin 4:1
#11	All Sanhedrin judges could argue for aquittal, but not all could argue for conviction.	Mishnah: Sanhedrin 4:1
#12	The high priest should not participate in the questioning.	
#13	Each witness in a capital case was to be examined individually, not in the presence of other witnesses.	Mishnah: Sanhedrin 3:6
#14	The testimony of two witnesses found to be in contradiction rendered both invalid.	Mishnah: Sanhedrin 5:2
#15	Voting for conviction and sentencing in a capital case was to be conducted individually, beginning with the youngest, so younger members would not be influenced by the voting of the elder members.	Mishnah: Sanhedrin 4:2
#16	Verdicts in capital cases were to be handed down only during daylight hours.	Mishnah: Sanhedrin 4:1
#17	The members of the Sanhedrin were to meet in pairs all night, discuss the case, and reconvene for the purpose of confirming the final verdict and imposing sentence.	Mishnah: Sanhedrin 4:1
#18	Sentencing in a capital case was not to occur until the following day.	Mishnah: Sanhedrin 4:1

Secondary Source	Actual Practice
Laurna L. Berg, "The Illegalities of Jesus' Religious and Civil Trials," (*Bibliotheca Sacra*, Vol. 161, No. 643, July - September, 2004), 330 - 342	Jesus was taken to Annas, Caiaphas, and the Sanhedrin at night.
Ibid.	The trials occurred at night during the Passover celebration.
Ibid.	Jesus was taken before the Sanhedrin at night for questioning and was immediately delared "guilty." Only His official sentencing took place during the day.
Ibid.	Jesus was first taken to Annas, then Caiaphas, before He was put before the Sanhedrin.
Ibid.	We don't know how many judges were present. The trials took place at night during a festival.
Ibid.	The Sanhedrin convicted Jesus on His own words and did not see the need for witnesses.
Darrell L. Bock, "Jesus v. Sanhedrin: Why Jesus 'lost' his trial," (*Christianity Today*, Vol. 42, No. 4, April 6, 1998), 49.	No one spoke for Jesus and when He objected to the illegality of the proceeding, He was struck in the face.
	The prosecution sought witnesses against Jesus, but their testimony conflicted.
	Witnesses were sought against Jesus for the purpose of conviction, not to aquit Him or even find the truth.
Berg, "Illegalities"	No one spoke in Jesus' defense, neither before the accusations, nor after.
Ibid.	The chief priests and the council sought witnesses against Jesus.
Bock, "Jesus v. Sanhedrin"	Both Annas and Caiaphas interrogated Jesus directly, asking questions designed to incriminate Him.
Berg, "Illegalities"	We don't know how many witnesses were brought to testify at any given time.
Ibid.	
Ibid.	The members of the Sanhedrin voted simultaneously and nearly rioted.
Ibid.	The Sanhedrin convicted Jesus and condemned Him right away, then reconvened the next day to give the appearance of order.
	We see only a rush to judgment and no indication that the judges met for any reason, least of all to find Jesus "not guilty."
Ibid.	The Sanhedrin convicted Jesus and condemned Him right away, then reconvened the next day to give the appearance of order.

At the east end of the Royal Portico in the temple, seventy-one elders sat in semicircular rows around an area resembling a threshing floor. The Sanhedrin officially met here to set national and religious policy and to rule on civil and criminal cases. All of their deliberations and decisions were open to the public.

the object of the trial was not to discover truth; that is why Jesus had refused to cooperate. Without another word, "Annas sent Him bound to Caiaphas" (18:24). He had hoped Jesus would make things easier by implicating Himself, but the Lord deftly applied the Sanhedrin's own rules of jurisprudence—and He had the truth on His side. Convicting Jesus of a capital crime and making it credible for the sake of popular opinion would not be easy.

— 18:25-27 —

Unlike Matthew and Mark, John does not include the details of the Lord's trial before Caiaphas, who officially held the position of high priest (unlike his father-in-law). Unfortunately, justice didn't fare any better in this trial than the last (Matt. 26:57-68; Mark 14:53-65). While the hearing appeared more legitimate—conducted by the actual high priest and attended by several members of the Sanhedrin—it violated many of the same rules. The trial was held in secret, at night, and in the high priest's palace instead of the council's meeting hall. Furthermore, no advocate for the accused had been provided, and the council pressed the case against Jesus rather than impartially weighing evidence.

To maintain at least the appearance of propriety, the council disbanded before daylight. According to their rules, the members were to meet in pairs, share a sparse meal, and discuss the case exhaustively in preparation for a final ruling the following day. Instead, they took turns abusing the accused. Meanwhile, out in the courtyard, Peter fulfilled His Master's prophecy. Two more denials completed his failure.

• • •

As the first two trials of Jesus came to a close, we see how He would respond to the injustice of the next four. The Lord accepted that He would not receive justice from men. He knew that the world was—then as now—polluted with sin and ruled by corrupt people. So He did not expect justice from the courts, nor did He seek the approval of people. Instead, the Son submitted to the will of the Father, who permitted injustice to advance His plan. If someone asked a question for the sake of greater understanding, Jesus simply and directly spoke truth in response. Moreover, He refused to allow anger or bitterness on His part to distract anyone from seeing that truth—should anyone truly desire to. Throughout His ordeal, He entrusted Himself to the One who will ultimately and inevitably judge every soul righteously.

APPLICATION: JOHN 18:1-27

Enduring Injustice with Grace

I can think of few situations more personally challenging than enduring injustice alone and unnoticed. Because we bear the image of God, justice satisfies a deep-seated, God-given need; however, because we are polluted with sin, our desire for justice becomes a supremely selfish pursuit. Outrage demands satisfaction. Bitterness demands revenge. A self-centered hopelessness begs heaven for relief. Desperate isolation longs for an advocate, while an uncaring world idly watches our suffering. In that lonely crucible of unfairness, the silence of heaven can be deafening.

Perhaps you are currently suffering in obscurity. Slander has sullied your reputation. Gossip has isolated you from those you respect. A false accusation has turned the course of your life. Persecution has fallen upon you instead of those who are genuinely guilty. Let me assure you, the Lord does hear your cries for help and hope, and He has not ignored you. Justice will be served, although not as you might want—or when.

Jesus promised neither to take us out of the world nor to prevent the world's oppression. Instead, He prayed that we would be preserved through trials and persecutions (John 17:15). Therefore, He will not preserve us *from* injustice; rather, He has promised to preserve us *through* injustice. Moreover, He promised glory on the other side of our suffering. The agony you suffer—though it feels overwhelming—will not go to waste. If you allow it, this experience can be the means by which God brings you His greatest blessings.

George Matheson expressed this well in his book *Thoughts for Life's Journey:*

> My soul, reject not the place of thy prostration! It has ever been thy robing-room for royalty. Ask the great ones of the past what has been the spot of their prosperity; they will say, "It was the cold ground on which I once was lying." Ask Abraham; he will point you to the sacrifice on Moriah. Ask Joseph; he will direct you to his dungeon. Ask Moses; he will date his fortune from his danger in the Nile. Ask Ruth; she will bid you build her monument in the field of her toil. Ask David; he will tell you that his songs came from the night. Ask Job; and he will remind you that God answered him out of the whirlwind. Ask Peter; he will extol his submersion in the sea. Ask John; he will give the palm to Patmos. Ask Paul; he will attribute his inspiration to the light which struck him blind. Ask one more—the Son of Man. Ask Him whence has come His rule over the world. He will answer, "From the cold ground on which I was lying—the Gethsemane ground; I received My sceptre there." Thou too, my soul, shalt be garlanded by Gethsemane. The cup thou fain wouldst pass from thee will

be thy coronet in the sweet by-and-by. The hour of thy loneliness will crown thee. The day of thy depression will regale thee. It is thy *desert* that will break forth into singing; it is the trees of thy silent *forest* that will clap their hands. . . .

The voice of God to thine evening will be this, "Thy treasure is hid in the ground where thou wert lying."[4]

Shortly after His prayer on our behalf, Jesus endured the worst injustice any human can experience. No one was ever more innocent than Jesus. Few were ever more hypocritical and corrupt than Annas, Caiaphas, the temple elite, or Herod Antipas. Perhaps reflecting on how Jesus conducted Himself during that awful time, Peter wrote to Christian slaves facing persecution, "What credit is there if, when you sin and are harshly treated, you endure it with patience? But if when you do what is right and suffer for it you patiently endure it, this finds favor with God" (1 Pet. 2:20).

One day, the Lord will return and He will restore justice. In the last day, truth will reign supreme and all who have suffered injustice will be vindicated, just as Jesus was vindicated by His resurrection. In the meantime, submit your need to be heard to the sovereign plan of God. Stop striving for vindication. Speak the truth in love and without apology to appropriate parties. Take comfort in the fact that your Savior understands your struggle.

Rush to Judgment
JOHN 18:28–19:16

NASB

28 Then they led Jesus from Caiaphas into the ªPraetorium, and it was early; and they themselves did not enter into the ªPraetorium so that they would not be defiled, but might eat the Passover. 29 Therefore Pilate went out to them and said, "What accusation do you bring against this Man?" 30 They answered and said to him, "If this Man were not an evildoer, we would not have delivered Him to you." 31 So Pilate said to them, "Take Him yourselves, and judge Him according to your law."

NLT

28 Jesus' trial before Caiaphas ended in the early hours of the morning. Then he was taken to the headquarters of the Roman governor.* His accusers didn't go inside because it would defile them, and they wouldn't be allowed to celebrate the Passover. 29 So Pilate, the governor, went out to them and asked, "What is your charge against this man?"

30 "We wouldn't have handed him over to you if he weren't a criminal!" they retorted.

31 "Then take him away and judge

NASB

The Jews said to him, "We are not permitted to put anyone to death," ³²to fulfill the word of Jesus which He spoke, signifying by what kind of death He was about to die.

³³Therefore Pilate entered again into the Praetorium, and summoned Jesus and said to Him, "Are You the King of the Jews?" ³⁴Jesus answered, "Are you saying this ªon your own initiative, or did others tell you about Me?" ³⁵Pilate answered, "I am not a Jew, am I? Your own nation and the chief priests delivered You to me; what have You done?" ³⁶Jesus answered, "My kingdom ªis not of this world. If My kingdom were of this world, then My servants would be fighting so that I would not be handed over to the Jews; but as it is, My kingdom is not ᵇof this realm." ³⁷Therefore Pilate said to Him, "So You are a king?" Jesus answered, "You say *correctly* that I am a king. For this I have been born, and for this I have come into the world, to testify to the truth. Everyone who is of the truth hears My voice." ³⁸Pilate said to Him, "What is truth?"

And when he had said this, he went out again to the Jews and said to them, "I find no guilt in Him. ³⁹But you have a custom that I release someone ªfor you at the Passover; do you wish then that I release ªfor you the King of the Jews?" ⁴⁰So they cried out again, saying, "Not this Man, but Barabbas." Now Barabbas was a robber.

19:1 Pilate then took Jesus and ªscourged Him. ²And the soldiers twisted together a crown of thorns and put it on His head, and put a purple robe on Him; ³and they *began* to come up to Him and say, "Hail, King of the Jews!" and to give Him slaps *in the face.* ⁴Pilate came out again and said to them, "Behold, I

NLT

him by your own law," Pilate told them.

"Only the Romans are permitted to execute someone," the Jewish leaders replied. ³²(This fulfilled Jesus' prediction about the way he would die.*)

³³Then Pilate went back into his headquarters and called for Jesus to be brought to him. "Are you the king of the Jews?" he asked him.

³⁴Jesus replied, "Is this your own question, or did others tell you about me?"

³⁵"Am I a Jew?" Pilate retorted. "Your own people and their leading priests brought you to me for trial. Why? What have you done?"

³⁶Jesus answered, "My Kingdom is not an earthly kingdom. If it were, my followers would fight to keep me from being handed over to the Jewish leaders. But my Kingdom is not of this world."

³⁷Pilate said, "So you are a king?"

Jesus responded, "You say I am a king. Actually, I was born and came into the world to testify to the truth. All who love the truth recognize that what I say is true."

³⁸"What is truth?" Pilate asked. Then he went out again to the people and told them, "He is not guilty of any crime. ³⁹But you have a custom of asking me to release one prisoner each year at Passover. Would you like me to release this 'King of the Jews'?"

⁴⁰But they shouted back, "No! Not this man. We want Barabbas!" (Barabbas was a revolutionary.)

19:1 Then Pilate had Jesus flogged with a lead-tipped whip. ²The soldiers wove a crown of thorns and put it on his head, and they put a purple robe on him. ³"Hail! King of the Jews!" they mocked, as they slapped him across the face.

⁴Pilate went outside again and said to the people, "I am going to bring

am bringing Him out to you so that you may know that I find no guilt in Him." [5]Jesus then came out, wearing the crown of thorns and the purple robe. *Pilate* said to them, "Behold, the Man!" [6]So when the chief priests and the officers saw Him, they cried out saying, "Crucify, crucify!" Pilate said to them, "Take Him yourselves and crucify Him, for I find no guilt in Him." [7]The Jews answered him, "We have a law, and by that law He ought to die because He made Himself out *to be* the Son of God."

[8]Therefore when Pilate heard this statement, he was *even* more afraid; [9]and he entered into the [a]Praetorium again and said to Jesus, "Where are You from?" But Jesus gave him no answer. [10]So Pilate said to Him, "You do not speak to me? Do You not know that I have authority to release You, and I have authority to crucify You?" [11]Jesus answered, "You would have no authority [a]over Me, unless it had been given you from above; for this reason he who delivered Me to you has *the* greater sin." [12]As a result of this Pilate [a]made efforts to release Him, but the Jews cried out saying, "If you release this Man, you are no friend of Caesar; everyone who makes himself out *to be* a king [b]opposes Caesar."

[13]Therefore when Pilate heard these words, he brought Jesus out, and sat down on the judgment seat at a place called [a]The Pavement, but in [b]Hebrew, Gabbatha. [14]Now it was the day of preparation for the Passover; it was about the [a]sixth hour. And he said to the Jews, "Behold, your King!" [15]So they cried out, "Away with *Him,* away with *Him,* crucify Him!" Pilate said to them, "Shall I crucify your King?" The chief priests answered, "We have no king but Caesar."

him out to you now, but understand clearly that I find him not guilty." [5]Then Jesus came out wearing the crown of thorns and the purple robe. And Pilate said, "Look, here is the man!"

[6]When they saw him, the leading priests and Temple guards began shouting, "Crucify him! Crucify him!"

"Take him yourselves and crucify him," Pilate said. "I find him not guilty."

[7]The Jewish leaders replied, "By our law he ought to die because he called himself the Son of God."

[8]When Pilate heard this, he was more frightened than ever. [9]He took Jesus back into the headquarters* again and asked him, "Where are you from?" But Jesus gave no answer. [10]"Why don't you talk to me?" Pilate demanded. "Don't you realize that I have the power to release you or crucify you?"

[11]Then Jesus said, "You would have no power over me at all unless it were given to you from above. So the one who handed me over to you has the greater sin."

[12]Then Pilate tried to release him, but the Jewish leaders shouted, "If you release this man, you are no 'friend of Caesar.'* Anyone who declares himself a king is a rebel against Caesar."

[13]When they said this, Pilate brought Jesus out to them again. Then Pilate sat down on the judgment seat on the platform that is called the Stone Pavement (in Hebrew, *Gabbatha*). [14]It was now about noon on the day of preparation for the Passover. And Pilate said to the people,* "Look, here is your king!"

[15]"Away with him," they yelled. "Away with him! Crucify him!"

"What? Crucify your king?" Pilate asked.

"We have no king but Caesar," the leading priests shouted back.

NASB

¹⁶So he then handed Him over to them to be crucified.

18:28 ªI.e. governor's official residence
18:34 ªLit *from yourself* 18:36 ªOr *is not
derived from* ᵇLit *from here* 18:39 ªOr *to
you* 19:1 ªOr *had Him scourged* 19:9 ªI.e.
governor's official residence 19:11 ªLit *against*
19:12 ªLit *was seeking to* ᵇOr *speaks against*
19:13 ªGr *The Lithostrotos* ᵇI.e. Jewish Aramaic
19:14 ªPerhaps 6 a.m.

NLT

¹⁶Then Pilate turned Jesus over to them to be crucified.

So they took Jesus away.

18:28 Greek *to the Praetorium;* also in 18:33.
18:32 See John 12:32-33. 19:9 Greek *the
Praetorium.* 19:12 "Friend of Caesar" is a
technical term that refers to an ally of the
emperor. 19:14 Greek *Jewish people;* also
in 19:20.

By the time the first two trials had ended, Jesus was bleeding and badly bruised, but still, no official sentence had been handed down. The trials took place under cover of night and therefore would not have been considered legitimate by anyone the Sanhedrin hoped to impress: either the common Jews or their Roman overlords. John's narrative omits any mention of the third trial, perhaps because his point had been made sufficiently clear. The third Jewish trial was merely for show; it changed nothing.

Around six o'clock in the morning, the high priest summoned the council to the official place of judgment, a semicircular hall at the east end of the Royal Portico of the temple. The place was designed to resemble a threshing floor (see illustration, p. 348). In ancient times, farmers met at the place where wheat was separated from chaff in order to sort truth from evil. It was at the threshing floor where all matters of justice were decided before the entire community. While the trial took place in the light of day, in the proper venue, and before the eyes of the public, the religious leaders still violated their own rules. Their purpose was not to uncover the truth, but to find a charge that would satisfy a very specific set of requirements.

By the end of the third trial, the religious leaders settled on the charge of treason against Rome. Jesus had claimed to be the Christ, whom Jews widely regarded as their hope of expelling their Roman oppressors. This would convince the Roman governor to execute Jesus while discrediting Him as a blasphemer. They were convinced they could please everyone. The empire would be rid of a potential revolutionary; and once Jesus had been executed, the people would reject Him as just another false Messiah. It was an ideal solution that brought together an unlikely coalition of Pharisees (mostly scribes and lay teachers), Sadducees (aristocratic chief priests), and Zealots (underground revolutionaries).

As the religious leaders hauled Jesus from the temple to be condemned before the Roman procurator, Pontius Pilate, the charge against Jesus changed from blasphemy to treason. He would be judged by Roman law rather than the code of the Jews. His trial before Pilate followed a common four-step process:

- Accusation (18:28-29)
- Interrogation (18:33-35)
- Defense (18:36-38a)
- Verdict (18:38b)

— 18:28-29 —

The Roman overseer normally resided 70 miles (113 kilometers) north-west of Jerusalem in Caesarea, a city built by Herod the Great in honor of Caesar Augustus and designed to resemble Rome. When visiting Jerusalem, Pilate occupied the official residence of the procurator, called the *Praetorium*, which had been the palace of Herod the Great. Since it was the home of a Gentile, Jews were unwilling to enter the Praetorium for fear of becoming ritually defiled. John uses this irony to great effect. The religious authorities remained ritually pure even as they corruptly handed their victim over to Gentiles for execution.

www.HolyLandPhotos.org

After Herod Archelaus was deposed and banished to Gaul, the family palace became the official residence of the Roman procurator, which was Pilate at the time of Jesus' trials. To avoid ritual defilement during the Passover festival, the religious leaders refused to enter Pilate's house. He most likely heard their complaints in the courtyard bounded by the three towers on the left side of the photo.

Pontius Pilate was a personal friend of Lucius Sejanus, the de facto leader of Rome during Emperor Tiberius's extended retirement on the Isle of Capri. Soon after rising to power, Sejanus granted his friend one of the most coveted posts in the empire: procurator of Judea.

PONTIUS PILATE

JOHN 18:28-29

By the time Jesus began His public ministry, Emperor Tiberius had retired to a lavish villa on the island of Capri, leaving the day-to-day administration of the empire in the hands of his trusted right-hand man, Lucius Sejanus. Sejanus had earned the emperor's trust by transforming a small regiment of the imperial bodyguard into the Praetorian Guard, a kind of secret police force that became an influential factor in Roman politics. Moreover, he shrewdly eliminated all of his political rivals through slick maneuvering and violent intrigue. One of the rivals he destroyed was Drusus, the emperor's own son, whom he slowly poisoned with the help of the unfortunate man's wife.

With Drusus dead of seemingly natural causes, Sejanus enjoyed ruling as the de facto leader of Rome and he saw to it that his friend Pontius Pilate received one of the most prestigious appointments in the empire: procurator of Judea. While extremely challenging, the post offered unlimited potential for political greatness in the empire. Sejanus wanted a strong ruler to keep Judea peacefully subservient despite the Judeans' mounting discontent.

The historian Philo of Alexandria described Pilate as "a man of a very inflexible disposition, and very merciless as well as very obstinate."[5] Pilate's inflexibility had served him well in the past, but it nearly became his undoing in Judea. Where finesse was required, he brought brute force. He failed to understand the delicate balance between autonomy and control needed to govern Judea. Soon after taking command from his headquarters in Caesarea-by-the-Sea, Pilate sent a clear message to Jerusalem, letting them know that he was in charge. Normally, the procurator's army wintered in Caesarea, but Pilate ordered them to spend the winter in Jerusalem. Moreover, he ordered them to bear Caesar's image on their shields and to display it in key locations throughout the city. He determined that Jerusalem should be treated like all other conquered nations. Unfortunately, this violated Jewish law prohibiting "graven images" (Deut. 4:15-18).

Before long, a large delegation of temple leaders marched en masse to Caesarea in protest. The resulting standoff became a test of wills. For Pilate, to remove the images would be a humiliating show of weakness, yet keeping the peace was his sole responsibility. The Jewish leaders refused to go home until the images were removed, which caused Pilate to respond with force. The Jewish historian Josephus described the procurator's means of breaking the stalemate.

> On the sixth day [of the protest] he ordered his soldiers to have their weapons [hidden], while he came and sat upon his judgment seat, which seat was so prepared in the open place of the city, that it concealed the army that lay ready to oppress them: and when the Jews petitioned him again, he gave a signal to the soldiers to encompass

them round, and threatened that their punishment should be no less than immediate death, unless they would leave off disturbing him, and go their ways home. But they threw themselves upon the ground, and laid their necks bare, and said they would take their death very willingly, rather than the wisdom of their laws should be transgressed; upon which Pilate was deeply affected with their firm resolution to keep their laws inviolable, and presently commanded the images to be carried back from Jerusalem to Caesarea.[6]

Not long after, Pilate engaged in another standoff, which he ended with a brutal slaughter. Within days, Judean leaders petitioned Tiberius for Pilate's removal. At last, the procurator's hostile policies caught up with him, and at a very unfortunate time. Back in Rome, Tiberius had discovered that Sejanus had poisoned his son and ordered him executed. As the citizens of Rome dragged the mutilated body of Sejanus around the streets, Pilate suddenly found himself without a friend in the world.

— 18:30-32 —

The exchange between the Jewish officials and their governor illustrates the animosity that existed between them. Their sarcastic reply said, in effect, "If this man were not guilty of something serious, we wouldn't be here, Pilate." Moreover, they appeared to expect Pilate's unquestioning cooperation. Romans were not opposed to killing an individual in exchange for civil peace, and Pilate certainly didn't mind killing Jews. However, he already had two strikes against him, so he proceeded with caution.

When Pilate challenged the Jewish leaders to prosecute Jesus according to Jewish law, the leaders revealed their problem. Rome generally allowed conquered civilizations to govern themselves, but reserved capital punishment for itself. The Jews wanted Jesus dead but lacked the authority to kill Him.

John's editorial note refers to Jesus' prediction that He would be "lifted up" on a cross (3:14; 8:28; 12:32-33), not stoned per the Jewish method of execution.

— 18:33-38 —

Once an accusation was made, the defendant was interrogated. This was his opportunity to tell his side of the story. Pilate asked Jesus *the* pertinent question, presumably because he already knew the official charge against Jesus. It's very likely Pilate had witnessed His Triumphal

Entry just days earlier (12:13). He wanted to know if Jesus was, in fact, in the process of overthrowing the government in Judea. There was no simple answer to the procurator's question. Jesus didn't come to lead the Hebrews in a military or political uprising, yet the coming of God's kingdom would, in fact, change everything.

Pilate wanted to know if Jesus was a threat to the rule of Rome. He was, but not in the way Pilate feared. Kingdoms of earth are founded upon power—military might, intellectual prowess, political cunning, financial abundance, social advantage. The kingdom of heaven is founded upon truth, and the arrival of the Messiah on a lonely Bethlehem night was an invasion. Consequently, each individual must choose which kingdom he or she will serve: the kingdoms of earth or the kingdom of God, kingdoms founded upon power or the kingdom founded upon truth.

Jesus reassured Pilate, in effect, "Not to worry, Procurator. Because My kingdom is founded upon truth, not power, My followers are not arming for a physical war."

Pilate spurned Jesus' choice for truth over power.

"What is truth?" indeed! The Roman world was not much different from ours today. Pilate didn't rise to power and prominence by championing the cause of truth. The Romans were relentlessly pragmatic. Truth is the tool of expediency. In their minds, "history is written by the victors" and truth is whatever the powerful say it is. But according to Jesus, choosing between truth and expediency is how one chooses which kingdom he or she will serve.

Jesus presented Pilate with a choice—the same choice He offers us: compromise truth and advance your status in the kingdom of this world, or walk in the light of truth and receive unseen rewards of God's kingdom.

Pilate could not afford the political no-win scenario presented to him that morning. His friend Sejanus had been executed as a traitor, so Pilate would not likely survive another disagreement with Jewish aristocrats. Each time they had appealed to Rome, they always gained the upper hand. And the last letter he received from Tiberius made it clear he had better respect Jewish sensibilities or suffer the end of his career . . . or worse. Now Jesus stood before him, innocent of any crime against Rome yet condemned by a riotous crowd that insisted He was a serious threat to Tiberius.

John does not record the Lord's fifth trial before Herod Antipas. According to Luke 23:6-12, Pilate tried to pawn off his problem by sending

Jesus to Antipas, son of Herod the Great and the current ruler of Galilee. But Antipas would have none of it. After humiliating Jesus, he returned Him to Pilate wearing one of his own royal garments as a joke. Pilate's gesture had gained him a much-needed friend in Antipas, but Jesus remained his problem to solve.

Eventually Pilate had to render a verdict. Having heard the accusation, interrogated the defendant, and heard His defense (John 18:36), Pilate declared, "I find no guilt in Him" (18:38).

— 18:39-40 —

Antipas wouldn't take Jesus off Pilate's hands, so he needed to resolve the issue another way. A potential solution sat in a cell roughly two thousand feet from the Praetorium: a known "robber." But don't mistake him for a petty thief; the Greek term describes what we would call a terrorist. Rome hated robbers and pirates, who disrupted trade over land and sea. But in Judea, robbery and murder came with a political agenda.

The man's name was reported to be Barabbas, which has the nonsensical meaning "son of a father." It might have been a "John Doe" kind of alias adopted for the sake of protecting his family from Roman retribution. Regardless, he was a notorious enemy of the state, a thief and a killer, the kind of man Rome relished the opportunity to kill in the most excruciating manner known: crucifixion.

According to the custom of Pilate's predecessors, one man could be released from prison during the Passover festival. He thought he could tempt the mob into releasing Jesus by giving them a less attractive option. If the Jews chose to release Barabbas, a genuine enemy of Rome, they risked their friendship with Tiberius. Certainly they would choose to release the innocent man rather than invite the wrath of Caesar. But Pilate underestimated the religious leaders' hatred for Jesus.

— 19:1 —

Pilate's scheme didn't solve his problem; it merely tightened the political vise closing around him. They had called his bluff and now *he* would be the one turning a dangerous criminal loose to harass Rome further. Desperate to find a solution and reluctant to release Barabbas, Pilate hoped to satisfy the mob's bloodlust by sentencing Jesus to "the halfway death."

John's simple statement, "Pilate then took Jesus and scourged Him," is shockingly plain. Jesus was led to the Roman garrison (the Fortress of

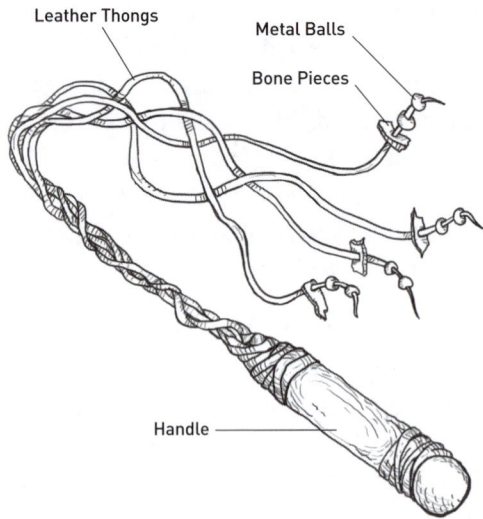

Leather Thongs

Metal Balls

Bone Pieces

Handle

Robert Gaither

A *flagrum*, the brutal whip used by Roman torturers (see note on 19:1).

Antonia) adjacent to the temple and given over to an expert in torture called a *lictor,* who used a whip with long, leather tails called a *flagrum.* The leather straps could be merely knotted or, if the *lictor* wanted to inflict more damage, he could choose a whip with small, metal weights or even bits of sheep bone braided into the straps. "The iron balls would cause deep contusions, and the leather thongs and sheep bones would cut into the skin and subcutaneous tissues. Then as the flogging continued, the lacerations would tear into the underlying skeletal muscles and produce quivering ribbons of bleeding flesh."[7] According to a forensic pathologist, the scourging typically resulted in "rib fractures and severe lung bruises and lacerations with bleeding into the chest cavity and partial or complete pneumothorax (collapse of the lung)."[8] The *lictor* was an expert in the art of torture and knew exactly how to beat a man within an inch of his life.

— 19:2-3 —

Because a scourging could potentially send the victim into shock in less than five minutes, the soldiers turned the event into a spectacle, taking delight in humiliating the victim. Three or four lashes would be followed by taunting. Then, as the victim recovered, more lashes. This continued until the victim could bear no more without dying.

When the *lictor* completed his gruesome task, he draped Antipas's royal cloak over Jesus' tattered, swollen flesh and sent Him back to Pilate wearing a crown of thorns, in mockery of His alleged kingship.

— 19:4-7 —

Pilate hoped that seeing Jesus humiliated and beaten nearly to death would satisfy the angry mob in his courtyard, but they would accept nothing less than a sentence of crucifixion. Pilate challenged the religious leaders to defy Rome by carrying out the death sentence themselves. But their reply took the procurator off guard. The title "Son of God" was particularly meaningful to Romans. In fact, Caesar Augustus declared himself the son of a god because he was heir to the power and titles of Julius Caesar, who had been declared a god. Moreover, the title "Son of God" cast new light on the Lord's earlier statement, "My kingdom is not of this world" (18:36).

— 19:8-11 —

At this point, Pilate began to panic. Before, he had written off Jesus as a harmless lunatic. His earlier question, "Are You the King of the Jews?" (18:33), was patronizing, prompting Jesus' question in return, "Are you asking this on your own initiative?" (my rendering). This time, Pilate asked in earnest, "Where are You from?"

Jesus had already answered the question, so there was no need to answer again. When Pilate threatened to exercise power over the Son

Ritmeyer Archaeological Design

Long before Herod the Great began construction on the temple complex, the Hasmonean rulers (a priestly family of Jews) constructed a citadel. Herod fortified and expanded the structure in order to secure and guard his new temple complex. To allay Roman fears that he was preparing for war, he named it Antonia, after his friend Mark Antony. Soon after his death, the fortress became a garrison for Roman soldiers as Jerusalem fell under direct Roman control.

of God, Jesus clarified His earlier statement about the kingdoms of earth and the kingdom of heaven. The world has changed. The rule of evil, which prizes power over truth, will fall. Its days are numbered. Truth trumps power—if not sooner, then ultimately. That's because no one on earth can exercise power unless it is permitted by God. And each must give account for his or her use of power, whether in defense of truth or in seeking its destruction. Jesus reminded Pilate that his power had been granted from above and that he was subject to divine judgment.

This was a final plea for Pilate to submit to the kingdom of God rather than the kingdom of Tiberius (or any other earthly kingdom).

In Jesus' final statement to Pilate, He pronounced a grave judgment on "he who delivered me to you." The "he" could have been Satan, Judas, Annas, or Caiaphas; each played a key role in trying to destroy Jesus. They did not act alone, however. The priests were culpable, as were the members of the Sanhedrin, and the crowd that called for crucifixion. Therefore, I suggest that the "he" applies to each Hebrew who took part in delivering Jesus over for execution. It is likely the Lord's accusers could hear this dialog, so He may have said this as a warning to be personally applied by each individual.

While Pilate ultimately rejected truth in order to preserve his power, Jesus recognized that he sinned in ignorance. The people who had handed Him over for execution committed the "greater sin" because they did so with every benefit of divine revelation. They prized the Lord's covenant with Abraham. They memorized the Scriptures. They studied the prophecies. Yet, despite their daily interaction with divine truth, they chose to sin. While Pilate disposed of a political nuisance, the Hebrew leaders plotted to execute their Messiah.

— 19:12-16 —

By now, Pilate was frantically searching for a way to release Jesus without losing the favor of the Jewish aristocracy and jeopardizing his advancement in the kingdom of Tiberius. Finally, he brought Jesus out to them and tried to shame the crowd into backing down. But the mob wielded the ultimate threat: they planned to inform Tiberius that Pilate had supported another king.

Pilate had to choose. Tiberius or Jesus? The kingdoms of earth or the kingdom of heaven? Power or truth?

The pressure of the world proved too great for Pilate. As is true of most politicians, public popularity trumped personal integrity. When

forced to choose, he elected to trust in power, to serve a kingdom of the world. Without another word, he moved to the official place of judgment called the *bema*. This was a raised platform from which official decrees were read, including verdicts and sentences in criminal trials. Pilate decided to appease the Jewish authorities. "Behold, your King!" The mob shouted back its choice: "We have no king but Caesar." And with that, the crowd sided with the kingdoms of the world.

John notes the time as noon on the day of preparation of the Passover; that is, the fourteenth day of Nisan. John's reference to time and day always has theological or symbolic meaning. At noon on the day of preparation, priests in the temple began slaughtering the Passover lambs in keeping with Exodus 12:6. Because they had so many worshipers to serve—as many as 100,000 pilgrims—the priests worked through the afternoon until sundown. John wanted to stress that Jesus had been sentenced at noon and would be hanging on the cross as the Passover lambs were being sacrificed in the temple.

• • •

The trials of Jesus Christ—all of them unfair and prejudiced—are now history. Centuries have reduced the bodies of Jesus' enemies to nothing. God only knows about their souls. Nevertheless, the choice they faced remains ours today: Truth or power? God's way or the way of the world? Faith or works? Grace or pride? Pilate tried in vain to seek a middle way, a scheme in which he could serve both or neither without having to choose, but there is none. Jesus calls all people to serve His kingdom rather than the kingdoms of the world. And so we must choose.

APPLICATION: JOHN 18:28-19:16

The Road Not Taken

In 1920, Robert Frost intrigued us with the opening lines of his classic poem:

Two roads diverged in a yellow wood,
And sorry I could not travel both
And be one traveler, long I stood . . .[9]

Unfortunately, our journey through life brings us to forks in the road that are not so wistful or winsome. The choice we face is not between convention and curiosity as much as it is between truth and power, riches on earth or treasure in heaven, earthly success or spiritual purity, short-term comfort or eternal reward. And the urge to preserve our comfort in the here and now can powerfully override our decision to obey God. Let's face it: His rewards are often intangible and almost always delayed, which makes obedience a matter of trust.

Pontius Pilate stood at a critical juncture—for him, a choice having eternal impact. He had to decide which kingdom he would serve. To render a "not guilty" verdict and release Jesus would have certainly destroyed his political career and may have invited severe punishment from Rome. So, instead of submitting to the kingdom of God, Pilate set truth aside for the sake of power, earthly success, and short-term comfort.

Before we pass judgment and count ourselves righteous, let me challenge your ethics with a test. What if you were a clerk in the German army, busily typing out orders, and the command to round up Jews and dissenters crossed your desk? In a totalitarian regime, disobedience will almost certainly result in severe punishment, if not death. And for what? You will not likely be remembered for your stand. Another nameless, faceless clerk will be pressed into service after your removal anyway. What would be gained? Certainly the satisfaction that you did what was right. But that will likely come at the expense of great suffering.

How about a situation not so clear-cut? You have been asked by the highest-ranking member of your employer's office—the person with the most power and least accountability—to do something your conscience clearly tells you is wrong. What do you do? No lives are at stake. It's unlikely anything tragic will result. Besides, what would be gained by refusing? When you are fired, would the satisfaction of doing what is right taste as sweet? Or, as you tell the story to your coworkers and share their outrage, will you shrug off your responsibility with the words, "A command is a command; I'm only following orders"?

The road we travel forks more than once. Our initial decision to trust in Jesus Christ is the most crucial choice we will make, but it is the first of many. Each and every day, we must choose which kingdom we will serve. Will you submit to truth or succumb to power?

Death on a Cross
JOHN 19:17-37

NASB

17 They took Jesus, therefore, and He went out, ᵃbearing His own cross, to the place called the Place of a Skull, which is called in ᵇHebrew, Golgotha. 18 There they crucified Him, and with Him two other men, one on either side, and Jesus in between. 19 Pilate also wrote an inscription and put it on the cross. It was written, "JESUS THE NAZARENE, THE KING OF THE JEWS." 20 Therefore many of the Jews read this inscription, for the place where Jesus was crucified was near the city; and it was written in ᵃHebrew, Latin *and* in Greek. 21 So the chief priests of the Jews were saying to Pilate, "Do not write, 'The King of the Jews'; but that He said, 'I am King of the Jews.'" 22 Pilate answered, "What I have written I have written."

23 Then the soldiers, when they had crucified Jesus, took His outer garments and made four parts, a part to every soldier and *also* the ᵃtunic; now the tunic was seamless, woven ᵇin one piece. 24 So they said to one another, "Let us not tear it, but cast lots for it, *to decide* whose it shall be"; *this was* to fulfill the Scripture: "THEY DIVIDED MY OUTER GARMENTS AMONG THEM, AND FOR MY CLOTHING THEY CAST ᵃLOTS." 25 Therefore the soldiers did these things.

But standing by the cross of Jesus were His mother, and His mother's sister, Mary the *wife* of Clopas, and Mary Magdalene. 26 When Jesus then saw His mother, and the disciple whom He loved standing nearby, He said to His mother, "Woman, behold, your son!" 27 Then He said to the disciple, "Behold, your mother!" From that hour the disciple took her into his own *household*. 28 After this, Jesus, knowing that

NLT

17 Carrying the cross by himself, he went to the place called Place of the Skull (in Hebrew, *Golgotha*). 18 There they nailed him to the cross. Two others were crucified with him, one on either side, with Jesus between them. 19 And Pilate posted a sign on the cross that read, "Jesus of Nazareth,* the King of the Jews." 20 The place where Jesus was crucified was near the city, and the sign was written in Hebrew, Latin, and Greek, so that many people could read it.

21 Then the leading priests objected and said to Pilate, "Change it from 'The King of the Jews' to 'He said, I am King of the Jews.'"

22 Pilate replied, "No, what I have written, I have written."

23 When the soldiers had crucified Jesus, they divided his clothes among the four of them. They also took his robe, but it was seamless, woven in one piece from top to bottom. 24 So they said, "Rather than tearing it apart, let's throw dice* for it." This fulfilled the Scripture that says, "They divided my garments among themselves and threw dice for my clothing."* So that is what they did.

25 Standing near the cross were Jesus' mother, and his mother's sister, Mary (the wife of Clopas), and Mary Magdalene. 26 When Jesus saw his mother standing there beside the disciple he loved, he said to her, "Dear woman, here is your son." 27 And he said to this disciple, "Here is your mother." And from then on this disciple took her into his home.

28 Jesus knew that his mission was

NASB

all things had already been accomplished, to fulfill the Scripture, said, "I am thirsty." 29 A jar full of sour wine was standing there; so they put a sponge full of the sour wine upon *a branch of* hyssop and brought it up to His mouth. 30 Therefore when Jesus had received the sour wine, He said, "It is finished!" And He bowed His head and gave up His spirit.

31 Then the Jews, because it was the day of preparation, so that the bodies would not remain on the cross on the Sabbath (ªfor that Sabbath was a high day), asked Pilate that their legs might be broken, and *that* they might be taken away. 32 So the soldiers came, and broke the legs of the first man and of the other who was crucified with Him; 33 but coming to Jesus, when they saw that He was already dead, they did not break His legs. 34 But one of the soldiers pierced His side with a spear, and immediately blood and water came out. 35 And he who has seen has testified, and his testimony is true; and he knows that he is telling the truth, so that you also may believe. 36 For these things came to pass to fulfill the Scripture, "NOT A BONE OF HIM SHALL BE ªBROKEN." 37 And again another Scripture says, "THEY SHALL LOOK ON HIM WHOM THEY PIERCED."

19:17 ªLit *bearing the cross for Himself* ᵇI.e. Jewish Aramaic 19:20 ªI.e. Jewish Aramaic 19:23 ªGr *khiton,* the garment worn next to the skin ᵇLit *from the upper part through the whole* 19:24 ªLit *a lot* 19:31 ªLit *for the day of that Sabbath was great* 19:36 ªOr *crushed* or *shattered*

NLT

now finished, and to fulfill Scripture he said, "I am thirsty."* 29 A jar of sour wine was sitting there, so they soaked a sponge in it, put it on a hyssop branch, and held it up to his lips. 30 When Jesus had tasted it, he said, "It is finished!" Then he bowed his head and released his spirit.

31 It was the day of preparation, and the Jewish leaders didn't want the bodies hanging there the next day, which was the Sabbath (and a very special Sabbath, because it was the Passover). So they asked Pilate to hasten their deaths by ordering that their legs be broken. Then their bodies could be taken down. 32 So the soldiers came and broke the legs of the two men crucified with Jesus. 33 But when they came to Jesus, they saw that he was already dead, so they didn't break his legs. 34 One of the soldiers, however, pierced his side with a spear, and immediately blood and water flowed out. 35 (This report is from an eyewitness giving an accurate account. He speaks the truth so that you also may continue to believe.*) 36 These things happened in fulfillment of the Scriptures that say, "Not one of his bones will be broken,"* 37 and "They will look on the one they pierced."*

19:19 Or *Jesus the Nazarene.* 19:24a Greek *cast lots.* 19:24b Ps 22:18. 19:28 See Pss 22:15; 69:21. 19:35 Some manuscripts read *that you also may believe.* 19:36 Exod 12:46; Num 9:12; Ps 34:20. 19:37 Zech 12:10.

Regardless of one's position on the merits or morality of execution as a form of justice, everyone should agree there is nothing pleasant or attractive about putting someone to death. All instruments of death are ugly and brutal by their very nature, and trying to make them less horrific would be absurd. Nevertheless, execution has come a long way since the days of Christ; even the last one hundred years have seen significant changes.

Modern methods of carrying out capital punishment differ from ancient methods in two significant ways. First, modern executions are done in private, keeping the gallery of witnesses as small as possible. Ancient executions were public spectacles with an almost carnival-like atmosphere. The express purpose of a public execution was its perceived value as a deterrent to similar crimes. Second, modern executions are designed to bring on death as swiftly and painlessly as possible. Ancient methods were painstakingly crafted to extend the process of dying as long as possible, while maximizing agony.

Of all methods of execution, whether ancient or modern, none rival the practice of crucifixion in terms of cruelty. The ancient orator Cicero described crucifixion as "the worst extreme of the tortures inflicted upon slaves."[10] Tacitus called it a "despicable death."

According to the Greek historian Herodotus, the Persians invented the practice after experimenting with other means of delaying death, such as stoning, drowning, burning, boiling in oil, strangulation, and flaying. Eventually, the Persians began impaling particularly detestable criminals or enemies in order to keep them from defiling the ground, which their god, Ormuzd, had made sacred. Alexander the Great adopted crucifixion, which influenced the four generals who succeeded him, who passed it to the Carthaginians. The Romans inherited the practice from the Carthaginians and then found new ways to extend death and maximize pain.[11]

Crucifixion combined four qualities the Romans prized most in an execution: unrelenting agony, protracted death, public spectacle, and utter humiliation.

The victim typically endured scourging before crucifixion. The *lictor* could affect how long a person would survive on a cross by adjusting the degree to which he injured the victim. If the executioner wanted the victim to die very quickly, a scourge with jagged bits of sheep bone braided into the tails would rapidly cause shock so that death occurred swiftly. On the other hand, a lighter scourging with simple leather straps could result in the person lasting as long as a week on the cross. Merrill Unger states that there are "instances on record of persons surviving for nine days."[12]

This was the physical character of crucifixion that Jesus faced. The spiritual dimensions of His suffering are literally unimaginable. In taking my place on the cross, He bore the penalty of my sin, which is eternity in torment. He also suffered your penalty, which is also eternity in torment. This penalty, compounded by the sin of countless billions of individuals, poured out on the Son as He hung on the cross. By this act of sacrifice, Christ confronted evil on a cosmic level and through His suffering ensured its defeat. But we should not cling to the notion that Jesus was a helpless victim of a failed plan. Jesus did not die a martyr's death, nor did He die before completing His intended mission. On the contrary, while Pilate deluded himself with the notion that he wielded the power of life and death over Jesus, he in fact had none. He handed down the death sentence in obedience to his own inescapable compulsions and in perfect harmony with God's sovereign plan (Ps. 22; Isa. 53; Acts 2:22-23; 3:18).

At the appointed hour, Jesus began His lonely march toward His destined glory. But before entering the light of resurrection, He had to travel through darkness and suffering.

— 19:17 —

None of the Gospels mention much about the Lord's procession to the place of crucifixion, probably because it was a familiar sight to first-century readers all across the empire—as common as a funeral procession. The victim stood at the center of an imaginary square, with a soldier posted at each corner and the commander of the detail in the lead. The execution detail was called a *quarternio,* which served under the command of an *exactor mortis.*

The victim was typically forced—if he was physically able after scourging—to carry the crossbeam (called the *patibulum*) to the waiting vertical post (called the *stipes*). A sign called a *titulus* hung around the victim's neck bearing his name and a list of his crimes. The sign was nailed above the victim's head so that, once he was lifted up on the cross, everyone would know why he was hung to die.

The Romans had designated a place outside Jerusalem for the purpose of crucifying criminals. The locals nicknamed it "the place of the skull," perhaps because an outcropping of rock looked like a skull, or merely because it was a place of death. Three had been sentenced to die that day. Undoubtedly, more would suffer there within the next week.

— 19:18 —

John's readers needed no more description of Jesus' mode of execution than the short phrase, "they crucified Him." The details of the method were indelibly etched on their minds. However, twenty-first century Westerners need the help of historians and scientists to understand the nature of this terrible ordeal.

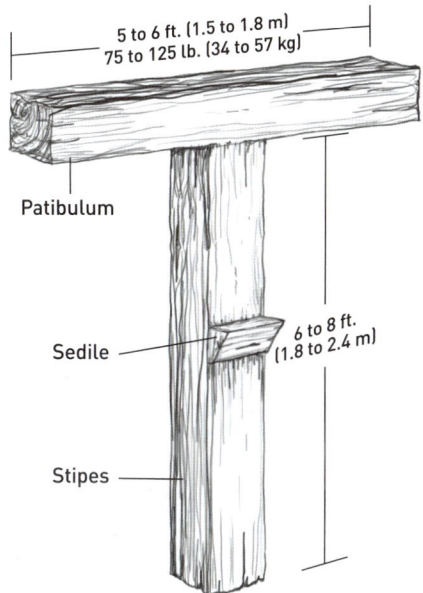

5 to 6 ft. (1.5 to 1.8 m)
75 to 125 lb. (34 to 57 kg)

Patibulum

Sedile — 6 to 8 ft. (1.8 to 2.4 m)

Stipes —

Robert Gaither

The Romans wasted nothing in the macabre art of execution, including wood and nails. Everything would be used again. Therefore, the *patibulum* (crossbeam) was attached to the top of the *stipes* (vertical member) with a mortise and tenon joint, which allowed them to dismantle the cross for the next victim more easily. Sometimes, to delay death and to prolong the victim's agony, the executioner attached a *sedile* (seat) between the victim's legs.

The execution detail laid the *patibulum* on the ground and attached it to the top of the *stipes,* using a mortise and tenon joint to form a giant capital *T.* The victim was stripped naked and placed against the wood and attached to the cross with his arms outstretched and feet flat against the face of the *stipes.* The victim was usually tied to the cross rather than nailed. Nails were expensive and the Romans wanted to extend the process of dying, which took much longer when suspended with rope instead of nails.

If, however, the executioner wanted to hasten death, he nailed the victim to the cross through the base of the palms and through the tops of the feet. Simulations, along with close examination of historical records, reveal that death usually came by way of exposure, dehydration, starvation, or fatigue asphyxia. In the case of asphyxia, the victim became too exhausted, dehydrated, and malnourished to pull in his next breath, which led to suffocation.

A victim nailed to a cross, like someone tied in place, also had to keep his body in constant motion to relieve the pain in his arms, chest, and legs, which only agitated the damaged nerves in the nail wounds.

Unless the guards broke the legs of the victim, the primary causes of death for nailed victims were likely hypovolemic shock (excessive blood loss), traumatic shock, or cardiac and respiratory arrest.[13]

We know Jesus was nailed to the cross because, later in John's Gospel, the disciple Thomas refers to the imprint of the nails in Jesus' hands (20:25-27). Furthermore, the Romans remained sensitive to Jewish sensibilities, so they hastened death to ensure the men would not be left hanging on their crosses during a very special Sabbath.

— 19:19-22 —

Pilate ordered the *titulus* prepared for Jesus to list His "crime" as being the King of the Jews, which enraged the temple officials, whom John refers to as "the chief priests of the Jews." Ordinarily, he called them "chief priests" or "Jews"—never both. In this case, he retained "of the Jews" to stress the irony of Jesus' title, "King *of the Jews*." The temple officials had earlier clarified their allegiance—"We have no king but Caesar" (19:15)—so, they demanded the *titulus* be altered. However, Pilate had grown sick of their demands. He had set truth and justice aside to retain their political favor and to avoid the wrath of Tiberius, so he refused to back down on this one detail.

Clearly, Pilate had been impacted by his encounter with Jesus and, apparently, saw some credence in His claims. However, we have credible evidence Pilate later clashed with the Samaritans and was recalled to Rome, where he was banished to Gaul and died by his own hand.

— 19:23-24 —

Before being nailed to the cross, Jesus was stripped naked, as were all victims of this humiliating death. Jews typically wore a *chiton* (undergarment against the skin) and at least one layer of *himation* (robe or cloak). Because cloth was a valuable commodity, His outer garments were ripped apart at the seams and divided among the *quarternio*. However, His seamless undergarment would have been far less valuable if torn.

John includes this detail to demonstrate the remarkable level of detail with which Jesus' crucifixion fulfilled prophecy given almost a thousand years before. David envisioned these details of the Messiah's crucifixion centuries before the method had been invented (Ps. 22).

— 19:25-30 —

John includes his eyewitness account of an intimate exchange between Jesus and His mother at the base of the cross. As a final detail of life,

Jesus placed His mother in John's care and then asked for something to drink. According to John, He did this in fulfillment of Scripture (either Ps. 22:15 or 69:21 is likely).

Someone nearby placed a sponge at the end of a hyssop branch, which tied in with the imagery of Passover. Later that evening, Jews would dip hyssop branches in the blood of their sacrificed lamb and then apply it to their doorposts and lintels (Exod. 12:22). The "sour wine" was commonly given with meals to soldiers and workers as an aid in reducing fever and giving refreshment.

After drinking the wine, Jesus drew in one last breath and cried, "*Tetelestai!*" [5055]. John chose this Greek term to translate Jesus' Aramaic. Archeologists have found papyrus tax receipts with *Tetelestai* written across them, meaning "paid in full." With Jesus' last breath on the cross, He declared the debt of sin canceled, completely satisfied. Then—as John declares emphatically—Jesus willingly gave over His spirit in death. No one took Jesus' life (John 10:17-18).

— 19:31-34 —

Jesus' death came relatively quickly. The combination of the "halfway death" scourging that He endured earlier, the blood loss and shock from the nails, and sheer exhaustion from the sleepless night before were enough to kill any man swiftly. However, it is best to take the phrase "gave up His spirit" (19:30) at face value. His life ended by choice. His life was not taken from Him.

Jews considered it an abomination to leave a corpse hanging overnight (Deut. 21:22-23), especially on the Sabbath and a feast day, so they requested the men's legs be broken to bring about death before nightfall. Some scientists have suggested the victims would quickly suffocate without the ability to push up with their legs. However, more recent research by a forensic pathologist offers a more plausible explanation.

> A single closed femoral (thigh bone) fracture may result in the loss of 2 liters of blood, and up to 4 liters of blood may be lost with fractures of both femoral bones. . . . The marked hemorrhage from the breaking of the legs and the severe pain would deepen the level of hypovolemic and traumatic shock, with a consequent drop in blood pressure and rapid development of congestion in the lower extremities, resulting in unconsciousness, coma, and death.[14]

Having taken a heavy maul to the legs of the other two victims, the soldiers found Jesus already dead. To be certain of death, one soldier took a short spear and rammed it into Jesus' body, probably through the rib cage, piercing the pericardial sac. He found what he was looking for. Blood mixed with clear fluid was an unmistakable sign of death.

— 19:35-37 —

John breaks his narrative with an extended parenthetical aside. John offers eyewitness testimony that Jesus did in fact die. More than sixty years later, a number of heresies would infect the communities of believers. Ironically, few false teachers in John's day doubted the deity of Christ; they challenged the reality of His humanity! One heresy, called "Docetism," claimed that Jesus merely seemed to be human, but was instead a divine apparition that could be seen and touched. Some of the so-called "Gnostic gospels" spin fanciful stories of Jesus appearing to eat without actually consuming food and then never needing to get rid of waste.

Some ancient critics may have claimed that Jesus didn't actually die, that he merely "swooned"; however, this was not likely John's chief concern. He fought hard against the notion that the Son of God was not fully human. John's detailed account of the physical evidence proved that Jesus inhabited a body like ours and died just as certainly as all humans will. This will bear witness to the literal bodily resurrection later in his narrative.

John augments his eyewitness testimony with Passover imagery (Exod. 12:46; Num. 9:12) and biblical prophecy (Ps. 34:20; Zech. 12:10).

• • •

I have often wondered what Barabbas later thought of the gift he received from a man he never knew. Did Barabbas want to know who endured his scourging, who carried his cross to the outskirts of town, who endured the gruesome, shameful death he had earned? Barabbas undoubtedly felt overwhelmingly relieved to avoid the cross, but did he ever understand that Jesus suffered death on behalf of all sinners— including him?

Make no mistake; we are guilty of sin and we deserve to suffer death as the just penalty of rebellion against our Creator. Justice cannot be set aside. This rebellion demands a penalty, and that penalty is eternal separation from God in a place of torment. Nevertheless, our Judge has delayed His final verdict. God so loved the world that He gave His one and only Son, so that everyone who believes in Him will not suffer eternal death, but have eternal life (John 3:16).

Jesus, though absolutely innocent, took the place of another man, a hopeless sinner, on the cross. Yes, Barabbas went free, but his unmerited freedom is merely a metaphor for a greater, more personal truth: It was *your place* on the cross He took. Jesus died *for you!*

APPLICATION: JOHN 19:17-37

A Fate Worse than Death on a Cross

In the quest to devise the most painful mode of execution possible, no one exceeded the Romans' capacity for cruelty in their particular variation on crucifixion. The Romans reserved crucifixion for slaves, deserters, revolutionaries, and the very worst criminals—people they considered less than human. Cicero wrote, "To bind a Roman citizen is a crime, to flog him is an abomination, to slay him is almost an act of murder: to crucify him is—what? There is no fitting word that can possibly describe so horrible a deed."[15]

Crucifixion gave the Romans extraordinary opportunity to inflict agony along with humiliation. Therefore, it became "one of the strongest means of maintaining order and security. Governors imposed this servile punishment especially on freedom fighters who tried to break away from Roman rule."[16]

So, imagine Pilate's surprise when the angry mob demanded the innocent take the place of the guilty on a cross. Imagine Barabbas's shock! As he sat on death row listening to the trial, he couldn't hear Pilate's side of the conversation. All he could hear was the roaring crowd in the distance:

"Barabbas . . . Crucify Him! Crucify Him! . . . His blood shall be on us and on our children!" (Matt. 27:21-23, 25)

Barabbas must have been overcome with dread upon hearing the guards approach his cell. I can only imagine his utter amazement to feel his shackles fall from his hands. The relief he felt must have been overwhelming as he was led to the end of the cell block and out into the light of day. His just punishment had been passed over. He was free!

I sometimes wonder, *What if Barabbas had said, "Freedom? I appreciate the offer, but I'd rather suffer the most excruciating death imaginable."* No one in his or her right mind would decline the offer to avoid death on a cross. So, why do people reject the opportunity to avoid a much worse fate: eternal torment in a place of eternal death? Why would anyone refuse to accept the free gift of eternal life, purchased for them by the suffering and death of Jesus Christ in their place?

What has been your response to the offer of grace?

A Miraculous Resurrection
JOHN 19:38–20:10

NASB

38 After these things Joseph of Arimathea, being a disciple of Jesus, but a secret *one* for fear of the Jews, asked Pilate that he might take away the body of Jesus; and Pilate granted permission. So he came and took away His body. 39 Nicodemus, who had first come to Him by night, also came, bringing a ᵃmixture of myrrh and aloes, about a hundred ᵇpounds *weight*. 40 So they took the body of Jesus and bound it in linen wrappings with the spices, as is the burial custom of the Jews. 41 Now in the place where He was crucified there was a garden, and in the garden a new tomb in which no one had yet been laid. 42 Therefore because of the Jewish day of preparation, since the tomb was nearby, they laid Jesus there.

20:1 Now on the first *day* of the week Mary Magdalene came early to the tomb, while it was still dark, and saw the stone *already* taken away from the tomb. 2 So she ran and came to Simon Peter and to the other disciple whom Jesus loved, and said to them, "They have taken away the Lord out of the tomb, and we do not know where they have laid Him." 3 So Peter and the other disciple went forth, and they were going to the tomb. 4 The two were running together; and the other disciple ran ahead faster than Peter and came to the tomb first; 5 and stooping and looking in,

NLT

38 Afterward Joseph of Arimathea, who had been a secret disciple of Jesus (because he feared the Jewish leaders), asked Pilate for permission to take down Jesus' body. When Pilate gave permission, Joseph came and took the body away. 39 With him came Nicodemus, the man who had come to Jesus at night. He brought about seventy-five pounds* of perfumed ointment made from myrrh and aloes. 40 Following Jewish burial custom, they wrapped Jesus' body with the spices in long sheets of linen cloth. 41 The place of crucifixion was near a garden, where there was a new tomb, never used before. 42 And so, because it was the day of preparation for the Jewish Passover* and since the tomb was close at hand, they laid Jesus there.

20:1 Early on Sunday morning,* while it was still dark, Mary Magdalene came to the tomb and found that the stone had been rolled away from the entrance. 2 She ran and found Simon Peter and the other disciple, the one whom Jesus loved. She said, "They have taken the Lord's body out of the tomb, and we don't know where they have put him!"

3 Peter and the other disciple started out for the tomb. 4 They were both running, but the other disciple outran Peter and reached the tomb first. 5 He stooped and looked in and saw the linen wrappings lying there,

he saw the linen wrappings lying *there;* but he did not go in. ⁶And so Simon Peter also came, following him, and entered the tomb; and he saw the linen wrappings lying *there,* ⁷and the face-cloth which had been on His head, not lying with the linen wrappings, but rolled up in a place by itself. ⁸So the other disciple who had first come to the tomb then also entered, and he saw and believed. ⁹For as yet they did not understand the Scripture, that He must rise again from the dead. ¹⁰So the disciples went away again to their own homes.

19:39 ªTwo early mss read *package of* ᵇLit *100 litras* (12 oz each)

but he didn't go in. ⁶Then Simon Peter arrived and went inside. He also noticed the linen wrappings lying there, ⁷while the cloth that had covered Jesus' head was folded up and lying apart from the other wrappings. ⁸Then the disciple who had reached the tomb first also went in, and he saw and believed—⁹for until then they still hadn't understood the Scriptures that said Jesus must rise from the dead. ¹⁰Then they went home.

19:39 Greek *100 litras* [32.7 kilograms].
19:42 Greek *because of the Jewish day of preparation.* **20:1** Greek *On the first day of the week.*

Dr. Frank Morison was not the kind of person you would find in church on Sunday morning, but he was a man respected by everyone—a well-educated Englishman, an attorney by profession, and a supremely moral man, but a skeptic in matters of faith. By his own account, he was a man moved only by irresistible logic and verifiable fact. He preferred the theology of German critics, Dr. Matthew Arnold of Oxford, Charles Darwin, and Sir Thomas Huxley. Therefore, he rejected the possibility of miracles and the supernatural, and he supposed that all of Christian tradition should be stripped of its "overgrowth of primitive beliefs and dogmatic suppositions" to find the real Jesus, whom he considered "an almost legendary figure of purity and noble manhood."¹⁷ Naturally, this meant he believed in the historical reality of a man named Jesus who died at the hands of Rome, but he denied the historic Christian belief in the resurrection of Jesus Christ from the dead.

Determined to discover a Jesus Christ unadorned by religion, Morison set out to study Jesus' last days and uncover the truth of the subsequent week. He chose to pursue the study from a purely intellectual point of view, using the documents of Scripture, history, and archaeology, committed to allow the facts to shape his conclusions. And with the dogged curiosity and relentless logic of a Sherlock Holmes, he unraveled the mystery of Jesus. The results of his findings and personal transformation are published in his book, *Who Moved the Stone?* In the preface, Morison writes,

[This book is] the inner story of a man who originally set out to write one kind of book but found himself compelled by the sheer force of circumstances to write quite another.

It is not that the facts themselves altered, for they are recorded imperishably in the monuments and in the pages of human history. But the interpretation to be put upon the facts underwent a change. Somehow my perspective shifted—not suddenly, as in a flash of insight or inspiration, but slowly, almost imperceptibly, by the very stubbornness of the facts themselves.

The book, as it was originally planned, was left high and dry.[18]

Obviously, there is no resurrection without a corpse. The miracle of the empty tomb depends upon the certainty of Jesus' death. The need to substantiate this fact is made necessary by the critics who declare he never died. Entire books have been written claiming that Jesus lapsed into a coma and lay unconscious in the burial cave. Then, inside the damp cool of the tomb, He revived, pushed aside the stone, slipped past the guards, and then escaped into the night, claiming to have been raised from the dead.

John described and defended the resurrection of Jesus against other kinds of repudiation, but his words—inspired and preserved by the Holy Spirit—are useful for us today. Not only for the sake of correct theology, but for something more basic: "so that you also may believe" (John 19:35).

— 19:38 —

Ancient people weren't as insulated from death as we are in the modern, developed nations of the twenty-first century. Certainly the men who earned their living by putting other men to death knew when their task was complete. And, unlike today, people prepared their own dead for burial. By the age of thirty, most everyone had seen dozens of corpses up close and personal. We might be fooled by a comatose body, but not the people of Jesus' day.

After death had been confirmed by the soldier's spear, two of Jesus' secret disciples in the Sanhedrin requested permission to take their friend's body. Normally, the Romans would have disposed of His remains in an unmarked grave with other enemies of the state, but Pilate probably wanted to avoid offending more Jews than he already had. According to Philo of Alexandria, extending this courtesy was not uncommon.

I have known instances before now of men who had been crucified when this festival and holiday was at hand, being taken down and given up to their relations, in order to receive the honours of sepulture, and to enjoy such observances as are due to the dead; for it used to be considered, that even the dead ought to derive some enjoyment from the natal festival of a good emperor, and also that the sacred character of the festival ought to be regarded.[19]

— 19:39-42 —

Joseph and Nicodemus waited for the soldiers to lower the body of Jesus from the cross. Then, they would have had to flex and massage His arms in order to relax the rigor mortis, which had certainly set in hard due to the dropping temperature and His physical exertion before death. After pulling His arms down out of the V position, they would have washed His body and anointed it with oil before wrapping it in a single linen cloth. They would have tied a separate cloth under His chin and over His head to keep His mouth closed once rigor mortis ended and His muscles relaxed.

The "burial custom of the Jews" referred to by John required the men to wrap the body of Jesus from head to toe in strips of linen soaked in a mixture of spiced resin. John described the amount as one hundred Roman *litrai*. Each litra weighed roughly 12 ounces (325 grams), so they would have used around 75 pounds (33 kilograms) of aromatic spices to counteract the smell of decomposition. Then they were to place His body in a burial cave, hewn from a limestone hill. After the body decomposed on a burial shelf in the tomb, Jesus' family would make room for a subsequent burial by gathering His bones and placing them in the family ossuary, or "bone box," along with those of His forefathers.

Because the sun was setting soon, the burial party had to act quickly. The holy day began at sunset and they were to be indoors with family for the Passover celebration; yet Deuteronomy 21:22-23 required the body of someone who had been executed to be buried that same day. They undoubtedly applied only the first layers of linen and resin before hastily placing His body in the tomb, intending to return on Sunday to complete the burial process (Mark 16:1-3; Luke 23:54–24:1). Once His body was inside, a team of men rolled a massive stone over the entrance so that grave robbers and wild animals would stay out and the smell of decomposition would stay in.

— 20:1-2 —

John assumed the reader was very familiar with the Synoptic accounts of Jesus' resurrection (Matt. 28:1-8; Mark 16:1-8; Luke 24:1-12), so his purpose was to bring something different to the story. The combined accounts reveal that several women, including Mary Magdalene, had come to the garden to complete the burial process. They came separately, but arrived around the same time. Upon discovering the empty tomb, the women split up. Matthew, Mark, and Luke tell us what happened to the other women (Luke 24:10), while John's record focuses on the experience of Mary Magdalene—while the other women moved in for a closer look, she immediately ran to inform Peter and John.

Because we view this story with 20/20 hindsight, we mustn't be too hard on Mary. Imagine returning to the grave of a very close friend or family member just a couple of days after the funeral. As you approach the burial site to leave flowers, you see that the dirt has been moved back from the grave, the coffin is lying open beside the hole, and the body is missing. Naturally, you would be shocked—and you would assume the body had been exhumed for some reason.

While Jesus had predicted His resurrection, His followers could only see events through natural eyes. Supernatural insight is the gift of the Holy Spirit.

— 20:3-8 —

The Greek language has six verbs translated "to see," but they have different nuances and specific uses. In 20:5-8, John uses three different forms—*blepō* [991] (20:5), *theōreō* [2334] (20:6), and *eidon* [1492] (20:8)—to describe the different kinds of "seeing" that he and Peter experienced.

Upon hearing Mary's report, John and Peter raced to the tomb to investigate. John arrived first, stopped at the cave opening, and peered in. He "observed without necessarily understanding" (*blepō*) the linen wrappings (20:5). Peter arrived moments later, only to push his way into the burial cave, where he "examined for the purpose of investigation" (*theōreō*) the curious condition of the burial wrappings (20:6). The general sense of John's description is that the resin and linen had formed a cocoon, only hollow where the body had been. Someone stealing the body would have taken everything—or at least unwrapped the linens and thrown them aside. Furthermore, the cloth used to tie Jesus' jaw shut had been rolled up and set aside. If this were a hoax, it was very elaborately accomplished!

Finally, John entered the tomb, at which point he "perceived with understanding" (*eidon*) and believed (20:8). He "got it." As we would say, "it clicked." He put it all together and realized that Jesus had risen from the dead.

— 20:9-10 —

John explains the reason for the disciples' slowness to comprehend the full meaning of what they saw (cf. 2:22). They did not understand the necessity of the Messiah's resurrection. Certainly prophecy alluded to His rising from the dead (Ps. 16:10-11; Hos. 6:2); however, it was more a logical necessity.

By the first century, Jewish scholars struggled to understand how the Messiah could suffer and die for the sake of His nation, yet overcome their enemies, lead them to prosperity, and establish a worldwide empire. One theory suggested the messianic prophecies foretold the rise of two individuals, one who would sacrifice his life and another who would reign in his place. The seemingly conflicting prophecies remained a conundrum until . . .

John recognized that the bodily, miraculous resurrection of the Messiah resolved everything. In more ways than one!

• • •

Unlike Morison, who pushed his books aside one evening and confessed, "I believe," Will Durant, the famous agnostic lecturer of Columbia University, faced death with overwhelming gloom. Someone close to Durant recorded his final words—the words of a man who had rejected faith in Jesus Christ and openly denied the fact of His resurrection. He wrote,

> God, who was once the consolation of our brief life, and our refuge in bereavement and suffering, has apparently vanished from the scene; no telescope, no microscope discovers him. Life has become, in that total perspective which is philosophy, a fitful pullulation of human insects on the earth, a planetary eczema that may soon be cured; nothing is certain in it except defeat and death—a sleep from which, it seems, there is no awakening.
>
> We are driven to conclude that the greatest mistake in human history was the discovery of "truth." It has not made us free, except from delusions that comforted us and restraints that preserved us. It has not made us happy, for truth is not beautiful,

and did not deserve to be so passionately chased. As we look on it now we wonder why we hurried so to find it. For it has taken from us every reason for existence except for the moment's pleasure and tomorrow's trivial hope.[20]

Will Durant died in 1981.

Dr. Robert Ingersoll, the American lawyer and Attorney General for the state of Illinois, lectured widely defending his agnostic beliefs. He often shocked audiences by standing on a stage and dramatically shouting to the sky, "If there is a God, let Him strike me dead. I'll give You ten minutes." Of course, the Lord graciously let his insolence pass. Ingersoll attended his brother's funeral and offered the following words: "Life is a narrow veil between the cold and barren peaks of two eternities. We strive in vain to look beyond the heights. We cry aloud, and the only answer is the echo of a wailing cry."[21]

Robert Ingersoll died in 1899.

Each of us must come to terms with the evidence of Jesus' resurrection. If Morison, Durant, and Ingersoll could return from wherever they are to offer their counsel, I wonder what they would say.

No, I don't wonder. I know. And, in your heart of hearts, so do you.

APPLICATION: JOHN 19:38–20:10

The Politics of Christ's Resurrection

Earlier, during His ministry in the temple, Jesus challenged Israel's religious and governmental leaders on the issue of freedom (John 8:31-38). They were surprisingly out of touch with their current political situation, boasting, "We are Abraham's descendants and have never yet been enslaved to anyone; how is it that You say, 'You will become free'?" (8:33). Ironic, considering their subservience to Rome at the time. This prompted Jesus to speak to the reality of their bondage, both political and spiritual.

Gentile expositors usually interpret the teaching of Jesus on freedom from an exclusively spiritual standpoint, but we must remember that the Messiah is the King of the Jews. The temple officials wanted political freedom and thought they had achieved it by maintaining peaceful relations with Rome, such that Rome allowed them to worship in peace.

Jesus clarified the issue, saying, in effect, "Because you are slaves to sin, you also lack political freedom." Then He boldly declared—as their King—"If the Son makes you free, you will be free indeed" (8:36). This was an invitation to submit to Him as the King of Israel.

The promise of freedom is both spiritual and political. And it is not for Israel only. All who believe in a living Jesus Christ may enjoy this freedom, both spiritual and political.

Belief in a living Christ is a crucial matter with broad ramifications and profound impact on the world. The implications of the resurrection aren't limited to history or philosophy. To deny the resurrection is to deny Scripture. To deny Scripture is to deny the existence of God. To deny the existence of God is to deny the reality of truth or meaning. And if nothing exists beyond our short sojourn in a meaningless universe, then we shouldn't waste our energies on such delusions as morality, love, purpose, or human worth.

Even people who reject the resurrection understand this, if only on a subconscious level. As each formerly Christian culture drifts further away from belief in a living Christ—and therefore all the implications of His resurrection—that society experiences moral decline. Love gives way to general disregard for one another. Public policies fail to protect those who cannot protect themselves, such as the aged, terminally ill patients, and the unborn. Violent acts of hopelessness—killing sprees that end in suicide—become commonplace. Justice gives way to the whims of dictators. Eventually, all we hold dear as civilized people vanishes, leaving only anarchy or despotism to fill the void. As Benjamin Franklin wrote in a letter on April 17, 1787, "Let me add, that only a virtuous people are capable of freedom. As nations become corrupt and vicious, they have more need of masters."[22]

Therefore, the question of Christ's resurrection is a supremely practical one. Whoever does not submit to the risen Christ has no master other than self. And according to Jesus, that's no freedom at all, as history has so amply proven.

I fear for my own nation, as I do for all nations that have cast off belief in the living Christ. Now, more than ever, Christians must proclaim the good news: HE IS RISEN!

Reactions to the Resurrected Lord
JOHN 20:11-31

[11] But Mary was standing outside the tomb weeping; and so, as she wept, she stooped and looked into the tomb; [12] and she saw two angels in white sitting, one at the head and one at the feet, where the body of Jesus had been lying. [13] And they said to her, "Woman, why are you weeping?" She said to them, "Because they have taken away my Lord, and I do not know where they have laid Him." [14] When she had said this, she turned around and saw Jesus standing *there*, and did not know that it was Jesus. [15] Jesus said to her, "Woman, why are you weeping? Whom are you seeking?" Supposing Him to be the gardener, she said to Him, "Sir, if you have carried Him away, tell me where you have laid Him, and I will take Him away." [16] Jesus said to her, "Mary!" She turned and said to Him in ªHebrew, "Rabboni!" (which means, Teacher). [17] Jesus said to her, "Stop clinging to Me, for I have not yet ascended to the Father; but go to My brethren and say to them, 'I ascend to My Father and your Father, and My God and your God.'" [18] Mary Magdalene came, announcing to the disciples, "I have seen the Lord," and *that* He had said these things to her.

[19] So when it was evening on that day, the first *day* of the week, and when the doors were shut where the disciples were, for fear of the Jews, Jesus came and stood in their midst and said to them, "ªPeace *be* with you." [20] And when He had said this, He showed them both His hands and His side. The disciples then rejoiced when they saw the Lord. [21] So Jesus said to them again, "Peace *be* with you; as the Father has sent Me, I also send you." [22] And when He had said

[11] Mary was standing outside the tomb crying, and as she wept, she stooped and looked in. [12] She saw two white-robed angels, one sitting at the head and the other at the foot of the place where the body of Jesus had been lying. [13] "Dear woman, why are you crying?" the angels asked her.

"Because they have taken away my Lord," she replied, "and I don't know where they have put him."

[14] She turned to leave and saw someone standing there. It was Jesus, but she didn't recognize him. [15] "Dear woman, why are you crying?" Jesus asked her. "Who are you looking for?"

She thought he was the gardener. "Sir," she said, "if you have taken him away, tell me where you have put him, and I will go and get him."

[16] "Mary!" Jesus said.

She turned to him and cried out, "Rabboni!" (which is Hebrew for "Teacher").

[17] "Don't cling to me," Jesus said, "for I haven't yet ascended to the Father. But go find my brothers and tell them, 'I am ascending to my Father and your Father, to my God and your God.'"

[18] Mary Magdalene found the disciples and told them, "I have seen the Lord!" Then she gave them his message.

[19] That Sunday evening* the disciples were meeting behind locked doors because they were afraid of the Jewish leaders. Suddenly, Jesus was standing there among them! "Peace be with you," he said. [20] As he spoke, he showed them the wounds in his hands and his side. They were filled with joy when they saw the Lord! [21] Again he said, "Peace be with you. As the Father has sent me, so I am sending you." [22] Then he breathed

this, He breathed on them and said to them, "Receive the Holy Spirit. ²³ If you forgive the sins of any, *their sins* ^ahave been forgiven them; if you retain the *sins* of any, they have been retained."

²⁴ But Thomas, one of the twelve, called ^aDidymus, was not with them when Jesus came. ²⁵ So the other disciples were saying to him, "We have seen the Lord!" But he said to them, "Unless I see in His hands the imprint of the nails, and put my finger into the place of the nails, and put my hand into His side, I will not believe."

^{26a} After eight days His disciples were again inside, and Thomas with them. Jesus came, the doors having been ^bshut, and stood in their midst and said, "Peace *be* with you." ²⁷ Then He said to Thomas, "Reach here with your finger, and see My hands; and reach here your hand and put it into My side; and do not be unbelieving, but believing." ²⁸ Thomas answered and said to Him, "My Lord and my God!" ²⁹ Jesus said to him, "Because you have seen Me, have you believed? Blessed *are* they who did not see, and *yet* believed."

³⁰ Therefore many other ^asigns Jesus also performed in the presence of the disciples, which are not written in this book; ³¹ but these have been written so that you may believe that Jesus is ^athe Christ, the Son of God; and that believing you may have life in His name.

20:16 ^aI.e. Jewish Aramaic 20:19 ^aLit *Peace to you* 20:23 ^aI.e. have previously been forgiven 20:24 ^aI.e. the Twin 20:26 ^aOr *A week later* ^bOr *locked* 20:30 ^aOr *attesting miracles* 20:31 ^aI.e. the Messiah

on them and said, "Receive the Holy Spirit. ²³ If you forgive anyone's sins, they are forgiven. If you do not forgive them, they are not forgiven."

²⁴ One of the twelve disciples, Thomas (nicknamed the Twin),* was not with the others when Jesus came. ²⁵ They told him, "We have seen the Lord!"

But he replied, "I won't believe it unless I see the nail wounds in his hands, put my fingers into them, and place my hand into the wound in his side."

²⁶ Eight days later the disciples were together again, and this time Thomas was with them. The doors were locked; but suddenly, as before, Jesus was standing among them. "Peace be with you," he said. ²⁷ Then he said to Thomas, "Put your finger here, and look at my hands. Put your hand into the wound in my side. Don't be faithless any longer. Believe!"

²⁸ "My Lord and my God!" Thomas exclaimed.

²⁹ Then Jesus told him, "You believe because you have seen me. Blessed are those who believe without seeing me."

³⁰ The disciples saw Jesus do many other miraculous signs in addition to the ones recorded in this book. ³¹ But these are written so that you may continue to believe* that Jesus is the Messiah, the Son of God, and that by believing in him you will have life by the power of his name.

20:19 Greek *In the evening of that day, the first day of the week.* 20:24 Greek *Thomas, who was called Didymus.* 20:31 Some manuscripts read *that you may believe.*

John's account of Jesus' life, ministry, death, and resurrection is written from a unique perspective, that of a man nearing the end of life. Younger people typically swaddle their fear of death and nothingness in convenient delusions or distract themselves with compelling diversions. But an old man stands close enough to the threshold of death to peer into the potential abyss of eternity and seriously question what he truly believes. As John approached this ultimate moment of truth, he cast an earnest look over his shoulder and called to all of us who inevitably follow him, "Believe!" That is the sole concern of his Gospel: "that believing you may have life in His name" (John 20:31).

As John nears the end of his narrative, he presents four encounters with the risen Christ, each highlighting a crisis in belief:

- Peter and John (20:1-10)
- Mary Magdalene (20:11-18)
- Disciples (20:19-23)
- Thomas (20:24-29)

We have already examined the first; three remain.

— 20:11-14 —

The combined Gospel accounts show the followers of Jesus in a state of chaos on the morning of His resurrection. They scrambled around, piecing together random bits of information, trying to make sense of what one had seen and another heard. Peter and John returned to their respective homes, reasonably sure that Jesus had risen from the dead. At some point, Jesus appeared to Peter (Luke 24:34; 1 Cor. 15:5), but it's difficult to determine when. The other women had already been sent on their mission by the angels (Matt. 28:5-8; Mark 16:6-8; Luke 24:5-9). Meanwhile, Mary Magdalene returned to the empty tomb, perhaps after telling other disciples the same news, and then sat down, weeping. As she peered into the burial cave and studied the hollow cocoon of linen and resin, two angels asked the rhetorical question, "Why are you weeping?" They knew Mary had cause only for rejoicing, if she understood the truth. The question served to engage her in a dialogue that would help her understand. She quite naturally thought someone had moved the body of Jesus. Ironically, Jesus was standing right behind her in plain sight.

Mary turned from the tomb to notice someone standing nearby, and with a short glance addressed a man she assumed to be the caretaker.

— 20:15-18 —

Jesus repeated the angels' question—"Why are you weeping?"—presumably for the same reason. But she failed to recognize Him, either by sight or sound. Some have suggested Jesus had altered His appearance or Mary's eyes were prevented from recognizing Him (cf. Luke 24:16), but this is doubtful given the context. She immediately recognized Him when He called her name as if to arrest her attention. More likely, a combination of factors prevented her seeing the Lord. Jesus looked very different from His last moments on the cross, and He was the last person Mary expected to see alive. Moreover, the phrase "she turned and said to Him," suggests she initially glanced toward the "gardener" and then spoke to Him while turned away.

Mary's request for the body of Jesus was probably made in the same spirit as that of Joseph and Nicodemus (John 19:38). She wanted nothing more than to bury her Master with dignity and then get on with putting the pieces of her life back together. When Jesus called her name, Mary turned to look at Jesus—really look at Him—and accepted the fact of His resurrection.

The meaning of Jesus' gentle reproof is not immediately obvious, mostly because older translations have created undue confusion. The old King James Version, "Touch Me not," was not helpful. The NASB more accurately renders the command, "Stop clinging to Me." Mary was so overwhelmed with relief, supposing she had her Lord back in the same manner as before, she embraced Him and held on as though letting go would cause her to lose Him again.

Jesus reassured Mary that she would see Him again, as He had not yet ascended to the Father. He instructed her to give the same message to His other followers. However, His message confirmed two truths. First, His physical presence on earth was temporary; before long, He would ascend to take His place in glory. Second, His relationship with His followers would then change. Mary's physical clinging would have to give way to another kind of bond, a relationship of faith.

Reduced to its bare essence, Jesus' rebuke consists of three imperative verbs, three commands. "Stop clinging . . . go . . . say . . ." (20:17). Her immediate response to His command: obedience. She did exactly as she was told.

— 20:19-20 —

Before the day of Jesus' resurrection had ended, His followers began to congregate in what was probably a familiar meeting place (cf. Luke 24:33). The doors were closed and locked in anticipation of persecution from the temple leaders.

Despite the locked doors, Jesus suddenly appeared among the

congregation of followers. Luke tells us that His appearance was so inexplicable by conventional means that the disciples thought Him a ghost; nevertheless, He possessed flesh and bones that could be sensed by touch (Luke 24:37-39). He greeted the frightened followers by reminding them of the "peace" He had promised earlier (John 14:27).

John includes this detail to illustrate for the first time in his narrative the different nature of Christ's resurrected body. Lazarus had been revived from death and restored to good health, but he lived with the same limitations, suffered illness and injury, and eventually died again. The resurrection of Jesus was fundamentally and profoundly different. It was, in fact, superior. His resurrection body, while still completely human, possessed supernatural qualities. He was raised to a new kind of life, never to die again.

Apparently, the disciples were slow to accept what they saw as the authentic presence of their risen Master. John's description applies to the whole group, which included a broad spectrum of responses. Peter and John were likely present and had already accepted the reality of Christ's resurrection; nevertheless, the group as a whole was slow to believe. Unlike Mary, who embraced Christ almost at once, the group of followers needed more evidence.

This increased need for objective proof, by the way, is a pattern in this segment of John's narrative.

— 20:21-22 —

Once the disciples' joy replaced their fear—which fulfilled the Lord's promise in the upper room (14:27)—He recommissioned them to fulfill God's great plan of redemption (17:18). Jesus then reaffirmed His earlier promise of the Holy Spirit (14:26; 15:26; 16:13; see also Jer. 31:31-34; Ezek. 37:14; Joel 2:28-32). He illustrated His promise of the coming Holy Spirit by breathing on the disciples, recalling the act of creation (Gen. 2:7) and Old Testament image of dry skeletons becoming live people again (Ezek. 37). This was either a temporary foretaste of Pentecost (Acts 2) or merely a symbolic gesture.

— 20:23 —

Entire Master's theses have been written on this verse and its parallels, Matthew 16:19 and 18:18. Some expositors claim these verses grant apostolic authority to be Christ's proxy on earth. These same expositors claim this apostolic authority has been passed on to succeeding generations to this very day, men from whom the forgiveness of heaven may be sought, usually in return for acts of penance.

Indeed, the apostles were granted authority—the same authority granted to all believers, all redeemed men and women who carry the Holy Spirit within them. The Lord commissioned and empowered believers to proclaim His message of forgiveness. The phrase rendered "have been forgiven them" in the NASB is in the passive voice and perfect tense, describing an action already taken by God (known to scholars as the "divine passive") that has ongoing results. The sins of believers have already been forgiven by God. If "any" respond with belief to the disciples' proclamation of the gospel, the disciples have the authority to pronounce them forgiven.

This is consistent with how Jesus saw His own ministry. While He both healed and forgave certain individuals, He said it was their faith that saved them, healed them, or made them whole (John 5:24, also Matt. 9:29; 15:28; Mark 5:34; 10:52; Luke 7:50; 8:48; 17:19; 18:42). And while His presence became a moment of moral crisis for some, it was their unbelief that condemned them (John 3:18-19; 5:22; 9:39-41).

— 20:24-25 —

When Jesus visited His followers huddled in their secret room, Thomas was absent. Sometime after Jesus' crucifixion, he may have returned to his home in Galilee. Upon his return to Jerusalem, he heard stories of Jesus' resurrection from the other followers; however, he refused to believe their testimony—including that of Peter and John! This has earned Thomas the nickname "doubting," but it's more accurate to call him pessimistic or melancholy—or better still, reflective. The only recorded statements of Thomas reveal a downcast, pitiful outlook:

"Let us also go, so that we may die with Him" (11:16).

"Lord, we do not know where You are going, how do we know the way?" (14:5).

Thomas wanted concrete proof, not to satisfy his doubt, but to overcome his hopelessness. He said, in effect, "Risen? This is too good to be true. I will not allow myself to hope until I can be sure my hope will not be dashed."

— 20:26-29 —

Eight days after the Lord's first visit to the disciples' hideout, Jesus appeared as He had before and offered the same greeting, "Peace be with you." He immediately gave attention to the neediest man in the room.

I am comforted by the Lord's gentle approach. While belief was the issue to be addressed with Thomas, Jesus knew the disciple's trouble to be hopelessness—or perhaps tough-minded pragmatism—not obstinate unwillingness to believe. Even though Thomas's statement was obvious hyperbole, the Lord offered Thomas the reassurance he wanted. His gentle rebuke said, in effect, "It's okay to place complete confidence in Me; I won't let you down. I am here, I am real, and I won't abandon you."

Thomas didn't need to touch the Lord's wounds. And his confession is a pinnacle moment in John's narrative: "My Lord and my God!" Jesus affirmed the disciple's confession of faith and then responded with a blessing on all those who had accepted the truth of His resurrection because of faith in God's promises rather than physical evidence (cf. 4:50).

This blessing on the faith of past believers suggests similar blessing on the generations of future believers.

— 20:30-31 —

John has illustrated four different faith responses to the resurrection of Jesus Christ. In each encounter, the subjects considered evidence and then chose whether or not to believe. And with each passing episode, the tension between tangible evidence and belief increased as each subject required more proof than the last. Finally, Jesus blessed all those who believe without the benefit of tangible proof. And with that, John turns to us, the reader.

Jesus performed "signs" which convinced reasonable men and women that Jesus is the Christ, the hope of eternal life for all people. "These" things were written so that we might believe and enter that eternal life.

• • •

Dying people aren't interested in opinions. Matters of belief become critically important, for death renders all truth undeniable, yet without second chances.

Many years ago, a close friend of mine asked me to visit a man in the hospital. His name was David. He had been a specimen of health until severe headaches forced him to seek the help of a neurosurgeon. But it was too late. Surgery revealed an inoperable malignant tumor that would soon affect his ability to reason and to communicate. Death would soon follow.

After gaining permission from the family and the hospital staff, I walked into the man's room. His head was shaved and heavily wrapped. His face gave away the pain he bravely endured. His son sat holding his hand. I introduced myself and then explained the reason for my visit. "David, I don't want to beat around the bush. All of us need to come to terms with death and what comes after, and your time is growing short."

He said, "Go ahead."

"Listen to the record of a man named John: 'God has given us eternal life, and this life is in His Son. He who has the Son has [eternal] life; he who does not have the Son of God does not have [eternal] life' (1 Jn. 5:11-12). David, by receiving Jesus Christ as your personal Savior, even though your earthly future is very, very uncertain and very bleak, you can have the assurance of eternal life."

He said, "I want that. I take that! I accept that! Right now." As I explained the good news, how Christ died to pay the penalty of our sins so that those who believe will have the assurance of life in heaven, I heard muffled weeping from his son.

I held out my hand and said, "David, let's pray." So he gripped my hand harder than I had ever felt before and we prayed. In those brief moments, David passed from death unto life. And within a few months, his faith gave way to visible, tangible reality as he stepped into eternity.

APPLICATION: JOHN 20:11-31

Responding to the Risen Lord

In chapter 20, John describes the responses of people confronted with evidence of Jesus' resurrection. They generally reacted in one of four ways:

1. *Some believed with indirect evidence.* They responded to the initial report with curiosity, and when they viewed the empty tomb and saw the hollow grave wrappings, they knew He had risen (20:1-10).
2. *Some believed with direct evidence.* They were either confused or doubtful until they saw the risen Lord with their own eyes (20:11-18).

3. *Some were slow to believe with direct evidence.* They initially responded to the Lord's presence with fear and then slowly accepted the reality of His resurrection (20:19-23, 26-28).
4. *Some believed without evidence, indirect or direct.* They believed based on the promises of Old Testament Scripture, the predictions of Jesus, and the testimony of credible witnesses (20:29).

Jesus never questioned the need for evidence in matters of faith, which is why He offered "signs" to validate His identity and to authenticate His message. However, He was selective in His use of tangible evidence, for He knew that no amount of proof will satisfy a skeptic. During His public ministry, Jesus rarely used "signs" to convince unwilling hearts. Instead, He offered tangible evidence to willing hearts in order to add confidence to their trust. And He followed the same model after His resurrection.

Note that after rising from the dead, Jesus appeared only to believers.[23] If His followers doubted His resurrection, it was not because they doubted the truthfulness of His claims; they merely thought His resurrection was too good to be true. Therefore, Jesus welcomed their belief, while tenderly offering evidence to build their confidence in the truth. Nevertheless, He praised those who believed in His resurrection without much need for proof.

Faith and evidence are not unrelated in the spiritual life of a Christian; however, our starting point is crucial. Trust in God must come first; *then* evidence is helpful. Apart from belief, evidence is virtually meaningless. I like to think of it this way:

Refusal to believe + Evidence = Confusion
Willingness to believe + Evidence = Confidence

Whenever I encounter a skeptic—someone who demands evidence before belief—I avoid offering proof of anything. I have wasted enough time on pointless debates. Instead, I focus on the real issue at hand: their sinfulness and their need for the Savior. When a lost person comes to terms with his or her sinfulness—genuinely so—belief is their next logical step. Then, ironically, they find great comfort and confidence in the historical fact of Christ's resurrection.

Our Weakness . . . His Strength
JOHN 21:1-23

NASB

[1] After these things Jesus ᵃmanifested Himself again to the disciples at the Sea of Tiberias, and He manifested *Himself* in this way. [2] Simon Peter, and Thomas called ᵃDidymus, and Nathanael of Cana in Galilee, and the *sons* of Zebedee, and two others of His disciples were together. [3] Simon Peter said to them, "I am going fishing." They said to him, "We will also come with you." They went out and got into the boat; and that night they caught nothing.

[4] But when the day was now breaking, Jesus stood on the beach; yet the disciples did not know that it was Jesus. [5] So Jesus said to them, "Children, you do not have ᵃany fish, do you?" They answered Him, "No." [6] And He said to them, "Cast the net on the right-hand side of the boat and you will find *a catch*." So they cast, and then they were not able to haul it in because of the great number of fish. [7] Therefore that disciple whom Jesus loved said to Peter, "It is the Lord." So when Simon Peter heard that it was the Lord, he put his outer garment on (for he was stripped *for work*), and threw himself into the sea. [8] But the other disciples came in the little boat, for they were not far from the land, but about ᵃone hundred yards away, dragging the net *full* of fish.

[9] So when they got out on the land, they saw a charcoal fire *already* laid and fish placed on it, and bread. [10] Jesus said to them, "Bring some of the fish which you have now caught." [11] Simon Peter went up and drew the net to land, full of large fish, a hundred and fifty-three; and although there were so many, the net was not torn.

[12] Jesus said to them, "Come *and* have breakfast." None of the

NLT

[1] Later, Jesus appeared again to the disciples beside the Sea of Galilee.* This is how it happened. [2] Several of the disciples were there—Simon Peter, Thomas (nicknamed the Twin),* Nathanael from Cana in Galilee, the sons of Zebedee, and two other disciples.

[3] Simon Peter said, "I'm going fishing."

"We'll come, too," they all said. So they went out in the boat, but they caught nothing all night.

[4] At dawn Jesus was standing on the beach, but the disciples couldn't see who he was. [5] He called out, "Fellows,* have you caught any fish?"

"No," they replied.

[6] Then he said, "Throw out your net on the right-hand side of the boat, and you'll get some!" So they did, and they couldn't haul in the net because there were so many fish in it.

[7] Then the disciple Jesus loved said to Peter, "It's the Lord!" When Simon Peter heard that it was the Lord, he put on his tunic (for he had stripped for work), jumped into the water, and headed to shore. [8] The others stayed with the boat and pulled the loaded net to the shore, for they were only about a hundred yards* from shore. [9] When they got there, they found breakfast waiting for them—fish cooking over a charcoal fire, and some bread.

[10] "Bring some of the fish you've just caught," Jesus said. [11] So Simon Peter went aboard and dragged the net to the shore. There were 153 large fish, and yet the net hadn't torn.

[12] "Now come and have some breakfast!" Jesus said. None of the disciples dared to ask him, "Who are you?" They knew it was the Lord.

disciples ventured to question Him, "Who are You?" knowing that it was the Lord. ¹³Jesus came and took the bread and gave *it* to them, and the fish likewise. ¹⁴This is now the third time that Jesus ᵃwas manifested to the disciples, after He was raised from the dead.

¹⁵ So when they had finished breakfast, Jesus said to Simon Peter, "Simon, *son* of John, do you ᵃlove Me more than these?" He said to Him, "Yes, Lord; You know that I ᵇlove You." He said to him, "Tend My lambs." ¹⁶He said to him again a second time, "Simon, *son* of John, do you ᵃlove Me?" He said to Him, "Yes, Lord; You know that I ᵇlove You." He said to him, "Shepherd My sheep." ¹⁷He said to him the third time, "Simon, *son* of John, do you ᵃlove Me?" Peter was grieved because He said to him the third time, "Do you ᵃlove Me?" And he said to Him, "Lord, You know all things; You know that I ᵃlove You." Jesus said to him, "Tend My sheep.

¹⁸Truly, truly, I say to you, when you were younger, you used to gird yourself and walk wherever you wished; but when you grow old, you will stretch out your hands and someone else will gird you, and bring you where you do not wish to go." ¹⁹Now this He said, signifying by what kind of death he would glorify God. And when He had spoken this, He said to him, "Follow Me!"

²⁰Peter, turning around, saw the disciple whom Jesus loved following *them;* the one who also had leaned back on His bosom at the supper and said, "Lord, who is the one who betrays You?" ²¹So Peter seeing him said to Jesus, "Lord, and what about this man?" ²²Jesus said to him, "If I want him to remain until I come, what *is that* to you? You follow Me!" ²³Therefore this saying went out among the brethren that that disciple would not die; yet Jesus did not

¹³Then Jesus served them the bread and the fish. ¹⁴This was the third time Jesus had appeared to his disciples since he had been raised from the dead.

¹⁵After breakfast Jesus asked Simon Peter, "Simon son of John, do you love me more than these?*"

"Yes, Lord," Peter replied, "you know I love you."

"Then feed my lambs," Jesus told him.

¹⁶Jesus repeated the question: "Simon son of John, do you love me?"

"Yes, Lord," Peter said, "you know I love you."

"Then take care of my sheep," Jesus said.

¹⁷A third time he asked him, "Simon son of John, do you love me?"

Peter was hurt that Jesus asked the question a third time. He said, "Lord, you know everything. You know that I love you."

Jesus said, "Then feed my sheep.

¹⁸"I tell you the truth, when you were young, you were able to do as you liked; you dressed yourself and went wherever you wanted to go. But when you are old, you will stretch out your hands, and others* will dress you and take you where you don't want to go." ¹⁹Jesus said this to let him know by what kind of death he would glorify God. Then Jesus told him, "Follow me."

²⁰Peter turned around and saw behind them the disciple Jesus loved— the one who had leaned over to Jesus during supper and asked, "Lord, who will betray you?" ²¹Peter asked Jesus, "What about him, Lord?"

²²Jesus replied, "If I want him to remain alive until I return, what is that to you? As for you, follow me." ²³So the rumor spread among the community of believers* that this disciple wouldn't die. But that isn't what Jesus said at all. He only said,

say to him that he would not die, but *only*, "If I want him to remain until I come, what *is that* to you?"

21:1 °Or *made Himself visible* 21:2 °I.e. the Twin 21:5 °Lit *something eaten with bread* 21:8 °Lit *200 cubits* 21:14 °Or *made Himself visible* 21:15 °Gr *agapao* °Gr *phileo* 21:16 °Gr *agapao* °Gr *phileo* 21:17 °Gr *phileo*

"If I want him to remain alive until I return, what is that to you?"

21:1 Greek *Sea of Tiberias*, another name for the Sea of Galilee. 21:2 Greek *Thomas, who was called Didymus.* 21:5 Greek *Children.* 21:8 Greek *200 cubits* [90 meters]. 21:15 Or *more than these others do?* 21:18 Some manuscripts read *and another one.* 21:23 Greek *the brothers.*

When Peter first met Jesus and then responded to His call to follow, he probably thought he was doing the Messiah a big favor. The new King of Israel would need a man like him—a bold, brave, take-charge leader of men. He was strong, decisive, a hard worker, quick with a blade, and even quicker to decide what should be done and how to do it. Peter was the kind of man who got things done by sheer force of will.

After his failure in the courtyard during Jesus' trials, Peter wasn't so high on himself. He undoubtedly winced every time he recalled his impulsive commitment in the upper room: "Lord, why can I not follow You right now? I will lay down my life for You" (John 13:37). Indeed, when surrounded by six hundred men, he was ready to take them on with a blade only slightly longer than a dagger. But in the courtyard, he feared for his life and he lied like a coward.

Failure of any kind is difficult enough to overcome, but moral failure in the realm of ministry is a killer. After a particularly ugly moral blunder, one might ask, "What good can I possibly do now?"

The answer to that question may be surprising.

— 21:1-3 —

John establishes the setting of this event as Galilee, sometime after Jesus' confrontation with Thomas in or near Jerusalem. We have no way of knowing how long after the resurrection this took place, but it was not likely more than a month (Acts 1:3). Five of the Twelve are named, while another two disciples are left anonymous, perhaps because they were not of the Twelve. Regardless, Peter and the "sons of Zebedee" (James and John) shared a lot of history with this region. This was where Jesus had extended His call for the men to follow, promising to transform them into "fishers of men" (Mark 1:17).

For no less than three years, these men followed their Messiah, learning from Him and fully expecting Him to reign as King of the Jews. Then suddenly, in a matter of hours, everything changed. He was arrested, tried, judged, crucified, and laid in a tomb. When the followers of Jesus buried their Messiah, they buried their fondest expectations with Him. And when He emerged from the tomb, their dreams were left behind with His grave clothes. This long period of quiet undoubtedly became an eerie state of limbo for them. The Messiah died, but was no longer dead. Jesus communed with them on a remarkably intimate level at times, but before the coming of the Holy Spirit, they were without daily leadership. The coming kingdom was not to be what they had all hoped, so for them it remained a shapeless, unfixed future.

Human nature cannot abide limbo for very long. So, when we cannot move forward, we cannot help but return to the familiar—even a past we were happy to leave. But, as the old adage goes, "You can never go home again." Even if home has not changed—and it always does—you have changed.

"I'm going fishing" was not merely a plan to pass the unbearable meantime. Peter, ever the man of action, saw no future for himself in service to Christ, so he returned to his successful, pre-Christ vocation. Unfortunately, Peter's efforts to catch fish fared no better than his prospects of catching men (Luke 5:10).

— 21:4-6 —

One of the qualities about the Lord I love the most is His grace—and not just in the theological sense. I mean His charming manner of accepting and loving His own. Peter and his friends returned to the familiar, so the Lord met them there. He even used their overdependence on the past to their mutual advantage.

The Lord's question rendered in Greek anticipates a negative response, not unlike saying, "So, you haven't caught anything, right?" Moreover, He called them *paidia* [3813], the plural form of the word for a small child. According to one lexicon, "it may also denote 'servant' (social position). Figuratively it carries the sense of undeveloped understanding but is also used in affectionate address."[24]

The disciples had been in this situation before. These very men had spent a wasted night on the sea when Jesus instructed them to recast their nets. When their obedience netted them a record catch, He promised them similar success in ministry (Luke 5:5-11). Now, after so much had happened, their resurrected Lord instructed them to recast their nets. Surely, one of the men must have suspected the stranger on the shore was Jesus. Once the top line of the net stretched to the point of breaking, however, there was no question.

Let us not forget the full context of this event. Jesus did not merely see a large school of fish from one hundred yards out, as some have suggested. He's the Creator. He *made* fish. And He *caused* those fish to be where the disciples could pull them into their nets.

— 21:7-8 —

The phrase "stripped for work" does not mean Peter was naked, merely that he had removed his outer robe and girded his *chiton,* or "undergarment," between his legs and around his waist. In characteristic Peter style, he plunged into the sea and swam to shore, delighted to see his Master again. Meanwhile, the other disciples pulled in a full net of fish.

— 21:9 —

John includes three significant details:

Jesus had prepared a charcoal fire. This is a deliberate literary allusion to Peter's failure in the courtyard, which occurred over a charcoal fire (see 18:18).

Jesus had fish cooking on the fire. The Lord does not depend upon the efforts of humanity to accomplish His will.

Jesus had loaves of bread waiting. The wilderness in which Jesus fed the multitude with five loaves and two small fish lay just behind them.

— 21:10-11 —

Peter, in his impulsive exuberance, left the other disciples to haul in the load of fish. Jesus' invitation for him to add his fish to the fire is significant. While the Lord can do all things without any help from anyone, he invited Peter to contribute the fruit of his efforts. The Lord wants to enjoy the victory we accomplish together, not because He *needs* us, but because He *wants* us!

So, Peter returned to the nets with his comrades and processed the extraordinary results of divine help given to human effort.

— 21:12-14 —

John clarifies that the men knew they were in the presence of the Lord. And his image of Jesus distributing the bread and fish is no accident— it is a clear allusion to the abundance He created in the wilderness (6:11).

John notes that this is the third time Jesus was "manifested" after His resurrection. The term means "to make visible what was not previously seen."

— 21:15-17 —

As if to take Peter back to the beginning, before he was "the Rock," Jesus looked across the charcoal fire and addressed the dejected disciple by his original given name: Simon, the son of John. "Simon" is based on the Hebrew name "Simeon," which in turn is based on the Hebrew verb *shama* [H8085], "to hear, to hearken, to heed."

The time had come for Jesus to address Peter's deepest wound. Were it not for the Lord's perfect compassion, His question might have been considered a cruel taunt. The added phrase, "more than these," was an unmistakable reference to Peter's bold declaration of loyalty in the upper room (13:37; see also Matt. 26:33; Mark 14:29; Luke 22:33).

The Greek language has three words for *love*. *Erōs* describes the euphoric, "in-love" feelings of romance; that is, before the honeymoon ends. *Philia* [5373] describes the warm affection shared by friends, close family members, and even romantic lovers after intimacy has cemented their union. The verb form, *phileō* [5368], means "to treat somebody as one of one's own people."[25] The Greeks held *philia* in high regard as a deeply emotional connection between people.

A third word, *agapē* [26], is rarely found outside Jewish and Christian literature. Unlike short-lived *erōs, agapē* is not impetuous, but steady and deliberate. Whereas *philia* describes affection, *agapē* speaks of loyalty: "Here is a love that makes distinctions, choosing its objects freely. Hence it is especially the love of a higher for a lower. It is active, not self-seeking love."[26] The New Testament writers drew upon this word to express the kind of love Jesus lived and taught. *Agapē* loves God first, loves neighbor as self, and loves enemies and friends alike. While strongly emotive, *agapē* is not fueled by emotion. This Christlike love places high value on tangible expressions of kindness rather than emotions that accomplish nothing.

Jesus asked Simon about his *agapē;* Simon responded with *philia*. Scholars and expositors do not agree about the significance of the different terms chosen by John to render their conversation from Aramaic. However, I don't think John's deliberate choice of Greek terms was irrelevant. On the contrary, I am convinced his word choice reflects the sentiments of each man. Note the pattern of their dialogue:

Simon, son of John, do you love [*agapaō*] Me more than these?
Yes, Lord; You know that I love [phileō] You.
Tend My lambs.

Simon, son of John, do you love [*agapaō*] Me?
Yes, Lord; You know that I love [phileō] You.
Shepherd My sheep.

Simon, son of John, do you love [*phileō*] Me?
Lord, You know all things; You know that I love [phileō] You.
Tend My sheep.

The confidence and passion that had earlier fueled Peter's decisions—both wise and foolish, heroic and cowardly—had been crushed out of him. This impulsive zeal distracted Peter from acknowledging a lifelong problem. As long as there were external foes to fight, challenges to meet, difficulties to overcome, quandaries to solve, he didn't have to face that he was, in fact, quite powerless.

Peter's *philia* fell short of what either man desired, but he deserved high marks for honesty. Furthermore, it acknowledged the truth of Peter's love. His affection for Jesus could not be denied, but he was powerless to avoid future failure—and he knew it. Now—with proud self-confidence a thing of the past—Peter was ready to depend upon the Lord to accomplish ministry.

Just as Jesus gently rescued Thomas from his hopelessness—or perhaps dogged pragmatism—the Lord pulled Peter from his despondency. And he invited the humbled disciple to recast his nets for another miraculous catch . . . only this time, for the souls of people.

— 21:18-19 —

I suspect Jesus allowed time for His invitation to sink in. Then, as an expert mentor, He encouraged His disciple. Having dealt with Simon's past, He revealed Peter's future. In the past, Simon was a self-confident, willful man who directed his own life. He even attempted discipleship on his own terms, with tragic results. Then he behaved like a coward to distance himself from Christ.

Following this disappointment, while Peter was at his lowest depths of despair and discouragement, Jesus assured him of a Christ-worthy death. His reference to outstretched arms alludes to being laid on a cross. The verb translated "to gird" literally means "to fasten." This is a cleaver pun, obviously referring to being fastened to a cross with nails or rope. In the past, Simon decided what to wear and where to go; in the future, Peter would submit to the leading of his Master, and he would "wear" a cross to his own honorable death.

Jesus punctuated His encouragement with "Follow Me!"—a

command reminiscent of Simon's original calling (Matt. 4:19; Mark 1:17; Luke 5:10).

— 21:20-23 —

Evidently, this portion of the conversation between Master and servant took place as they strolled along the shore. Peter noticed John following along behind them. Of all the disciples, John behaved the most honorably. While he fled the assault on Gethsemane (Matt. 26:56; Mark 14:50), he soon returned and remained close to Jesus throughout His trials and crucifixion. While Simon kept his distance and denied his discipleship in the courtyard, John stood in the courtroom. While Simon cowered during the crucifixion, John stood at the base of the cross.

Personal failure usually leads to comparisons. We either push others down to feel less inferior, or we allow shame to bury us at the bottom of the world. Neither response is from God. "What about this man?" Peter was indicating John. Jesus rebuked Peter's question, saying in effect, "You do what you're supposed to do; let me manage John." Then He repeated His earlier call with greater emphasis: "You—keep on following Me!" (my literal translation).

John concludes his description of their encounter with a humorous footnote. Long before he prepared his narrative, this particular story circulated as oral history. Peter undoubtedly told it often as a means of encouraging other down-and-out believers. Peter spent much of his later life tackling false teaching concerning Jesus, so he probably relished the irony of having to put down an error involving himself!

Many took Jesus' correction of Peter to mean that He planned to return before John died. Believers during John's lifetime didn't suppose he would exceed a normal life expectancy; they used Jesus' comment to support their own wishful thinking that He would return soon. John's comment clarified before his death that this was a false rumor.

• • •

The corporate world, like all kingdoms of the world, looks for leaders among those who have exceptional natural abilities. Nations look for charisma and innate people skills in their politicians. The military has adopted the motto "Up or out," because an officer is expected to rise through the ranks until he or she can rise no further . . . or retire. In virtually every sphere of life, a significant failure usually means termination or demotion—"Shape up or ship out!" But not in the kingdom of God.

Chuck Colson, at one time, was one of the most powerful men in the world. As a confidant and advisor to Richard Nixon during his presidency, Colson was also one of the most feared, earning for himself the nickname "the Hatchet Man." Years later, he trusted in Jesus Christ, but by then he had lost everything—power, position, prestige, even his freedom. In his book *Born Again,* he writes,

> I have prayed especially for honesty in my writing, knowing only too well that my basic nature would want to present myself in the most favorable light. As I have fallen down, picked myself up, and fallen down again during the past few years, I am learning how God can break us in order to remake us. And through my dependence on Him has come a surprising sense of freedom—and an exhilaration in my spirit.[27]

Peter emerged from his failure a transformed man, one ready to acknowledge his own inabilities and ready to exchange self-confidence for Christ-confidence. With the sound of the miracle haul of fish flopping in the background, Peter was finally ready to accept the Lord's call. "You—keep on following Me!"

Have you failed the Lord? That's His call to you as well.

Keep on following.

APPLICATION: JOHN 21:1-23
Coming to Terms with Your Calling

In Christian circles, we tend to think of full-time vocational ministers as "called" by God. However, they are not the only people called by God to fulfill a divine purpose. *All* believers have been called to bring glory to God in whatever we do. Therefore, I think it is appropriate to extend the range of "calling" to include any vocation a believer chooses to pursue.

With that in mind, allow me to offer three thoughts from John 21:1-23 that will help us come to terms with our calling.

First, *we must come to terms with our limitations.* While we should do our best and always pursue excellence, never forget that, ultimately, success is not up to us. Peter and his business partners ran a lucrative fishing enterprise and were experts in their vocation. They had years of experience and all the right equipment, yet their nets came up empty.

Only with the Lord's help did the men find success. The miracle haul of fish illustrated that without the Lord's help, our expertise and diligence will come to nothing.

Second, *we must come to terms with our priorities.* All believers have been called as disciples and all are commissioned to "make disciples" (Matt. 28:19-20), regardless of how each individual earns a living. Moreover, we have all been called to bring glory to God in whatever we do (1 Cor. 10:31). So, students, tradesmen, homemakers, professionals, ministers, laborers . . . "Whatever you do, do your work heartily, as for the Lord rather than for men" (Col. 3:23).

What is your attitude toward work? If you start the day thinking, *Ugh! Back to the grind!* it's time for a change. If a new job isn't possible, then the change might have to be internal. Begin by committing every aspect of your job to the Lord for His purposes and His glory. "Lord, I'm Yours today. This is Your desk. This is Your office. These are Your tools. This is Your computer. Now help me become the very best worker I can possibly be. And in the process of time, let's catch some fish. Let's make some disciples."

Third, *we must come to terms with our imperfection.* Peter laid aside his calling of "catching men" (Luke 5:10) because of his failure and took up a vocation in which failure wouldn't cause as much damage to the kingdom—at least in his way of thinking. While he wanted to put it in the past and make the best of a lesser future, Jesus met it head-on. He didn't deny, minimize, rationalize, or ignore Peter's failure. Instead, He emphasized it three times, each time calling the dejected disciple to "tend My sheep." The Lord said, in effect, "Yes, Peter, you blew it. And you'll blow it again. Nevertheless, I want you to fulfill your calling."

Failure is inevitable. And the Lord is *never* surprised when we fail. It's not as though He called us to follow Him without knowing the future! With the penalty of our sins paid in full, failure for the believer is merely a reminder to depend upon Him rather than self—to replace self-confidence with Christ-confidence.

When I served as the pastor of a church in Waltham, Massachusetts, I met a particularly gifted evangelist named Bob. He worked at what I came to call the Greater Boston Metropolitan Evangelistic Center, which also happened to be the gas station he owned and operated in Arlington. Early on in his life, Bob recognized that his vocation and his calling were one and the same.

Bob's service station became well-known as *the* place to go for a full service fill-up, as well as tires, tune-ups, winterizing, and repairs. It was not uncommon to see half a dozen cars lined up bumper-to-bumper before two pumps in front of that little station, waiting to be served by that man. Now, mind you, he had no "Jesus Saves" flags, no religious slogans or fish symbols or big cross displayed anywhere. No banners hung over the street reading, "Bring your car to Bob and take your soul to Jesus"—nothing like that. Bob simply did his job with excellence and provided superb customer service . . . and it was remarkable the impact he had on the eternal destinies of countless patrons. I lost count of the people directed to our church and into the kingdom as a result of that little service station because of one man who saw his vocation as his calling.

Years later, Bob retired with some money in the bank. He sold his business, moved to Florida, and paid cash for a home. When he later visited me in California, I could see that retirement didn't suit him well. Sure enough, a few months later, I received a letter from Bob.

Dear Chuck,
I hated Florida because I hated retirement. My ministry cannot retire.

He went on to tell me about his venture in tire sales and the opportunity for making Christ known among his clientele.

He'll do that until his body quits. He can't help it. That's the way it ought to be. He had found his calling.

Many Other Signs . . . Many Other Things
JOHN 21:24-25

NASB

24 This is the disciple who is testifying to these things and wrote these things, and we know that his testimony is true.

25 And there are also many other things which Jesus did, which if they were written in detail, I suppose that even the world itself would not contain the books that would be written.

NLT

24 This disciple is the one who testifies to these events and has recorded them here. And we know that his account of these things is accurate.

25 Jesus also did many other things. If they were all written down, I suppose the whole world could not contain the books that would be written.

As a minister of the gospel, I share a wonderful privilege with ship captains, judges, and justices of the peace. I am authorized to join two people in a state of marriage—a holy union and a legal partnership. Before the big day, the couple must go to the courthouse and obtain a marriage license. Then, after the ceremony, I place my signature at the bottom of the license as a testimony to the court—and therefore all who are concerned—that two individuals have been united. Furthermore, two additional witnesses sign the document, testifying to the fact that I conducted the service and affirming that the officiator's signature is mine.

It was also customary in Rome, and throughout the empire, to have *all* legal documents signed and sworn, testifying to their authenticity. As John blotted the ink on his original scroll and prepared to roll it up for distribution to the churches, he added his sworn statement, testifying to the truth of all he had written under the inspiration and guidance of the Holy Spirit. And he was joined by others, who witnessed his signature.

— 21:24 —

John's seal of authenticity affirmed three important facts:

First, *every record contained in this scroll is the account of an eyewitness;* not only one of the Twelve, but one of Jesus' closest friends. "This . . . disciple" refers to the individual present with Peter and Jesus on the shore (21:20-23), the same disciple rumored to be alive at the Lord's return.

Second, *every word contained in this scroll was written by this same eyewitness.* It is very likely John prepared this statement in the first person plural, "we," to include the elders present with him as he completed the manuscript. Though debatable, tradition holds that he wrote this Gospel in Ephesus, home of the most influential church in Asia Minor, which was a renowned stronghold of doctrinal purity.[28]

Third, *every word contained in this scroll is truth.* John not only witnessed the events and recalled them accurately, he wrote under the inspiration of the Holy Spirit, who guided his editorial choices and prevented him from error.

— 21:25 —

John closed his narrative with an editorial caveat, perhaps to counter the inevitable criticism all biographers face: "How could you leave out such an important thing as . . . ?" And, let's face it, when your subject is the Son of God, critics would be standing in line for years to come!

John affirmed that he was selective about which events to include. He was not only selective but strategic. He did not intend to provide an exhaustive (or exhausting) account, but to make a case for belief (20:31). Besides, including everything would not have been feasible. Our knowledge of Christ will never be exhaustive, because He is God and God is infinite.

Rather than try to describe every detail of Christ's earthly ministry, John paints a compelling portrait of Christ's life. His narrative, like so many other things in this realm of existence, is limited. Everything here is less than the very least in the life to come. Therefore, John was content to write only what was absolutely necessary to bring readers to belief in Christ. If that were accomplished, then he thrilled at the prospect of having them learn about the Son of God firsthand.

So, if exhaustive knowledge of the God-man, Jesus, is what you want, then belief will give you an eternity to know Him as deeply and as thoroughly as you desire (Rev. 22:3-5).

APPLICATION: JOHN 21:24-25

The Final Chapter

John's Gospel is in a sense unfinished. John wrote down every word the Holy Spirit directed him to express, yet the story remains incomplete. That's because it is yours to write.

John concludes his account of Christ's earthly ministry with a story of how he and his friend Simon Peter were impacted. The Lord's story set their life stories in motion. Peter would be martyred. John would live so long, people wondered if he would ever die. Both had destinies to fulfill as a result of their time with Christ. Jesus urged both men to "keep on following Me."

And so it is with you—Jesus urges you to follow Him. So, I have a few questions for you. Please consider each carefully.

1. *What will you do with what you have seen in the pages of John's Gospel?* The greatest requirement and risk in all the world is to be exposed to biblical truth. We who live in the light have no business trafficking in the dark. We have learned truths about abiding, washing feet, resting, and what it means to be holy and dedicated even unto

death. How will your life change now that you have these divine truths bouncing around in your consciousness?

2. *What is your part in God's redemptive plan for the world?* God had plans for John and Peter, not merely because they were part of "the Twelve" but because they were Christ's followers, called out of their old lives, given new life, and commissioned to build His kingdom. The same is true of you if you have, indeed, believed. If you haven't discovered your calling, your purpose, begin asking Him to guide you toward it now. God never hides His will; ask Him to reveal your role in His plan.

3. *How much hardship are you willing to bear for the sake of Christ?* Earlier, Jesus warned that to be in His kingdom is to become the enemy of "the world," which will hate you and persecute you (John 15:18-21). Peter would be martyred. John would minister alone, long after his friends had died. Life is not likely to get easier if you are meaningfully engaged in Jesus' agenda. Have you counted this cost? Are you prepared to bear hardships? To what will you devote yourself? His plan to redeem the world from evil, or your comfortable arrangement safely outside the fray?

The Lord's story promises to launch your life story—if you will let Him.

ENDNOTES

INTRODUCTION

1   Quoted by I. Howard Marshall, *The Epistles of John*, 2nd ed. (Grand Rapids: Wm. B. Eerdmans Publishing Company, 1994), xi. (WA 28, 183).
2   Some consider His illustration in 10:1-18 to be a parable, but I suggest it is merely an analogy, a word picture. Parables are short stories, illustrations that feature characters and a plot.

PROLOGUE (JOHN 1:1-18)

1   While some see similarity between Paul's use of *sarx* and that of Greek philosophy and religion, the apostle's is quite unique. For the apostle, *sarx* is the material aspect of humanity that is not inherently evil, but was corrupted along with the rest of the material world after the fall of humanity (Gen. 3:14-19). Paul's theology uses *sarx* to denote our sinful, rebellious manner of thought and deed that reveres the perverted world system as a result of Adam's sin.
2   Gerhard Kittel and Gerhard Friedrich, eds., *Theological Dictionary of the New Testament: Abridged in One Volume,* trans. Geoffrey W. Bromiley (Grand Rapids: Wm. B. Eerdmans, 1985), 290.
3   Ibid., 291.
4   "Does Sodom Love Gomorrah?" *Time,* March 20, 1964.
5   "The verb tense where the writer portrays an action in process or a state of being that is occurring in the past with no assessment of the action's completion." (Michael S. Heiser, *Glossary of Morpho-Syntactic Database Terminology,* "Imperfect" [Logos Bible Software, 2005].)
6   A. W. Tozer, *The Knowledge of the Holy: The Attributes of God; Their Meaning in the Christian Life* (San Francisco: Harper & Row, 1978), 39.

PRESENTATION OF THE WORD (JOHN 1:19–4:54)

1   Kittel and Friedrich, eds., *Theological Dictionary of the New Testament: Abridged in One Volume,* 38.
2   Ibid.
3   Ibid., 567.
4   See ibid., 1015.
5   While the high priest and royal officials were mostly Sadducees, the Sanhedrin and rabbis were principally Pharisees. The priests held official positions of authority over the temple, while the Pharisees claimed moral authority over worshipers.
6   *Merriam-Webster's Collegiate Dictionary,* 11th ed. (Springfield, MA: Merriam-Webster, 2003), s.v. "religious."
7   The NLT renders the Greek word for "son" as "chosen one" in keeping with some early manuscripts. The Old Testament sometimes calls the anointed king of Israel the "chosen one" (Ps. 89:3, 19; Isa. 42:1) or "anointed one" (Pss. 2:2; 18:50; 20:6). Furthermore, a descendant of David who occupied the throne was

expected to share a figurative father-son relationship with God (2 Sam. 7:14; Ps. 2:7). In the case of Jesus, the figurative title "son of God" was literal.

8 J. Oswald Sanders, *Spiritual Leadership*, rev. ed. (Chicago: Moody Press, 1980), 230.

9 Ibid.

10 Karl Marx, *Karl Marx and Frederick Engels: Selected Works in Two Volumes,* (Moscow: Foreign Languages Publishing House, 1949), 2:367.

11 Karl Marx and Friedrich Engels, *The Communist Manifesto of Karl Marx and Friedrich Engels,* ed. D. Ryazanoff (New York: Russell & Russell, 1963), 68.

12 *The NET Bible Notes* (Peabody, MA: Biblical Studies Press, 2003; available at bible.org), note on John 1:39.

13 Josephus, *The Jewish Wars,* 2.15.3.

14 Johannes P. Louw and Eugene Albert Nida, *Greek-English Lexicon of the New Testament: Based on Semantic Domains,* 2nd ed. (New York: United Bible Societies, 1989), 1:381.

15 Merrill Tenney, "John," in *Expositor's Bible Commentary* (Grand Rapids: Zondervan, 1981), 9:47.

16 Ibid.

17 Helmut Thielicke, *Encounter with Spurgeon,* trans. John W. Doberstein (Philadelphia: Fortress, 1963), 14.

18 F. B. Meyer, *John the Baptist* (Fort Washington, PA: Christian Literature Crusade, 1983), 97.

19 *The Westminster Standards* (Philadelphia: Great Commission Publications, 1986), 35.

20 D. James Kennedy, *Evangelism Explosion,* 4th ed. (Carol Stream, IL: Tyndale), 46.

21 Ibid., 47.

AUTHENTICATION OF THE WORD (JOHN 5:1–12:50)

1 See Kittel and Friedrich, eds., *Theological Dictionary of the New Testament: Abridged in One Volume,* 178.

2 Jess Moody, *A Drink at Joel's Place* (Waco, TX: Word Books, 1967), 80–81.

3 Many thanks to Josh McDowell for his excellent book, *Evidence that Demands a Verdict,* and to C. S. Lewis for writing *Mere Christianity.*

4 Sometimes, on the battlefield, a drum became an ad hoc writing desk in a hastily formed court, set up on the spot to try and convict someone for crimes committed during battle. A guilty verdict was almost always a foregone conclusion with punishment carried out immediately.

5 Gerald L. Borchert, *John 1–11,* New American Commentary 25A (Nashville: Broadman & Holman, 1996), 258.

6 On *skandalizō,* see Gerhard Kittel and Gerhard Friedrich, eds., *Theological Dictionary of the New Testament,* ed. and trans. Geoffrey W. Bromiley (Grand Rapids: Wm. B. Eerdmans, 1973), 7:339–358.

7 Aristophanes, *Acharnenses,* 687; cited in Kittel and Friedrich, eds., *Theological Dictionary of the New Testament,* 7:340.

8 Robert Jamieson, A. R. Fausset, and David Brown, *A Commentary, Critical and Explanatory, on the Old and New Testaments* (Grand Rapids: Wm. B. Eerdmans, 1945), 392.

9 *The NET Bible Notes* (Biblical Studies Press, 2003), notes on John 7:23.

10 *Parade Magazine,* February 11, 1962.

11 Adapted from Charles R. Swindoll, *Parenting: From Surviving to Thriving* (Nashville: Thomas Nelson, 2006), 236–238. Used by permission.

12 H. V. Morton, *In the Steps of the Master* (New York: Dodd, Mead, 1937), 180.

13 Ibid., 179.

14 Around 250 BC, the Hebrew Scriptures were translated into Greek by

approximately seventy Jewish scholars. Most Jews living in Jesus' time were likely to know the Old Testament in their spoken language rather than Hebrew or Aramaic. Sometimes the term "Septuagint" is abbreviated "LXX," the Roman numeral for seventy.

[15] The journey from a town in southern Galilee, such as Jezreel, to Bethany is approximately 50 miles. A man could cover 25 miles in a twelve-hour day (11:9).

[16] *Genesis Rabbah* 100.7; *Leviticus Rabbah* 18.1.

[17] See Hersh Goldwurm and Yekutiel Friedner, *History of the Jewish People* (New York: Mesorah, 1982), 1:58.

[18] See comments on Romans 1:24-25 in Charles R. Swindoll, *Insights on Romans* (Carol Stream, IL: Tyndale, 2014).

[19] "Leprosy" referred to any chronic or acute skin condition, not just the incurable form we know as Hansen's disease.

[20] Adapted from Swindoll, *Insights on Romans;* see discussion on Romans 9:14-18.

CONFIRMATION OF THE WORD (JOHN 13:1–17:26)

[1] Gladys M. Hunt, "That's No Generation Gap!," *Eternity,* October 1969, 15.

[2] Chart adapted from Kittel and Friedrich, eds., *Theological Dictionary of the New Testament,* 1:37.

[3] Unknown author.

[4] The Bible does not condemn feelings of anxiety, distress, or worry. We are counseled to avoid worry over worldly concerns, such as physical needs the Lord has promised to supply. A parent's worry over the spiritual welfare of his or her children is quite in order! However, anxiety should prompt us to approach problems constructively, especially by employing God's remedy for worry: prayer (Phil. 4:6-7). Let us set aside the notion that worry is a sin; it is not. Worry is counterproductive *by itself.* Worry is unnecessary if no further action is taken, particularly in prayer. But worry should not cause us to add shame to an already overloaded emotional burden.

[5] It is not my intention to oversimplify fear. Serious phobias often require intensive help from psychological professionals. However, I am convinced these biblical truths are foundational to the treatment of chronic, debilitating fear.

[6] Kittel and Friedrich, eds., *Theological Dictionary of the New Testament,* 1:185.

[7] Warren W. Wiersbe, *The Bible Exposition Commentary* (Wheaton, IL: Victor Books, 1994), 1:356.

[8] Samuel Taylor Coleridge, "The Rime of the Ancient Mariner," in *The Collected Works of Samuel Taylor Coleridge: Poetical Works I, Poems (Reading Text): Part 1,* ed. J. C. C. Mays (Princeton: Princeton University Press, 2001), 391.

[9] Samuel Taylor Coleridge, "Youth and Age," in *The Collected Works of Samuel Taylor Coleridge: Poetical Works I, Poems (Reading Text): Part 2,* ed. J. C. C. Mays (Princeton: Princeton University Press, 2001), 1012.

[10] Charles Dickens, *A Tale of Two Cities* (Oxford: Oxford University Press, 1987), 358.

[11] Archibald Thomas Robertson, *Word Pictures in the New Testament* (Nashville: Broadman, 1932), 5:262.

[12] Ibid., s.v. 15:27.

[13] See Kittel and Friedrich, eds., *Theological Dictionary of the New Testament: Abridged in One Volume,* 1036.

[14] A. W. Tozer, *God Tells the Man Who Cares* (Harrisburg, PA: Christian Publications, 1970), 154–155.

[15] Kittel and Friedrich, eds., *Theological Dictionary of the New Testament: Abridged in One Volume,* 222.

[16] Ibid., 315.

[17] Ibid.

18 Josephus, *Antiquities* 11.8.4-5.
19 See Kittel and Friedrich, eds., *Theological Dictionary of the New Testament: Abridged in One Volume,* 707.

VINDICATION OF THE WORD (JOHN 18:1–21:25)

1 See Kittel and Friedrich, eds., *Theological Dictionary of the New Testament,* 9:3.
2 *International Standard Bible Encyclopedia* (Grand Rapids: Wm. B. Eerdmans, 1979), 1:128.
3 Ibid.
4 George Matheson, *Thoughts for Life's Journey* (New York: Hodder and Stoughton, 1908), 266–267.
5 Philo of Alexandria, *The Works of Philo: Complete and Unabridged,* trans. C. D. Yonge (Peabody, MA: Hendrickson, 1993), 784.
6 Flavius Josephus, *The Works of Josephus: Complete and Unabridged,* trans. William Whiston (Peabody, MA: Hendrickson, 1987), 392.
7 W. D. Edwards, MD, W. J. Gabel, MDiv, and F. E. Hosmer, MS, "On the Physical Death of Jesus Christ," *The Journal of the American Medical Association* 255, no. 11 (March 21, 1986): 1457.
8 Frederick T. Zugibe, *The Crucifixion of Jesus: A Forensic Inquiry* (New York: Evans, 2005), 22.
9 Robert Frost, "The Road Not Taken" in *The Road Not Taken: An Introduction to Robert Frost,* ed. Louis Untermeyer (New York: Holt, Rinehart and Winston, 1968), 270.
10 Cicero, *The Verrine Orations,* trans. L. H. G. Greenwood (Cambridge, MA: Harvard University Press, 1976), 2:655.
11 On the history of crucifixion, see Kittel and Friedrich, eds., *Theological Dictionary of the New Testament,* 7:573.
12 Merrill F. Unger, *The New Unger's Bible Dictionary* (Chicago: Moody Press, 1982), 265.
13 Edwards, Gabel, and Hosmer, "On the Physical Death of Jesus Christ," 1461.
14 Zugibe, *The Crucifixion of Jesus,* 106.
15 Cicero, *The Verrine Orations,* 2:655–657.
16 Kittel and Friedrich, eds., *Theological Dictionary of the New Testament,* 7:573.
17 Frank Morison, *Who Moved the Stone?* (Downers Grove, IL: InterVarsity Press, 1981), 10–11.
18 Ibid., 8.
19 Philo of Alexandria, *The Works of Philo,* 732.
20 Will Durant, *On the Meaning of Life* (New York: Ray Long and Richard R. Smith, 1932), 5.
21 Robert Green Ingersoll, *Complete Lectures of Robert G. Ingersoll* (New York: Freethought Press, 1944), 60.
22 Benjamin Franklin, *The Writings of Benjamin Franklin,* ed. Albert Henry Smyth (New York: Macmillan, 1907), 9:569.
23 The apostle Paul on the road to Damascus is a notable exception (Acts 9:1-19), as is James, the brother of Christ, who did not believe until after His resurrection.
24 Kittel and Friedrich, eds., *Theological Dictionary of the New Testament: Abridged in One Volume,* 760.
25 Ibid., 1262.
26 Ibid., 7.
27 Charles Colson, *Born Again* (Old Tappan, NJ: Fleming H. Revell, 1977), 12.
28 A dubious second-century document known as "The Acts of John" contains a collection of stories about the apostle. While the stories are not credible, they may contain kernels of genuine history, such as where he resided.